THE DECLINE OF
FERTILITY IN GERMANY,
1871–1939

This book is the second in a series on
the decline of European fertility.
A publication of the Office of Population Research
Princeton University

The Decline of Fertility

in Germany, 1871-1939

BY JOHN E. KNODEL

PRINCETON UNIVERSITY PRESS

PRINCETON, NEW JERSEY

Copyright © 1974 by Princeton University Press

All Rights Reserved

LCC: 72–9944

ISBN: 0–691–09359–8

This book has been composed in Monotype Times Roman

Printed in the United States of America
by Princeton University Press, Princeton, New Jersey

For my parents
to whom I owe my interest in Germany

Foreword

This book is the second in a series of country studies that are part of a cooperative investigation that began in 1964 at the Office of Population Research in Princeton. The purpose of the project, which is supported by the National Institutes of Health, is to examine the circumstances under which fertility declined in each of the more than 700 provinces of Europe. Accurate records of births, deaths, and of the size and composition of populations are more widely prevalent and extend over a longer period of time in Europe than in any other equally large or diverse part of the world, and during the era covered by such statistics there has been a reduction of nearly 50 percent in the rate at which women of childbearing age bear children in virtually all of the European provinces.

Many well-informed observers have asserted that a reduction in the rate of childbearing is a natural consequence of modernization and industrialization. This view has apparently been developed as a somewhat impressionistic generalization of European experience, confirmed by a further impression of declines accompanying modernization in northern America, Australia and New Zealand, and Japan.

The large project of which this book is a part is a more thorough examination of the European record to see what aspects of modernization or industrialization (if any) have, in fact, been linked with the decline in fertility that virtually all of the provinces seem to have experienced.

In this book Dr. John Knodel examines the decline in all provinces of Germany. He has assembled and collated the voluminous German demographic statistics since the unification of the country in 1871, supplemented by an examination of data extending back to the beginning of the nineteenth century in certain German areas. Indices of overall fertility, marital fertility, illegitimate fertility, and of proportions married were constructed and analyzed. He has carefully re-examined most of the proposed explanations of the fall in fertility of married women, a fall that began in most of the German provinces between 1870 and 1910, and has presented evidence and offered his own explanation in cautious and sober terms. The book, like its predecessor in this series, *A Century of Portuguese Fertility* by Massimo Livi Bacci, is a contribution to the social history of a European country during a period of profound change. Like its predecessor and, we hope, like its successors in the series, it is also a building block in our eventual understanding of the circumstances under which a major decline in fertility occurs.

Ansley J. Coale
Director
Office of Population Research

Preface

One of the great advantages of working at the Office of Population Research at Princeton University is the opportunity to meet a large number of professional colleagues in an atmosphere conducive to informal discussion and mutual aid. During the five years I spent there I must have discussed my research on the German fertility decline with at least a score of fellow demographers. I would like to express my appreciation to all of them for their interest and support of my research. My greatest debt is due Ansley Coale, the director of both OPR and the European Fertility Project of which this monograph is a part. He provided valuable guidance and encouragement through every stage of research and writing. My colleague Etienne van de Walle also deserves to be singled out for the many research suggestions he contributed both through his own work and through the countless informal discussions we had during coffee, coke, and grape soda breaks. He also read through several versions of the manuscript and made numerous helpful suggestions and criticisms. A note of appreciation is due Joel Cohen of Harvard University who spent the summer of 1971 at Princeton and generously provided methodological advice when it was most urgently needed.

Edward Shorter of the University of Toronto and Michael Haines of Cornell University were kind enough to read through the entire manuscript prior to publication and make extensive comments which were an aid in making final revisions. Norman Ryder also read through earlier versions of several chapters and made insightful and valuable comments.

I would like to thank the Deutsches Wirtschaftsinstitut in East Berlin and the Bayerisches Statistisches Landesant in Munich for allowing me to use their excellent library facilities. Their collections of German statistical source books are truly exceptional. While I was in Berlin during the first year of research for this monograph, my work was greatly facilitated by Herbert Hübner who generously made his office and a calculating machine constantly available to me.

The secretarial staff at the Office of Population Research deserves mention not only for their fine typing services but also for their pleasant attitude toward the task. In particular my thanks go to Hazel Chafey, who always managed to find time for my manuscript no matter how late I gave it to her or how busy she was. Additionally, assistance provided by Hilary Page and Patricia Taylor in editing and preparing the tables, graphs, and maps for publication is gratefully acknowledged. They not only managed a long and tedious job efficiently but kept a cheerful attitude in the process.

Finally, I would like to acknowledge the support of the National Institutes of Health which has made possible the analysis of the decline of fertility in Europe.

John E. Knodel
Bangkok
May 1973

Contents

List of Tables

LIST OF TABLES

List of Maps and Figures

THE DECLINE OF
FERTILITY IN GERMANY,
1871–1939

CHAPTER 1: Introduction

Since the beginning of the nineteenth century most European countries have experienced major economic, social, and demographic transformations which collectively social scientists today label modernization. The Industrial Revolution, which had begun towards the end of the eighteenth century in Great Britain, spread throughout much of Europe in the century that followed. The changes that occurred during this modern period of history were much broader, however, than those directly involved in the emergence of modern industry. Among the most important of the concomitant developments was the shift from moderately high birth and death rates to substantially lower ones. By the economic depression of the 1930s, this demographic transition, as it is often labeled, had reached the point in much of Northern, Western, and Central Europe where the populations were reproducing themselves at a level near or below replacement despite the substantially reduced levels of mortality.

The transformation of Germany from a predominantly rural agrarian state to a highly urban industrialized society occurred in the main between the political unification of Germany in 1871 and the beginning of World War II. At the time of unification industry consisted typically of handicrafts pursued in the home and small workshops. By 1910, industry was based on coal and iron and factory production. Germany's industrialization, although temporarily checked by defeat in World War I and the Great Depression, had more than fully recovered before the defeat in World War II. The magnitude of some of the social and economic changes that comprised the modernization of Germany are evident from the statistical series presented in Table 1.1. In 1871, almost two thirds of the population lived in rural areas. Within four decades this situation was reversed. In the same period the percentage of the population living in cities with over 100,000 population had increased more than fourfold. Between 1882 and 1939 the proportion of the population that was dependent on agriculture and other primary industries for their livelihood was reduced by more than half. Women became increasingly

INTRODUCTION

TABLE 1.1

SOCIAL AND ECONOMIC INDICES: 1852 TO 1939

Year	Rural population (percent)	Metropolitan population (percent)	Population dependent on primary industry (percent)	Females, 14+, employed in manufacturing & trade (percent)	Secondary industry concerns with over 50 employees (number)	Railroad track (Km)	Per capita output (in 1913 marks)
1852	67.3[a]	2.6[a]	--	--	--	ca6,000	267
1871	63.9	4.8	--	--	--	21,482	379
1875	61.0	6.2	--	--	8,186	27,981	407
1880	58.6	7.2	42.5	9.4	9,481	33,645	409
1885	56.3	9.5	--	--	--	37,189	470
1890	53.0	12.1	--	--	--	41,818	493
1895	49.8	13.9	35.8	11.7	17,941	45,203	554
1900	45.6	16.2	--	--	--	49,878	589
1905	42.6	19.0	28.6	14.3	29,033	54,680	637
1910	40.0	21.3	--	--	--	59,031	693[e]
1925	35.4[b]	26.6[b]	23.0	18.0	32,759	55,841[d]	776
1933	32.8[c]	30.1[c]	21.0	17.9	19,690	58,185[d]	703
1939	30.1	31.6	18.2[d]	19.4	33,587	70,452	--

NOTES: Rural population is that living in municipalities of under 2,000.
Metropolitan population is that living in municipalities of over 100,000.
Employment data included in indices for 1905 refer to 1907; those for 1925
and 1933 exclude the Saar.
Per capita output is calculated as $\frac{\text{net domestic product}}{\text{average population}}$ and is based on
statistics from Hoffmann 1965, pp.33,172-174, for five-year periods
beginning 1850.
1852-1910 data are for pre-World War I boundaries; 1925-1939 data are for
post-World War I boundaries, excluding areas annexed after 1937.

[a] Prussia only.
[b] Including results from the 1927 census of the Saar.
[c] Including results from the 1935 census of the Saar.
[d] Excluding the Saar.
[e] Data calculated from four-year period (1910-1913).

involved in the nonagricultural labor force. Large manufacturing
concerns proliferated particularly rapidly during the decades prior to
World War I while the network of railroads continued the expansion
begun during the mid-nineteenth century. One of the effects of these
changes was a practically steady rise in per capita output to a level in
1925 triple that of seven decades earlier.

This same period was also characterized by sweeping demographic
changes. From 34 million inhabitants in 1843, the population of Germany practically doubled by 1913. Population density increased from
62 per square kilometer to over 120. Mortality and fertility fell to
much lower levels (Table 1.2). Life expectancy at birth rose by 24
years between the 1870s and the 1930s. Infant mortality was reduced
to only a small fraction of its previous level. During the same decades
the crude birth rate declined by more than 50 percent. In fact, after a

TABLE 1.2

VITAL TRENDS: 1851 TO 1939

Date	Crude birth rate	Crude death rate	Infant mortality rate	Life expectancy (years)	Annual growth rate (percent)
1851-1860	35.3	26.3	--	--	0.7
1861-1870	37.2	26.8	239[a]	--	0.8
1871-1875	38.8	28.2	244[b]	} 37.0	0.9
1876-1880	39.3	26.1	227		1.1
1881-1885	37.0	25.7	226	} 38.7	0.7
1886-1890	36.5	24.4	224		1.1
1891-1895	36.3	23.3	221	} 42.3	1.1
1896-1900	36.0	21.2	213		1.5
1901-1905	34.3	19.9	199	} 46.6	1.5
1906-1910	31.7	17.5	174		1.4
1911-1915	26.3	17.7	160	--	1.0
1916-1920	17.9	19.1	145	--	--
1921-1925	22.2	13.3	120	57.4[c]	0.7[e]
1926-1930	18.4	11.8	94	--	0.6
1931-1935	16.5	11.2	75	61.3[d]	0.5
1936-1939	19.5	11.9	63	--	1.0

NOTES: The infant mortality rate is defined as deaths to infants under
one-year old per 1,000 live births.
Boundaries for data presented for 1851-1922 are those existing
at the time; boundaries for data presented after 1922 are
those existing at the end of 1937.

[a] 1867, excluding several small states which together represent less
than 5 percent of the population.
[b] 1872-1875.
[c] 1924-1926.
[d] 1932-1934.
[e] 1922-1925.

period of fluctuation in the middle of the nineteenth century, both
birth and death rates declined almost steadily until just prior to World
War II, when fertility was well below replacement, despite the great
reduction in mortality.

Most discussions of the demographic transition link the long term
changes in vital rates to the process of industrialization or moderniza-

tion. It is clear that all countries today which can be considered as fully part of the developed world experienced a substantial secular decline in fertility and mortality. In Germany, as the tables above have shown, there was a general coincidence between industrialization and demographic transition. How close the connection is between these two major processes in Germany or in the rest of Europe, however, is much less clear. Perhaps the principal reason for the uncertainty has been the absence of research empirically documenting the demographic changes in anything more than their crudest outlines.

The task of the present study is to examine in detail the secular decline in fertility that occurred in Germany between unification and World War II. Mortality trends are investigated only with respect to their possible consequences for long term changes in fertility. Efforts to study the German fertility decline are not new. From the time when a declining birth rate was first evident until the recovery of fertility during the Third Reich, scores of German scholars wrote about the *Geburtenrückgang*. Many merely decried the falling birth rate as a sign of moral decay and national degeneration. Others, however, were more analytical in their discussion. As the literature proliferated, bitter controversies developed over causes and consequences. Treatments of the subject were generally polemical although occasionally attempts were made to reconcile divergent positions (e.g. Müller, 1922; Kosic, 1917). Opponents used *ad hoc* theorizing as well as statistical data to support their views. The onset of the Third Reich with its ambitious population programs and the concurrent rise in natality eclipsed concern among German demographers about the past decades of falling fertility. During the post-World War II period little work has emerged from Germany concerning the historical transition from high to low fertility that occurred in the seven decades before the war.

In view of the vast amount of detailed demographic data available for German states during the period of fertility decline, it is surprising that previous studies have not exploited this material more fully in order to present a comprehensive description of fertility trends. Many studies relied solely on crude birth rates. Even the relatively sophisticated treatments of the fertility decline that utilized more refined measures left much to be desired. No attempts were made to estimate the date of the onset of the decline or the rate of the decline for the different areas of Germany. The explanations offered for the decline were also unsatisfactory. Most writers suggested one or another single factor as the prime mover in the decline rather than attempting to utilize a more general perspective. Many of the disputes found in the earlier literature resulted from a confusion of the levels of explanation involved.[1] Thus one writer would argue that increased use of contraception was responsible for declining fertility, another would stress increased employment of women, and neither would recognize that the two explanations were not necessarily incompatible. With the recent interest in a thorough reassessment of the demographic transition and in particular in the decline of fertility in Europe, a new analysis of the German experience is in order. The past studies, however, can be helpful in suggesting directions to this research.

The present study attempts both to describe and to analyze the German fertility decline. The task of description is the easier although not necessarily the less important since a comprehensive knowledge of the facts is a prerequisite for any adequate explanation. The main part of the description is concerned with identifying and depicting geographical and sociological differentials in the fertility decline. Thus fertility trends of administrative areas of Germany are described in detail. The use of these geographical areas as a basic unit of observation is dictated largely by the fact that censuses and vital statistics present data on this basis. Moreover, to the extent that the spread of the fertility decline followed geographical patterns, such a unit of analysis is useful in identifying these patterns. The description of demographic trends for each area includes factoring overall fertility into three components of marital fertility, illegitimate fertility, and proportions married.

In addition to a full description of the fertility decline in each administrative area of Germany, an attempt is made to delineate the differential trends in fertility among the various sectors of the German society. The choice of variables which can be used in categorizing the German population for this purpose is restricted largely to those for

[1]Müller (1922) in a brief review of the German literature made the same point.

which data are available in the published census and vital statistics reports. This allows classification of fertility trends by residence (rural-urban), occupation, and religion. In addition, some indirect evidence is available with respect to fertility differences according to wealth and ethnic affiliation. This data is used to identify sociological differentials in the timing and extent of decline.

An analysis of the fertility decline in Germany beyond pure description of trends and differentials is considerably more difficult, particularly if it attempts to identify underlying causes. In the first place, of the many possible factors which might have brought about a basic change in fertility behavior, very few can be identified through available statistics. Thus only a limited number of crude indices can be used in an attempt to explain changes which are most likely intricate and complex. Second, there are various levels of causation, and it is not always clear which are the most appropriate. Third, causal analysis through statistical manipulation, the basic method to which demographers are usually confined, is rarely conclusive. Possible associations with factors not held constant inherently plague interpretations.

The search for factors associated with the fertility decline is limited in the present study to a consideration of hypotheses that can be tested with the available statistics. The main approach is to associate changes in independent variables with the onset or course of the fertility decline in different geographical areas or in different social groups. Since the data described and analyzed refer generally to areas or groups and not to individuals, the danger of the "ecological fallacy" runs high. In fact it would be logically incorrect to try to determine the characteristics of individual families that limit fertility by analyzing data that supplies only averages for large aggregates. The most that can be expected, even with the best of luck and analytical skill, is an identification of the broad social and economic circumstances that made Germany susceptible to a decline in fertility.

Two working hypotheses are prominent in determining the strategy of the present study. First, the emphasis is on the course of *marital fertility* rather than other demographic components of fertility trends. This is based on the working hypothesis (subject to verification later) that the secular decline in fertility that occurred over the last century in Germany, and indeed in the rest of Europe, was due essentially to a

[8]

reduction of births within marriage. Overall fertility is a product not only of marital fertility but of illegitimacy and the proportions married as well. Thus an index of marital fertility is a more appropriate instrument for analyzing the fertility decline than an index of overall fertility. Since the conditions affecting secular changes in marital fertility are not necessarily the same as those that influence the other components of overall fertility, marital fertility should be more sensitive to the factors underlying the fertility decline. Illegitimate fertility and nuptiality patterns will not be ignored, and their role in determining patterns of overall fertility will be considered, but relatively minor attention will be given them.

A second working hypothesis (subject to partial verification later) defines the fertility decline that occurred in Germany during the latter decades of the nineteenth century and the first half of the twentieth century as a unique, clearly identifiable, and irreversible phenomenon in the course of German demographic history. Prior to the onset of this decline, marital fertility is assumed to be high and relatively constant for a long period of time. Such an assumption need not rule out the possible existence of limited fertility control within marriage during the predecline period. It does mean, however, that if such control existed it was not widespread or that it was not practiced either extensively or efficiently. Fluctuations in predecline fertility over time are considered probable, but any long term trends would be either gradual or inconclusive. The modern fertility decline, in contrast, represents a distinct break from past trends. Through the adoption, increased use, or diffusion of fertility control within marriage, the practice of intensive family limitation became customary. The result was a rapid unprecedented reduction of marital fertility. Subsequent fluctuations in marital fertility in response to changing social and economic conditions took place and will continue to do so, but the possibility of a return to the much higher predecline levels is precluded.

Administrative and Geographical Subdivisions

During the years between unification in 1871 and World War II, Germany was subdivided at several levels for administrative purposes. The broadest division separated Germany into states (*Staaten*). These were subdivided into small districts (*Kreise* or *Ämter*). In addition, the larger states were divided into middle level administrative areas. Prussia had a dual system of middle level areas. In 1900, for example, the Prussian State was divided into 14 provinces (*Provinzen*) which in turn contained a total of 35 smaller units (*Regierungsbezirke*). Bavaria, Saxony, Württemberg, Baden, Hesse, and Oldenburg all possessed a single system of middle level administrative areas. The states themselves differed greatly from each other in population size and territorial area. In 1900, for example, more than 60 percent of Germany's 56 million inhabitants resided in Prussia, which covered almost two-thirds of the national area. In contrast less than 34 thousand lived in the smallest state, Schaumburg-Lippe.

Because of the inordinate differences in population size, the state per se is not the appropriate unit for the present study of regional demographic trends. The small administrative districts are also unsuitable. There are too many of them, well over 1,000 and detailed vital statistics and census data are not generally available on the basis of such small units. Instead a combination of middle level administrative areas, where they exist, and states, where they do not, can best serve as the basic geographical units in the present study. In Prussia the smaller *Regierungsbezirke* rather than the larger *Provinzen* are used.

Most states and middle level administrative areas remained intact as administrative units between 1871 and the mid-1930s. In fact most existed long before 1871. Thus continuous statistical series on these levels can be assembled. In several instances, however, changes did occur. States or middle level areas were either consolidated or redivided. For the present study, the larger units (when either consolidation or redivision occurred) were chosen to permit comparison over time.[2] Table 1.3 indicates the number and title of the adminis-

---

[2]The following combined areas are used throughout most of the present study: AREA 01 OSTPREUSSEN consists of the Prussian *Regierungsbezirke* Königsberg and Gumbinnen until 1905 and thereafter includes Allenstein. The total area of Ostpreussen is the same before and after 1905 since Allenstein was formed from parts of the area which formerly belonged to Königsberg and Gumbinnen. AREA 07 STETTIN-STRALSUND is a combination of the Prussian *Regierungsbezirke* Stettin and Stralsund. AREA 27 KASSEL includes both the *Regierungsbezirk* Kassel and the small principality of Waldeck except in indices refer-

TABLE 1.3

TYPE AND AVERAGE POPULATION OF ADMINISTRATIVE AREA
USED AS UNIT OF ANALYSIS, BY STATES IN 1900

| State | Administrative areas used in study | | |
	Type	Number	Average population (000)
Prussia	Regierungsbezirk	34	1,016
Bavaria	Regierungsbezirk	8	772
K. Saxony	Kreishauptmannschaft	3	1,401
Württemberg	Kreis[a]	4	542
Baden	Kreis[a]	4	467
Hesse	Provinz	3	373
Gd. Oldenburg	Landesteil[b]	3	133
Alsace-Lorraine	Bezirk	3	573
Remaining States	The state itself	9	465
Germany	--	71	783

[a] Distinct from a much smaller administrative district also called <u>Kreis</u>.
[b] Before 1920, one <u>Landesteil</u> was a duchy (<u>Herzogtum</u>) and the other two
principalities (<u>Fürstentümer</u>).

trative unit used in the present study for each German state. The
average population size of all the administrative areas within each
state is shown for 1900.

In the remainder of this study the small states and middle level
administrative areas which serve as the basic geographic units in the
study will be referred to simply as the administrative areas of Germany. Map 1.1 shows these areas according to their 1900 boundaries.
The German names for the administrative areas used in the official

---

ring to the censuses of 1867, 1895, and 1905. AREA 43 DRESDEN includes *Kreishauptmannschaften* Dresden and Bautzen. AREA 45 ZWICKAU includes *Kreishauptmannschaften*
Zwickau and Chemnitz. AREA 50 KONSTANZ consists of the *Kreise* Konstanz, Villingen,
and Waldshut. AREA 51 FREIBURG consists of the *Kreise* Freiburg, Lorrach, and Offen-
burg. AREA 52 KARLSRUHE consists of *Kreise* Baden and Karlsruhe. AREA 53 MANNHEIM
consists of *Kreise* Mannheim, Heidelberg, and Mosbach. AREA 57 MECKLENBURG consists of the two states Mecklenburg-Schwerin and Mecklenburg-Strelitz except in indices
referring to the 1867 census in which case it refers only to the former. AREA 58 THÜRIN-
GEN consists of the eight small states of Sachsen-Weimar, Sachsen-Meiningen, Sachsen-
Altenburg, Sachsen-Coburg-Gotha, Schwarzburg-Sonderhausen, Schwarzburg-Rudel-
stadt, Reuss ältere Linie, and Reuss jüngerer Linie.

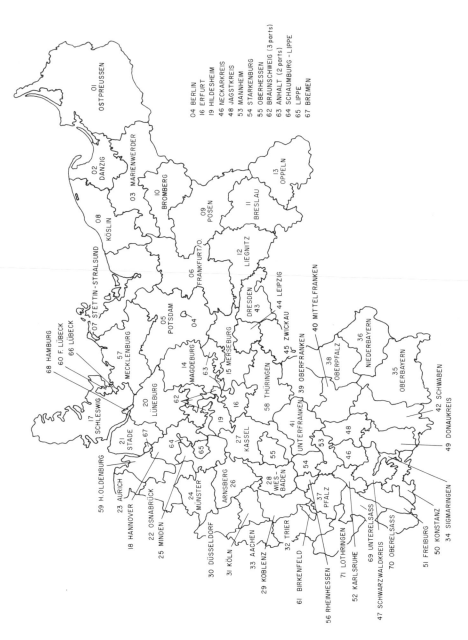

Map 1.1. Administrative Areas of Germany: 1900

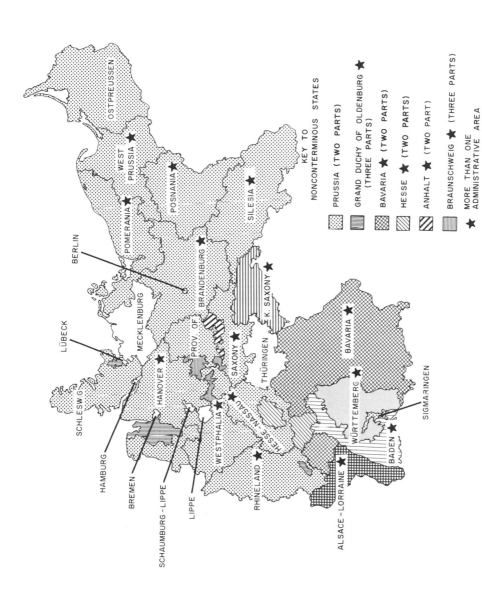

Map 1.2.   States of Germany and Provinces within Prussia: 1900

statistics have been retained and will be used as such in the text and tables.[3] For convenience sake each area was given a number which is also shown on the map. Map 1.2 shows the German states and Prussian provinces.[4] States or provinces for which equivalent English names exist, such as Prussia (Preussen) or Bavaria (Bayern), are referred to by their English name on the map as they will be in the text and tables.[5] The only exception to this rule will be provinces or states which themselves are administrative areas. In order to avoid confusion, their German name will be used whether they are being referred to as administrative areas or as provinces or states.[6]

[3]Special note should be taken of the distinction between area 60 F. Lübeck (standing for Fürstentum Lübeck), which is part of the larger state of Oldenburg, and area 66 Lübeck, which refers to the free city-state of Lübeck.

[4]K. Saxony (Kingdom of Saxony), which is an independent state, should not be confused with the Prussian province of P. Saxony (Province of Saxony). Hesse (Grand-duchy of Hesse), an independent state, should not be confused with the Prussian province of Hesse-Nassau. Also Gd. Oldenburg (Grand-duchy of Oldenburg) should not be confused with area 59 H. Oldenburg (Herzogtum Oldenburg), which is only one of the three parts of this state. Likewise area 09 Posen is only one of the two areas constituting the province of Posnania (Posen in German) and area 18 Hannover in only one of the five areas which constitute the province of Hanover (Hannover in German).

[5]A complete list of the German names and the English equivalents used in the text and tables include the following states and provinces:

Westpreussen = West Prussia
Pommern = Pomerania
Posen = Posnania
Schliesen = Silesia
Provinz Sachsen = Province of Saxony
Hannover = Hanover
Westfalen = Westphalia
Hessen-Nassau = Hesse-Nassau
Rheinland = Rhineland
Preussen = Prussia
Bayern = Bavaria
Königreich Sachsen = Kingdom of Saxony
Hessen = Hesse
Grossherzogtum Oldenburg = Grand-duchy of Oldenburg
Elsass-Lothringen = Alsace-Lorraine

[6]Thus Ostpreussen (East Prussia), Thüringen (Thuringia), and Braunschweig (Brunswick) all have English equivalents, but since they also are single administrative areas their German names will be used when referring to them as states or provinces. The two administrative areas, Schleswig and Sigmaringen, are also Prussian provinces. In official statistical publications when they were treated as provinces (rather than as *Regierungsbezirke*) they were called Schleswig-Holstein and Hohenzollern respectively. However, to avoid confusion, they will be referred to as Schleswig and Sigmaringen whether they are being treated as an administrative area or a province.

Following World War I, Germany lost a significant part of its territory to foreign powers. The three administrative areas of Alsace-Lorraine were returned to France. Most of the territory of four Prussian areas comprised the newly formed Polish Corridor and the free city of Danzig, although two new administrative areas were formed from the parts of those areas that remained with Prussia. In addition, small parts of other areas were lost to Poland, Lithuania, Czechoslovakia, Denmark, and Belgium. Map 1.3 shows the lost territory and the newly formed administrative areas.[7] The lost areas will be considered in the present study for the periods during which they formed part of Germany.

One of the central questions of this study is whether or not the fertility decline in Germany was characterized by distinctive regional patterns. In other words, we want to direct attention to the question of whether there is a closer association in the fertility experience of populations that are located in the same geographical region than would be expected on the basis of the variables conventionally associated with fertility. Are populations of administrative areas within the same region more homogeneous in their fertility behavior than we would expect from knowledge of solely nongeographical variables such as infant mortality, literacy, urbanization, religion, etc.? We could argue that such regional differences are to be expected since the population of a region might well share a common cultural heritage, history, or dialect which would facilitate interaction and communication within a regional population more than it would between regional populations. There is already evidence from studies of the secular fertility decline in other countries that there is indeed a pronounced association between regional location and various demographic variables (Leasure, 1963; Livi Bacci, 1971).

[7]The newly established *Regierungsbezirk* Westpreussen (area 3A) should not be confused with the much larger former province of West Prussia (Westpreussen in German) although it was formed from parts of this older province. When referring to the administrative area in the text, the German name Westpreussen is used; when referring to the larger province the term West Prussia is used. Westpreussen was officially incorporated into the province of Ostpreussen. In the present study, however, it is retained as a separate administrative area. Likewise the newly created *Grenzmark* Posen-Westpreussen (area 9A) should not be confused with the larger areas of the former *Regierungsbezirk* Posen (area 09) or the even larger former provinces of Posnania or West Prussia.

[15]

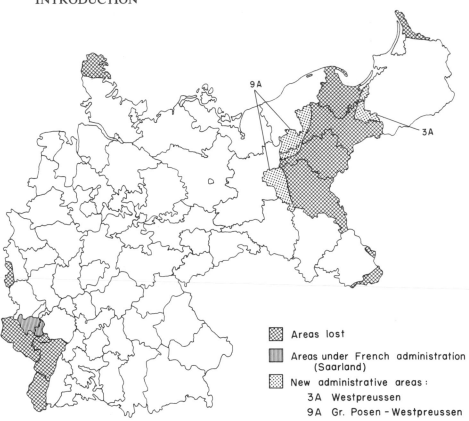

Map 1.3. Boundaries of Germany: After World War I

In order to examine the importance of regional influences on the German fertility decline it is necessary to group the 71 administrative areas into a smaller number of regions, each of which consists of two or more contiguous administrative areas. Ideally the regional groupings should possess some apparent economic, political, or other sociocultural identity. This raises the question of the appropriate delineation of regions. Unfortunately, there is no conventionally accepted set of regional groupings of German administrative areas which could be adopted in the present study. Traditional political subdivisions, namely states, are unacceptable since, as already described, they vary too much with regards to the number of areas they encompass. Indeed many include only one administrative area. Another possibility might be to group together into regions areas which share a common dialect. Although the intuitive logic of such an approach is particularly appealing, it was not adopted in the present study (see Appendix 1A). Linguistic maps of German dialects reveal that the boundaries of dialect regions do not always coincide with the political boundaries of the administrative areas. In fact in several cases the dialect boundaries run through the middle of administrative areas.

The German Statistical Bureau has used several different regional classifications for grouping together contiguous administrative areas. Prior to World War I official presentations of census results grouped together middle level administrative areas solely on the basis of the political subdivisions of the nation, that is by state in the event a state comprised of more than one administrative area as defined here. The 1925 census however delineated six larger regions in Germany and frequently used this as a basis of grouping together contiguous administrative areas in their presentation of the census results.[8] The criteria which the German Statistical Bureau used in order to delineate the regions was not made explicit in their publications.[9] They are referred to merely as the six large geographical regions of Germany. The publications of the 1933 census used a somewhat different regional classification which combined the administrative areas into five regions.[10] Again the rationale behind the delineation of the regional boundaries was unspecified. The 1925 and the 1933 classifications are quite similar The main difference, although not the only one, results from the combination of two of the 1925 regions into a single region. The borders of both sets of regions probably represent some undefined mix of natural, historical, and cultural boundaries. It should also be noted that in both the 1925 and 1933 censuses several other regional classifications are used in addition, although much less frequently than the two referred to above.[11] Thus it appears that the division of Germany into large geographical regions is to some extent

[8]See for example, Germany, Statistisches Reichsamt, *Statistik des Deutschen Reichs*, vol. 401, part II, pp. 512–513.

[9]The current officials of the Federal Statistical Office are also unaware of the criteria used (personal communication dated September 1, 1970 from Dr. Hermann Schubnell, the present head of the Division of Population and Cultural Statistics in the Federal Statistical Office).

[10]See for example, Germany, Statistiches Reichsamt, *Statistik des Deutschen Reiches*, vol. 451, part I, pp. 45–51.

[11]See for example, *ibid*, vol. 401, part II, p. 542, and *ibid*, vol. 451, part I, p. 23.

an arbitrary matter. The substantial agreement among the various regional classifications used in the census publications as well as the considerable overlap between these regions and those that could be formed using a linguistic map is somewhat encouraging. For the present study, a modified version of the main regional classification scheme employed in the 1925 census was adopted. A description of the method used to choose among the several alternative regional classifications is presented in Appendix 1A.

The seven regions of Germany specified for use in this study are shown in Map 1.4. They are identical to the regions specified in the

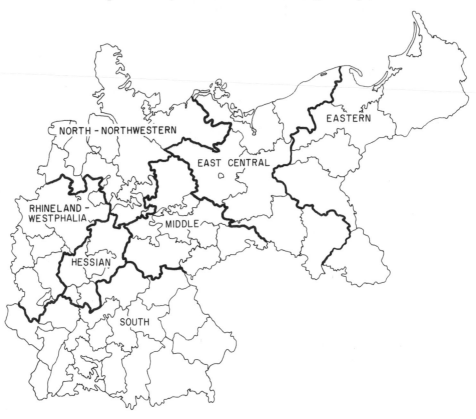

Map 1.4. Geographic Regions of Germany

1925 census except that the eastern administrative areas have been divided into two regions rather than grouped into a single one. In 1925 much of the easternmost region no longer belonged to Germany as it had been lost after World War I. This may account for the fact that no separate region covering this area was specified in the 1925 census. However, since most of the administrative areas which constitute this region contained substantial proportions of the population that was ethically and linguistically not German, the region has a character distinct from the east central German region and thus is identified separately in the classification employed in the present study. The regions and their constituent administrative areas are listed in Table 1.4.

The Demographic Statistics of Germany

The present study is based on two main sources of demographic information: census data and vital statistics. German officials have a worldwide reputation for rigor and precision which is shared by the statistics they issue. Nevertheless, questions concerning data quality, especially when historical statistical trends are being investigated, are too important to be dismissed on the basis of general reputation. Therefore a few introductory remarks about the development of the German statistical system and several tests of data consistency are presented as an aid to evaluating the quality of the data which forms the basis of the present study.

The historical development of censuses and vital registration is more complicated in Germany than in many other European states which had achieved some earlier semblance of national political unity.[12] Prior to the nineteenth century, population data for large parts of Germany were neither abundant nor precise enough to be of great value. Modern censuses evolved in Germany during the nineteenth century. In 1800 the country was divided into some hundred states, but no central agency existed for instituting an exact census on a uniform plan. The formation of the *Deutscher Bund* in 1815

[12]The following treatment of the development of German censuses is based in part on a discussion by Zahn in the introduction to the 1900 census, *ibid*, vol. 150, and on "70 Jahre Volkszählung im Deutschen Reich," *Wirtschaft und Statistick*, vol. 21 (1941), pp. 409 ff.

INTRODUCTION

TABLE 1.4

ADMINISTRATIVE AREAS BY GEOGRAPHICAL REGION

I. Eastern Region	V. Rhineland-Westphalia Region
01 Ostpreussen	24 Münster
02 Danzig	25 Minden
03 Marienwerder	26 Arnsberg
09 Posen	29 Koblenz
10 Bromberg	30 Düsseldorf
13 Oppeln	31 Köln
	32 Trier
II. East Central Region	33 Aachen
	61 Birkenfeld
04 Berlin	65 Lippe
05 Potsdam	
06 Frankfurt/Oder	VI. Hessian Region
07 Stettin-Stralsund	
08 Köslin	27 Kassel
11 Breslau	28 Wiesbaden
12 Liegnitz	54 Starkenburg
	55 Oberhessen
III. Middle Region	56 Rheinhessen
14 Magdeburg	
15 Merseburg	VII. Southern Region
16 Erfurt	
43 Dresden	34 Sigmaringen
44 Leipzig	35 Oberbayern
45 Zwickau	36 Niederbayern
58 Thüringen	37 Pfalz
63 Anhalt	38 Oberpfalz
	39 Oberfranken
	40 Mittelfranken
IV. North-Northwestern Region	41 Unterfranken
	42 Schwaben
17 Schleswig	46 Neckarkreis
18 Hannover	47 Schwarzwaldkreis
19 Hildesheim	48 Jagstkreis
20 Lüneburg	49 Dcnaukreis
21 Stade	50 Konstanz
22 Osnabrück	51 Freiburg
23 Aurich	52 Karlsruhe
57 Mecklenburg	53 Mannheim
59 H. Oldenburg	69 Unterelsass
60 F. Lübeck	70 Oberelsass
62 Braunschweig	71 Lothringen
64 Schaumburg-Lippe	
66 Lübeck	
67 Bremen	
68 Hamburg	

SOURCE: Regions I and II constructed by the author; Regions III - VII, 1925
          official census.

effected little change in this respect, and it was left to the individual states to decide the manner in which the census should be taken.

Between 1816 and 1969 four periods can be distinguished with regard to the development of German population censuses. The first period ends in 1834. During this time most states of the *Deutscher Bund* compiled frequent, often annual, population counts. The police generally used household registers for this purpose and the entire process frequently took several months. Uniform guidelines were lacking both within and between the individual states. In contrast to later years, census counts during this initial period usually had no special significance for the various customs of trade agreements which existed. The customs pact between Bavaria and Württemberg in January 1828 was the first which incorporated a regulation that the net proceeds would be divided according to population size and the exact population counts would be taken each three years for this purpose.

Starting in 1834, the second period of census-taking in Germany began. According to the agreements of the newly formed *Zollverein*, censuses were to take place every three years in all member states (which included most of Germany).[13] These censuses were to be taken during the month of December by community police officials to determine the number of long term residents of the state. The results yielded the *Zollabrechnungsbevölkerung*, which served as the basis for distributing the revenue of the *Zollverein*. Enough detail was to be recorded to allow distinction between civil and military population and the population over and under 14 years of age by sex. Starting in 1843, the census was to take place on a single fixed day rather than over the entire month of December. More important, however, direct house-to-house counts of individuals were required and no longer could the count be based simply on the dwelling unit registers. In addition, each community was to keep complete lists of all inhabitants explicit for use during census-taking. This method had proved highly

---

[13]By 1843 the *Zollverein* included Prussia, Bavaria, K. Saxony, Württemburg, Hesse-Nassau, Gd. Hesse, the Thüringen States, Anhalt, and the two duchies of Hohenzollern. Membership increased during the following decades and by 1867 only Mecklenburg, Lauenburg, and the free cities of Lübeck, Bremen, and Hamburg were not members.

successful in improving population counts in Prussia, where it had been in general use by 1840. In 1864, the census became truly nominative. The census taker was to list each person by name rather than merely count inhabitants. This regulation had already been in force in some of the large states. The last census of this second period was in 1867, when for the first time the census took place simultaneously in all German states, including those that were not members of the *Zollverein*.[14] In addition, most states for the first time counted the *de facto* population (*Ortsanwesende*).

The third period in the development of German population censuses dates between 1871 and 1910. By 1867 it was evident that the purpose of population counts had changed. The narrow aim of determining the basis for the distribution of customs revenue was replaced by much broader administrative purposes including military recruitment and determination of electorate power. Therefore a much wider range of information was required through the census than previously. Standard census guidelines were established by a central commission. Following German unification in 1871, uniform census statistics were published in substantial detail for all states. However, even after unification the state statistical bureaus continued to maintain considerable autonomy, frequently publishing data in greater detail than the national *Statistisches Reichsamt*. In addition it should be noted that several states published census data in great detail even prior to unification. Between 1875 and 1910 a census was taken every five years. All counts during this third period were based on the *de facto* population.

The last period of German censuses prior to World War II includes three censuses taken in 1925, 1933, and 1939. For the first time, population counts were combined with occupation and industrial censuses (*Berufs- und Betriebszählungen*). The census day was moved to the middle of the year and *de jure* population (*Wohnbevölkerung*) was tabulated. The censuses in 1933 and 1939 contained extensive questions on fertility (children ever born). This information was tabulated on a cohort basis.

Until the last quarter of the nineteenth century ecclesiastical registers served as the official source for data on vital events (births, deaths, and marriages) in most German states. Not until 1875 were civil

14Excluding Alsace-Lorraine, which at that time was still part of France.

registers established throughout Germany, although some states had instituted a civil system several years earlier. Uniform regulations governing the information to be collected were legislated in 1870. Uniform vital statistics were published for all states from this date on by the *Statistisches Reichsamt*. Both prior to and after unification the individual states maintained autonomy with regard to the detailed vital statistics they chose to publish on their own. Because of the relative independence of the individual state statistical bureaus, the amount of detail and format of both vital statistics and census data beyond the minimum required for national publications varies considerably from state to state and year to year.

Since the present study is limited largely to the analysis of demographic trends after the 1860s, tests of data reliability prior to this time are given only cursory consideration. It is worth noting, however, that some of the improvements in census-taking techniques during the first half of the nineteenth century resulted in increasing completeness of enumerations. Thus growth rates in the population determined from comparing successive population counts during this period are spuriously high. Table 1.5 illustrates this by comparing the apparent

TABLE 1.5

POPULATION INCREASE, CENSUSES VS. VITAL STATISTICS, PRUSSIA: 1817 TO 1849

| | Absolute increase | | Annual percentage increase | |
Date	Census counts	Vital registration	Census counts	Vital registration
1817-1820	923,451	642,950	2.14	1.51
1832-1837	1,059,165	763,064	1.30	0.95
1838-1840	830,376	486,937	1.91	1.13
1841-1849	1,402,686	1,410,604	1.00	1.00

increase in population in Prussia indicated by successive censuses and the increase indicated by the surplus of births over deaths during the intervening period. [15] In Prussia, the 1820 census was an improvement over the previous censuses because a tax list was drawn up during 1820

[15]The examples and the following discussion are based largely on von Fircks, *Preussische Statistick* (1879), pp. 8–11.

which covered about nine tenths of the population. This list was an aid in the census which took place at the end of the year. Another possible explanation for the discrepancy between the figures is, of course, that births relative to deaths were underregistered. However, the rate of natural increase that the birth and death rates suggest is not at all unreasonable. It is also unlikely that any significant net in-migration took place during the period. Thus the difference in increase indicated by the census results and the surplus of births over deaths appears to be a result of improved census coverage. Major improvements in census methods were again introduced prior to the 1837 census and prior to the 1840 census. Both censuses indicated considerably greater increases in the population than would be expected from the vital registration data. There may have been some net in-migration during the 1830s, but it is unlikely that it can account for most of the difference. In contrast, the increase indicated by the surplus of births over deaths during 1841–1849 agree very closely with the census results. During this time no major changes were introduced in enumeration methods.

The high quality of German censuses during the latter part of the nineteenth century is illustrated in Figure 1.1, which plots the single year age distributions for the 1871, 1880, 1890, and 1900 censuses. Each census was taken at the beginning of December. The birth year of respondents was recorded rather than current age. Since infants born during the year of the census constitute roughly 11/12 of the full year cohort at the time of the census, the figures have been adjusted to allow for the births that would occur during the month of December.[16] The number of successive cohorts enumerated in each census is plotted according to the year of birth. Two features stand out. First, very little age-heaping is evident. Age-heaping would be expected to occur more around birth years ending in 5 or 0 than around ages ending 5 or 0 since age was not directly asked in the census. Actually, for all but the 1871 census, ages ending in 5 or 0 roughly corresponded to birth years ending in 5 or 0. Thus on December 1, 1880 all persons

[16]For the 1871 and 1880 census these adjustments were included in the census publication. For the 1890 and 1900 censuses, the number of infants aged 0-1 year were taken rather than the birth cohort of the census year.

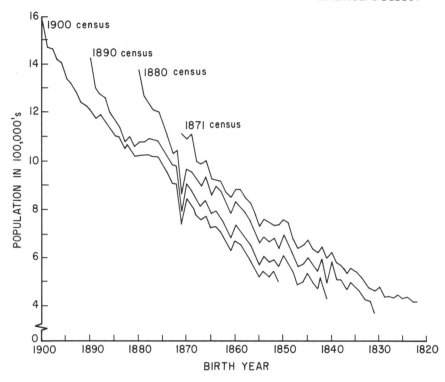

Figure 1.1. Population by Year of Birth: Census of 1871, 1880, 1890, and 1900

40 years old had been born during the year 1840 except the few born in December 1839. Slight age-heaping is evident for birth years 1860, 1850, and 1840. This is less so in the 1871 census than the other three, perhaps because in December 1871 if the last digit of a person's age were 0 or 5, the last digit of his birth year would be 1 or 6, and thus a compounding effect for age-heaping did not exist. Incidentally, no age-heaping is apparent around birth years ending in 5. The jump in the distributions for birth year 1845 reflects a genuine excess of births in that year relative to 1844 and 1846. The second striking feature of Figure 1.1 is the parallelism between the age distributions of the four censuses. The relatively small birth cohort of 1871, for example, stands out sharply in each successive census. However, less spectacular dips and peaks also recur. This consistency attests to the reliability of German censuses.

[25]

INTRODUCTION

A rough impression of the completeness of birth registration can be obtained by examining trends in the ratio of stillbirths to total births. It seems plausible that stillbirths are more likely to suffer from under-registration than live births. Thus a trend of increasing proportions of stillbirths is usually a result of improving registration rather than deteriorating health conditions. Also, in any given period areas with particularly low ratios of stillbirths to total births are suspect unless convincing evidence exists that prenatal care or other health factors are relatively better in that area.

Rising proportions of stillbirths are indicated by Prussian birth statistics during the first half of the nineteenth century (Table 1.6).

TABLE 1.6

STILLBIRTH RATE, PRUSSIA AND ALL GERMANY: 1816 TO 1900

Date	Prussia	All Germany
1816-1820	31.1	--
1821-1830	33.3	--
1831-1840	37.0	--
1841-1850	38.4	39.0
1851-1860	40.7	40.5
1861-1870	41.2	40.7
1871-1880	40.7	39.6
1881-1890	38.4	37.1
1891-1900	32.7	32.4

NOTE: The stillbirth rate refers to the number of still-
         births per 1,000 total births.

Stillbirth ratios appeared to level off by the 1860s and apparently declined during the latter part of the century. For all of Germany such data are available only after 1840. Not much increase is evident in Germany after this date. The increasing proportions of stillbirths in Prussia is probably an indication of greater completeness of stillbirth registrations. Von Fircks, writing for the Prussian Statistical Bureau, expressed this opinion. However he felt stillbirth registration was essentially complete following 1850 in Prussia (von Fircks, 1879, pp. 36–37). In fact during the period 1855–1864 only two of the 27 Prus-

[26]

sian areas (*Regierungsbezirke*) for which data are available showed less than 3 percent of total births registered as stillbirths. In the period 1865–1874 and the year 1880 among the 34 Prussian administrative areas, the comparable number was 2 and 1 respectively.

If we examine data for each of the 71 administrative areas of Germany during the decade of the 1870s, only a few areas indicate less than 3 percent of total births being born as stillbirths, and the number dwindles rapidly during the first few years of the decade. In 1872 twelve areas indicate less than 3 percent stillbirths, whereas in 1875 only half that number do. It is unlikely however that the low proportions of stillbirths indicate underregistration in most of these areas. Almost every area with less than 3 percent stillbirths during the 1870s had extremely high marital fertility rates, suggesting rather complete registration (assuming complete census statistics for married women). It is more likely that in these areas stillbirths were frequently registered as live births for religious reasons. In every area with less than 3 percent stillbirths the majority were Catholic, and in most of the cases Catholics represented over 80 percent of the population. As Grassl (1904, pp. 283–284) has commented in discussing the frequency of stillbirths in Bavaria, Catholics are more likely to consider a stillbirth as a live one in order to baptize it before it is considered dead.

A considerably more exacting test of the reliability of census and vital registration data is achieved through a comparison of one with the other. If such data were completely accurate we would expect, for example, the number of infants 0–1 years old in an area to equal the number of births in the previous 12 months minus the number of deaths occurring to those born during the year plus the net increment caused by migration. Since families with small infants are not likely to migrate, the net migration effect is probably negligible. Detailed vital statistics for Prussia concerning births by month and infant deaths by year of birth (as well as by month of birth in 1864) and by year of occurrence are available. Thus, for example, for 1864 it is possible to calculate according to the vital statistics how many infants born that year would be alive at the beginning of December when the census was taken. The number of infants that were born in 1864 and died during December 1864 was estimated from the distribution of deaths in 1864 classified by month of birth. It was assumed that the proportion of infant deaths occurring in December to infants born in each month of the year equalled the proportion that would be expected according to the 1875–1876 life table values for Prussian infants given by month of life for the first year of life.[17] Since the census enumerated the population by year of birth, a comparison between the enumerated number of infants and the expected number according to vital registration can be made. The results of such comparisons for 1864, 1867, 1880, and 1900 are presented in Table 1.7.

The reasonably close agreement between census results and vital registration results in all four years testifies to the high quality of demographic statistics already achieved by the 1860s in Prussia. Although deficiencies in both sets of data in the same area would cancel each other out and thus not be evident in the above comparison, there is no reason to expect such compensating errors. The areas of eastern Prussia show lower ratios suggesting some undercount in the census. However, the areas experienced particularly heavy outmigration which might account for at least some of the deficit. The ratio for the entire state of Prussia is very similar for all three years although the results for the states show greater uniformity in 1880 and 1900.

A further illustration of the quality of Prussian demographic statistics appears in Table 1.8, which compares the number of children by single years of birth enumerated in the 1871 and 1875 censuses to the number of children which would be expected according to vital registration, ignoring the effects of migration.[18] Again the agreement between the two sources of data is striking, although some slight age misreporting is apparent. During the period prior to 1871 out-migration is thought to have exceeded in-migration, and yet several of the older age groups show a larger enumerated population than would be expected from registration without taking account of any loss through migration. This excess probably results in part from the inclusion of some younger children in the older age groups. This would help also to explain the relative deficit of children in the youngest birth cohorts. The same phenomenon is apparent in the 1875 census as well.

[17]The life table values for infants according to age in months (and weeks) were taken from von Fricks (1879), pp. 88–89.

[18]For a detailed description of the calculations, see von Fircks (1879), pp. 11–15.

TABLE 1.7

RATIO OF INFANTS ENUMERATED IN CENSUS TO INFANTS EXPECTED TO BE
SURVIVING ACCORDING TO VITAL REGISTRATION,
BY ADMINISTRATIVE AREA, PRUSSIA: 1864, 1867, 1880, AND 1900

	Area	1864	1867	1880	1900
01	Ostpreussen	.93	.92	.95	.94
02	Danzig	.94	.93	.95	.95
03	Marienwerder	.91	.89	.93	.94
04	Berlin	.98	.97	.98	.96
05	Potsdam	--	.99	1.00	1.01
06	Frankfurt/Oder	.96	.96	1.01	.99
07	Stettin-Stralsund	.96	.95	.97	.97
08	Köslin	.97	.95	.98	.97
09	Posen	.98	.94	.96	.95
10	Bromberg	.96	.93	.95	.94
11	Breslau	.98	.97	.99	.98
12	Liegnitz	.99	.98	.99	.99
13	Oppeln	.99	.96	.96	.96
14	Magdeburg	.96	.97	.99	.98
15	Merseburg	.96	.99	.99	.99
16	Erfurt	.99	.97	.98	.99
17	Schleswig	--	1.02	.98	.98
18	Hannover	--	.94	.98	.97
19	Hildesheim	--	.95	.99	.98
20	Lüneburg	--	.96	.99	.98
21	Stade	--	.98	.98	.98
22	Osnabrück	--	.94	.96	.97
23	Aurich	--	.96	.98	.97
24	Münster	.99	.98	.98	.98
25	Minden	.97	.95	.98	.97
26	Arnsberg	.96	.95	.98	.99
27	Kassel	--	.94	.98	.98
28	Wiesbaden	--	.96	.99	.99
29	Koblenz	.98	.97	.99	.99
30	Düsseldorf	.98	.98	.99	.98
31	Köln	1.00	.96	.97	.96
32	Trier	.99	.97	.98	.98
33	Aachen	1.02	1.00	.99	.99
34	Sigmaringen	.94	.94	.99	.97
	Prussia	.97	.96	.98	.97

NOTE: Censuses were taken at the beginning of December. For 1864 and 1867,
the ratios refer to infants aged 0 to 11 months at the beginning
of December; in 1867, the number of who were born in 1867 but who
died in December 1867 was estimated according to the comparable
proportions estimated for 1864 by the author. For 1880 and 1900,
the ratios refer to infants aged under one year at year end;
although the 1880 and 1900 census took place at the beginning of
December, the published results include estimates of the number of
infants aged under one year at year end. Presumably these
published estimates were determined by adding to the enumerated
infants aged 0 to 11 months the excess of births in December over
deaths occurring in December to infants born in the census year.

TABLE 1.8

COMPARISON OF CHILDREN ENUMERATED IN CENSUS AND CHILDREN
EXPECTED TO BE SURVIVING ACCORDING TO VITAL REGISTRATION,
BY SINGLE YEARS OF AGE, PRUSSIA: 1871 AND 1875

	1871			1875		
Age	Enumer-ated in census	Expected from vital registra-tion	Ratio of enum-erated to regis-tered	Enumer-ated in census	Expected from vital registra-tion	Ratio of enum-erated to regis-tered
0-1	675,426	693,202	.974	866,233	882,989	.981
1-2	669,690	698,689	.958	727,396	748,688	.972
2-3	680,980	672,804	1.012	698,536	711,831	.981
3-4	613,979	616,338	.996	675,130	677,972	.996
4-5	605,982	604,651	1.002	553,064	544,710	1.015
5-6	615,831	597,740	1.030	611,074	616,665	.991
6-7	577,743	575,410	1.004	624,008	617,664	1.010
7-8	572,092	571,333	1.001	--	--	--
Total	5,011,723	5,030,167	.996	4,755,441	4,800,519	.991

SOURCE: von Fircks, 1879, pp. 14-15.
NOTES: Boundaries for 1871 data are those existing prior to 1867;
        boundaries for 1875 include all acquisitions except Lauenburg.
        Census enumerations are adjusted to allow for births and deaths in
        December of census year.

This brief testing of the quality of German (and Prussian) demographic data helps substantiate the assertion that censuses and vital
registration were virtually complete and accurate in their coverage by
the 1860s. Thus, the published data are accepted at face value and no
attempts are made in the present study to correct possible deficiencies.

Population Size and Growth

The population size of each administrative area of Germany is given
in Table 1.9 for three census years: 1870, 1900, and 1933. Also included is the area in square kilometers according to the 1900 boundaries. Although population size of these areas is not uniform, it is
much less variable than the states as single units.

During the nineteenth century the population increased rapidly in

[30]

TABLE 1.9

GEOGRAPHICAL SIZE OF ADMINISTRATIVE AREAS IN 1900
AND POPULATION OF ADMINISTRATIVE AREAS IN 1871, 1900, AND 1933

Administrative area	Size (sq.km.)	Population (000)			Administrative area	Size (sq.km.)	Population (000)		
		1871	1900	1933			1871	1900	1933
01 Ostpreussen	21,108	1,823	1,997	2,056	37 Pfalz	5,928	615	832	986
02 Danzig	7,957	525	666	--	38 Oberpfalz	9,652	498	554	652
03 Marienwerder	15,578	790	898	--	39 Oberfranken	6,999	541	608	786
3A Westpreussen	--	--	--	277	40 Mittelfranken	7,583	584	816	1,037
04 Berlin	63	826	1,889	4,243	41 Unterfranken	8,402	586	651	796
05 Potsdam	20,639	1,002	1,929	1,415	42 Schwaben	9,824	583	714	878
06 Frankfurt/O.	19,198	1,035	1,179	1,311	43 Dresden	6,807	1,008	1,622	1,917
07 Stettin-Str.	16,089	879	1,047	1,236	44 Leipzig	3,567	589	1,061	1,368
08 Köslin	14,031	552	588	686	45 Zwickau	4,619	959	1,520	1,912
09 Posen	17,519	1,017	1,198	--	46 Neckarkreis	3,330	549	746	1,036
9A Gr.Posen-Wes.	--	--	--	338	47 Schwarzwaldkreis	4,776	448	509	621
10 Bromberg	11,452	567	689	--	48 Jagstkreis	5,141	385	400	430
11 Breslau	13,484	1,415	1,698	1,944	49 Donaukreis	6,266	437	514	609
12 Liegnitz	13,610	983	1,103	1,260	50 Konstanz	4,168	276	297	353
13 Oppeln	13,225	1,310	1,868	1,483	51 Freiburg	4,748	435	510	631
14 Magdeburg	11,513	855	1,176	1,304	52 Karlsruhe	2,567	366	517	688
15 Merseburg	10,211	879	1,190	1,486	53 Mannheim	3,598	385	543	741
16 Erfurt	3,532	369	466	611	54 Starkenburg	3,019	349	490	666
17 Schleswig	19,004	1,045	1,388	1,590	55 Oberhessen	3,287	254	282	343
18 Hannover	5,717	405	648	905	56 Rheinhessen	1,375	250	348	421
19 Hildesheim	5,352	407	527	594	57 Mecklenburg	16,056	655	710	805
20 Lüneburg	11,344	384	473	622	58 Thüringen	12,332	1,067	1,420	1,660
21 Stade	6,786	303	375	468	59 H. Oldenburg	5,383	244	318	467
22 Osnabrück	6,205	269	329	467	60 F. Lübeck	541	34	37	48
23 Aurich	3,108	193	240	311	61 Birkenfeld	503	36	43	59
24 Münster	7,253	436	700	1,561	62 Braunschweig	3,672	312	464	513
25 Minden	5,261	474	637	872	63 Anhalt	2,299	203	316	364
26 Arnsberg	7,697	866	1,851	2,607	64 Schaumburg-L.	340	32	43	50
27 Kassel	11,203	823	948	1,149	65 Lippe	1,215	111	139	176
28 Wiesbaden	5,617	633	1,008	1,436	66 Lübeck	298	52	97	136
29 Koblenz	6,206	555	682	763	67 Bremen	256	122	225	372
30 Düsseldorf	5,473	1,328	2,600	4,079	68 Hamburg	415	339	768	1,218
31 Köln	3,977	613	1,022	1,545	69 Unterelsass	4,784	600	659	--
32 Trier	7,184	592	841	498	70 Oberelsass	3,505	459	495	--
33 Aachen	4,155	491	615	748	71 Lothringen	6,223	490	565	--
34 Sigmaringen	1,142	66	67	73					
35 Oberbayern	16,725	842	1,324	1,777	Germany	540,743	41,010	56,368	65,218
36 Niederbayern	10,757	604	678	770					

NOTE: Population data based on official censuses of 1871, 1900, and 1933.

Germany as illustrated by Table 1.10. The relatively high rates of increase between 1816 and 1825 as well as between 1834 and 1843 probably reflect improving census methods. The high rate between 1871 and 1880 on the other hand results from the particularly large numbers of births in that decade. The faster decline of the death rate than the birth rate resulted in the higher levels of growth between 1890 and 1910. By 1925–1933, the decling birth rate had more than compensated for the reduction in death rates, and thus the rate of increase is substantially reduced.

Differences in regional rates of growth are apparent particularly

TABLE 1.10

TOTAL POPULATION: 1816 TO 1933

Territory	Year	Population (000)	Average annual growth rate
Boundaries of	1816	24,831	--
1910	1825	28,111	.014
	1834	30,609	.009
	1843	33,722	.011
	1852	35,930	.007
	1861	38,137	.007
	1871	40,997	.007
	1880	45,095	.011
	1890	49,241	.009
	1900	56,046	.013
	1910	64,568	.014
- - - - - - - - - -	- - - - -	- - - - - - - - -	- - - - - - - - - - - - -
Boundaries of	1910	58,451	--
1933, including	1925	63,181	.005
the Saarland	1933	66,030	.006

SOURCE: Statistisches Bundesamt, <u>Statistisches Jahrbuch für die Bundesre-publik Deutschland 1963</u>, p. 33 and Statistisches Reichsamt, <u>Statistik des Deutschen Reichs</u>, vol. 451, 1, p. 15.

TABLE 1.11

POPULATION GROWTH INDEX, BY REGION: 1825 to 1871, AND 1871 TO 1933

Region	Population growth index 1825 to 1871 (1825 population set at 100)						Population growth index 1871 to 1933 (1871 population set at 100)						
	1825	1834	1843	1852	1861	1871	1871	1880	1890	1900	1910	1925	1933
Eastern	100	109	128	138	152	167	100	108	111	121	134	--	--
E.Central(excl.Berlin)	100	109	125	137	147	154	100	107	110	117	125	133	137
Berlin	100	120	160	206	244	371	100	124	210	291	401	432	455
Middle	100	113	125	137	150	165	100	113	129	148	165	174	180
North-Northwestern	100	105	113	118	124	132	100	110	121	139	162	175	183
Rhineland-Westphalia	100	111	123	132	144	158	100	114	133	167	210	239	252
Hessian	100	110	120	123	125	129	100	110	118	133	155	166	173
Southern	100	107	113	116	118	124	100	108	114	125	140	150	157
Germany	100	109	120	128	136	146	100	111	122	140	161	174	182

NOTE: Boundaries for all data are those existing in 1934, with the exception of the Eastern Region for which 1910 boundaries were used. For this index, 61 Birkenfeld is included in the North-Northwestern Region, the Saarland is included in the Rhineland-Westphalia region, and Alsace-Lorraine is excluded.

during the period of rapid industrialization and the resultant internal migration. This is clear from Table 1.11 which shows population growth in the various regions of Germany during the periods 1825–1871 and 1871–1933. Berlin, the important center of administration, clearly grew fastest during both periods. Important differences in growth rates among the other regions did exist however between the two periods. Prior to German unification in 1871, Middle Germany and Rhineland-Westphalia as well as the agrarian eastern and east central regions of Germany were above average in growth. In southern Germany growth was particularly slow. After unification the situation was changed. Eastern and east central Germany grew at a considerably slower rate than previously and much slower than the rest of Germany. The western industrial area of Rhineland-Westphalia, the major recipient of migration of eastern regions, grew rapidly. The southern region again lagged somewhat below the average.

The Demographic Indices

A set of interrelated demographic indices developed by Coale are employed in this study to describe trends in fertility and nuptiality (Coale, 1965 and 1969). The index of overall fertility (I_f) measures the extent to which women in a given population approach the number of births they would have if all were subject to the highest schedule of age-specific fertility on reliable record: the fertility of married Hutterite women in 1921–1930.[19] Thus,

$$I_f = \frac{B}{\sum w_i F_i},$$

where B is the annual number of births to all women in a given period, w_i is the number of women in each five-year age interval from 15

[19]The standard schedule as given by Henry (1961, p. 84) indicates the following number of births per married women per year in each age group:

20–24	.550
25–29	.502
30–34	.447
35–39	.406
40–44	.222
45–49	.061

through 49, and F_i is the fertility of married Hutterite women in each age interval. An index of marital fertility (I_g) indicates how closely married women approach the number of births they would produce if they experienced the Hutterite fertility. Specifically,

$$I_g = \frac{B_L}{\sum m_i F_i},$$

where B_L is the annual number of legitimate births and m_i is the number of married women in each five-year age interval. An index of illegitimate fertility (I_h) indicates how closely the fertility of unmarried women approaches that of the married Hutterites. Thus,

$$I_h = \frac{B_I}{\sum u_i F_i},$$

where B_I represents the annual number of illegitimate births and u_i are the number of unmarried women in the corresponding age interval.

These three basic fertility indices take into account in their computation the maximum amount of data typically available for German states from the vital statistics and censuses: i.e. births by legitimacy and age distributions by marital status. Age-specific marital fertility rates or other more refined measures would be more useful analytically in identifying the onset of family limitation and fertility decline. Long series of births by age of mother or other more specific data, however, are not available for most German states during much of the period under investigation. The three fertility indices used in this study do have the particular advantage of lending themselves to intuitive interpretations; that is, they can be considered ratios of the number of births actually had by women to the plausible maximum they could experience.

The Hutterite schedule of marital fertility was selected as the standardizing schedule because it represents the highest reliable schedule of natural fertility on record. Natural fertility is used here to mean, as it is defined by Henry, fertility existing in the absence of deliberate birth control (Henry, 1961). Although the absolute value of the fertility indices would be affected if alternative schedules of natural fertility were employed instead of the Hutterite rates, the relative change measured by such indices would be practically identical. Thus, a 57 percent decline in marital fertility in Germany between 1875 and 1925 is indicated regardless of which of the 12 possible schedules of natural fertility proposed by Henry is used (Henry, 1961, p. 84).[20]

A fourth index (I_m) summarizes the proportion married among women in the childbearing ages by comparing the number of children married women would bear if experiencing the Hutterites' marital fertility rates to the number all women would bear if subject to the same fertility schedule. More precisely,

$$I_m = \frac{\sum m_i F_i}{\sum w_i F_i}.$$

This index indicates how much marriage is contributing to the achievement of the highest potential fertility of the given population. It depends on the average age of marriage, on the proportion of women who never get married, and on the frequency of widowhood, divorce, and remarriage. Perhaps I_m is best thought of as a weighted index of the proportion of women married giving a large weight to the proportion of married women in the most fertile years.

The four indices just described are related in such a manner that

$$I_f = I_g \cdot I_m + I_h \cdot (1 - I_m)$$

Thus, when illegitimacy is negligible, the level of overall fertility can be expressed as the product of marital fertility and proportion married.

As Coale has pointed out, I_m is not free from the effects of the female age distribution (Coale, 1969, pp. 5–6). Indeed none of the four indices described above is completely independent of the populations age structure. However, since we know the proportions of women married at each age, it is possible to construct an alternative index of proportion married (I_m*) which eliminates completely the influence of age structure. Defined in terms of the symbols used above

$$I_m* = \frac{\sum F_i \frac{m_i}{w_i}}{\sum F_i}.$$

[20]For women 15–19 a value of .300 was assigned to represent the annual marital fertility rate in all schedules.

This index would be identical to I_m if the age distribution of women 15–49 were rectangular. I_m then bears a similar relationship to I_{m*} as I_f bears to the total fertility rate which implies a rectangular age distribution. Similar alternative indices could be constructed for I_f, I_g and I_h in order to eliminate the influence of age structure on them if age-specific fertility rates were known. Since age-specific data are rarely available, however, such alternative indices are of only hypothetical interest.

The correlation between the two indices of proportion married for the different areas of Germany is high in any given year. In fact, the correlation coefficient r ranges between .957 and .985 for the eight census years from 1871 through 1933 for which tabulations of marital status and age are available. Changes in the two indices over time are also relatively consistent with each other although some difference does emerge (Table 1.12). As might be expected, since the index I_{m*}

TABLE 1.12

PROPORTION MARRIED (I_m & I_m*), CORRELATION BETWEEN CHANGES IN THE TWO INDICES OVER THREE TIME PERIODS

Time Period	Correlation Coefficients	
	Absolute Change	Relative Change
1871-1900	.893	.883
1900-1933	.947	.956
1871-1933	.922	.931

eliminates the potentially disturbing influence of age distribution, values for this index are more consistent with each other from census to census than are values of I_m. This is evident from the correlations presented in Table 1.13. I_m values in 1871 are correlated with I_m values in later years. I_{m*} values in 1871 are similarly correlated with I_{m*} values in later years. The higher correlations between I_{m*} values reflect the greater consistency.

In the ensuing chapters, the description of fertility and nuptiality will be primarily in terms of the four interrelated demographic indices just discussed with the additional inclusion of I_{m*} when it is likely that

TABLE 1.13

PROPORTION MARRIED (I_m & I_m^*), CORRELATIONS BETWEEN
1871 LEVELS AND SUBSEQUENT LEVELS:
1880, 1900, 1925, AND 1933

Year	I_m 1871	I_m^* 1871
1880	.911	.965
1900	.857	.888
1925	.687	.764
1933	.723	.776

presentation of I_m alone might cause misleading conclusions. However for years prior to 1871 in some German states and prior to 1867 in most of the others, census data are frequently not detailed enough to permit calculation of these indices. Thus for the earlier part of the nineteenth century more conventional but less refined indices of fertility and nuptiality will have to serve as substitutes. This raises the question of comparability. In addition, the indices used in the present study are probably unfamiliar to most readers. Therefore it would be useful to make a comparison between the indices used here and more conventional fertility and nuptiality measures. Appendix 1B presents an empirical comparison of these measures based on the German experience between 1880 and 1925. The findings given in Appendix 1B suggest that the substitute indices used to measure fertility prior to 1870 yield trends that are quite comparable to the trends in marital and overall fertility depicted after that date.

CHAPTER 2: Trends in German Fertility and Nuptiality

This chapter presents and discusses in some detail the trends in the basic demographic indices described in the previous chapter for Germany between the mid-nineteenth century and the beginning of World War II. Because of its size, Appendix Table 2.1, which contains the basic indices for all administrative areas (as well as for states and provinces consisting of more than one area) is presented in Appendix 2A. The indices were calculated for all years during the period between 1867 and 1939 for which sufficient census tabulations and vital statistics were available. For some periods the requisite data were available for only some states. Hence the completeness of the series varies from one administrative area to another. The indices have generally been calculated from data on live births and census age distributions (in five-year age groups) of married and total women. Occasionally minor adjustments of the birth and census data were required in order to increase comparability of the indices. The two most common adjustments involved estimating the number of live illegitimate births from raw data which did not distinguish live from still-born illegitimate births, and dividing census age distributions given in ten-year age groups into five-year age groups. Appendix 2B provides a description of the specific adjustments.

Table 2.1 and the accompanying graphs in Figure 2.1 summarize the national trends in fertility and nuptiality as measured by our demographic indices. Prolonged and precipitious declines are apparent not only in overall and marital fertility, but in illegitimate fertility as well. On the other hand, the predominant trend in the two indices of proportions married during the same period was towards an increase. The bulk of this chapter will be devoted to a detailed examination of these trends in fertility and nuptiality.

The series of indices presented in Appendix Table 2.1 constitute the basic input data used in the following analysis of the fertility decline within Germany. Before such an analysis can proceed, however, it is necessary to explore two preliminary questions:

1. Did fertility start to decline prior to the 1870s, the first decade for which the indices could be calculated for the entire country?

TABLE 2.1

DEMOGRAPHIC INDICES: 1867 to 1961

Census year	Birth registration period	Actual levels					Relative levels (1871 set at 100)				
		Overall fertility I_f	Marital fertility I_g	Illegitimate fertility I_h	Proportion married I_m	I_{m*}	Overall fertility I_f	Marital fertility I_g	Illegitimate fertility I_h	Proportion married I_m	I_{m*}
1867	1866–1868	.389	.761	.079	.454	.501	98	100	111	96	98
1871	1869–1873	.396	.760	.071	.472	.511	100	100	100	100	100
1875	1874–1877	.428	.791	.073	.495	.534	108	104	103	105	105
1880	1878–1882	.404	.735	.072	.501	.543	102	97	101	106	106
1885	1883–1887	.395	.726	.073	.494	.538	100	96	103	105	105
1890	1888–1892	.386	.706	.070	.497	.544	97	93	99	105	106
1900	1898–1902	.373	.664	.066	.513	.557	94	87	93	109	109
1910	1908–1912	.312	.542	.059	.524	.564	79	71	83	111	110
1925	1923–1927	.185	.334	.041	.490	.525	47	44	58	104	103
1933	1931–1935	.157	.264	.033	.534	.526	40	35	46	113	103
1939	1938–1939	.202	.316	.038	.590	.568	51	42	54	125	111
1950	1948–1952	.173	.291	.035	.537	.530	44	38	49	114	104
1961	1959–1963	.200	.301	.032	.625	.627	51	40	45	132	123

NOTES: Data refer to boundaries of the census year except for the following:

1867 - several small states excluded.
1939 - Austria and 3A Westpreussen excluded; areas of Sudetenland annexed by Silesia and Bavaria included.
1950 - West Germany, with West Berlin excluded.
1961 - West Germany, with West Berlin included.

2. Are we justified in assuming that the transition to modern low levels of controlled fertility was essentially complete by the 1930s, the last decade for which indices could be calculated for many areas?

Fertility before 1870

For the purposes of the present study we will rely primarily on a brief survey of fertility trends confined to the several decades pre-

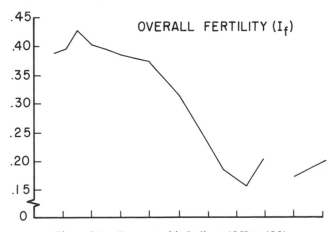

Figure 2.1. Demographic Indices: 1867 to 1961

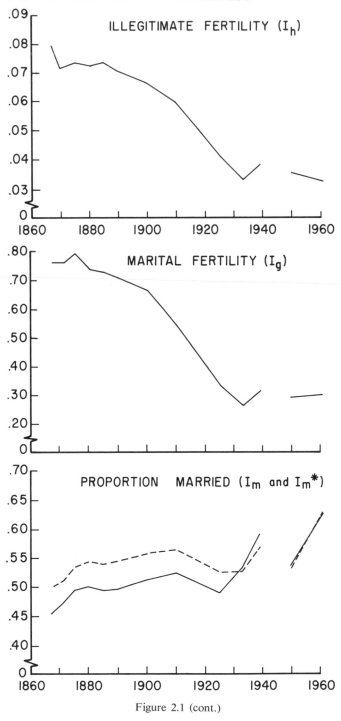

Figure 2.1 (cont.)

ceding 1870 to determine whether or not the sustained decline experienced after this date had begun earlier. It is possible, of course, that an even earlier secular decline in fertility occurred prior to the nineteenth century. Such a decline, although it would be of great demographic interest if it were established, is of no immediate importance in describing the *continuous* decline which concluded in the twentieth century.

Unfortunately, the requisite data needed for the calculation of the basic demographic indices are not available for many German states prior to 1867. Even for the few areas for which the data do exist, they do not cover any extended period of time. Table 2.2 presents the index

TABLE 2.2

MARITAL FERTILITY (I_g), SELECTED AREAS: 1840 TO 1871

Census year	Birth registration period	17 Schleswig	59 H.Oldenburg	60 F. Lübeck	61 Birkenfeld	67 Bremen	Württemberg
1840	1838-1842	.667	--	--	--	--	--
1845	1843-1847	.665	--	--	--	--	--
1855	1854-1856	.667[a]	.656	.588	.636	--	--
1858	1857-1859	--	.674	.620	.675	--	--
1861	1860-1862	.656[b]	.664	.610	.672	.719	.852
1864	1863-1865	--	.692	.608	.686	.726	
1867	1866-1868	.686	.695	.644	.652	.746	.881
1871	1869-1873	.680	.691	.648	.704	.728	.877

[a]Births 1853-1857
[b]Census year 1860, and births 1858-1862

of marital fertility for the five administrative areas and the one state for which it could be calculated for a period extending back at least one decade prior to Unification. In none of these areas does it appear that the continuous fertility decline which characterized them after Unification began in the decades prior to the 1870s.

In a monumental volume of *Preussiche Statistick*, von Fircks (1879) surveys in detail population trends in Prussia from 1816 to 1874. In his opinion, vital statistics registration was virtually complete during the entire period (p.10). Our earlier analysis suggests however that a few areas may have had deficient birth registration. Von Fircks questioned the completeness of the census data before 1840. He pointed out that prior to this date successive population counts indicated increases in excess of the growth represented by the surplus of births over deaths. He attributed most of this excess increase to improving census coverage. Suspiciously high rates of intercensal growth correspond closely with the introduction of improvements in data collection methods during this period. Thus the declining fertility rates indicated in several provinces between 1816 and 1840 appear to be largely a product of greater completeness in the population counts used as the denominator for these rates in combination with an absence of a compensatory improvement in birth registration.

If von Fircks' opinion that census coverage following 1840 was virtually complete is correct, then we can at least rule out the possibility of changing census quality affecting rates in Prussia for three decades prior to the 1870s. Table 2.3 shows general fertility rates for Prussian administrative areas. Most experienced a higher fertility for 1862–1867 than during the previous decades. Many of the areas showing the greatest increases were also areas which appear to have sex ratios at birth that deviate substantially from 105 to 106. This suggests that part of the increase may be merely an artifact of improving registration. Only in a few areas is a slight decline evident. It should be added that fertility was considerably higher in almost all areas during the 1870s. This is apparent in Table 2.4, which shows crude marital fertility rates for the Prussian provinces for periods between 1841 and 1875. All provinces except Ostpreussen exhibit a crude marital fertility rate higher in the years 1872–1875 than in 1865–1867. In Ostpreussen marital fertility as measured by the I_g is very stable between 1870 and 1900 and hence the small decline in the crude rate just after mid-century can hardly be considered the beginning of a continuous decline. The statistical evidence thus does not indicate the beginning of a continuous fertility decline in Prussia before 1870. If any tendencies toward decline existed prior to 1870, they were reversed during the 1870s when fertility was unusually high. Even the capital city of Berlin, which later outpaces almost every other area in Germany with regard to declining fertility, shows no sign of decline until after the 1870s.

TABLE 2.3

GENERAL FERTILITY RATE, BY ADMINISTRATIVE AREA, PRUSSIA: 1841 TO 1867

Area		Actual levels			Relative levels (1862-1867 set at 100)		
		1841-1855	1856-1861	1862-1867	1841-1855	1856-1861	1862-1867
01	Ostpreussen	170	178	181	94	98	100
02	Danzig	178	178	186	96	96	100
03	Marienwerder	199	194	200	100	97	100
04	Berlin	125	136	146	86	93	100
05	Potsdam	164	161	160	103	101	100
06	Frankfurt /O.	164	161	162	101	99	100
07	Stettin-Str.	167	167	167	100	100	100
08	Köslin	171	172	175	98	98	100
09	Posen	180	166	176	102	94	100
10	Bromberg	200	190	195	103	97	100
11	Breslau	158	155	161	98	96	100
12	Liegnitz	144	141	146	99	97	100
13	Oppeln	181	186	186	97	100	100
14	Magdeburg	160	166	164	98	101	100
15	Merseburg	163	172	174	94	99	100
16	Erfurt	151	153	158	96	97	100
17	Schleswig	--	142	147	--	96	100
18	Hannover	134	146	148	91	99	100
19	Hildesheim	135	145	147	92	99	100
20	Lüneburg	124	134	134	93	100	100
21	Stade	150	151	156	96	97	100
22	Osnabrück	127	133	141	90	94	100
23	Aurich	132	140	141	94	99	100
24	Münster	123	125	127	97	98	100
25	Minden	164	158	156	105	101	100
26	Arnsberg	160	174	181	88	96	100
27	Kassel	--	--	--	--	--	--
28	Wiesbaden	--	--	--	--	--	--
29	Koblenz	155	151	153	101	99	100
30	Düsseldorf	164	168	171	96	98	100
31	Köln	163	159	157	104	101	100
32	Trier	142	158	165	86	96	100
33	Aachen	153	152	153	100	99	100
34	Sigmaringen	141[a]	149	153	92[a]	97	100
	Prussia	164	165	168	98	98	100

NOTES: General fertility rate refers to live and stillbirths per 1,000 women aged 14-44.

Schleswig data do not include Lauenburg and are for the years 1856-1859 and 1867.

[a] 1850-1855.

TABLE 2.4

CRUDE MARITAL FERTILITY RATE, BY PROVINCE, PRUSSIA: 1841 TO 1875

Province	Actual levels					Relative levels (1865-1867 set at 100)				
	1841- 1845	1856- 1861	1862- 1864	1865- 1867	1872- 1875	1841- 1845	1856- 1861	1862- 1864	1865- 1867	1872- 1875
Ostpreussen	226	242	236	223	220	101	109	106	100	99
West Prussia	261	257	265	256	258	102	100	104	100	101
Berlin	233	227	220	223	230	104	102	99	100	103
Brandenburg	210	205	199	196	210	107	105	102	100	107
Pomerania	226	222	219	218	223	104	102	100	100	103
Posnania	266	251	256	254	259	105	99	101	100	102
Silesia	217	211	212	213	223	102	99	100	100	105
P. Saxony	204	204	203	202	215	101	101	100	100	106
Westphalia	214	217	222	226	261	95	96	98	100	115
Rhineland	231	224	231	236	263	98	95	98	100	111
Sigmaringen	--	199	195	204	232	--	95	96	100	114
Prussia	225	222	224	222	236	101	100	101	100	106

NOTES: Crude marital fertility rate refers to legitimate births (including stillbirths)
        per 1,000 married women.
        Boundaries for data exclude provinces acquired in 1867.

The only other state besides Prussia for which it was possible to calculate a series of crude marital fertility rates for any length of time prior to 1870 was the kingdom of Saxony. Again marital fertility shows no tendency to decline during this period (Table 2.5).

For the remaining areas of Germany, the only measure of fertility available for the decades prior to unification is the crude birth rate (Table 2.6). Admittedly this is a rather inexact measure of fertility and is particularly inappropriate during the 1860s since in many areas of Germany nuptiality was increasing.[1] Nevertheless, in the absence of more precise measures the crude birth rate will have to serve as our indicator of fertility prior to 1870 for much of Germany. It is clear that the crude birth rate was higher in 1866–1870 than in 1861–1865

[1] For a description of increased marriage rates during the 1860s and 1870s see Knodel, 1967.

[44]

TRENDS IN FERTILITY AND NUPTIALITY

TABLE 2.5

CRUDE MARITAL FERTILITY RATE, KINGDOM OF SAXONY: 1833 TO 1868

Date	Rate	Date	Rate
1833-1838	195	1857-1862	201
1839-1844	192	1863-1865	203
1845-1850	198	1866-1868	201

NOTE: Crude marital fertility rate refers to live legitimate births per 1,000 married women.

TABLE 2.6

CRUDE BIRTH RATE, BY STATE: 1841 TO 1870

State	Actual levels				Relative levels (1866-1870 set at 100)			
	1841-1850	1851-1860	1861-1865	1866-1870	1841-1850	1851-1860	1861-1865	1866-1870
Prussia	38.2	38.1	39.2	39.3	97	97	100	100
Hesse-Nassau	34.9	32.7	34.9	37.0	94	88	94	100
Bavaria	35.2	34.4	36.8	39.5	89	87	93	100
K. Saxony	43.4	43.4	42.2	42.4	102	102	100	100
Württemberg	42.6	37.4	41.2	43.7	97	86	94	100
Baden	39.2	34.2	37.2	39.3	100	87	95	100
Hesse	35.1	32.6	35.2	37.1	95	88	95	100
Mecklenburg	34.6	33.1	33.0	33.3	104	99	99	100
Thüringen	34.6	33.2	36.4	36.8	94	90	99	100
Gd. Oldenburg	30.5	31.5	32.5	32.8	93	96	99	100
Braunschweig	32.3	33.7	34.1	35.0	92	96	97	100
Anhalt	32.4	37.8	38.2	38.0	85	99	101	100
Schaumburg-Lippe	30.1	31.1	31.4	33.4	90	93	94	100
Lippe	36.9	33.6	34.9	36.9	100	91	95	100
Lübeck	26.6	29.2	31.2	32.8	81	89	95	100
Bremen	32.6	32.4	33.9	37.8	86	86	90	100
Hamburg	33.6	30.8	32.0	34.8	97	89	92	100
Alsace-Lorraine	33.2	30.9	33.5	33.5	99	92	100	100
Germany	37.6	36.8	38.4	39.1	96	94	98	100

NOTES: Crude birth rates include stillbirths.
Boundaries for Prussian data include all areas acquired prior to 1871.

for almost every area listed. Nowhere was a consistent decline evident between 1841 and 1870. Thus the crude birth rate at least lends no support to a hypothesis that the fertility decline began before 1871.

In addition to the statistical evidence provided by the publications of the state census and vital statistics bureaus, we can also find some information about fertility in Germany prior to 1870 from studies of local population history, most of which concern single villages or parishes. Such studies exist for a moderate number of German villages and are based either directly on the parish records of births, deaths, and marriages (or baptisms, burials, and weddings) or else on village genealogies (*Ortssippenbücher*) which themselves are based largely on parish records.[2] Since the parish records often extend back as far as the seventeenth century, long series of fertility (as well as mortality and nuptiality) measures can be calculated from them. In addition, since the raw information of birth, death, and marriage dates were usually organized into family histories of vital events for individual nuclear family units, a wider variety of fertility measures could be calculated than is usually permitted by conventional tabulations of census and vital statistics data.

One indication of marital fertility that most of the local population studies included is completed family size per marriage. Since the authors of most of the studies used reconstituted family histories as the basis of their demographic analysis, it was a simple matter for them to compute the average number of births per married couple. Some fluctuations can be expected in family size over time in any particular village as a result of changes in the age of marriage, changing frequency of marital dissolutions through widowhood prior to the completion of the couple's fecund years (unless this has been specifically controlled as it was in several studies), or simply because of the small number of cases on which the studies are based. Nevertheless any major decline in marital fertility would probably make itself evident through a reduction in children born per marriage. Table 2.7 summarizes trends in average family size for most of the German

[2]For a description of *Ortssippenbücher* and their potential as a source of demographic data see Knodel and Espenshade, 1972 and Knodel, 1972. For an example of a local population study based on an *Ortssippenbüch* see Knodel, 1970.

TABLE 2.7

CHILDREN EVER BORN PER MARRIAGE, BY DATE OF MARRIAGE, SELECTED VILLAGES: MARRIAGES CONTRACTED PRE-1750 TO 1899

Village or parish	Administrative area or state	Pre-1750 Children born (average)	Families studied (number)	1750-1799 Children born (average)	Families studied (number)	1800-1849 Children born (average)	Families studied (number)	1850-1869 Children born (average)	Families studied (number)	1870-1899 Children born (average)	Families studied (number)
Kuhbier[a]	Potsdam	--	--	5.6[b]	--	4.1[b]	--	2.9[e]	--	2.3[f]	--
Hainholz, Litz, and Vahrenwald	Hannover	--	--	4.5	143	3.9	109	4.4	44	3.9	33
Kirchrode	Hannover	--	--	4.8	62	4.4	65	--	--	--	--
Misburg	Hannover	--	--	4.2	20	6.0	19	--	--	--	--
Lamstedt	Stade	5.9	--	6.2	--	5.5	--	5.9	--	5.7	--
Mulsum	Stade	6.1	43	5.5	41	5.5	64	5.3	28	5.2	47
Homburg	Düsseldorf	--	--	6.0	--	6.7[d]	--	7.4	--	5.7	--
Carl	Trier	4.7	39	4.5	87	4.6	77	4.3	38	5.8	49
Lauf	Baden	--	--	6.2[c]	147	6.5	391	6.5	140	--	--
Finken-Würder	Hamburg	5.5	--	5.8	--	6.5	--	--	--	--	--
Böhringen	Schwarzwald-kreis	7.7	91	7.8	127	9.0	139	8.5	62	6.4	122
Göttel-fingen	Schwarzwald-kreis	7.0	82	6.8	84	7.0	148	6.2	67	6.3	110

Village or parish	Administrative area or state	Pre-1750 Children born (average)	Families studied (number)	1750-1799 Children born (average)	Families studied (number)	1800-1849 Children born (average)	Families studied (number)	1850-1899 Children born (average)	Families studied (number)
Frommern	Schwarzwald-kreis	--	--	7.3	108	7.1	208	7.2	190
Hambühren	Lüneburg	--	--	4.2	25	3.4	23	2.8	13
Moordorf	Aurich	--	--	4.8	62	5.7	173	3.4	113
Giesmar	Kassel	--	--	4.8	166	4.6	224	4.5	184
Goddelsheim	Kassel	--	--	5.4	--	4.8	--	4.9	--
Anhausen	Schwaben	5.0	80	5.0	90	4.7	70	5.6	70
Streumen	Dresden	--	--	6.0	43	6.7	47	6.3	54
Lohmen	Mecklenburg	--	--	5.7	35	5.2	69	4.7	42
Sühlen	Mecklenburg	--	--	6.1	64	5.6	92	4.0	120

Village or parish	Administrative area or state	Pre-1700 Children born (average)	Families studied (number)	1700-1799 Children born (average)	Families studied (number)	1800-1899 Children born (average)	Families studied (number)
Tottleben	Thüringen	4.8	76	3.6	173	4.9	188
Wiegleben	Thüringen	--	--	4.2	103	4.1	157

SOURCES: Lamstedt and Mulsum: Klenck, 1959. Carl: Simonis, 1939. Anhausen: Knodel, 1970. Böhringen: Heckh, 1939.
Göttelfingen: I. Müller, 1939. Tottleben: Trübenbach, 1962. Wiegleben: Trübenbach, 1959. Finkenwürder:
Scheidt, 1932. All others taken from Wülker, 1940.

NOTES: General restrictions on data are as follows:

Farmers only - Kuhbier, Hainholz, Litz, Vahrenwald, Kirchrode, Misburg, Hambühren, and Frommern.
First marriages for both spouses - Mulsum, Homburg, Giesmar, Goddelsheim, Streumen, Böhringen, Göttelfingen,
Frommern, Lauf, Kirchrode, Misburg, and Sühlen.
Spouses surviving to the end of the wife's fecund period - Lamstedt, Mulsum, Böhringen, and Göttelfingen.

[a] Marriages of 10 years duration or more.
[b] Unweighted average of two 25-year-period averages.
[c] 1770-1799.
[d] Unweighted average of decade averages.
[e] 1850-1874.
[f] 1875-1899.

villages that have been subjects of historical demographic studies. The evidence that emerges is more or less consistent with the contention that a prolonged decline in marital fertility had not been taking place prior to German unification. In the vast majority of the villages, family size shows no consistent downward trend for couples married before 1870. Indeed most of the studies reviewed in Table 2.7 give the impression that marital fertility was high and reasonably constant for at least a century prior to German unification. The most notable exceptions to this generalization, namely Kuhbier, Hambühren, Lohmen, and Söhlen, deserve a few additional words of comment, however.

Since the number of families included in the Kuhbier study was not given, it is difficult to know what to make of it. A breakdown of the results into marriages by each quarter century indicates a higher family size (4.4) for couples marrying between 1825 and 1849 than the family size (4.1) for couples marrying during the last quarter of the eighteenth century. Thus the apparent decline was also characterized by fluctuations. In the case of Hambühren the number of cases is so small that very little confidence can be placed in the reliability of the trend. A greater degree of confidence can be attributed to the results shown for Lohmen and Söhlen, at least on the basis of the number of cases used in each study. It might also be added that by the time the marital fertility series presented in Appendix Table 2.1 begin, both Mecklenburg, the administrative area in which these two villages are located, and Lüneburg, the area in which Hambühren is situated, are characterized by particularly low fertility in comparison to the rest of Germany.

Several of the village studies include measures which are intended to be more sensitive in detecting the onset or existence of family limitation than simply the average number of children ever born per family. One sign of family limitation, for example, is a low maternal age at the last birth for couples in which wives are at risk to the end of the childbearing period. The results of four village studies which included calculations of this measure are reproduced in Table 2.8. Although a slight trend towards a younger maternal age at last birth prior to 1870 is evident in all series, only in Remmesweiler is the extent of the decline more than of minimal magnitude. In Remmesweiler, interestingly enough, the decline appears to have occurred mainly between marriages occurring prior to the beginning of the nineteenth

TABLE 2.8

AGE OF MOTHER AT LAST BIRTH, BY DATE OF MARRIAGE, SELECTED VILLAGES: MARRIAGES CONTRACTED PRE-1750 TO 1899

Village	Admini-strative area	Date of marriage									
		Pre-1750		1750-1799		1800-1849		1850-1869		1870-1899	
		Age (Years)	Women (Number)	Age (Years)	Women (Number)	Age (Years)	Women (Number)	Age (Years)	Women (Number)	Age (Years)	Women (Number)
Remmesweiler	Trier	--	--	39.6^a	57	34.3^b	48	35.1^c	53	35.6	55
Anhausen	Schwaben	40.8	12	40.4	42	39.9	42	39.3^d	47	--	--
Bőhringen	Schwarzwald-Kreis	41.1	--	40.9	--	41.1	--	40.0	--	39.7	--
Gőttelfingen	Schwarzwald-Kreis	39.6	--	40.3	--	39.7	--	38.8	--	39.0	--

SOURCES: Remmesweiler: Houdaille, 1970b. Anhausen: Knodel, 1970. Bőhringen: Heckh, 1939. Gőttelfingen: I. Mϋller, 1939.

NOTES: All data are for marriages which remained intact at least until the wife reached the end of her fecund years. Data for villages of Bőhringen and Gőttelfingen are for first marriages for both partners; figures represent unweighted averages of decade averages.

[a] Pre-1810.

[b] 1810-1839.

[c] 1840-1869.

[d] 1850-1899.

century and those occurring later. For marriages occurring during the nineteenth century, the age of the mother at the last birth is actually increasing slightly.

Still other, perhaps even more sensitive indices, have been computed to test the possibility of the spread of family limitation prior to the beginning of the secular decline in fertility associated with Germany's demographic transition (Houdaille, 1970a,b; Knodel, 1970). The results are not entirely consistent, but even in the instances where there is some evidence of family limitation beginning prior to the end of the nineteenth century, either the extent to which it was practiced or its increase appears to be minimal in comparison to the magnitude of the changes in reproductive behavior which characterize the decades following German unification. A fuller understanding of demographic behavior in Germany prior to the latter half of the nineteenth century and the beginning of the systematic collection of accurate and detailed census and vital statistics, probably awaits the extension of microlevel studies based on parish records to more villages in more regions of Germany.[3] At this point, sequences of fertility measures

[3] For a discussion of several potential sources for microlevel historical demographic studies of Germany see Knodel, 1968 and 1972.

either from official statistical sources or from studies of local populations suggest that the secular decline in German fertility which culminated in low levels characteristic of more recent times had its temporal origin in the decades immediately following German unification and not earlier. The image of a plateau of relatively high and constant fertility seems appropriate for at least the century or so preceding 1870.

The End of the Fertility Decline

Before the magnitude and rate of the fertility decline can be established, the dates of both the start and the end of the decline must be determined. We turn first to the date at which fertility stopped declining because, as defined here, it is a relatively simple matter. In the previous chapter, the working hypothesis was set forth that the decline was continuous. Once fertility has begun to fall it should not reverse this trend until the transition from high to low levels has been completed. An interruption in the trend toward decline by an increase in marital fertility would signal the completion of the transition, provided it is not followed by a quick resumption of the trend toward lower levels. An increase followed by fluctuations would suggest marital fertility was under sufficient control to respond to short run changes in social and economic conditions and that the secular movement from high to low levels had reached its end. Drifts to slightly higher or lower levels within the range of post-decline fertility are not viewed as contradictions to the transition. A substantial rise to former predecline levels however would negate this hypothesis. A substantial drop (excluding unusual circumstances such as wars) to much lower levels after a sustained period of fluctuations would also require modification of our conception of the decline as "continuous."

A close examination of Appendix Table 2.1 reveals that in every area of Germany a major and essentially continuous decline in marital fertility took place prior to the low levels reached in 1931–1935. In contrast, every area experienced a rise in marital fertility between 1931–1935 and 1938–1939. Even those areas with the highest levels in 1931–1935 show an increase, although sometimes more moderate than those areas which reached lower levels by the beginning of the decade.

Unfortunately the 1939 census was not detailed enough to permit computation of I_g for the usual administrative areas in the large states, and thus the results just referred to apply only to the states themselves and to Prussian provinces. However, Table 2.9 shows crude birth

TABLE 2.9

CRUDE BIRTH RATE, BY ADMINISTRATIVE AREA: 1931-1935 AND 1938-1939

Area	1931-1935	1938-1939	Increase (percent)	Area	1931-1935	1938-1939	Increase (percent)
				35 Oberbayern	15.8	19.4	23
01 Ostpreussen	21.7	25.0	15	37 Pfalz	18.1	19.0	5
3A Westpreussen	22.2	26.2	18	36 Niederbayern	23.2 }	} 25.2	} 9
04 Berlin	10.6	16.0	51	38 Oberpfalz	22.9		
05 Potsdam	15.6	17.4	12	39 Oberfranken	18.4 }	} 21.1	} 26
06 Frankfurt/O.	16.0	18.9	18	40 Mittelfranken	15.7		
07 Stettin-Str.	18.4	21.9	19	41 Unterfranken	19.0	23.2	22
08 Köslin	20.2	23.1	14	42 Schwaben	16.8	21.0	25
9A Posen-Wes.	20.8	22.6	9	43 Dresden	12.8	16.8	31
11 Breslau	18.4	21.5	17	44 Leipzig	13.0	16.0	23
12 Liegnitz	17.1	20.4	19	45 Zwickau	13.2	15.8	20
13 Oppeln	24.6	26.7	9	46 Neckarkreis	15.1 }		
14 Magdeburg	15.5	19.1	23	47 Schwarzwald-			
15 Merseburg	17.0	19.7	16	kreis	17.5 }	} 21.3	} 28
16 Erfurt	16.3	20.8	28	48 Jagstkreis	17.5		
17 Schleswig	16.5	21.5	30	49 Donaukreis	17.0 }		
18 Hannover	13.9	18.2	31	50 Konstanz	17.5 }		
19 Hildesheim	16.6	19.7	19	51 Freiburg	17.7 }	} 20.2	} 19
20 Lüneburg	16.6	19.5	17	52 Karlsruhe	16.6 }		
21 Stade	17.3	19.5	13	53 Mannheim	16.5 }		
22 Osnabrück	21.0	24.6	17	54 Starkenburg	15.8 }		
23 Aurich	21.5	25.1	17	55 Oberhessen	16.3 }	} 18.3	} 16
24 Münster	20.5	23.6	15	56 Rheinhessen	15.8 }		
25 Minden	17.3	20.8	20	57 Mecklenburg	18.0	22.5	25
26 Arnsberg	16.2	19.9	23	58 Thüringen	15.7	19.1	22
27 Kassel	16.8	20.9	24	59 H. Oldenburg	20.8 }	} 25.3	} 23
28 Wiesbaden	13.4	16.8	25	60 F. Lübeck	17.3 }		
29 Koblenz	17.8	20.4	15	62 Braunschweig	14.7	17.6	20
30 Düsseldorf	15.6	19.0	22	63 Anhalt	16.2	20.9	29
31 Köln	15.0	18.2	21	64 Schaumburg-			
32 Trier	19.3	20.8	8	Lippe	14.7	19.5	33
33 Aachen	18.0	19.7	9	65 Lippe	16.7	19.9	19
34 Sigmaringen	16.9	20.3	20	67 Bremen	14.4	21.7	51
				68 Hamburg	12.9	17.3	34
				Saarland	17.6[a]	22.1	26
				Germany	16.5	20.0	21

NOTES: Boundaries for area 17 Schleswig incorporate those of 66 Lübeck.
Boundaries for area 29 Koblenz incorporate those of 61 Birkenfeld.
The Saarland consists of areas formerly belonging to Trier and Pfalz.

[a] 1933.

rates for most of the individual administrative areas. In every case a rise in fertility is indicated. The reason for the abrupt reversal of the fertility decline is not fully clear. The National Socialists, in particular, claimed it was a response to their appeals of race and *Volk* and their material inducements to childbearing.[4] In contrast Dudley Kirk (1942) has argued that most of the increase is simply an expected reaction to massive re-employment. In any event the response of rising fertility to changing social conditions is indicative of a population which has fertility under substantial voluntary control.

Following World War II, the large loss of territory, the division of the remaining territory into East and West Germany, and the vast re-organization of states within divided Germany makes it impossible to continue the series of the basic demographic indices for many administrative areas past 1938–1939. A continuation of the decline for the whole of Germany, however, is not evident if we compare figures for West Germany with those for pre-World War II Germany (see Table 2.1). A comparison of West German administrative areas with their pre-war equivalents (Table 2.10) indicates that in most cases marital fertility in 1959–1963 was above the levels experienced during the early 1930s. Only in a couple of the administrative areas which had particularly high marital fertility during 1931–1935 are the recent levels very much lower. Niederbayern and Oberpfalz are most notable in this respect. The predominantly higher or only slightly lower levels of I_g which characterized most areas suggest we will not go too far astray by treating the 1931–1935 period as the end of the fertility transition in Germany. Measures of the rate and magnitude of decline will be calculated accordingly.

Marital Feritility

(a) *Levels 1871, 1900, 1933.* Every area of Germany for which a continuous series of I_g is available between unification and the beginning of the 1930s experienced a substantial reduction in marital fertility which ranged from over 40 to almost 80 percent. Even in the areas lost by Germany following World War I a drop in marital fertility is evident by 1908–1912, the last period for which I_g can be computed on

[4]An extensive literature exists which attempts to analyze the causes of the rise in German fertility after 1933. The main factors stressed have been the material inducements provided under the National Socialists, the suppression of abortion and birth control propaganda, and the alleged revitalization of the German people. For an extensive review of both the German and non-German contemporary literature on the subject see Glass, 1940, pp. 269–313.

[52]

TABLE 2.10

MARITAL FERTILITY (I_g), BY ADMINISTRATIVE AREA WITHIN WEST GERMANY: 1931-1935 AND 1959-1963

Area		1931-1935	1959-1963	Change (percent)	Area		1931-1935	1959-1963	Change (percent)
04	Berlin	.152	.213	40	36	Niederbayern	.473	.365	-23
17	Schleswig	.259	.310	20	37	Pfalz	.288	.299	4
18	Hannover	.210	.270	29	38	Oberpfalz	.455	.356	-22
19	Hildesheim	.264	.296	12	39	Oberfranken	.305	.300	-2
20	Lüneburg	.259	.314	21	40	Mittelfranken	.247	.276	12
21	Stade	.280	.327	17	41	Unterfranken	.355	.351	-1
22	Osnabrück	.444	.415	-7	42	Schwaben	.345	.336	-3
23	Aurich	.411	.358	-13	46	Neckarkreis	.263 ⎫		
24	Münster	.364	.344	-5	48	Jagstkreis	.389 ⎬ .319[d]		--
25	Minden	.330			34	Sigmaringen	.399 ⎫		
65	Lippe	.305	.322[a]	--	47	Schwarzwaldkreis	.355 ⎬ .382[e]		--
26	Arnsberg	.253	.282	11	49	Donaukreis	.388 ⎭		
27	Kassel	.284	.303	7	54	Starkenburg	.238 ⎫		
28	Wiesbaden	.218	.262[b]	--	55	Oberhessen	.261 ⎬ .278[f]		--
			.327[c]		56	Rheinhessen	.255	.294	15
29	Koblenz	.345	.327	-5	59	H. Oldenburg	.367	.376	2
30	Düsseldorf	.243	.271	11	62	Braunschweig	.214	.262	22
31	Köln	.245	.278	13	67	Bremen	.220	.263	20
32	Trier	.442	.390	-12	68	Hamburg	.192	.244	27
33	Aachen	.332	.300	-9		Saarland	.305[g]	.309	1
35	Oberbayern	.275	.284	3		Germany	.264	.301	14

NOTE: Boundaries for data for Berlin and Germany are for the entire city and country in 1931-1935 and for only West Berlin and West Germany (including West Berlin) in 1959-1963.

[a] Regierungsbezirk Detmold.
[b] Present day Regierungsbezirk Wiesbaden.
[c] Regierungsbezirk Montabaur.
[d] Nordwürttemberg.
[e] Südwürttemberg-Hohenzollern.
[f] Regierungsbezirk Darmstadt.
[g] 1935. The Saarland consists of areas formerly belonging to Trier and Pfalz.

the basis of German statistics. A close examination of Appendix Table 2.1 reveals, almost without exception, that once the I_g declined more than a few percent, it followed an uninterrupted downward course until the beginning of the 1930s. The radically changing complexion of marital fertility within Germany is evident from Maps 2.1, 2.2, and 2.3 which show the levels of I_g in each administrative area at the time of unification, at the turn of the century, and in the early 1930s. During 1869–1873 only two areas experienced an I_g below .600, and just

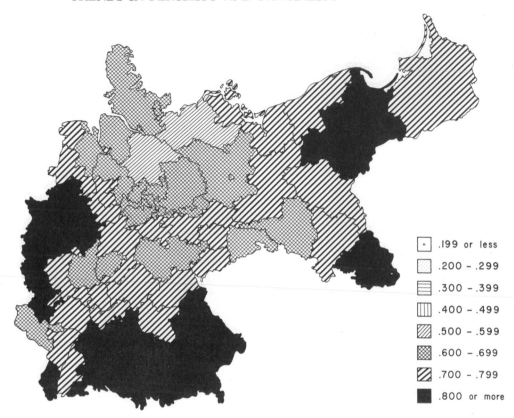

.199 or less

.200 – .299

.300 – .399

.400 – .499

.500 – .599

.600 – .699

.700 – .799

.800 or more

Map 2.1.   Marital Fertility (I_g), by Administrative Area: 1869–1873

barely so at that. Indeed most were substantially higher. In sharp contrast, by 1931–1935 no area was characterized by an I_g above .500. In fact most areas were well below this level. Both at the time of unification and at the turn of the century the areas of lower fertility appear concentrated in the central areas of Northern Germany near Berlin. Areas of quite high fertility are generally in the more peripheral regions. Thus in 1869–1873, I_g is above .800 in all Württemburg, Southern Bavaria, and Westpreussen and in most of Baden, the Rhineland, and Westphalia. By 1900 this pattern of differentials is even more pronounced although marital fertility is somewhat lower in many areas. Pockets of very high fertility still remain in the easternmost and westernmost regions as well as in parts of Bavaria. Even

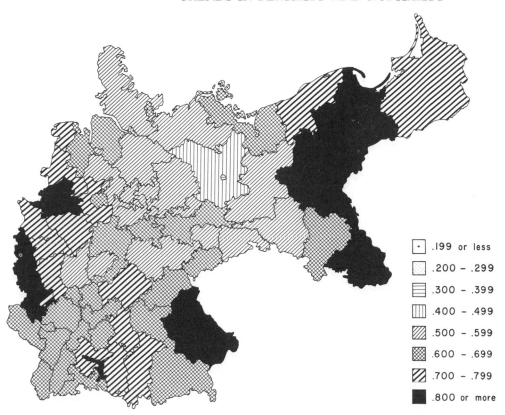

.199 or less
.200 – .299
.300 – .399
.400 – .499
.500 – .599
.600 – .699
.700 – .799
.800 or more

Map 2.2.   Marital Fertility (I_g), by Administrative Area: 1898–1902

by 1931–1935 some remnants of this pattern persist although marital fertility is substantially lower in every area and nowhere is I_g above the .500 level.

(b) *Problems in assigning a date to the fertility decline.* The problem of determining the time at which fertility begins the transitional descent from relatively high to relatively low levels is of considerable interest. Provided there is a sufficient spread in the date of the fertility decline among the areas of Germany, some clues to the circumstances of the decline should emerge through the analysis of the social, economic, and, demographic settings which differentiate areas experiencing early declines from those in which the decline occurs later.

Two alternative approaches can be employed to determine the date

[55]

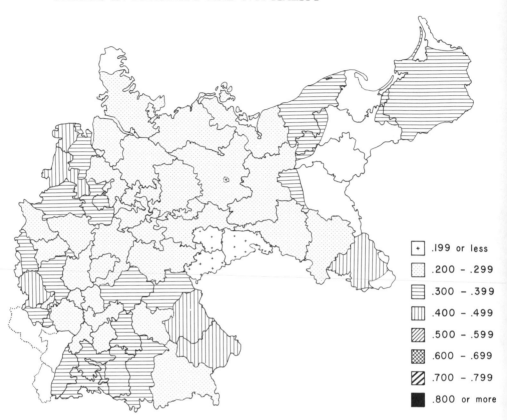

+	.199 or less
	.200 - .299
☰	.300 - .399
⦀	.400 - .499
▨	.500 - .599
▨	.600 - .699
▨	.700 - .799
■	.800 or more

Map 2.3.   Marital Fertility (I_g), by Administrative Area: 1931–1935

that fertility undergoes its transitional fall to lower, modern levels. In one approach the date of the decline corresponds to the year during which fertility has declined to some arbitrarily set level considered to be either distinctly modern or distinctly within the range of transitional fertility. For example, the date of the decline could be set equal to the year during which the index of marital fertility (I_g) reached a value of .600 or .500. Such an approach presents few problems and is usually a simple matter of interpolation between two census years. The disadvantage of this approach is that the date attributed to the decline reflects not only when fertility began to decline but also the level from which the decline started. Although this method does not suffice then to date the beginning of the fertility transition, it does produce results which are of some interest in themselves. An alternative approach to dating the decline concerns itself with the year by which the fertility index has dropped an arbitrarily set percent or absolute amount from the predecline level. Thus the date of the beginning of the decline could be considered the year during which I_g reached a level of 10 percent below its predecline level, never to return again within this range. By requiring an initial 10 percent decline, many of the problems created by predecline fluctuations for dating the decline are eliminated.

The main difficulty with this second approach is the determination of the predecline level of fertility. In fact, this difficulty was the basis of considerable controversy over the date of the beginning of the German decline among the German scholars who wrote about the *Geburtenrückgang* at the beginning of this century. Mombert (1907, pp. 122–125), for example, dated the start of the national fertility decline in the 1870s. Indeed, fertility indices show a relatively continuous decline from this date. Würzburger (1914, pp. 1261–1264), on the other hand, dates the beginning of national decline just after the turn of the century. In considering the crude birth rate, he argues that it is misleading to regard the unusually high birth rates of the 1870s as the starting point of the decline since the relatively large number of births at that time was due to exceptionally high number of marriages following the Franco-Prussian War of 1870–71. The relatively large number of young marriages led to a corresponding increase in births. This effect dissipated itself by the early 1880s, which resulted in a decrease in the birth rate. Würzburger argues that the relatively constant birth rates between 1883 and 1901 prove that this earlier decline represented a return to the normal situation and thus should not be considered as part of the *Geburtenrückgang*. Still others date the decline as beginning sometime in between the 1870s and 1900 (Oldenburg, 1911, p. 331; J. Müller, 1924 pp. 1–6).

This controversy among German scholars at the beginning of this century reflects the main difficulty in determining dates for the beginning of the fertility decline within Germany. In most areas, fertility was higher during the 1870s than it was either before or after. This is particularly true for measures of overall fertility, although marital fertility is also somewhat higher. For Germany as a whole, I_f increased 10 percent from 1866–1868 to 1874–1877, whearas I_g increased only 4 percent during the same period. The difference was due to the large increase in marriages occurring during the 1870s resulting from liberalized marriage legislation and freedom of movement laws, the return of soldiers from France, and the general atmosphere of national economic prosperity following victory in the Franco-Prussian War (Knodel, 1967). The increase in marital fertility may also be due to the increased marriages since an unusually high proportion of married couples in the childbearing ages would be newlyweds. Even in populations which do not practice contraception, marriages in short durations have relatively higher fertility.

In determining the date and rate of the fertility decline, the indices for 1874–1877 will be excluded from consideration. This appears to be the most reasonable procedure since the fertility indices for this period are usually uniquely high and thus unrepresentative of predecline levels. Also since 1874–1877 rates are available only for some areas and not for others, the comparability of results is increased by excluding this period from consideration for all areas. The period 1866–1868 and 1869–1873 both encompass war years which had some effect on subsequent marriages and births. Thus deficits in marriages and births occured in 1867 following the "six weeks war" in 1866 between Austria (and most other German states) and Prussia, and in 1871 following the Franco-Prussian War in 1870 between Prussia (with the Southern German States as allies) and France. However, the increases in marriages following the wars essentially compensated for the earlier deficit. Evidence that the net result of these wars and their aftermath on maritial fertility was negligible for these periods is provided by the few states (see Table 2.2) for which I_g is available for the periods earlier than 1866–1868. If anything, marital fertility appears to be higher during the war period than in the preceding years.

In the present study preference is given to the second of the above mentioned approaches to dating the fertility decline. More specifically, the preferred index of the date of decline will be the estimated year in which I_g attained a sustained reduction of 10 percent from its maximum predecline value. The main reason for favoring this measure over those which could be derived from the first approach stems from its clearer interpretation as an index of the *onset* of the fertility transition. One of the main concerns with the present study is to attempt to identify the circumstances which gave rise to the *start* of an irreversible transition from high to low fertility. Thus there is necessity for a measure which differentiates areas with respect to the time when the transition began. In the following analysis which relates the date of decline with the magnitude and rate of decline, however, two additional measures of the date of decline based on the first approach are used for comparative purposes. These measures are the estimated year in which I_g reaches the .600 level and the .500 level.

(c) *The range of predecline fertility.* Before launching into a detailed analysis of the date and rate of fertility decline, a brief discussion of the levels of marital fertility just prior to its decline seems in order. One striking result emerging from an analysis of the indices shown in Appendix Table 2.1 is the great regional diversity in the predecline levels of marital fertility within Germany. The range of predecline fertility is summarized in Table 2.11 which shows the distribution of the maximum values of I_g (excluding the 1874–1877 period) attained in the 71 administrative areas of Germany. Two possible explanations for the diversity come to mind. First, it is possible that the differences in predecline marital fertility represent diverse levels of natural fertility, i.e., fertility in the absence of deliberate birth control. The causes for these differences would then be sought in such factors as breastfeeding customs, social customs governing sexual behavior, prevalence of sterility and subfecundity, health conditions, frequency of miscarriages, etc., but not in factors which reflect deliberate decisions to limit family size. No doubt there are marked variations in fertility among populations in which deliberate birth control is not practiced. If I_g's were to be calculated for the populations cited by Henry (1961) as examples of natural fertility they would range from .57 to .99.[5] The range within Germany is thus very similar to the range

[5] Assuming a rectangular age distribution of married women. The range would be .56 to .99 if the age distribution of married women in Germany 1871 were used as a standard. The marital fertility schedules are given in Henry (1961, p. 84). Even if the calculations were limited to the "western" populations included in the table, the range of I_g would be from .69 to .99.

TABLE 2.11

DISTRIBUTION OF ADMINISTRATIVE AREAS BY MAXIMUM RECORDED
MARITAL FERTILITY (I_g)

Maximum I_g	Areas	
	Number	Percent
.57-.59	1	1
.60-.69	18	25
.70-.79	27	38
.80-.89	21	30
.90-.95	4	6
TOTAL	71	100%

NOTE: Data for the 1874-1877 time period are excluded.

among Henry's populations but is more difficult to explain within the context of natural fertility since, *prima facie*, we would expect more homogeneity within a national population than among such diverse populations as those he cites. In addition, when marital fertility is analyzed for geographical units smaller than the administrative areas considered in this study, equally large differences in I_g's appear.[6] An attempt to account for differences in predecline fertility levels within Bavaria with regard to regional variations in breastfeeding did not succeed (Knodel and van de Walle, 1967). Although districts in which breastfeeding was uncommon frequently had higher fertility, this association disappeared when differences in infant mortality were taken into account. However it should be added that the results of another study of fertility in three Bavarian villages based on data for individual families indicate that breastfeeding can prolong interbirth intervals substantially (Knodel, 1968).

An alternative explanation would hold that at least some sectors of the populations practiced birth control before the onset of the fertility

[6]For example, within the administrative area Oberbayern, I_g's in 1880 range at least between .56 and .90 among the *rural* districts alone. Within Niederbayern the same range is between. .76 and 1.06.

[60]

decline. Predecline differentials would then reflect variations in the voluntary control of marital fertility. Carlsson (1966) and Buissink (1971) interpret regional differences in Swedish and Dutch marital fertility prior to the secular decline in this way. Carlsson (1970) also argues that nineteenth-century fertility oscillations give further support to this interpretation. If predecline fertility control existed, social and economic conditions as well as differences in levels of infant mortality could be introduced as explanative factors during the predecline period.

This second interpretation is not without problems. For example, the relatively constant fertility which existed at very different levels, at least for several decades before the decline began then becomes problematical. Did the areas with low marital fertility which are presumed to be practicing contraception at the onset of the decline ever have higher levels of natural fertility? If so, when did the transition occur from high levels of natural fertility to the levels experienced just prior to the decline? It would appear particularly difficult to argue that marital fertility had declined much in the areas where I_g indicated a fertility of 90 percent or more of the Hutterite level. What then differentiated areas with long traditions of family limitation from others where it went unpracticed? In addition, even if the predecline regional differences in Germany did result from variations in the use of birth control, the questions would still remain whether a low level meant that all social strata of a region's population were practicing a limited degree of control, or if limited strata were practicing a substantial amount of control. This cannot be determined by our regional data per se.

Regardless of the explanation of regional differences in fertility during the mid-nineteenth century, it is clear that in all areas of Germany a sharp decline in fertility occurred by the second decade of the twentieth century representing a distinct departure from past trends and, as stated earlier, it is this decline which is our present concern.

(d) *The magnitude, date, and rate of decline.* The magnitude, date, and rate of the decline in marital fertility in each administrative area in Germany is summarized in Table 2.12. The magnitude of the decline can be expressed either in terms of the absolute or relative differences

[61]

TRENDS IN FERTILITY AND NUPTIALITY

TABLE 2.12

MARITAL FERTILITY (I_g), MAGNITUDE, DATE, AND RATE OF DECLINE, BY ADMINISTRATIVE AREA

Area	Magnitude			Date			Annual rate	
	Maxi-mum I_g	Mini-mum I_g	Decline (percent)	10% decline	I_g= .600	I_g = .500	Abso-lute	Rela-tive
01 Ostpreussen	.800	.384[a]	52.0	1907	1916	1923	1.29	1.80
02 Danzig	.821	.366[a]	55.4	1909	1917	1922	1.55	2.10
03 Marienwerder	.868	.366[a]	57.8	1911	1918	1922	1.87	2.40
04 Berlin	.648	.147	77.3	1881	1879	1889	.99	1.70
05 Potsdam	.680	.225	66.9	1891	1892	1900	.92	1.51
06 Frankfurt /O.	.704	.236	66.5	1896	1899	1908	1.07	1.68
07 Stettin-Stralsund	.733	.278	62.1	1897	1903	1910	1.06	1.61
08 Köslin	.801	.349[b]	56.4	1905	1915	1921	1.34	1.86
09 Posen	.834	.382[b]	54.2	1911	1918	1923	1.70	2.26
10 Bromberg	.855	.382[b]	55.3	1911	1919	1923	1.76	2.28
11 Breslau	.749	.289	61.4	1901	1907	1915	1.19	1.76
12 Liegnitz	.671	.258	61.5	1899	1899	1911	1.01	1.67
13 Oppeln	.870	.442	49.2	1912	1923	1929	1.62	2.07
14 Magdeburg	.673	.212	68.5	1893	1893	1904	.97	1.61
15 Merseburg	.736	.225	69.4	1897	1903	1910	1.23	1.85
16 Erfurt	.741	.245	66.9	1891	1902	1911	1.00	1.49
17 Schleswig	.686	.259	62.2	1898	1899	1909	1.01	1.64
18 Hannover	.679	.210	69.1	1893	1896	1904	1.00	1.64
19 Hildesheim	.661	.264	60.1	1900	1900	1909	1.01	1.70
20 Lüneberg	.573	.259	54.8	1903	1867	1905	.86	1.67
21 Stade	.688	.280	59.3	1904	1906	1914	1.16	1.87
22 Osnabrück	.749	.444	40.7	1911	1918	1928	1.05	1.56
23 Aurich	.765	.411	46.3	1909	1917	1925	1.16	1.69
24 Münster	.886	.364	58.9	1911	1921	1926	1.95	2.44
25 Minden	.798	.330	58.6	1902	1912	1920	1.25	1.74
26 Arnsberg	.839	.253	69.8	1903	1912	1918	1.69	2.23
27 Kassel	.731	.284	61.1	1895	1904	1913	1.00	1.51
28 Wiesbaden	.700	.218	68.9	1884	1890	1906	.84	1.34
29 Koblenz	.799	.345	56.8	1902	1912	1920	1.21	1.68
30 Düsseldorf	.872	.243	72.1	1895	1909	1914	1.42	1.81
31 Köln	.872	.245	71.9	1893	1908	1914	1.35	1.73
32 Trier	.844	.442	47.6	1907	1925	1930	1.23	1.61
33 Aachen	.931	.332	64.3	1904	1917	1923	1.75	2.09
34 Sigmaringen	.888	.399	55.1	1900	1916	1923	1.22	1.53
35 Oberbayern	.842	.275	67.3	1886	1905	1912	1.02	1.35
36 Niederbayern	.923	.473	48.8	1914	1924	1931	1.85	2.23
37 Pfalz	.776	.288	62.9	1895	1907	1915	1.08	1.55
38 Oberpfalz	.896	.455	49.2	1910	1923	1930	1.50	1.87
39 Oberfranken	.717	.305	57.5	1902	1906	1917	1.09	1.70
40 Mittelfranken	.762	.247	67.6	1886	1902	1909	.94	1.37
41 Unterfranken	.782	.355	54.6	1901	1913	1922	1.08	1.54
42 Schwaben	.948	.345	63.6	1884	1916	1921	1.03	1.21
43 Dresden	.651	.186	71.4	1893	1891	1903	1.01	1.73
44 Leipzig	.730	.179	75.5	1891	1896	1904	1.13	1.72
45 Zwickau	.786	.181	77.0	1892	1902	1908	1.30	1.83
46 Neckarkreis	.846	.263	68.9	1883	1904	1910	.99	1.30
47 Schwarzwald-kreis	.892	.355	60.2	1889	1913	1919	1.01	1.26
48 Jagstkreis	.859	.389	54.7	1890	1914	1922	.90	1.16
49 Donaukreis	.921	.388	57.9	1886	1915	1922	.93	1.12
50 Konstanz	.848	.356	58.0	1881	1910	1919	.78	1.03
51 Freiburg	.742	.343	53.8	1887	1905	1915	.71	1.06
52 Karlsruhe	.851	.284	66.6	1881	1906	1914	.92	1.21
53 Mannheim	.737	.267	66.1	1893	1907	1914	1.11	1.57
54 Starkenburg	.763	.238	68.8	1883	1904	1910	.89	1.30
55 Oberhessen	.627	.261	58.4	1884	1874	1904	.62	1.09
56 Rheinhessen	.759	.255	66.4	1885	1901	1908	.89	1.31
57 Mecklenburg	.616	.272	55.8	1892	1871	1902	.70	1.26
58 Thüringen	.644	.220	65.8	1901	1896	1908	1.11	1.91
59 H.Oldenburg	.710	.367	48.3	1906	1910	1919	1.01	1.58
60 F. Lübeck	.672	.282	58.0	1903	1904	1913	1.07	1.77
61 Birkenfeld	.708	.291	58.9	1908	1911	1920	1.40	2.20
62 Braunschweig	.623	.214	65.7	1898	1886	1904	.99	1.76
63 Anhalt	.672	.217	67.7	1892	1893	1904	.96	1.58
64 Schaumburg-Lippe	.717	.222	69.0	1885	1889	1906	.89	1.37
65 Lippe	.767	.305	60.2	1899	1909	1918	1.12	1.63
66 Lübeck	.651	.201	69.1	1889	1886	1904	.88	1.50
67 Bremen	.746	.220	70.5	1879	1891	1905	.84	1.26
68 Hamburg	.666	.192	71.2	1884	1884	1899	.84	1.39
69 Unterelsass	.793	.305[c]	61.5	1883	1901	1909	.85	1.20
70 Oberelsass	.802	.290[d]	63.8	1888	1902	1908	1.01	1.39
71 Lothringen	.695	.344[e]	50.5	1902	1905	1916	.96	1.53
Germany	.761	.264	65.2	1895	1905	1913	1.11	1.62

NOTES: The pre-World War II minimum I_g was reached in the 1931-1935 time period for all but administrative area 04 Berlin, where minimum I_g was reached 1923-1927.
Dates of decline estimated by the author.
Rates of decline calculated from formula devised by author (See footnote 9 to this chapter); the absolute decline is expressed in terms of I_g points multiplied by 100.

[a] 3A Westpreussen.
[b] 9A Gr. Posen-Westpreussen.
[c] French department Rhin Bas, 1929-1933.
[d] French department Rhin Haut, 1929-1933.
[e] French department Moselle, 1929-1933.

between the maximum (excluding 1874–1877 levels) and the minimum levels of I_g. Berlin experienced its minimum I_g during 1923–1927. In all other areas, the pre-World War II minimum was achieved during the 1931-1935 period. For the entire country, I_g declined 65 percent between unification and the early thirties. Among the administrative areas, the extent of the decline ranged from 41 percent in Osnabrück to 77 percent in Berlin and Zwickau. The vast majority of areas however experienced declines between 50 and 70 percent. I_g fell by 60 percent or more in over half (41 of the 71 administrative areas, to be exact). In only 7 did I_g decline less than 50 percent.

Three different measures for the date of the decline in marital fertility are also included in Table 2.12. The year by which fertility had declined by 10 percent can be considered as the estimated date of the onset of the fertility transition. The other two measures can more properly be considered as estimates of the year by which I_g reached a level which is clearly within the range of transitional fertility. For all three measures, the year was estimated by linear interpolation between the census years which were used in the calculation of the series of marital fertility presented in Appendix Table 2.1.[7] It should be

[7]Three minor technical problems involved in the determination of the dates of fertility decline in Germany merit comment. In estimating the year by which I_g fell by 10%, we need to determine the predecline level from which it started. Even after excluding the 1874–1877 period from consideration, there are more observations of the basic indices available for some administrative areas than for others. Thus the year in which I_g achieved its highest predecline value is affected by whether or not observations are available for periods earlier than 1869–1873. The disturbance introduced by this factor, however, does not appear to be significant. In no area for which data were available did an irreversible decline of more than 3% occur between the earliest period and 1869-1873, the first period for which indices were available for all areas. More specifically in the 14 administrative areas which exhibit a maximum I_g before 1869–1873 all but one experience this maximum in the period 1866–1868. In only 13 areas are the indices not available for 1866–1868 or any earlier period. Four of these 13 areas compose Württemburg which as a whole shows a rise in I_g between 1860–1862 and 1866–1868 and only a 0.5% decline between 1866–1868 and 1869–1873. An additional four compose Baden which as a whole shows a maximum I_g in 1863–1865. This maximum however is only 1% higher than the value for I_g in 1869–1873. Thus the unavailability of I_g's for the 13 areas before 1869–1873 is unlikely to substantially affect the results of the analysis of the date and rate of decline.

A second technical problem arises from the fact that in several areas lost after World War I I_g had either not yet declined by 10% by the time our series of fertility indices end (in these cases 1908–1912) or even more commonly I_g was still above the .600 or .500 level. For the administrative areas of Danzig and Marienwerder the fertility indices for

stressed that the dates are not intended to be taken at face value as literal historical dates but rather as indices of the differences in the timing of the fertility decline within Germany.[8]

In terms of setting a date for the onset of the decline in I_g, it appears that the criteria of 10 percent reduction as the sign of the start of the transition is appropriate for Germany. In almost every area once I_g declined by 10 percent it continued to decline uninterruptedly to the low levels reached in 1931–1935. The national level of I_g registered a 10 percent reduction by 1895. In the different administrative areas, the onset of the fertility transition is evenly distributed over the last two decades of the nineteenth century and first decade and a half of this century. Of the 71 areas, the estimates indicate that 20 began their transitional descent before 1890, 22 in the decade prior to 1900, 21 in the decade following 1900, and the remaining 8 by the next five years.

The differences in the timing of the fertility decline within Germany is almost as extensive as the national differences in the rest of Europe. Among 15 other European countries included in a recent study of the demographic transition, only France experienced a 10 percent decline in marital fertility before 1879, and only Ireland and Spain were listed as declining after 1914 (van de Walle and Knodel, 1967). Of course in the span of history, three and a half decades is a rather short period for a phenomenon as significant as the fertility transition to spread throughout Germany and even more so throughout most of Europe.

---

post-World War I *Regierungsbezirk* Westpreussen were used as proxies; for Posen and Bromberg the indices for Grenzmark Posen-Westpreussen served as proxies; for Lothringen the indices of the French department of Moselle were used.

The third minor problem concerns the date of the decline determined by an irreversible fall of I_g below the .600 level. In one area, Lüneburg, the maximum I_g recorded was slightly below the .600 level. Hence we do not know the date at which the crucial level was crossed. The date has arbitrarily been set at 1867, the first year for which we have information.

[8]The discrepancy between the literal date when I_g either began its decline or reached a level of .600 or .500 and the indexes presented in Table 2.12 is particularly clear for areas associated with dates falling between 1910 and 1925. The annual course of marital fertility between these two years must have been severely affected by World War I. Our measures are based on linear interpolation between the level of I_g in the 1908–1912 and the 1923–1927 period and thus imply that I_g was changing in a linear manner. Although the measures of the date of decline cannot be taken literally, it is assumed that they at least serve as a rough *index* of the timing of the decline.

In many respects the remarkable fact is the coincidence in timing rather than the diversity. Nevertheless the investigation of characteristics which differentiate regions of early and late decline may prove rewarding.

The geographical distribution of the date of 10 percent decline in I_g is shown on Map 2.4. The most striking feature of the map is the

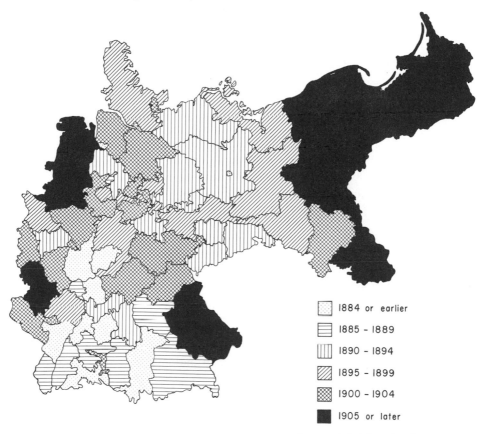

1884 or earlier

1885 - 1889

1890 - 1894

1895 - 1899

1900 - 1904

1905 or later

Map 2.4.   Marital Fertility (I_g), Date of 10% Decline, by Administrative Area

uniformly late date at which the fertility decline began in the eastern-most provinces. This area is populated by large numbers of persons who were Polish or belonged to some other non-German ethnic and linguistic group. However, before we can attribute the late start in the fertility transition to this sector of the population we would first need to demonstrate that the German speaking population behaved differently. The northwesternmost administrative areas also stand out as late decliners. The rest of Germany, however, resembles a patchquilt more than anything else. Bavaria, for example, contains areas of very early and very late decline as does most of southwestern Germany.

Since less emphasis is placed in this study on the estimated years in which I_g fell to .500 or .600 separate maps showing these distributions by administrative area are not presented. Such maps however would show more regular patterns than Map 2.4. In general the areas in central parts of Germany fell below these levels of marital fertility before the areas towards the nation's periphery did. This result is not surprising since dating the decline by estimating the year in which I_g fell below a certain level reflects not only when marital fertility began to decline but also its level prior to decline. Map 2.1 indicated that marital fertility prior to its decline (i.e., in 1869–1873) was also lower in the central areas and higher towards the periphery.

Table 2.12 includes the average annual decline in marital fertility expressed in both absolute and relative (percent) terms.[9] For both measures, the time period considered was the period following the estimated year by which I_g had fallen 10 percent from its maximum value in each particular administrative area. Although in the strictest terminology only the *percent* decline per year can be considered a true rate, for convenience sake we will refer to both measures as rates of decline.

The degree of association between the measures of the rate, date, and magnitude of decline is of interest in the description of the fertility transition. Several hypotheses have been put forth regarding the rate of decline to the effect that the later an area declines, the faster its fertility falls, and the higher the predecline level of fertility, the more rapid the decline (Kirk, 1971). These and other relationships are measured by correlation coefficients presented in Table 2.13.

[9]Absolute rate of decline =
$$\frac{(.9)\,(\text{maximum } I_g \times 100) - (\text{minimum } I_g \times 100)}{(\text{year } I_g \text{ reached minimum value}) - (\text{year of } 10\% \text{ decline})}$$
Relative rate of decline =
$$\frac{\text{absolute rate of decline}}{(.9)\,(\text{maximum } I_g)}$$

[66]

TABLE 2.13

MARITAL FERTILITY (I_g), CORRELATIONS BETWEEN MAGNITUDE, DATE, AND RATE OF DECLINE

| | | Magnitude | | | Date | | | Annual Rate | |
		Maximum I_g	Absolute decline	Percent decline	10% decline	I_g=.600	I_g=.500	Absolute	Relative
Magnitude	Maximum I_g	1.00							
	Absolute decline	.57	1.00						
	Percent decline	-.22	.67	1.00					
Date	10% decline	.16	-.43	-.65	1.00				
	I_g = .600	.81	.18	-.51	.55	1.00			
	I_g = .500	.73	-.07	-.75	.66	.91	1.00		
Annual rate	Absolute	.57	.23	-.22	.74	.67	.62	1.00	
	Relative	.16	-.02	-.15	.81	.39	.37	.90	1.00

NOTE: N = 71. Had areas lost after World War I been excluded, the resulting correlations would have been almost identical.

Several interesting results emerge. There appears to be very little relation between the date of a sustained decline of 10 percent in I_g and the level from which the I_g declined. Although the average maximum I_g of areas which were particularly late in beginning their fertility decline was relatively high, many areas with relatively high predecline levels of marital fertility declined much earlier. In contrast, a strong relationship exists between the maximum predecline level and the date I_g fell below either .600 or .500. Such a contrast underscores the fact that rather different results can be obtained by using one or the other of the two types of measures dating the fertility decline despite the moderate correlations between them. The date I_g falls below any specific level is clearly a product of both the date fertility begins to decline and the level from which it starts.

The maximum predecline level of marital fertility bears a positive relationship to the absolute amount I_g fell. This is not surprising since the higher is the predecline level of I_g, the larger is the potential magnitude of its decline. However the correlation is weak and in the opposite direction ($-.22$) when we consider the relative decline instead. The relationships between the level of predecline fertility and rate of decline are similar. The higher the maximum I_g the faster

[67]

marital fertility fell in absolute terms. This association practically disappears when we consider the relative rate of decline.

The date of the onset of the fertility transition is related to both the rate and extent of decline. More precisely, a later start in the transition is associated with a smaller fertility reduction. Nevertheless, there is a positive correlation between the date and rate of decline. Areas which start late in their fertility decline reach lower levels at a faster pace both relatively and absolutely even though the level reached is not as low as that experienced by areas which began their decline earlier. It is also true that the later an area enters into the range of clearly transitional or modern fertility (i.e., when I_g falls below .600 or .500) the faster is its decline. The relationships, however, are not as strong.

Nuptiality

Prior to the widespread acceptance of family limitation within marriage, the level of nuptiality itself was a most important factor affecting the level of reproduction in Europe. Illegitimate fertility in most parts of Germany during the nineteenth century was typically low although not negligible. Hence the proportions married in the population of childbearing ages combined with marital fertility to determine the level of overall fertility. We have already seen that the marital fertility component of overall fertility declined substantially between German unification and the beginning of World War II. Did changes in marriage patterns contribute to an even greater decline in overall fertility? This is the question we turn our attention to now.

Perhaps the most important parameters which can be used to describe marriage patterns in a population succinctly are the age at first marriage and the proportion who remain permanently single. Remarriage, divorce, and widowhood all exert some influence on a population's reproductive level, but in general they are of a second order of importance to the first two aspects. As an estimate of the proportion who never marry, we will use the proportion single indicated in the census for the population between 50 and 54 years of age. Very few persons marry for the first time after this age and for women this represents the proportion who do not marry before the end of the reproductive ages and who, therefore, do not contribute at all to the

[68]

marital fertility of the population. The mean age at first marriage is calculated from the proportions of single persons at each age in the censuses. Hajnal (1953a) has devised a method to estimate the mean age at first marriage from the age and marital status distribution of a single census. The method is appropriate, however, only in situations where marriage patterns have been stable during the recent past. Agarwala (1962, pp. 6–24) has modified the technique in a manner which renders it appropriate to circumstances of changing nuptiality as well. In the modified version the calculation is based on the proportions single at each age in two successive censuses and reflects the age of marriage characterizing the intercensal period. The results of these calculations, contained in Table 2.14, show a moderately stable situation existing during most of the period of the fertility decline although a gradual drift towards a younger age at first marriage is evident. World War I and its aftermath temporarily interrupt this trend which then seems to accelerate during the post-World War II years. The younger age of marriage characterizing the recent decades is not unique to Germany. It conforms to the "marriage boom" phenomenon found in many European countries (Hajnal, 1953b). Some discrepancy exists between the estimates based on single census distributions and those calculated by the intercensal method. The latter set of estimates more accurately represent the age of marriage of persons marrying during the intercensal period, while the former set is affected by both current and past experience. Thus during the first decade the intercensal estimates show little change, while the single census estimates decline substantially. The increases during the 1870s in the proportions married at all ages under forty or so result in a decline in the latter measure even though the age of persons marrying was not changing much.

The proportions of the population remaining single was also relatively constant during much of the period. Since persons age 50–54 were generally married between ages 25 and 30, changes in the proportion permanently single are particularly responsive to events two or three decades in the past. Thus the high proportions of women who were single in 1939 and 1950 probably reflect the shortage of men in marriageable ages following World War I.

[69]

TABLE 2.14

AGE AT FIRST MARRIAGE AND PERCENTAGE NOT MARRYING: 1871 TO 1966

| | Age at first marriage | | | | Percentage single (aged 50-54) | |
| | Single census estimate | | Intercensal estimate | | | |
Year	Male	Female	Male	Female	Male	Female
1871	28.8	26.3			9.3[b]	11.9[b]
1875	28.3	25.7	28.4	25.9	8.7[b]	11.5[b]
1880	28.1	25.5	28.3	25.8	8.4[b]	11.4
1885	28.3	25.6	28.3	25.9	7.9	10.7
1890	28.1	25.6	28.1	25.7	7.9	10.5
1900	27.8	25.5	27.8	25.4	8.2	10.1
1910	27.9	25.3	27.9	25.3	7.9	10.4
1925	27.5	26.1	--	--	6.4	10.1
1933	28.3	26.2	28.3	25.6	5.7	10.6
1939	28.2	24.5	27.7[a]	24.3[a]	5.8	12.3
1950	27.7	24.5	--	--	5.3	12.7
1961	26.2	23.3	26.7	23.7	4.9	9.7
1966	26.7	22.8	26.5	23.3	--	--

NOTES: 1939 data include Austria.   1950, 1961, 1966 data refer only
           to West Germany
         1966 data based on sample survey.

[a] 1939 data include Austria whereas 1933 data do not.
[b] 50-59.

It is clear at least on the national level that the changes in German
marriage patterns could not have been responsible for a decline in
overall fertility. The German fertility decline is essentially a matter of
declining marital fertility and not an artifact of higher ages of marriage or decreasing proportions of the population entering conjugal
unions. Thus one of the initial working hypotheses is confirmed, and
the rationale for concentrating on marital fertility as the major dependent variable is firmly established.

The two basic indices of proportions married, I_m and I_{m*}, described
in the previous chapter reflect the combined effect of the age at mar-

riage, the proportion ever marrying, and the proportions widowed or divorced in a population. Although the measures incorporate statistical weights based on the Hutterite marital fertility schedule, they are essentially measures of the marital state of the population. It should be recalled that I_m is somewhat influenced by the age distribution of the population; I_{m*} is not.

The national trend of the two indices (Table 2.1, Figure 2.1), which refer only to women, conforms more or less to the picture of nuptiality trends given by the age at first marriage and the proportion never marrying.

The sharp increase in these indices between 1867 and 1880 testifies to the increase in marriages which resulted from the repeal of restrictive marriage legislation and the general atmosphere of economic prosperity that followed victory in the Franco-Prussian War and unification. Following 1885 the indices continue to rise but in a slower steadier manner until 1910. The lower rates in 1925 reflect the shortage of eligible men resulting from casualties in World War I. The deficit of young men in the most marriageable ages is largely eliminated by 1933, which accounts for the sharp upturn in I_m. The fact that this is primarily an age-distribution effect and not a result of a genuine change in the propensity to marry is revealed by the absence of a similar rise in I_{m*}. Following 1933 a sharp increase in both indices occurs. As with marital fertility, the increase in marriage between 1933 and 1939 is probably due to widespread reemployment and the family incentive policies of the National Socialist regime. Again a world war resulted in a sharp drop in the indices, but during the 1950s the trend toward the new pattern of young and universal marriage resumed, and by 1961 I_m and I_{m*} were both at levels above any previously recorded.

There are substantial territorial variations in marriage patterns within Germany. The age of first marriage for women indicated by the intercensal method for 1880–1885 ranges from over 27 in Aachen and Oberbayern to below 24 in Arnsberg. The proportion single among women 50 to 54 years of age in 1880 ranged from just over 5 percent in Magdeburg to almost 24 percent in Niederbayern. The same differences are reflected in both I_m and I_{m*}, and despite the general increase in these indices over time the relative position of administrative areas alters only moderately. For example, I_m in 1871 correlates .86 with I_m in 1900 and .72 with I_m in 1933. Due to the persistence of differences in nuptial patterns among the administrative areas, Map 2.5 which rep-

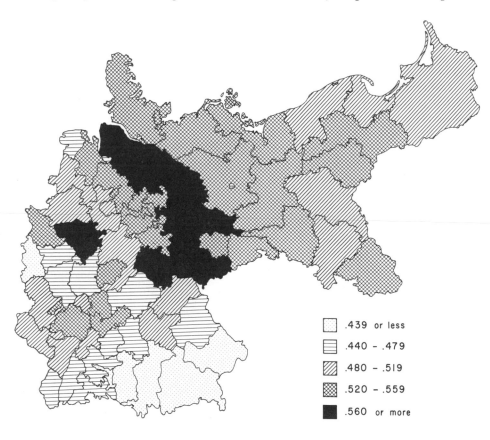

.439 or less

.440 – .479

.480 – .519

.520 – .559

.560 or more

Map 2.5.   Proportion Married (I_m), by Administrative Area: 1900

resents I_m in 1900 is a fairly good indicator of differences existing several decades before and after the turn of the century as well. Clearly distinctive patterns of I_m characterize broad clusters of administrative areas. Proportions married are comparatively low across southern Germany and uniformly high in central Germany. The eastern areas occupy a more intermediate position. Only in the western area, particulary in the Rhineland and Westphalia is a patchwork appearance evident. It also appears that with the exception of the 1870s when the aftermath of the repeal of marriage restrictions was still being felt, the initial levels of the proportions married have little effect on subsequent changes during the course of the fertility decline. The correlation between I_{m*} in 1880 and changes in this index between 1880 and 1900 is essentially nil ($+.03$). Furthermore, the levels in 1880 appear to bear no relation to the changes which occurred by 1933. I_{m*} in 1880 is correlated only .07 with changes in its level by 1933.

The relationship between *marital* fertility and the frequency and age of marriage is a different and more complex issue. From a static point of view, a simple Malthusian argument can be made that prior to widespread birth control higher marital fertility was associated with lower proportions married and vice versa. According to this argument population pressure could be checked by holding down one or the other of these components of overall fertility. From a more dynamic point of view, several alternative hypotheses exist relating long term changes in the two variables (van de Walle, 1968). The first hypothesis suggests that decreasing marital fertility reduces population pressure on land and resources and releases a natural propensity of populations for young and universal marriage, which had been latent during times of uncontrolled, higher marital fertility. According to this hypothesis a decline in marital fertility should precede an increase in marriage. An alternative hypothesis considers marriage patterns as the independent variable and holds that more frequent and earlier marriage creates pressure on the population to control fertility within marriage. Thus a trend toward increasing marriage precedes a decline in marital fertility.

Some evidence concerning the above-mentioned hypotheses is provided by the correlations between the indices of proportions married and I_g for successive censuses (Table 2.15). A weak inverse relationship exists between I_g and the marriage indices in 1871 lending only minimum support to a contention that nuptiality and marital fertility counteract each other during the predecline period. In fact, the correlations are remarkably constant through 1910. Only after I_g declines considerably does a stronger inverse relationship appear. This lends support to the hypothesis that reductions in marital fertility lead to rising marriage rather than the converse. Also the unprecedented high

TABLE 2.15

MARITAL FERTILITY (I_g), CORRELATION WITH PROPORTION MARRIED (I_m and I_{m^*}): 1871 TO 1933

| | Correlation coefficients | |
| | I_g and I_m | I_g and I_{m^*} |
Year		
1871	-.449	-.437
1880	-.451	-.382
1885	-.410	-.292
1890	-.381	-.302
1900	-.429	-.348
1910	-.454	-.290
1925	-.644	-.443
1933	-.653	-.526

NOTE: N = 71 for 1871 through 1910.
N = 66 for 1925 and 1933.

levels of I_m and I_{m^*} by the 1960s further support this possibility. The evidence of course is only suggestive and quite possibly a two-way process is at work. It seems unlikely that a major long term rise in the proportions married preceded the fertility decline. Since I_m and I_{m^*} were rather low in 1867, it is improbable that they could have risen much during the beginning of the nineteenth century. Since data on marriage patterns during this period are available only for local parish or village studies and not in the administrative area level for most of Germany, we can not adequately test our speculation with our data. However, it is possible to test whether marriage patterns just prior to the fertility decline influenced its onset and also to check if short run changes in the proportions married were related to the initial decline in marital fertility. To answer the first question we have correlated the predecline levels of I_m and I_{m^*} with the year I_g had fallen by 10 percent (Table 2.16). If higher proportions married in an area's population created pressure for an early reduction in marital fertility, we would expect a negative correlation between I_m or I_{m^*} and the date of decline. The results indicate a very weak relationship in the opposite direction. In other words, higher levels of the index of proportions married are weakly associated with later dates of decline. Also, allowing for the differences in the predecline level of marital fertility (represented by I_g in 1869–1873) through partial correlation actually in-

TABLE 2.16

DATE OF 10% DECLINE IN MARITAL FERTILITY(I_g),
CORRELATION WITH PROPORTION MARRIED (I_m & I_{m*})
IN 1871 AND 1880

Year	Index of proportion married	Correlation coefficients	
		Zero order	Partial controlling for I_g 1869-1873
1871	I_m	.21	.31
	I_{m*}	.26	.35
1880	I_m	.02	.20
	I_{m*}	.19	.36

N = 71

creases the strength of the relationship in the opposite direction than predicted.

Similarly, a correlational analysis of changes in marital fertility and changes in proportions married yields very weak coefficients. Changes in I_g between 1871 and 1900 are correlated only −.18 with changes in I_m and −.20 with changes in I_{m*} over the same period. The negative direction of the relationship indicates that the more I_g declines the more I_m or I_{m*} increase and thus are in the predicted direction but the values are too low to be considered important.

Illegitimacy

Illegitimate fertility in Germany has been high by European standards. During the last two decades of the nineteenth century the national level of I_h was above the level experienced even in the Scandanavian countries and exceeded only by Austria, Hungary, and Portugal.[10] After the turn of the century its relative position was somewhat less extreme, although it remained well above the European average (Shorter, Knodel, and van de Walle, 1971).

[10]For a short but comprehensive survey of illegitimate fertility in Germany during the last three decades of the nineteenth century see Prinzing, 1902; for a comparison between Germany and other European countries see Prinzing, 1911.

The contribution of illegitimacy to overall fertility $[I_h(1 - I_m)/I_f]$ fluctuated between 8 and 11 percent nationally from 1867 to 1939. It was considerably higher, however, in some of the individual administrative areas. In 1866–1868 for example, the impact of illegitimacy on I_f was almost 25 percent in much of Bavaria. This was reduced after the weakening of marriage and residence restrictions, but even after 1880 the contribution of I_h was close to 20 percent in Oberbayern and Niederbayern and close to or above 15 percent in the Kingdom of Saxony. In contrast illegitimacy made only a 3 percent contribution to I_f in Westphalia for much of the period under observation and barely a 4 percent contribution in most of the Rhineland.

The values of I_h for each area are included in Appendix Table 2.1 Area 1 differences in illegitimacy were rather persistent over time. For example, I_h in 1880 correlates .83 with I_h in 1933. The values of I_h in the administrative areas in 1900 correlate .96 with corresponding values in 1880 and .86 with the 1933 levels. Hence Map 2.6, which represents the distribution of I_h by administrative area for 1900 (1898–1902), provides a fairly good indication of the area differentials during the entire time under observation. Broader regional patterns are quite evident with respect to illegitimate fertility. The western administrative areas of Prussia exhibit very low levels of I_h, the eastern areas with a high proportion of Polish and Slavic ethnic groups (especially the province of Posnania and the administrative area of Oppeln) occupy a middle position, and the other provinces east of the Elbe experienced fairly high levels. Particularly high illegitimacy characterizes southeastern Germany, Thüringen, and Saxony, while somewhat more moderate levels prevail in the southwestern areas. Prinzing (1902) attributed the regional differences in illegitimacy to differences in customs as well as differences in the ratio of unmarried women to unmarried men. He suggested that situations where there is a shortage of eligible men for marriage are particularly conducive to high illegitimacy. Thus within Prussia he attributes the rather high illegitimacy in Bresslau and Liegnitz to the relative excess of unmarried women in comparison to unmarried men. The western provinces on the other hand were characterized by both low illegitimacy and a greater numerical availability of unmarried men. The substantial differences

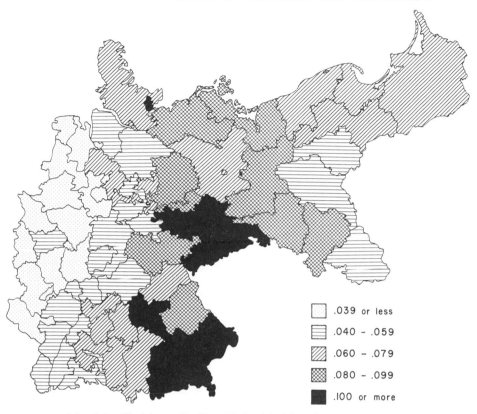

Map 2.6. Illegitimate Fertility (I_h), by Administrative Area: 1898–1902

.039 or less
.040 – .059
.060 – .079
.080 – .099
.100 or more

in the ratios of unmarried men to unmarried women that Prinzing points to were to a large extent the by-product of the flow of single men in working ages from the more agrarian eastern provinces to the industrial parts of Westphalia and the Rhineland.

Prinzing's thesis, which certainly merits further investigation, unfortunately can not be tested with our indices since I_m and I_{m*} refer to the ratio of unmarried women to women of all marital statuses and not to unmarried men. Nevertheless it is interesting to compare the index of non-marital fertility through correlational analysis with the indices of marital fertility and proportions married on a cross-sectional basis for successive periods (Table 2.17). The results indicate that I_h varies within Germany independently of marital fertility and the proportions married.

[77]

TABLE 2.17

ILLEGITIMATE FERTILITY (I_h), CORRELATIONS WITH MARITAL FERTILITY (I_g) AND
PROPORTION MARRIED (I_m AND I_{m*}):   1871 TO 1933

| Census year | Correlation coefficients between I_h and | | |
	I_g	I_m	I_{m*}
1871	-.041	-.086	-.148
1880	-.051	.082	-.003
1885	-.057	.149	.091
1890	-.080	.136	.094
1900	-.218	.144	.086
1910	-.296	.100	.077
1925	-.172	.197	.136
1933	-.073	.207	.186

NOTE: N = 71 for 1871 through 1910.
        N = 66 for 1925 and 1933.

Very much like the secular trend in marital fertility, illegitimate fertility in Germany underwent a substantial long run decline during the seven decades preceding World War II (Table 2.1). Between 1866–1868 and 1931–1935, I_h declined almost 60 percent at the national level. Perhaps the most remarkable feature of the national trend is the extent to which the decline parallels the course of marital fertility (see Figure 2.1). The initial drop in I_h between 1866–1868 and 1869–1873 is largely a result of the intervening repeal in many states of legislation restricting marriages (Knodel, 1967). Except for a slight lag in the decline of illegitimate fertility, the two curves are otherwise identical up to 1939. The similarity continues even through the increases in fertility experienced between 1931–1935 and 1938–1939. Possibly, aspects of the pro-natalist policies of the National Socialists account for some of this, since in certain places they not only encouraged marital fertility but were also extremely tolerant of illegitimacy (Glass, 1940, p. 304). Only in the 1950s do the trends diverge.

Neither the secular decline in illegitimate fertility nor the parallelism between it and the decline in marital fertility are unique to Germany; they appear to be general European phenomena (Shorter, Knodel, van de Walle, 1971; Cutright, 1971, p. 29). The coincidence in the declines in I_g and I_h, however, is not easy to explain since *a priori* there is little reason to expect both types of fertility to respond to the same social and economic forces. Normally we would expect that illegitimate fertility, except under unusual circumstances such as severe marriage restrictions or non-Western family customs, would represent unwanted births. Thus it seems plausible to assume that substantial motivation to avoid extramarital births existed long before the end of the nineteenth century and on one level of explanation at least the decline in I_h probably can be attributed to the introduction and spread of more effective birth control technology and practices throughout the German population. On the other hand the decline in marital fertility has frequently been considered largely a product of changing motivations for large families or a large number of births rather than a response to new and effective methods of contraception. Indeed there is some evidence that in Western Europe *coitus interruptus* rather than more modern or advanced techniques of birth control was the primary method used by married couples to reduce their fertility (Freedman, 1961–62, p. 52). If *coitus interruptus* was a "folk" method known throughout the population prior to the decline in marital fertility, as it is sometimes argued (Hawthorn, 1970, pp. 33–39), why was it not used more effectively earlier to control illegitimate fertility? Does then the simultaneous decline of I_g and I_h support the argument that the diffusion of contraceptive techniques, including *coitus interruptus*, was instrumental in initializing the decline in marital fertility? Or should the argument run in a different direction? Perhaps the increased desire to limit marital fertility resulted in pressure to develop and market more effective methods of birth control. Those involved in non-marital sexual relationships may simply have benefited from the availability of these techniques as well.

For individual areas the magnitude of the decline in I_h is only weakly associated with the corresponding amount of decline in I_g. Thus if we calculate the change in I_g and the change in I_h between 1878–1882 and 1931–1935, the absolute changes correlate .22 with

[79]

each other and relative changes correlate .24. A more interesting question concerns the association between the onset of the decline in I_h and I_g. This could be determined, for example, by correlating the date of the beginning of the decline in both types of fertility for the administrative areas. However, it is more difficult to determine in a meaningful manner the date of the start of the decline in non-marital fertility than it is for marital fertility. There is a relatively much wider range in the level of I_h among administrative areas than in I_g. Some areas experience levels of non-marital fertility almost ten times that of other areas. Hence the meaning of a 10 percent decline in I_h may depend heavily on the predecline level. For this reason a partial correlation between the date of a 10 percent decline in I_g and in I_h "controlling" for the maximum predecline level of I_h seems a more preferable measure of the relationship than a simple zero-order correlation. Actually, neither the partial correlation ($r = .01$) nor the zero order correlation ($r = .02$) indicate any relationship between the start of the declines in marital and non-marital fertility. These results are surprising in view of the parallel course of decline in I_g and I_h on the national level. Perhaps the absence of correlations result from imperfections in the measures of the dates of decline. The relationship between illegitimate and marital fertility, expecially over time, needs to be studied further. Such an investigation might very likely help illuminate the nature of the decline in each.[11]

Overall Fertility

The measure of overall fertility, I_f, used in this study is closely related to the other demographic indices $\left[I_f = I_g I_m + (1 - I_m) I_h \right]$. In the absence of illegitimacy, I_f is simply the product of I_g and I_m. Although I_h in many areas of Germany is not negligible, it is clearly of less importance in determining the level of I_f than are marital fertility and the proportions married. Furthermore, since I_m did not change greatly between the beginning of the fertility transition and 1933, it is not surprising that closely parallel courses are followed by I_f and I_g

[11] An exploratory study in this vein has been attempted using the data on non-marital fertility generated by the Princeton European Fertility Study. See Shorter, Knodel, and van de Walle, 1971.

(Table 2.1 and Figure 2.1). The slowly rising proportions married resulted in a slightly slower decline in I_f.

The values of I_f for each area are included in Appendix Table 2.1. The correlations between I_f and each of its components for successive periods shows some changes during the course of the decline (Table 2.18). I_f is most closely associated with I_g. The low correlations be-

TABLE 2.18

OVERALL FERTILITY (I_f), CORRELATIONS WITH OTHER DEMOGRAPHIC
INDICES: 1871 TO 1933

Census year	Correlation coefficients between I_f and			
	I_g	I_h	I_m	I_{m^*}
1871	.688	.368	.233	.206
1880	.746	.364	.153	.169
1885	.743	.377	.221	.301
1890	.734	.316	.273	.331
1900	.831	.066	.094	.162
1910	.934	-.133	-.150	.015
1925	.922	.092	-.360	-.143
1933	.876	.220	-.254	-.112

NOTE: N = 71 for 1871 through 1910.
       N = 66 for 1925 and 1933.

tween I_f and the indices of proportions married are interesting. They result from the inverse relation between I_g and I_m. By 1910 this effect was strong enough to produce a negative correlation between I_f and I_m.

The start of the decline in overall fertility can be dated in a similar way as the decline in marital fertility, i.e., using the criterion of the date I_f achieved a sustained decline 10 percent. The date of the decline in I_f is correlated .88 with the date of the decline in I_g. As with marital fertility, there is almost no relationship between the maximum pre-decline level of overall fertility and the date it begins its transition to lower levels ($r = .15$). Likewise, the maximum predecline I_f is not related to the relative decline in I_f between its maximum value and 1931–1935 ($r = .15$). The higher the predecline I_f, however, the greater the absolute decline ($r = .70$).

Not only are I_f and I_g highly correlated for different areas at any given period, but the declines in each variable are closely associated. The absolute decline from the maximum predecline values for these two indices of fertility are correlated .78 with each other, and a .86 correlation exists between the relative amounts of decline.

Territorial and Regional Variation in the Demographic Indices

A few comments on territorial and regional variation are offered to conclude our discussion of trends in the demographic indices in Germany. Three measures of variation, the range, the standard deviation, and the coefficient of variation (ratio of standard deviation to mean), are presented in Table 2.19. They enable us to evaluate the extent to which a divergence or convergence of fertility and nuptiality patterns took place during the historic process of the fertility transition. Examining the trend in marital fertility, we see that both the range and the standard deviation of I_g first increase and then decrease. The initial phase of increase is created by some areas beginning to decline while other continue to experience high, predecline fertility. Eventually all areas begin to decline, and since the late starting areas experience faster rates of decline, the amount of absolute variation between areas decreases. By 1933 both the range and the standard deviation of I_g are reduced to less than their predecline values. The relative variation, however, increases steadily between 1871 and 1933 as evident from the trend in the coefficient of variation.

The regional variation in I_f follows a very similar path. Both the range and the standard deviation increase and then decrease, while the coefficient of variation constantly becomes larger. In fact, the coefficient of variation for both I_g and I_f show very similar values until 1910. Thereafter the change in marriage patterns results in lower relative variation in I_f than in I_g. Areas with lower marital fertility become more strongly associated with higher proportions married.

A considerable reduction in both the range and the standard deviation of I_h occur after 1900. The coefficient of variation fluctuates in a

TABLE 2.19

TERRITORIAL VARIATION IN DEMOGRAPHIC INDICES AMONG ADMINISTRATIVE AREAS: 1871 TO 1933

Demographic index	Census year	Levels			Variation		
		Mean	High	Low	Range	Standard deviation	Coefficient of variation
Overall fertility (I_f)	1871	.388	.482	.314	.168	.0400	.103
	1880	.398	.487	.320	.167	.0410	.103
	1885	.388	.486	.283	.203	.0437	.113
	1890	.379	.479	.258	.221	.0452	.119
	1900	.370	.491	.217	.274	.0516	.139
	1910	.318	.447	.183	.264	.0564	.177
	1925	.197	.283	.085	.198	.0379	.192
	1933	.167	.244	.090	.154	.0319	.191
Marital fertility (I_g)	1871	.759	.942	.598	.344	.0871	.115
	1880	.732	.915	.554	.361	.0846	.116
	1885	.722	.917	.535	.382	.0893	.124
	1890	.705	.918	.494	.424	.0920	.130
	1900	.674	.912	.394	.518	.1144	.170
	1910	.562	.835	.303	.532	.1266	.225
	1925	.370	.599	.147	.452	.0969	.262
	1933	.293	.473	.152	.321	.0770	.263
Illegitimate fertility (I_h)	1871	.067	.140	.012	.128	.0282	.422
	1880	.066	.144	.016	.128	.0300	.455
	1885	.067	.139	.016	.123	.0301	.449
	1890	.064	.136	.014	.122	.0288	.450
	1900	.062	.126	.015	.111	.0265	.427
	1910	.056	.112	.014	.088	.0231	.413
	1925	.040	.090	.012	.078	.0182	.455
	1933	.033	.089	.010	.070	.0161	.488
Proportion married (I_{m*})	1871	.505	.597	.413	.184	.0465	.092
	1880	.542	.623	.462	.161	.0401	.074
	1885	.537	.619	.454	.165	.0414	.077
	1890	.542	.626	.454	.172	.0433	.080
	1900	.554	.641	.465	.176	.0440	.079
	1910	.563	.643	.467	.146	.0414	.074
	1925	.525	.599	.443	.156	.0390	.074
	1933	.525	.631	.407	.224	.0549	.105

NOTE: N = 71 for 1871 through 1910.
       N = 66 for 1925 and 1933.

narrow range between 1871 and 1925, with a small increase occurring by 1933.

Some convergence in marriage patterns as measured by I_{m*} is evident between 1871 and 1880. All three measures of variation decline. This was a period of rising nuptiality, during which areas with the lowest proportions married experienced the greatest increase. Following 1880, however, there is little change in the territorial variation until after World War I when a considerable increase takes place in both absolute and relative variation.

[83]

The question we turn to now is whether or not there existed a closer association in the fertility and nuptiality experience of administrative areas that are regionally associated than would be expected by chance. In our discussion of the various maps showing the territorial distribution of the demographic indices, it often appeared that wider regional patterns existed, extending over a number of adjacent administrative areas. In the introductory chapter a classification scheme was presented which grouped the 71 administrative areas in seven broader regions for the purpose of facilitating a precise, quantitative evaluation of regional patterns of demographic behavior in the context of the fertility transition. The statistical tool we use in our study of regional influence is the analysis of variance which enables us to compare the variation in fertility and nuptiality arising from the differences between the average regional values and the "grand mean" and the variation in values for administrative areas within the same region from the regional mean. The resulting F-ratio of "between region" variation to "within region" variation indicates if regional association exists and also if it is statistically significant.[12] Put more simply, it tests whether regional means differ from each other more than we can expect by chance. The strength of the relationship between regional location and whatever demographic indice is being examined can be measured by the "unbiased correlation ratio" (ϵ).[13] The values of F and ϵ for the demographic indices at successive periods are presented in Table 2.20. Several measures of the magnitude, date, and rate of decline (Table 2.21) indicate that regional differentials are substantial for every index during the entire six and a half decades under observation. For each measure, the F-ratio indicated a level of regional association significant at the .001 level or better except for I_f in 1925 and the percent decline in I_g from its maximum to 1933. The latter two were significant at .01 level. Hence the general impression of regional clustering conveyed by the maps of fertility and nuptiality are

[12]The reader should bear in mind, however, that the assumptions of the F-test are not strictly satisfied by the data and thus the results should be treated as only a rough indication of statistical significance.

[13]The "unbiased correlation ratio" is calculated according to the following formula:

$$\epsilon = \sqrt{1 - \frac{\text{mean square variance within regions}}{\text{total mean square varience}}}$$

TABLE 2.20

TERRITORIAL VARIATION IN DEMOGRAPHIC INDICES, ANALYSIS OF VARIANCE BETWEEN ADMINISTRATIVE AREAS AND BETWEEN GEOGRAPHICAL REGIONS: 1871 TO 1933

Census year	F-ratio					Unbiased correlation ratio (ε)				
	I_f	I_g	I_h	I_m	I_{m^*}	I_f	I_g	I_h	I_m	I_{m^*}
1871	9.8	15.8	12.6	9.3	12.8	.66	.75	.71	.64	.71
1880	8.3	14.6	10.3	5.8	8.1	.62	.73	.67	.54	.62
1885	8.3	12.9	9.9	9.1	9.2	.62	.71	.66	.64	.64
1890	9.7	13.0	9.4	14.0	11.4	.65	.71	.65	.73	.69
1900	10.3	14.4	9.2	11.3	10.6	.67	.73	.64	.69	.67
1910	8.6	12.6	8.5	5.7	8.2	.63	.71	.63	.54	.62
1925	3.3	6.6	8.3	10.7	7.4	.42	.59	.63	.69	.61
1933	5.0	7.4	11.8	12.8	10.5	.52	.61	.71	.72	.68

NOTE: df. = 6,64 for F-ratios for 1871 through 1910.
df. = 6,59 for F-ratios for 1925 and 1933.

TABLE 2.21

TERRITORIAL VARIATION IN DECLINE IN MARITAL FERTILITY (I_g), ANALYSIS OF VARIANCE BETWEEN ADMINISTRATIVE AREAS AND BETWEEN GEOGRAPHICAL REGIONS

Measure of decline		F-ratio	Unbiased correlation ratio (ε)
Magnitude	Absolute (maximum to 1910)	5.1	.51
	Percent (maximum to 1910)	6.3	.56
	Percent (maximum to 1933)	4.1	.46
Date	10% decline	6.9	.58
	I_g = .600	9.2	.64
	I_g = .500	9.4	.65
Rate	Absolute	14.2	.73
	Relative	12.6	.71

NOTE: df. = 6,64 for F-ratio.

confirmed. Although the degree of regional association in marital and overall fertility weakened somewhat after World War I when their levels were beginning to converge all over Germany, such was not the case for either non-marital fertility or the indices of proportions married.

The possibility of regional location as an important determinant of an administrative area's level of marital fertility or its date and rate of decline will have to be taken into consideration in the analysis of the relationship between other factors and marital fertility. In particular we will want to test if these observed regional associations are actually a result of regional clusterings of identifiable social-structural or demographic factors which are themselves the real determinants of marital fertility and its decline or if the reverse is true.

One last question needs to be answered before concluding the discussion of territorial and regional variations in fertility. The basic units of analysis in our study of the German fertility decline are the administrative areas described in the introductory chapter. Their choice was largely a matter of convenience since they were the smallest unit for which demographic and social statistical data were available in substantial detail. The choice of the units however carries with it the implicit assumption that the population of each administrative area is relatively homogeneous as far as our dependent variable, marital fertility, is concerned. We can test this assumption with the help of analysis of variance in the same way that we tested for regional associations. As indicated in Chapter 1, each administrative area was divided for administrative purposes into a number of local districts (*Kreise* or *Ämter*). Because of occasional divisions or consolidations, the total number of districts in Germany was not constant over time. At the turn of the century these numbered roughly a thousand. With the help of the *F*-test we can compare the variation of fertility within each administrative area at the district level with the variation between administrative areas. In other words, the *F*-ratio will indicate the ratio of the mean square variance "between" adminstrative areas to the mean square variance "within" the administrative areas. *F*-ratios substantially above one indicate that the fertility of districts within administrative areas is relatively homogeneous. We will have to content ourselves with the crude birth rate as our measure of fertility in this instance since it is not possible to compute more refined measures from published data. Specifically, the analysis of variance has been applied to the crude birth rate in 1894-1896 and 1909–1911 as well as to the change in the crude birth rate between these two periods. The results can be summarized as follows:

CBR 1894–1896; $F_{65,911} = 14.6$, E = .78
CBR 1909–1911; $F_{65,1060} = 12.8$, E = .65
Change in CBR; $F_{65,911} = 9.2$, E = .60

The large value of F (significant at well above the .001 for all three measures) indicated that a large portion of variance is between administrative areas, and only a small proportion within. In view of the fact that fertility was falling most rapidly in Germany precisely in the period bracketed by the dates of the crude birth rate measures used in the analysis, the relative homogeneity within administrative areas is particularly reassuring for the study of the fertility decline.

In conclusion to our survey of the trends in German fertility and nuptiality we can state that a decline in fertility of major proportions took place in every administrative area sometime between the political unification of Germany in 1871 and the outbreak of World War II. In almost every case this transition to modern levels of low fertility had a clear beginning and a clear end with no backtracking along the way. At the same time, the proportions married among the female population in the childbearing ages increased somewhat, particularly during the first and last decades of the period. Both marital and non-marital fertility fell precipitously, but since illegitimate births represented only a small portion of total births, the bulk of the overall fertility decline can be attributed to a reduction of births within marriage. An examination of the available statistical evidence suggests that no decline in fertility of any significance occurred in the decades preceding German unification; to the contrary, the predominant trend was of constant or slightly rising fertility in most administrative areas. By the 1930s the decline had run its course and fertility actually rose somewhat in all areas between 1933 and the outbreak of World War II.

In the next chapter we turn our attention away from the administrative area per se as our unit of analysis and focus instead on comparing fertility trends among various socially defined sectors of the German population. In particular, we will deal with differences according to rural-urban residence, economic activity, wealth, religion, and ethnic affiliation.

CHAPTER 3: Social Differentials in the German Fertility Decline

An important step in gaining a fuller understanding of the fertility transition in Germany is to identify social factors that differentiate subpopulations within Germany with respect to the timing and extent of their participation in the fertility decline. The previous chapter examined in detail geographical differences in demographic behavior using as the units of analysis fertility and nuptiality measures for administrative areas. We now turn to the task of delineating differential fertility trends for sociologically defined population aggregates. Our choice of variables to be used in categorizing the German population for this purpose is restricted largely to those for which data are available in the censuses and vital statistics. The greatest amount of data is available contrasting persons who resided in the cities on the one hand or in the countryside on the other. Thus a large portion of this chapter will be devoted to describing rural-urban differentials in the fertility decline. Some information is also available on fertility differences according to the husband's economic activity and according to religion. In addition some indirect evidence can be included regarding differences with regard to wealth and ethnic affiliation.

Several words of caution about social differentials in fertility are appropriate at this point. First it should be noted that for the study of the fertility decline it is particularly important to distinguish between differences in fertility levels and differences in trends or changes. Just as there was substantial variation in the predecline level of fertility among the populations of administrative areas in Germany, there are bound to be substantial differences in the predecline level of fertility for various socially defined subpopulations. Hence a lower fertility within any particular sector of the population at a given point of time is not sufficient evidence that it led other sectors in the fertility transition. The more crucial questions from the perspective of the present study then do not concern differences in levels of fertility at any one point in time but rather differentials in the timing and extent of decline.

The second point regards the distinction between the social differen-

[88]

tials and the social causes of the fertility decline. Identification of leaders and laggers with respect to any social change does not explain the change but rather provides more detail in its description. When we utilize a variable such as occupation or religion to classify the population for the investigation of fertility differentials, we are not able to relate changes in the variable to changes in fertility as we must do to establish causal relationships. Finding that fertility declined first in the urban areas, for example, is not evidence that urbanization brought about the changes. Nevertheless rural-urban differentials in pre- and post-decline fertility as well as in the rate and date of the decline are useful in outlining the pattern of the decline. Their presence or absence tell us that much more about the setting of the fertility transition and thus can provide clues for identifying the nature and direction of causality.

Rural-Urban Residence

Sufficient reasons exist to expect differences in the fertility behavior of urban and rural populations. A great deal has been written describing aspects of modern city life which logically would seem to inhibit high fertility. Explicitly or implicitly, a contrast is made with traditional rural life. Thus, in the modern city, space is at a premium creating housing problems, children cost more and contribute less to production that they did on the farm, secular values prevail, social mobility aspirations rise, women find employment away from the home, etc. The thrust of this argument then is not so much to explain why fertility fell in the city as it is to suggest why at any one time fertility should be lower in cities than in the countryside. On the other hand, to the extent that the reduction in fertility involved a modification in the importance of the family, in the force of tradition, and in attitudes towards the possibility of controlling one's own destiny, then the importance of the rural-urban dichotomy is that such changes tend naturally to take place in the cities first, and also perhaps to diffuse more rapidly through an urban than rural population. This hypothesis implies that one would expect urban populations in a given area to experience an earlier decline in fertility and perhaps a more rapid decline. The purpose of the present section is to review the empirical evidence bearing on two questions about the fertility decline: (1) What were the extent and direction of differences in rural and urban fertility prior to and during the fertility transition? (2) Are there rural-urban differentials in the timing and extent of the decline?

The national statistical bureau did not publish census age and marital status distributions or vital statistics according to a rural-urban cross-classification until after World War I. Thus it is not possible to compute rural-urban demographic trends on a national level. However, the capital city, Berlin, and the three independent city states (*Hansestädte*) of Hamburg, Bremen, and Lübeck each formed separate administrative areas for which the requisite statistics are available. A comparison of I_g in these four large metropolitan areas with the national trend in Germany provides some evidence on the timing and magnitude of the urban fertility decline. The basic demographic indices for these areas are included in Appendix Table 2.1. The trends in I_g which are represented graphically in Figure 3.1 in-

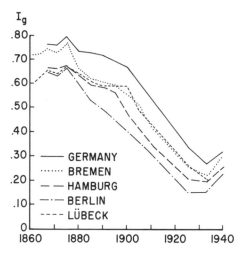

Figure 3.1 Marital Fertility (I_g), Selected
Cities and Germany: 1867 to 1939

dicate all four metropolitan areas started declining from lower levels than the national average and experienced lower marital fertility throughout the entire period of decline. All four cities began their declines earlier than Germany as a whole, as indicated by the year a sustained decline of 10 percent was achieved, or by the year that I_g

crossed the .600 and .500 levels (see Table 2.12 in the previous chapter). Despite differences in detail among the four metropolitan areas there is a striking parallel in their paths of decline, and indeed a general resemblance to the path followed by the nation as a whole.

A comparison between the Reich and the four metropolitan areas using the index of overall fertility (I_f) would yield essentially the same results. In 1866–1868, for example, I_f in all four cities was lower than the national average. The relative differences were even greater than for I_g since I_m was lower than in the rest of Germany. The date I_f declined was also earlier in all four cities than in the Reich. In each case, because I_m was rising during the 1870s, the date of a 10 percent decline in overall fertility is somewhat later than for marital fertility.

More direct data on rural-urban demographic trends are available from many of the state statistical bureaus, which often independently tabulated and published results from censuses and vital registration. Since substantial autonomy existed in the statistical offices of different states, each utilized its own scheme of rural-urban classification. Essentially two different systems were used. Occasionally the systems were combined as in Prussia. One categorized municipalities as rural or urban according to population size; the other classified a municipality as a city or not according to its legal status (the so-called *rechtliche Prinzip*). In the first case, the size which was used to designate an area as urban or which was used to cross-classify areas was not uniform. Frequently the crucial size for separation was 2,000, although pivotal values of 5,000, 20,000 or 100,000 were also employed occasionally. The use of the criterion of population size to determine urban status creates a problem for the calculation of statistical time series since the number of municipalities qualifying as urban may change from one census to another. This is particularly disturbing when trying to match vital statistics over a period of several years with the results of a census taken during a year midway in the period. Since different criteria might have been used to define municipality boundaries within different states some difficulties exist in interpreting comparisons between German states, not to mention between Germany and other countries, even when the population size criterion for urban classification is the same.

The alternative system classifies municipalities as towns or cities if they are legally considered as such. The legal definition is usually based on the municipality's historical importance. Thus, sometimes a community with under 500 inhabitants qualifies as a town while a neighboring community with a much larger population is considered rural. Since historical circumstances are different from area to area and state to state, comparisons of rural and urban areas classified according to the legal principle also require caution. In addition, towns tended to expand their boundaries over time and incorporate neighboring rural areas. Nevertheless considerable continuity in the rural-urban classification usually holds from census to census, thus facilitating the calculation of indices over time.

One last problem should be mentioned in connection with the calculation of rural-urban fertility rates. Until 1933 births were registered according to the place of occurrence rather than according to the place of residence of the parents.[1] To the extent that women residing outside the urban areas went to clinics or hospitals inside the city limits to give birth, the number of registered births in urban areas would include births that should be allocated to rural areas for the purpose of calculating fertility rates. The result would be to inflate artificially the urban rate and deflate the rural rate. However since only a small proportion of births actually occurred in hospitals or clinics before 1933 and particularly before World War I, the amount of distortion introduced into rural and urban rates can not be large. In 1890, for example, only about one percent of all births occurred in hospitals; during 1908–1910 2.6 percent occurred in medical institutions; by 1925 the figure rose to almost 8 percent, and in 1932 it was just over 15 percent. Of course the majority of mothers giving birth in hospitals undoubtedly lived in the city or town where the hospital was located, and thus the amount of distortion introduced into the rural or urban fertility rates by births being registered outside the mother's place of residence is substantially smaller than the percent of births that occurred in hospitals or clinics. Since most of the rural-urban series we examine in this chapter do not extend past World War I, dis-

[1] Communicated in a personal letter dated Nov. 2, 1970 from Dr. Hermann Schubnell, director of the Division of Population and Cultural Statistics in the Federal Statistical Office, Wiesbaden, Germany.

tortions arising from this problem need not be of great concern. What distortion exists is in the direction of overstating urban fertility, and understating rural to a gradually increasing extent.

(a) *Prussia*. The largest body of data permitting calculation of separate fertility measures for rural and urban areas is provided by Prussia. The basic demographic indices were calculated whenever possible for each administrative area for the following rural-urban categories: all rural communities (legally defined), all cities, each city with at least 20,000 population in 1880, and all cities with less than 20,000 population in 1880. These categories are not mutually exclusive. Thus the all-cities category consists both of cities with less than 20,000 population (in 1880) as well as larger cities. The entire administrative area of course consists of all cities and all rural communities. In order to eliminate problems which would arise from increases in the number of cities with at least 20,000 population, this category was limited to those that had reached the prescribed size by 1880.

The fact that cities frequently expanded by incorporating neighboring rural areas or towns into their city limits and also that municipalities occasionally changed their official status from rural to urban presents a problem when vital statistics over a period of several years are related to census distributions given for a single year. For example, if a city incorporated a rural area into its limits just prior to a census, a fertility rate based on the average annual number of births during the five years centered on the census year would be misleadingly low. On the other hand, if births for just the year of the census were used, the fertility rate might fluctuate too much because of year to year peculiarities. As a compromise, two-year birth averages based on births during the census year and during the following year were used. In the few situations when changes in boundaries or in number of urban communities occurred during the year following the census, the number of births were adjusted accordingly.[2]

[2]In situations where a city incorporated an adjacent area into its boundaries during the year following a census, the number of births that would have occurred in the city had the boundaries remained the same as they were at the time of the census was estimated by letting the births be equal to the number of births during the census year plus an annual increment in births equal to the average increment occurring to cities in its category in all of Prussia.

SOCIAL DIFFERENTIALS

The 1867 census was the first that included the necessary data for the calculation of the basic demographic indices for rural and urban categories in Prussia. Birth data were also published according to rural-urban categories. However, the values of the rural-urban fertility indices based on the 1867 census and birth data for 1867–1868 appear to be unreasonable for many administrative areas. A consistency test between the census and vital statistics suggests why. In Chapter 1 the number of infants aged 0–11 months old enumerated in the December 1867 census was compared with the number of births registered in the first 11 months of 1867 minus the number of deaths to these infants before December. Close agreement was found for each administrative area in Prussia. A similar test for the urban districts within each area yields quite different results (Table 3.1). Apparently the definition of urban areas or city boundaries used by the census did not match the

TABLE 3.1

RATIO OF INFANTS ENUMERATED IN CENSUS TO INFANTS EXPECTED TO BE SURVIVING ACCORDING TO VITAL REGISTRATION, BY URBAN AREA, PRUSSIA: 1867 AND 1880

Area	1867	1880	Area	1867	1880
01 Ostpreussen			17 Schleswig	1.34	.98
Königsberg	.79	.95	18 Hannover	1.28	1.17
Gumbinnen	.76	.96	19 Hildesheim	1.13	.98
02 Danzig	.89	.96	20 Lüneburg	1.27	.98
03 Marienwerder	.90	.95	21 Stade	2.28	.98
04 Berlin	.97	.97	22 Osnabrück	1.34	.95
05 Potsdam	1.07	1.00	23 Aurich	1.07	1.23
06 Frankfurt/O.	.95	.98	24 Münster	.71	1.01
07 Stettin-Stralsund			25 Minden	.90	.96
Stettin	1.01	.98	26 Arnsberg	.93	.99
Stralsund	.93	.95	27 Kassel	.86	.97
08 Köslin	.91	.98	28 Wiesbaden	.94	.97
09 Posen	.89	.97	29 Koblenz	.98	.98
10 Bromberg	.79	.97	30 Düsseldorf	.99	.99
11 Breslau	.97	.98	31 Köln	.93	.92
12 Liegnitz	.60	.97	32 Trier	.97	.98
13 Oppeln	.90	.98	33 Aachen	1.06	.99
14 Magdeburg	.99	.99	34 Sigmaringen	.95	1.02
15 Merseburg	.99	.99			
16 Erfurt	.97	.99	Prussia	.94	.98

NOTES: Ratios are presented for urban districts within each area.
Data for 29 Kassel excludes Waldeck.

definition used by the vital statistics. The results of this consistency test and the results of the fertility indice calculations match well. The urban areas with unreasonably high fertility rates show a low ratio of census-enumerated infants to "expected" infants according to the vital statistics. The reverse was true for areas with fertility rates which appeared too low. The next census tabulating age, sex, and marital status distributions by rural-urban categories in Prussia occurred in 1880. A test of consistency between the census results and the vital statistics yields much better results, indicating that the problem had been largely overcome. Only two administrative areas, Hannover and Aurich, indicate substantial disagreement between the census and the vital statistics. By 1890 these last two also fell in line. A similar consistency test for the 40 large Prussian cities for which separate statistics were available in 1867, indicates for 18 (45%), the vital registration and census figures differed by more than five percent, and for 7 (18%) they differed by more than ten percent. In contrast, in 1880, among the 68 large cities with separate statistics, only 10 (15%) showed more than a five percent disagreement and only 1 showed more than a ten percent disagreement. Due to the inherent difficulties in relating birth data in 1867–1868 to census distributions in 1867, the following analysis of rural-urban fertility in Prussia will be limited to trends from 1880 on. Rural-urban demographic indices were calculated for Prussia for all years with available requisite data.[3] A complete set of the marital fertility indices for each Prussian administrative area are presented in Appendix Table 3.1.[4]

---

[3] The basic demographic indices could be calculated for all rural-urban categories for 1880–1881, 1890-1891, 1895-1896, 1900–1901, and 1905–1906. For 1885–1886, the indices could be calculated separately only for cities with at least 20,000 population. For 1910–1911, the indices could be calculated only for all cities and rural areas and not separately for those cities which had at least 20,000 population in 1880. For periods after World War I, it is not possible to calculate comparable rural-urban fertility rates for Prussia.

[4] In order to increase the number of areas to be used in the analysis of rural and urban marital ferility in Prussia, the administrative area Ostpreussen (01) was subdivided into its component *Regierungsbezirke* Königsberg (1K) and Gumbinnen (1G) prior to 1905 with the addition of Allenstein (1A) starting in 1905. Since Allenstein was formed from parts of Königsberg and Gumbinnen, the series for these two areas are not directly comparable before and after 1905. The administrative area Stettin-Stralsund (07) was subdivided into its component *Regierungsbezirke* Stettin (7A) and Stralsund (7B).

The trends in all the demographic indices for rural-urban categories of the Prussian State are given in Table 3.2.[5] The course of marital

TABLE 3.2

DEMOGRAPHIC INDICES, URBAN/RURAL, PRUSSIA: 1867 TO 1911

Index	Urban/Rural category	1867–1868	1880–1881	1885–1886	1890–1891	1895–1896	1900–1901	1905–1906	1910–1911
Marital fertility (I_g)	Berlin	.650	.590	.536	.504	.439	.399	.361	.292
	Other large cities	--	.686	.677	.664	.625	.588	.530	--
	Small cities	--	.719	--	.702	.686	.651	.596	--
	All cities	(.727)	.689	--	.656	.625	.589	.536	.449
	Rural	(.750)	.758	--	.774	.779	.764	.716	.659
	State	.743	.733	.743	.727	.715	.685	.631	.554
Overall fertility (I_f)	Berlin	.329	.318	.278	.263	.234	.219	.207	.178
	Other large cities	--	.348	.338	.338	.320	.311	.289	--
	Small cities	--	.379	--	.376	.369	.361	.336	--
	All cities	(.354)	.359	--	.343	.328	.318	.297	.255
	Rural	(.405)	.424	--	.436	.441	.441	.416	.383
	State	.388	.399	.401	.396	.390	.383	.357	.316
Illegitimate fertility (I_h)	Berlin	.082	.079	.058	.060	.063	.061	.067	.073
	Other large cities	--	.062	.061	.059	.058	.057	.056	--
	Small cities	--	.058	--	.056	.058	.053	.050	--
	All cities	(.063)	.062	--	.058	.059	.056	.055	.054
	Rural	(.059)	.062	--	.063	.063	.058	.052	.050
	State	.060	.062	.064	.061	.061	.057	.054	.052
Proportion married (I_m)	Berlin	.434	.467	.459	.456	.455	.467	.477	.479
	Other large cities	--	.459	.450	.462	.461	.478	.491	--
	Small cities	--	.487	--	.495	.495	.516	.524	--
	All cities	.438	.473	--	.476	.475	.492	.503	.508
	Rural	.500	.520	--	.524	.528	.543	.549	.547
	State	.480	.502	.497	.503	.504	.519	.526	.527

NOTES: Other large cities are those with over 20,000 population in 1880, small cities are
those with less than 20,000 in 1880.
Data for the State do not correspond to those given in Appendix Table 2.1 because
different birth years were used for most dates.
Data in parentheses are of questionable reliability.

fertility is shown graphically in Figure 3.2. Caution must be exercised in interpreting the graph since the same number of points could not be plotted for each category. In the early phase of the decline, distinct differentials in the levels of marital fertility in rural and urban populations already existed. These differentials lie in the direction usually stated in demographic transition theory; the more urban the area, the lower the marital fertility. It is unfortunate that the indices for all rural-urban categories could not be extended back reliably before 1880. However there is considerable evidence to suggest that in Prus-

[5]The figures for the state do not correspond to those given in Appendix Table 2.1 because different birth years were used for most dates.

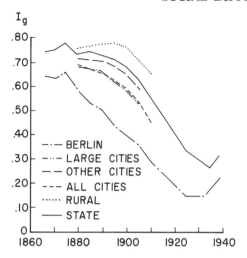

Figure 3.2. Marital Fertility (I_g), Urban/
Rural, Prussia: 1867 to 1939

sia the same differentials existed during the period just prior to the decline as well. Berlin, for which the statistics appear reliable, experienced distinctly lower marital fertility than Prussia in 1867–1868 even though, as documented in Chapter 2, no tendency to decline appeared during the several prior decades. It should be noted however that marital fertility in the surrounding administrative area of Potsdam was only slightly higher. In all but one of the 14 administrative areas which had the most reliable rural-urban statistics for 1867–1868, the rural marital fertility was higher than the urban.[6] In 1880–1881 only 3 administrative areas (excluding Berlin) experienced higher marital fertility in urban than in rural districts. In addition, in 23 of the 29 administrative areas for which reliable statistics were available, marital fertility in cities with at least 20,000 population was lower than in cities with smaller populations. Similar differentials appear in overall fertility (I_f).

In Prussia, then, prior to the decline, urban fertility was generally lower than rural fertility but the difference was small. For the entire state of Prussia, marital fertility was 15 percent higher in the rural

[6]This includes the 14 administrative areas which showed ratios of enumerated-to-expected infants in 1867 between .92 and 1.04.

areas than in the largest cities in 1880–1881 and 5 percent higher than in the other cities. If we consider the administrative areas separately, we find even less of a difference. The median difference in I_g between the rural areas and the large cities was 12 percent, and 4 percent between rural areas and the remaining cities. The contrast between rural-urban differentials for the Prussian state as an aggregate and the median difference in the separate administrative areas implies that larger cities have lower fertility and are located in areas where rural fertility is also low. The data for larger cities weight the state aggregate according to the size of their populations. Rural-urban differences in general need to be viewed both in terms of the state aggregate and the average or median values for the provinces. The aggregate differentials are not necessarily representative of the rural-urban differentials in the individual administrative areas.[7]

Rural-urban differences in overall fertility (I_f) are more pronounced than in marital fertility. For example, in 1880–1881, I_f is 18 percent higher in rural areas than in urban areas as opposed to a 10 percent difference for I_g. The difference is due to the higher proportions of rural women who are married.

It is also interesting to investigate differences in the date that fertility declined by 10 percent in rural and urban areas (Table 3.3). The method of calculation is similar to the one used to calculate the date of decline in Chapter 2. However since only some areas had reliable data for 1867–1868 and since indices could not be calculated separately for rural-urban categories using either the 1871 or 1875 census, the date of decline is based on indices from 1880–1881 and after. Thus the dates are not strictly comparable to those given earlier for the administrative areas as a whole. The dates are not intended to be taken as literal historical dates but rather to serve as indices of rural-urban differences in the onset of decline. In all cases, the cities experienced earlier declines than the rural areas. In addition, fertility usually started down sooner in the larger cities than in the smaller cities. The differences in the date of decline however are not great. For the aggregate Prussian state I_g in the large cities began to decline 13 years earlier than in the

[7] A similar finding with regards to rural-urban differences in marital fertility was found for Spain. See Leasure, 1963.

TABLE 3.3

MARITAL FERTILITY (I_g), DATE OF 10% DECLINE, URBAN/RURAL
BY ADMINISTRATIVE AREA, PRUSSIA

Area	Large cities	Small cities	All cities	Rural areas
01 Ostpreussen				
Königsberg	1897	1902	1901	1905
Gumbinnen	1894	1900	1900	1906
02 Danzig	1903	1910+	1903	1910+
03 Marienwerder	1902	1907	1906	1910+
04 Berlin	1886	--	1886	--
05 Potsdam	1891	1893	1891	1895
06 Frankfurt/O.	1894	1894	1894	1901
07 Stettin-Stralsund				
Stettin	1901	1900	1900	1901
Stralsund	1900	1902	1901	1904
08 Köslin	1910+	1903	1903	1908
09 Posen	1910+	1910	1908	1910+
10 Bromberg	1900	1910+	1907	1910+
11 Breslau	1899	1900	1899	1905
12 Liegnitz	1889	1894	1892	1904
13 Oppeln	1906	1907	1906	1910+
14 Magdeburg	1892	1896	1894	1898
15 Merseburg	1894	1895	1894	1901
16 Erfurt	1894	1895	1894	1905
17 Schleswig	1894	1901	1897	1903
18 Hannover	*	*	*	*
19 Hildesheim	1895	1900	1899	1903
20 Lüneburg	--	1901	1901	1908
21 Stade	--	1899	1899	1907
22 Osnabrück	1901	1910+	1906	1910+
23 Aurich	--	*	*	*
24 Münster	1902	1908	1907	1910
25 Minden	1891	1899	1896	1906
26 Arnsberg	1902	1907	1905	1906
27 Kassel	1903	1897	1898	1904
28 Wiesbaden	1897	1901	1896	1904
29 Koblenz	1901	1896	1897	1907
30 Düsseldorf	1894	1898	1895	1905
31 Köln	1895	1892	1893	1905
32 Trier	1902	1899	1902	1907
33 Aachen	1897	1901	1899	1908
34 Sigmaringen	--	1884	1884	1893
Prussia	1893	1900	1896	1906

NOTES: Calculations based on data from 1880-1910. The date was determined
by linear interpolation or extrapolation and represents when I_g declined
10% from the maximum value achieved during the entire period. If
extrapolation indicated a date of decline past 1910, the date is represented as 1910+.
Large cities are those with over 20,000 population in 1880; small cities
are those with less than 20,000 in 1880.
Data for 29 Kassel exclude Waldeck.

*Available data considered too unreliable.

rural areas and 7 years earlier than in the small cities. Again this difference is not typical of the separate administrative areas. The median
difference in the date of decline in marital fertility was only 7 years
between large cities and rural areas and 4 years between large and
small cities.

An examination of trends in I_f reveals a similar ordering in the dates of 10 percent decline with respect to the rural-urban categories.

The earlier declines in urban areas resulted in accentuating the differences in levels of fertility between rural and urban areas as the decline took place. Quite likely this was only a temporary effect and eventually the gap between rural and urban fertility closed considerably during the later stages of the decline. Since comparable data are not available after 1910–1911 for Prussia, however, this effect must remain undocumented.

The rural fertility of an administration area is highly correlated with the urban fertility of the same area. For 1880–1881 in Prussia, the I_g in the rural part of an administrative area was correlated .92 with the urban I_g. In addition there is a .87 correlation between the date I_g declined by 10 percent in the rural part and the date I_g declined in the urban part, indicating a close relationship within an administrative area in the timing of the rural and urban decline in fertility.

An analysis of variance helps to evaluate the importance of the rural and urban components of the fertility decline in Prussia. Both the level of fertility in 1880–1881 and the date that fertility declined by 10 percent are considered in this respect. The values of these two fertility measures for each of the three rural-urban categories (rural, cities under 20,000, cities with 20,000 or more) in each administrative area were considered for this test as independent observations.

The ratio of the mean square variance of I_g in 1880–1881 among administrative areas within each of three rural-urban categories to the mean square variance between the three categories was calculated in order to yield the value of the F-statistic. An F-ratio was also computed using the values of the date I_g declined by 10 percent. The following values of F and ϵ resulted:

$$F_{2,94} \text{ (using } I_g \text{ 1880–1881) } = 8.9; \; \epsilon = .38$$
$$F_{2,94} \text{ (using date of decline) } = 17.1; \; \epsilon = .50$$

The F-ratios indicate that there are significant differences between the rural-urban categories for both the level of I_g in 1880–1881 and the date of decline. In both cases the values of F are significant at the .001

level.[8] Nevertheless considerable variation in both fertility measures remain within each category as indicated by the low values of the measure of the degree of association.

(b) *The other German States.* Rural-urban series of the demographic indices could be calculated for at least part of the period covering the decline in fertility for Bavaria, K. Saxony, Braunschweig, Lübeck, Bremen, and Hamburg. Also, separate indices could be calculated for the city of Stuttgart in the administrative area Neckarkreis. The trends in marital fertility are presented graphically in Figure 3.3. Appendix Table 3.2 presents the demographic indices by rural-urban categories for Bavaria and the marital fertility index (I_g) for the eight Bavarian administrative areas. Appendix Table 3.3 shows values of rural-urban marital fertility (I_g) for each of the other areas included in Figure 3.3. Only in some cases could the series be extended to cover most of the period of the fertility decline, since the details in the statistics characteristic of the latter half of the nineteenth century apparently did not survive the demands for economy made in this

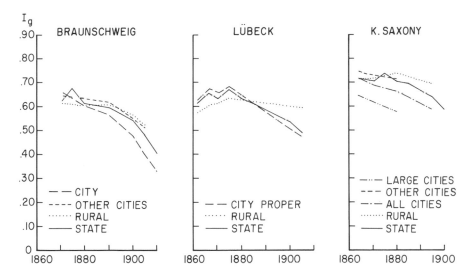

Figure 3.3. Marital Fertility (I_g), Urban/Rural, Selected Administrative Areas and States

[8]The reader should bear in mind, however, that the assumptions of the F-test are not strictly satisfied by the data, and thus these results should be treated as the roughest indication of statistical significance.

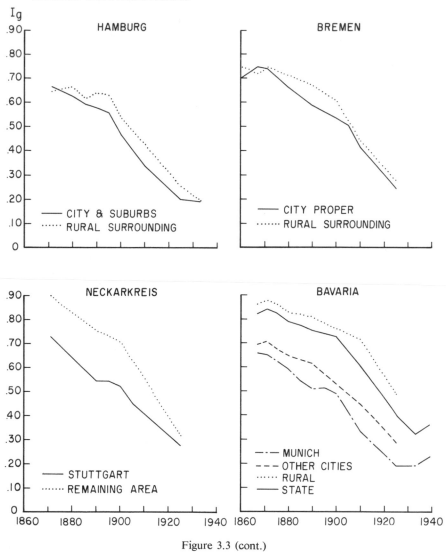

Figure 3.3 (cont.)

century. Also the series are frequently incomplete and gaps exist between dates for which indices for the different rural-urban categories could be calculated. Thus care must be exercised in interpreting the graphs since the same number of points are not necessarily plotted for each category.

For Bavaria, the data suggest that considerable differences in marital fertility existed between rural and urban areas. In the seven administrative areas for which the appropriate data were available, the rural I_g was higher than the urban in 1866–1868, the earliest period for which data was available. The lowest I_g was found for Munich, the largest city. In general the differences were considerably greater than those found in Prussia in 1880. For the entire state of Bavaria the rural I_g was 26 percent higher than the urban. In only one of the seven administrative areas was the difference less than 20 percent. In Neckarkreis, the I_g for Stuttgart for 1871–1873 was also much lower than for the rest of the population. The indications concerning predecline differentials in the level of fertility were not as consistent in the other German states. In Saxony the data suggest that marital fertility was lower in the large cities than in the rest of the state just prior to the decline. The smaller cities, however, apparently started their decline from a level higher than the rural areas. In Braunschweig, the capital had the highest marital fertility and the rural population experienced the lowest according to the earliest observations. In the three city-states of Hamburg, Bremen, and Lübeck the fertility of the city proper is compared to the fertility of the immediately surrounding rural areas. The differences were not large, but in two of the states the marital fertility was higher in the city proper according to the earliest observations. These exceptions to the more general pattern of higher predecline fertility in rural areas are perhaps not very meaningful, since the rural surroundings of these large cities might have been much more suburban in nature than other rural areas.

Additional information on predecline rural-urban fertility differentials is available for several other states for years prior to 1870 (Table 3.4). For most of the areas, the differences in marital fertility were rather small. The largest difference was in Hesse, where the I_g was higher in the cities than in the countryside. However because of the consistently higher proportion married in rural areas, the index of overall fertility (I_f) is lower for urban areas in every case.

The evidence suggests that in most German areas at the time just prior to the onset of the major decline of fertility, urban marital fertility was lower than rural. The difference between I_g in the large cities and in rural areas was fairly pronounced. Also in certain areas,

TABLE 3.4

DEMOGRAPHIC INDICES AT PREDECLINE LEVELS, URBAN/RURAL, BY SELECTED AREAS

Area	Census year	Birth registration period	Overall fertility (I_f)	Marital fertility (I_g)	Illegitimate fertility (I_h)	Proportion married (I_m)
Schleswig						
Cities	1840	1835–1845	.275	.660	.030	.389
Rural	1840	1835–1845	.314	.661	.029	.451
Holstein						
Cities	1840	1835–1845	.295	.636	.068	.399
Rural	1840	1835–1845	.365	.674	.051	.504
Anhalt						
Cities	1867	1866–1868	.374	.665	.086	.497
Rural	1867	1866–1868	.403	.656	.100	.544
Gd. Oldenburg						
Cities	1855–1864[a]	1855–1864	.285	.689	.031	.386
Rural	1855–1864[a]	1855–1864	.324	.664	.034	.460
Hesse						
Cities	1864	1863–1865	.341	.754	.109	.360
Rural	1864	1863–1865	.360	.690	.100	.441

NOTE: The former duchies of Schleswig and Holstein after 1866 comprise together administrative area 17 Schleswig.

[a]Average of several censuses; computed by Oldenburg Statistical Bureau.

especially in southern Germany, the differences in general were rather large. In Prussia the differences were usually less striking but still evident. In only a few areas urban I_g was higher than rural, and these cases can best be considered as exceptions to a more general pattern.

In areas where long standing predecline differentials in marital fertility existed, questions arise as to use of birth control. Did, for example, the lower fertility in the city in comparison to the country-side indicate a tradition of fertility control among some portions of the urban population? Comparison of marital fertility rates in the form of I_g's can not tell as much about birth control unless the differences are of great magnitude. Age specific marital fertility rates would be more useful as has been demonstrated in much of the current work in historical demography.[9] Unfortunately in Germany, births were rarely tabulated according to age of mother during the nineteenth century, thus prohibiting the calculation of such rates. Without further information it is difficult to conclude whether or not a long

[9]See for example Wrigley, 1966.

standing use of birth control accounts for the lower predecline fertility levels in the cities.

An examination of Figure 3.3 suggests that in Germany urban populations in general experienced a more abrupt decline in the initial phase of transition from high to low fertility than did rural areas. Even if urban areas started the decline at higher levels of I_g, they soon showed lower levels than the rural areas as the decline progressed. And in those areas where urban fertility was already lower, the differential increased during the initial phase.

If we calculate the date of a 10 percent sustained decline in I_g according to the method described in the previous chapter, we obtain the results presented in Table 3.5. The dates of decline are not shown

TABLE 3.5

MARITAL FERTILITY (I_g), DATE OF 10% DECLINE, URBAN/RURAL, SELECTED STATES

State	Urban/Rural category	Date
Bavaria	Munich	1879
	Other cities	1884
	Rural	1894
Braunschweig	City of Braunschweig	1883
	Other cities	1895
	Rural	1902
Hamburg	City proper	1884
	Rural	1897
Kingdom of Saxony	Large cities	1880
	All cities	1884
	Rural	After 1885
Bremen	City proper	1878
	Rural	1889

for Lübeck or Neckarkreis because of the large gaps in the data. However if the dates of decline were interpolated from the limited data, they would indicate earlier declines in the urban than in the rural population. Thus in all the non-Prussian states surveyed, the urban regions show earlier declines than the rural areas and the large cities experience the earliest decline of all. These results are similar to findings for the Prussian administrative areas and are in conformity with the usual description of rural-urban differentials incorporated by demographic transition theory. Whatever the causes were that precipitated the decline, they were apparently effective earlier in the cities than in the countryside. Although these factors are not revealed by the above data, they evidently spread quickly to the rural areas as indicated by the short time lag between rural and urban fertility declines.

There is also evidence that after the decline had run its course fertility remained higher in the rural than in the urban areas. Between 1933 and 1939 when the trend towards decline was reversed all over Germany, not only did fertility increase in both rural and urban populations, but the differences in the level of fertility persisted at least on a national level. Table 3.6 illustrates this. The net reproduction rate

TABLE 3.6

NET REPRODUCTION RATE AND GENERAL MARITAL FERTILITY RATE, URBAN/RURAL: 1933 AND 1939

Population of municipality	Net reproduction rate			General marital fertility rate		
	1933	1939	Absolute increase	1933	1939	Absolute increase
Over 100,000	.505	.740	.235	71.2	106.4	35.2
2,000-100,000	.691	.930	.239	100.8	134.4	33.6
Under 2,000	.931	1.168	.237	137.9	167.4	29.5

SOURCE: Data for net reproduction rate obtained from Wirtschaft und Statistik, vol. 23 (January 1943), p. 7.

NOTES: Boundaries for all data are those of 1934.
The general marital fertility rate refers to the number of legitimate births (including stillbirths) per 1,000 married women aged 15-44.

increased almost exactly the same amount in all three rural-urban categories between 1933 and 1939, leaving the differentials in the level of fertility unaltered. The index of marital fertility (I_g) could not be calculated for the separate rural-urban categories in 1939. As a substitute, the number of legitimate births per 1,000 married women are included in Table 3.6. Marital fertility also rose in each rural-urban category, though the increase was somewhat less in the smaller municipalities. The rural-urban differences are only slightly reduced by 1939 in comparison with 1933.

(c) *Rural-urban differentials revealed in census statistics on the family*. The German censuses of 1933 and 1939 provide another source of data concerning rural-urban differentials during the fertility decline.

Distributions of the number of children ever born in the current marriage were tabulated in both censuses for married women (or couples living together) and cross-classified by three rural-urban categories: muncipalities with less than 2,000 population, municipalities with between 2,000 and 100,000, and municipalities with 100,000 and more. Unfortunately for the study of the fertility decline, recent marriage and birth cohorts were emphasized and earlier cohorts were not broken down with great detail. Nevertheless some picture of the decline in family size as it proceeded from cohort to cohort is evident from the statistics. Family size by marriage cohorts rather than by birth cohorts are presented in this section since the breakdown of marriage cohorts in the censuses extended further back into the past. Table 3.7 shows the average number of children born in the current

TABLE 3.7

CHILDREN EVER BORN IN CURRENT MARRIAGE, URBAN/RURAL, BY DATE OF MARRIAGE: 1939
(average number)

Date of marriage	Germany	Population size of municipality		
		Over 100,000	2,000-100,000	Under 2,000
Pre-1904	4.67	3.86	4.76	5.29
1905-1909	3.58	2.74	3.65	4.42
1910-1914	3.07	2.28	3.12	3.91
1915-1919	2.58	1.90	2.62	3.37
Decline				
Absolute	2.09	1.96	2.14	1.92
Percent	45	51	45	36

SOURCE: 1939 census data as reported in Statistik des deutschen Reich, vol. 554, pp. 62, 82, 86, 90.

NOTES: Data are for births to married couples living together. Boundaries are of May 17, 1939, excluding Memelland.

marriage reported in the 1939 census by married couples living together. Only marriages of at least 20 years duration are included in order to ensure that the figures at least approximate the final number of children born to the marriage cohorts considered. Although the cohort married in 1915–1919 still experienced some births subsequent to the 1939 enumerations, the effect was almost certainly negligible. Also note that the figures refer to the boundaries of 1939 and therefore include Austria.

Clearly many couples married prior to 1905 took part in the fertility decline. It is unfortunate that the census tables did not present a more detailed breakdown for these couples, so that the start of the decline could be identified. These limited results are nevertheless consistent with data already presented. For any given cohort the family size is largest for couples living in the smallest municipalities and smallest for couples in the large cities. In fact the rural-urban differences which had existed during the decline may well be underestimated in this data since the fertility of the city couples (especially the older ones) includes persons married in the rural areas but who later moved to an urban area. Family size was declining in all three rural-urban categories, and if we consider the absolute decrease between couples married prior to 1905 and couples married in 1915–1919, the results are quite similar. However between the two earliest cohort groups (i.e. those married before 1905 and those married 1905–1909), the greatest decrease occurs among couples living in the big cities and the least decline among those living in the small municipalities. The declines between the last two cohort groups occur in the reverse order. This reflects the tendency for rural populations to begin their declines later than urban populations but then to "catch up" as the decline proceeds.

A more detailed picture of the fertility decline in rural and urban populations is presented for Prussia in the 1933 census. Children ever born to the current marriage as reported by married women (including those separated from their husbands but not divorced) are given by single years of marriage back as far as 1900. Unfortunately all marriages prior to 1900 are grouped together. Nevertheless the results, which are shown in Table 3.8, reveal a very smooth pattern of decline from cohort to cohort for all three rural-urban categories. Women married after 1913 are not included since their fertility was not completed by 1933. However women married between 1914 and 1918 and living in Prussia reported an average of 2.65 children ever born in the 1939 census, thus showing, as would be expected, a continuance of the decline. The most striking feature is the regularity of the decline from cohort to cohort. The average children ever born declines with each successive marriage cohort in all three rural-urban categories. The

TABLE 3.8

CHILDREN EVER BORN IN CURRENT MARRIAGE, URBAN/RURAL,
BY DATE OF MARRIAGE, PRUSSIA: 1933
(average number)

Date of marriage	Prussia	Population size of municipality		
		Over 100,000	2,000-100,000	Under 2,000
Pre-1899	5.05	4.38	5.27	5.46
1900	4.24	3.49	4.43	4.92
1901	4.19	3.40	4.38	4.91
1902	4.07	3.28	4.26	4.80
1903	3.94	3.15	4.11	4.69
1904	3.82	3.05	4.01	4.58
1905	3.65	2.89	3.82	4.46
1906	3.54	2.78	3.73	4.35
1907	3.45	2.69	3.63	4.28
1908	3.36	2.62	3.50	4.17
1909	3.25	2.51	3.38	4.07
1910	3.12	2.40	3.25	3.93
1911	3.04	2.31	3.17	3.87
1912	2.92	2.22	3.06	3.73
1913	2.83	2.16	2.94	3.63
Decline				
Absolute	2.22	2.22	2.33	1.83
Percent	44	51	44	34

SOURCE: 1933 census data as reported in Statistik des deutschen Reich, vol. 452, Heft. 1, pp. 11, 15.

NOTES: Boundaries are of 1934.
Data for municipalities between 2,000 and 100,000 in size calculated as the residual of the other two urban/rural categories from the total of Prussia.

tendency for the rural areas to "catch up" in the absolute amount of decline is also apparent among the Prussian cohorts.

   In conclusion, our survey of rural-urban differentials in marital fertility and their part in the German fertility decline reveals several patterns: (1) Just prior to the beginning of the fertility decline, marital fertility was generally higher in rural than urban populations. (2) The decline began first in the urban populations but was followed after a short time lag by a parallel decline in the rural population. (3) Considerable differences existed among adiministrative areas within each rural-urban category both with respect to the level of marital fertility at the onset of the decline and the date the decline began. (4) Rural-urban differentials in the level of fertility persisted during the decline and because of the later date of decline in the rural populations the differential increased during the initial phases. (5) By the time the decline had run its course in the early 1930s rural-urban differentials still existed but on much lower levels of fertility. (6) Both rural and urban populations experienced an increase in fertility between the beginning of the National Socialist period and World War II. The rise in marital fertility was somewhat less in the rural populations. Nevertheless, in 1939 rural-urban differentials in fertility were still clearly evident.

(d) *Rural-urban differentials in nonmarital fertility and marriage.* The indices of illegitimate fertility and proportions married for the state rural and urban populations in Prussia and Bavaria are given in Table 3.2 and Appendix Table 3.2 respectively. These indices have also been calculated for the Prussian and Bavarian administrative areas and provide interesting information on rural-urban differentials in nonmarital fertility and nuptiality. Since the main purpose of this study is to analyze marital fertility, however, only brief comments on rural-urban differentials in I_h and I_m follow and tables presenting the data for the individual administrative areas have not been included.

On theoretical grounds we could predict rural-urban differentials in nonmarital fertility to be in either direction during the period of the decline in marital fertility. On the one hand, if the knowledge and practice of deliberate fertility control were more widespread in the cities, then there would be reason to expect illegitimate fertility to be lower assuming that most nonmarital births were not desired by the couple at the time of conception. On the other hand, there is a commonplace notion that traditional values break down more easily in cities than in rural settings, particularly during periods of rapid social change such as the decades under observation. The urban social environment should be more conducive to socially deviant behavior such as illegitimacy than a rural setting where traditional social controls are in stricter force. Of course there are many intervening factors such as birth control practices and the probability of marrying once pregnant that operate between the socially deviant act of premarital or extramarital intercourse and an illegitimate birth (Cutright, 1971). The latter argument assumes that these intermediate factors operate in equivalent fashions in both settings, which is quite unlikely. Another possible source of higher illegitimacy rates in the city is a tendency for unmarried women becoming pregnant in the village to migrate to the city to have the illegitimate child away from the condemnation and surveillance of their home community.

An examination of the data for Germany does not confirm either prediction. From 1880–1881 to 1910–1911 rural and urban rates of illegitimacy (I_h) were very similar in Prussia (Table 3.2). Even Berlin, which usually had a higher I_h than the Prussian average during this time, had a lower rate than the rural population in surrounding Potsdam. In over half of the individual administrative areas in Prussia in 1880–1881 the index of illegitimate fertility was higher in the rural part than in the cities with 20,000 or more population. In only three administrative areas was the I_h twice as high in the large cities as in the countryside. In two administrative areas the reverse was true. By 1900–1901 the situation had changed little.

The experience in Bavaria was similar. Urban I_h was only slightly higher for the state than rural I_h. For the years prior to 1900, rural I_h was usually above the urban rate in half of the Bavarian administrative areas. By 1925, however, the urban rate was slightly higher in all.

In the several additional administrative areas for which the demographic indices could be calculated for years prior to the fertility decline, there are no consistent rural-urban differences in I_h (see Table 3.4). Usually, the illegitimacy rates were similar for both categories.

In general, the data for Germany indicate that where illegitimacy was high in the city, it was also high in the nearby countryside. And where it was low in the countryside, it was also low in the city. If unmarried girls went to the cities to have illegitimate births and then returned home afterwards, the pattern was not evident in the statistics.

An examination of rural-urban differences with respect to the index of proportion married (I_m) reveals a remarkably consistent pattern. At least until the beginning of World War I, I_m was highest in rural populations and lowest in the big cities. This is true, for example, not only for the state of Prussia (Table 3.2) but also for almost every individual Prussian administrative area. In 1867, for example, rural I_m was higher than urban I_m in all areas.[10] The differential presisted through 1910. Also in the larger cities (those with 20,000 or more in 1880) I_m was lower than in the remaining cities. For every census year from 1867 to 1905, such was the case in at least four-fifths of the Prussian administrative areas.

In Bavaria a similar situation prevailed. Prior to World War I, not only was the average rural I_m constantly higher than the average urban I_m in the state but also in every Bavarian administrative area. Munich consistently experienced lower proportions married than the smaller cities in the same vicinity. Following the war, the situation changed. The 1925 census shows a higher urban I_m for the state as a whole and for five of the eight administrative areas.

By the end of the fertility transition, rural-urban differences in the proportions married throughout Germany were apparently no longer as pronounced or distinctive as they were during the decades before World War I. On the basis of the 1933 census it is possible to calculate national figures for I_m for three categories of municipalities: those with less than 2,000 inhabitants, those with 2,000 to 100,000 populations, and those with 100,000 or more. The values of I_m were practically identical for the first two categories (.530 vs. .529) and only slightly lower (.508) for the large municipalities.

Economic Activity and Position

One of the most fundamental bases for social differentiation in human society is the range of the positions persons occupy in the economic structure. Perhaps the most succinct index of a person's position in this respect is his occupation. Countless studies have documented the relevance of occupation as a sociological variable. Not

[10]Although the 1867–1868 rural-urban fertility indices (I_f, I_g, and I_h) for Prussia have not been used in this chapter due to the apparent inconsistency between the census definition of each category and the vital statistics definition as discussed earlier, it seems justifiable to use the values of I_m which is based solely on census data and not on data from two separate sources.

only do the specific activities and social interactions that are associated with carrying out a job condition a person's attitudes, values, and perceptions of his environment but occupational position is also an important determinant of social class and thereby exerts substantial influence far beyond the work situation.

Occupation has been a prominent variable both in theoretical considerations and empirical investigations of fertility behavior. With respect to the transition from high to low fertility, it has generally been argued that middle- and upper-class couples were first to reduce their family size and that only after some time lag did the small-family norm and the acceptance of family limitations as a means to achieve it spread to the lower classes (e.g. Banks, 1954; Beshers, 1967). It should be interesting to examine the available evidence to see if this suggested pattern accurately reflects the experience in Germany.

In order to calculate conventional measures of fertility during a given period for occupational groups, statistics on births classified by the occupation of the parents (or the father) as well as statistics on the population classified by occupation (and preferably cross-classified by age, sex, and marital status) are required. Even when the necessary combination of data does exist, problems associated with insuring comparability in the occupational classifications in both sets of information are common. The classification scheme used in the census may not agree with the scheme used in the vital registration system. Even if the schemes are comparable, the same person may report a different occupation on each occasion. This problem is especially significant for persons employed in seasonal occupations. The job that a person has at the time of the census may differ from the job held at the time of birth of his child, and therefore may place him in a different occupational category on each occasion. This is particularly likely if the census and birth occur in different seasons.

Data on the occupational distribution of the German population is available from the special periodic occupation censuses (*Berufszählungen*).[11] These censuses provide data on the number of persons

[11]Between the unification of Germany and World War II, occupational censuses took place in1882, 1895, 1907, 1925, 1933, and 1939. The last three were taken in combination with the population census but the first three were taken independently of the population censuses.

working in different branches of industry as well as in different occupational positions within each branch. Data on births by occupation of parents, however, are available only for Prussia for any extended period of time. Hence the following discussion will be limited to a discussion of fertility indices for Prussia. In addition, the discussion will not deal strictly with occupational fertility since the data are not classified according to detailed occupations but rather according to branch of industry and broad occupational positions within each industry.

Two studies were published by the officials of the Prussian Statistical Bureau which describe differential fertility according to economic activity (von Fircks, 1889; Berger, 1912). Although these studies are very useful in describing problems associated with the basic data, they unfortunately rely primarily on the ratio of births to marriages as a measure of marital fertility. Both authors are aware of the shortcomings of this index, and indeed in the second study considerable effort is made to evaluate biases which might affect it (Berger, 1912, pp. 232–234). Of particular concern are persons who change their job shortly after marriage since their marriage is counted in the denominator of the rate for one category but their births are attributed to the numerator of the fertility rate for another category. In addition couples who marry in a particular year do not contribute a very substantial proportion of the legitimate births during that year. Only if the index refers to births over a longer span of time, perhaps ten or more years, and the marriages also cover the same span of time will the married couples in the denominator actually represent a substantial proportion of the population at risk to giving births. However if there are systematic shifts in the proportionate distribution of marriages by occupation during the same period, distortion in the fertility indices can result. Both of these problems are avoided if we use a marital fertility index which relates births to the married population in each occupational or industrial category rather than to marriages.[12] Marital fertility rates of this type are examined here as the basis for investigating differentials in fertility decline by economic activity.

[12]This approach was also used by Berger (1912) on the basis of the 1895 and 1907 occupational censuses.

Male marital fertility rates and their absolute and relative decline are given in Table 3.9 for various branches of industry in Prussia. Part A presents the crude rate which represents the annual number of legitimate births per 1,000 married men in each industry branch. Since there are substantial differences in the age distribution of married men in different branches of industry, a second rate is presented in Part B

TABLE 3.9

MALE MARITAL FERTILITY RATES, BY INDUSTRY, PRUSSIA: 1882 TO 1924

							Decline				
		Levels				Absolute			Percent		
Rate	Industry	1882	1895	1907	1924	1882-1907	1907-1924	1882-1924	1882-1907	1907-1924	1882-1924
Crude male marital fertility	Agriculture	204	203	190	134	14	56	70	7	29	34
	Mining, manufacturing, construction	224	215	197	99	27	98	125	12	50	56
	Mining only	239	276	278	156	+39	122	83	+16	44	35
	Trade and transportation	225	201	165	77	60	88	148	27	53	66
	Civil service, military, professional	179	171	139	74	40	65	105	22	47	59
General male marital fertility	Agriculture	317	332	308	236	9	72	81	3	23	26
	Mining, manufacturing, construction	290	278	246	137	44	109	153	15	44	53
	Mining only	277	321	315	194	+38	121	83	+13	38	30
	Trade and transportation	303	270	213	104	90	109	199	30	51	66
	Civil service, military, professional	262	237	188	103	74	85	159	28	45	61

NOTES: The crude male marital fertility rate refers to the number of legitimate births (including stillbirths) per 1,000 married men.
The general male marital fertility rate refers to the number of legitimate births (including stillbirths) per 1,000 married men under age 50. Married men under age 50 in 1895, 1907, and 1925 were estimated by multiplying the total married men in Prussia in each category by the ratio of married men under 50 to all married men in each category given for all Germany in the occupational censuses.
1882 data are averages of 1877-1886 period; 1895 data are averages of 1894-1896 period; 1907 data are averages of 1906-1908 period; and 1924 data represent the ratio of births in 1924 to married men enumerated in the 1925 occupational census.

which relates legitimate births to married men under 50 and has been called the general male marital fertility rate since it is roughly analogous to the better know general fertility rate referring to females. Although some births surely occurred to women married to men over 50 the number is very likely small, and we can therefore consider the denominator of the general male marital fertility rate as referring basically to the population capable of childbearing. Only the 1882 occupational census provided age distributions of married men by branch of industry for Prussia separately. Later occupational censuses gave the total number of married men by branch of industry in Prussia but did not indicate their age composition. Thus, the number of married men under 50 had to be estimated accordingly from the corresponding age distribution of married men by branch of industry for all of Germany. Neither crude nor general rates could be calculated after 1924 because of changes in the categorization scheme used in presenting published figures on births by branch of industry.

The categories used in Table 3.9 correspond to the main divisions shown in the Prussian statistics with two exceptions. First, a separate rate was calculated for persons engaged in mining since their fertility rate was found in the study by Berger (1912) to be substantially different from the average of other groups in secondary industry. Second, rates for a division comprised primarily of domestic servants and day laborers are not shown since they were obviously inflated. The primary reason for the erroneous inflation of these rates stems from the fact that many persons who during much of the year belonged in this category worked as agricultural workers during the time of the occupational censuses (June), and were classified as working in agriculture (Berger, 1912, pp. 228–229). In the vital statistics, which were a product of continuous registration throughout the year, they were often listed as belonging to the separate category mentioned above. Since this group contributes only a small proportion of all legitimate births, their inconsistent classification does not have much effect on the rate for the other branches of industry.[13]

Already in 1877–1886, the earliest years for which observations are available, substantial differences were evident in the fertility of the various branches of industry. The differentials revealed by the general male marital fertility rates are not in complete agreement with those evidenced in the crude rates, testifying to the considerable differences in the age distribution of married men of each industry branch. Thus in agriculture there was an unusually high proportion of married men over 50 which depressed the crude marital fertility rate whereas in mining the reverse was true. It is not possible to determine from the data given in Table 3.9 if the differentials in marital fertility found in 1877–1886 represented long standing differences in fertility or if they derived from differential changes in fertility during the preceding

[13]In 1895–1897, for example, they represented only 3.7 percent of the legitimate births.

years. There is little evidence of a substantial decline in the fertility of the entire Prussian population during the half century prior to 1880 (see Appendix Table 2.1). Thus it is unlikely that either of the first two branches of industry, which represented large proportions of the population, could have declined much since they would have noticeably affected the average for the state. But it is not impossible that fertility had declined for the group comprised of civil servants, military, and professionals since they represented a relatively small part of the population. In any event it is clear that differential changes in fertility level by 1895–1897 accentuated the differences in fertility levels among the various economic groups. Substantial declines are evident for persons engaged in trade and transportation as well as for the civil servant, military, and professional group. The sharp rise in fertility for those engaged in mining is striking. The rapid development of the coal industry in the Ruhr attracted many migrants particularly from the Eastern provinces. Perhaps the rapid influx of Polish-speaking Germans or other such groups predisposed to high fertility was sufficient to alter the composition of the rapidly growing number of miners to account in part for this rise. It should be reemphasized however that the indices presented here are both crude with respect to the categories used and inexact with respect to the fertility levels indicated. They suffice only to show the general pattern of differences and should be interpreted accordingly.

By 1906–1908 fertility had declined substantially for all groups except agriculture and mining. The result is that differentials in the level of fertility are even more pronounced than earlier. The unusually high fertility of the miners and their resistance to fertility decline can perhaps be best explained by the social and demographic composition of this group. A larger proportion of married miners was under 50 than for any other group and, more importantly, among miners under 50 an unusually high proportion was in the younger part of this age span and thus at relatively more fertile ages. Moreover the majority of miners was Catholic (e.g. 60 percent in 1907), whereas Catholics represent a minority of all the other economic groups. Also in the other groups a sizeable proportion was classed as owners, managers, or white collar employees. The overwhelming majority of miners however, were occupationally classed as workers (93 percent in 1907). As will be shown below, both Catholics and workers experienced high fertility and lagged behind other groups in reducing fertility. In addition, miners were predominately located in areas where fertility was generally high and slow to decline.

By 1924 all economic groups experienced substantial declines in marital fertility. Nevertheless, differences with respect to level and extent of decline are still pronounced. Persons engaged in agriculture and mining clearly lag behind persons in other sections of the economy.

Marital fertility rates for men in Prussia according to their occupational position in the various branches of industry are examined in Table 3.10. For each of the three main branches of industry, marital fertility is shown separately for workers on the one hand and for persons in higher positions on the other. Unfortunately a more refined division of occupational positions is not justified because of limitations of the data. Both crude and general rates are presented for 1906–1908 and 1924. A broader time span could not be covered because the categories used in the birth and census statistics did not match prior to 1902 or after 1924. Since the registration of births in public institutions did not include any indication of occupational position for the parents in 1906–1908, these births are not included in the data. However, only very few legitimate births (less than 1 percent in 1906–1908) occurred in such institutions (Berger, 1912, p. 226).

In 1906–1908 there were already substantial differences in marital fertility between owners and white collar employees on the one hand and workers on the other. The extent of these differences tends to be exaggerated by use of the crude rates since they do not take into account the relatively younger age distribution of workers. Nevertheless, differences between the two categories of occupational positions are still substantial even when age distribution is taken into account as evidenced by the general marital fertility rate. In each branch of industry, workers experienced higher fertility. It would be interesting to determine if the same differentials existed prior to the onset of the secular decline in fertility. Most likely, at least some of the difference between the workers and the persons in higher positions derives from

TABLE 3.10

MALE MARITAL FERTILITY RATES, BY INDUSTRY AND OCCUPATION, PRUSSIA: 1907 AND 1924

Rate	Industry and occupation	Levels		Decline	
		1907	1924	Absolute	Percent
Crude male marital fertility	Agriculture				
	Farm owners, managers, clerks, and officials	157	105	52	33
	Workers	242	187	55	23
	Mining, manufacturing, construction				
	Owners and white collar employees	154	70	84	55
	Workers	212	112	100	47
	Trade and transportation				
	Owners and white collar employees	133	67	66	50
	Workers	197	98	99	50
General male marital fertility	Agriculture				
	Farm owners, managers, clerks, and officials	268	199	69	26
	Workers	354	281	73	21
	Mining, manufacturing, construction				
	Owners and white collar employees	210	104	106	50
	Workers	253	150	103	41
	Trade and transportation				
	Owners and white collar employees	185	94	91	49
	Workers	235	123	112	48

NOTES: The crude male marital fertility rate refers to the number of legitimate
births (including stillbirths) per 1,000 married men.
The general male marital fertility rate refers to the number of legitimate
births (including stillbirths) per 1,000 married men under age 50.
Married men under age 50 were estimated by multiplying the total married
men in Prussia in each category by the ratio of married men under 50 to
all married men in each category given for all Germany in the occupational
censuses.
1907 data are averages of 1906-1908 period and do not include births in
public institutions.

differentials in fertility reduction during the immediately preceding
decades. Unfortunately it is not possible to document this from the
present data. It is interesting to note that if we consider each of the
two occupational categories separately, similar differences between
branches of industry existed for each in 1906–1908.

Between 1906–1908 and 1924, fertility declined for each occupational group in all three branches of industry. Within each branch of industry, the absolute and relative degree of fertility decline was similar for each occupational group. If we had figures for earlier periods, however, it seems likely that we would have found a considerably greater decline before 1906–1908 among persons with higher positions than among workers. For the three branches of industry it is clear that during the period between 1906–1908 and 1924 persons engaged in agriculture, whether as a worker or in a higher position, reduced their fertility less and experienced higher fertility than persons employed in other industries.

In sum, the data on marital fertility for Prussia confirm the differentials in fertility decline according to economic activity that have conventionally been described in most discussions of the demographic transition. Although it seems likely that some of the differentials in the level of fertility existed prior to the onset of the fertility decline, there can be no doubt that the leads and lags involved in the downward course of fertility created considerably more pronounced differentials during the transition process. Civil servants, independent professionals, and persons engaged in trade and transportation, all predominantly urban economic activities, led the decline, whereas persons in agriculture lagged behind. In all main branches of industry workers apparently were slower to reduce fertility than persons in higher positions.

The German censuses of 1933 and 1939 provide another source of information on differential fertility by economic activity during the fertility decline. Data on the number of children ever born to married couples by the year of marriage were cross-tabulated with the branch of industry in which the husband was employed and also with the occupational position of the husband within the branch of industry. As described earlier in the section of urban-rural fertility differentials, the fertility of recent marriage cohorts was given prime consideration in the census analysis so the data is of limited value for the study of cohorts which can be assumed to have completed their fertility by the census dates. In the 1933 census publications, marriages of twenty years duration or more are pooled together in cross-tabulation of children ever born with economic activity. Only in the 1939 census are marriage cohorts of over twenty years duration broken down further by year of marriage and cross-tabulated by economic activity. Hence the following discussion is restricted to data from the later census. It should be noted that all figures refer to Germany according to its boundaries in May 1939 and therefore include Austria.

Table 3.11 presents the statistics on the average number of children

TABLE 3.11

CHILDREN EVER BORN IN CURRENT MARRIAGE, URBAN/RURAL, BY INDUSTRY AND DATE OF MARRIAGE: 1939
(average number)

Population of municipality	Industry	Date of marriage				Decline	
		Pre-1905	1905-1909	1910-1914	1915-1919	Absolute	Percent
Over 100,000	Agriculture	4.47	3.48	2.96	2.49	1.98	44.3
	Nonagriculture	3.86	2.73	2.28	1.89	1.97	51.0
20,000 - 100,000	Agriculture	5.48	4.52	3.98	3.39	2.09	38.1
	Nonagriculture	4.70	3.57	3.05	2.56	2.14	45.5
Under 2,000	Agriculture	5.52	4.74	4.20	3.64	1.88	34.1
	Nonagriculture	5.16	4.13	3.65	3.16	2.00	38.8
All municipalities	Agriculture	5.49	4.67	4.14	3.57	1.92	35.0
	Nonagriculture	4.52	3.35	2.84	2.40	2.12	46.9

SOURCE: 1939 census data as reported in Statistik des deutschen Reich, vol. 554, pp. 62, 82, 84, 86, 88, 90, 92, 96.
NOTE: Boundaries are of May 17, 1939, excluding Memelland.

born to the current marriage for couples still living together according to whether or not the husband worked in agriculture. Only marriages of at least twenty years duration are considered to ensure that the figures at least approximate the final number of children born to each cohort. All marriages prior to 1905 are grouped together in the published census figures. Since the fertility decline was well on its way by 1905 in most segments of the population, even the earliest marriage cohort identified contains many couples which participated in the reduction of family size.

The data unfortunately do not permit non-agricultural couples to be further subdivided by branch of industry. Nevertheless it is clear that there are substantial differences in the reproductive performance of the two groups shown. For any of the four marriage cohorts included in the analysis, agricultural couples had more children than non-agricultural couples. However, the average number of children declines steadily with successive marriage years for both economic groups. The absolute and relative differences between the earlier and most recent cohort were greater for the non-agricultural couples. However the fact that the absolute decline between the two most recent marriage cohorts is greater for agricultural couples, suggests that differences in the average number of children ever born were beginning to diminish. Both the differences in fertility level and fertility decline hold up in almost every case when we control for size of municipality. It is interesting to note that for both agricultural and non-agricultural couples family size is smaller in larger municipalities.

Within agricultural and non-agricultural industry the census cross-tabulates children ever born with the occupational position of the husband. Within agriculture, five positions are differentiated: (1) independents, (2) members of the owner's immediate family who help on the farm, (3) officials, (4) salaried employees, and (5) workers. The first category represents farmers who own their property. The second category refers primarily to the couples who will inherit the farms when the parents die. They represent a very small proportion of all agricultural couples and in the subsequent analysis they are combined with farmers. The third group consists largely of officials in forestry, and the fourth group to farm inspectors, administrators, and clerks. The third and fourth groups are similar in that the positions require some reasonable amount of formal education and are basically white collar in nature. They have also been combined in the subsequent analysis. The above categories are ambiguous with regard to occupational prestige or social class. The first category of independent farmers is particularly heterogeneous since it groups together persons ranging from peasants farming small plots of land to wealthy landowners operating large agricultural enterprises. Perhaps the clearest contrast is between categories (3) and (4) on the one hand, which represent middle-class white collar workers, and category (5), which contains mostly farm laborers.

Non-agricultural couples were subdivided in the census into the same broad categories as the agricultural population with the addition of a sixth category comprising independent persons without occupations. This last category consists mainly of persons living from pensions or annuities and hence represents a large proportion of older couples. Most of these couples belonged in one of the other five categories during much if not all of their reproductive life. Since it is impossilbe to redistribute these couples according to their former occupational position, they are excluded from the analysis. For the non-agricultural population the category of independents includes a very diverse group ranging from small shopkeepers to medical doctors, and factory owners. The second category, family helpers, consists mainly of sons working in their father's business. They represent only a small fraction of the non-agricultural population and for purposes of convenience have been combined with the first category. The third and fourth category have been combined since together they represent largely white collar middle-class occupations. As with the agricultural population, the clearest contrast is between this latter group and the workers.

A summary of the results of the 1939 census inquiry on fertility by occupational position is presented in Table 3.12. Among the agricultural population, the average number of children born in marriages of workers is consistently the highest for all four marriage cohorts, whereas the fewest children are born in marriages of officials and salaried employees. Farmers and their family helpers occupy an intermediate position. The relationship holds for all three categories of municipality size. However the reduction in the number of children born, at least in absolute terms, as evidenced by the difference between the earliest and most recent marriage cohorts is less for officials and salaried employees than for the other groupings. This suggests that the differentials in fertility levels were diminishing. Probably pre-1905 marriage cohorts of agricultural officials and salaried employees had participated to a greater extent than the other groups in reducing their fertility and thus the initial cohort shown is already more advanced with respect to the transition from high to low fertility.

Similar differentials by occupational position both in the level and decline of fertility are evident for the non-agricultural population as well. Workers have the highest fertility, the amorphous group of

[123]

TABLE 3.12

CHILDREN EVER BORN IN CURRENT MARRIAGE, URBAN/RURAL, BY INDUSTRY, OCCUPATION,
AND DATE OF MARRIAGE: 1939
(average number)

Population of municipality	Industry	Occupation	Date of marriage				Decline	
			Pre-1905	1905-1909	1910-1914	1915-1919	Absolute	Percent
Over 100,000	Agriculture	Officials, salaried employees	3.18	2.57	2.13	1.85	1.33	41.8
		Independents, relatives	4.45	3.41	2.97	2.48	1.97	44.2
		Workers	4.66	3.76	3.12	2.66	2.00	42.9
	Nonagriculture	Officials, salaried employees	3.01	2.40	2.04	1.73	1.28	42.5
		Independents, relatives	3.30	2.40	1.98	1.61	1.69	51.2
		Workers	4.03	3.16	2.64	2.18	1.85	45.9
2,000-100,000	Agriculture	Officials, salaried employees	3.96	3.07	2.87	2.48	1.48	37.3
		Independents, relatives	5.44	4.51	3.97	3.37	2.07	38.0
		Workers	5.80	4.84	4.29	3.71	2.09	36.0
	Nonagriculture	Officials, salaried employees	3.73	3.07	2.62	2.23	1.50	40.2
		Independents, relatives	4.18	3.22	2.73	2.27	1.91	45.6
		Workers	4.88	4.05	3.49	2.91	1.97	40.4
Under 2,000	Agriculture	Officials, salaried employees	4.15	3.40	2.93	2.60	1.55	37.3
		Independents, relatives	5.42	4.64	4.10	3.52	1.90	35.0
		Workers	6.18	5.38	4.87	4.26	1.92	31.1
	Nonagriculture	Officials, salaried employees	4.32	3.63	3.17	2.67	1.65	38.1
		Independents, relatives	4.89	3.99	3.42	2.85	2.04	41.7
		Workers	5.38	4.62	4.04	3.51	1.87	48.3
All municipalities	Agriculture	Officials, salaried employees	4.01	3.23	2.84	2.48	1.53	38.1
		Independents, relatives	5.40	4.59	4.06	3.48	1.92	35.6
		Workers	6.05	5.20	4.68	4.08	1.97	32.6
	Nonagriculture	Officials, salaried employees	3.44	2.80	2.39	2.03	1.41	40.9
		Independents, relatives	4.04	3.10	2.61	2.16	1.88	46.5
		Workers	4.67	3.82	3.27	2.76	1.91	40.9

SOURCE: 1939 census data as reported in Statistik des deutschen Reich, vol. 554.

NOTES: Boundaries are of May 17, 1939, excluding Memelland.
Data refer to births to married couples living together at the time of the census.

independents experience intermediate levels in fertility and officials and salaried white collar employees have the fewest children. The difference between this last group and the first two however, at least in absolute terms, is less for the more recent cohorts because of differences in cohort to cohort fertility reduction. In fact, the difference between independents on the one hand and officials and salaried employees on the other is almost erased for the 1915–1919 cohort. The same patterns are observed for all three size-classes of muncipalities. It is interesting to note that when we do not take into account the size of the municipality, the fertility of the agricultural population is higher for each occupational class than for the equivalent class of the non-agricultural population. When we control for size of muncipality, this holds only for the independents and workers. Officials and salaried employees of both the agricultural and non-agricultural population experience roughly equivalent fertility.

Some additional information on the fertility of farm families is available from the 1939 census and is presented in Table 3.13. The number of children ever born to farm couples is cross-classified by the size of their farm, which is expressed in hectares (1 hectare = 2½

TABLE 3.13

CHILDREN EVER BORN IN CURRENT MARRIAGE, FARMERS, BY SIZE OF FARM
AND DATE OF MARRIAGE: 1939
(average number)

Size of farm (in hectares)	Date of marriage				Decline	
	Pre-1905	1905-1909	1910-1914	1915-1919	Absolute	Percent
Under .5	4.95	3.79	3.31	2.77	2.18	44.0
.5 - 2	5.12	3.89	3.42	2.94	2.18	42.6
2 - 5	5.38	4.43	3.85	3.29	2.09	38.8
5 - 10	5.61	4.73	4.13	3.51	2.10	37.4
10 - 20	5.77	4.87	4.27	3.65	2.12	36.7
20 - 50	6.05	5.02	4.37	3.75	2.30	38.0
50 - 100	5.76	4.74	4.16	3.54	2.22	38.5
Over 100	4.66	4.12	3.69	3.28	1.38	29.6
All farms	5.56	4.67	4.12	3.52	2.04	36.7

SOURCE: 1939 census data as reported in Statistik des deutschen Reich, vol. 554, p. 182.

NOTES: Boundaries are of May 17, 1939, excluding Memelland.
Data refer to births to married couples living together at the time of the census.

acres). For each of the four marriage cohorts shown, the average number of children first increases with the size of the landholdings and then decreases for farmers with particularly large farms. One possible explanation is offered in the text commentary of the 1933 census with respect to a similiar finding. Small and middle-size farms are still basically family-operated farms, whereas farms of over 50 hectares usually depended on labor from outside the family to assist in its operation. The greater utility of additional children for the operation of larger family farms than for smaller ones may explain the increase in children ever born with farm size within the range of small and middle-size farms. The advantage of additional children, according to this argument, is no longer valid for very large farms which depend primarily on non-familial labor.[14] It is also possible that differences in age at marriage may contribute to the relationship between number of children and size of farm. Stys (1957) found this to be true in a study of peasant families in Poland. The census data, however, are not cross-tabulated by age of marriage and hence do not permit this hypothesis to be tested. In any event, regardless of the size of the farm, the average number of children born per couple was considerably lower for those married between 1915–1919 than for earlier marriages. The decline in fertility, measured in terms of the absolute difference in the average number of children, is very similar for all categories except for the most wealthy farmers who held land covering areas exceeding 100 hectares. The low fertility of the couples married before 1905 in this category suggest that the 1939 census data do not extend far enough into the past to detect much of the intercohort fertility reductions which otherwise would probably be evident.

In sum, data on children ever born from the 1939 German census are less than ideal for the study of the secular decline of fertility. They do not permit unambiguous identification of the socio-economic groups which led or which lagged in the transition to lower fertility levels. The earliest marriage cohorts identified in the data already showed signs of having participated in the decline. In addition the classification scheme employed to divide the population according to

[14]This explanation is given for a similar finding in the 1933 census. Statistisches Reichsamt, *Statistik des Deutschen Reichs*, vol. 452, part 1, pp. 36–39.

economic activity and occupational position leaves much to be desired. Nevertheless they do permit several conclusions about fertility patterns during the demographic transition in Germany. First, they demonstrate quite clearly that for couples married after the turn of the century, the average number of children born was declining for successive marriage cohorts for all economic segments of society identified in the census tabulations. The same decline in each economic group was found in small, middle-sized and large municipalities. Second, to the extent that differentials in the level and decline of fertility were evident, they appeared to conform to the expectations about fertility differentials which are incorporated in the conventional statements of demographic transition theory. For marriages of at least twenty years duration, workers experienced higher than average fertility, middle-class white collar couples experienced lower than average fertility, and persons with independent positions were intermediate. This relationship held for both the agricultural and non-agricultural population as well as rural and urban municipalities. In terms of the decline in fertility evident from cohort to cohort changes in the average number of children ever born, it seems likely that the smaller reductions found for the officials and salaried employees were due to the fact that this group probably led the fertility decline during the end of the nineteenth century and therefore the marriage cohorts shown in the 1939 data were only extending a decline that was already well on its way.

Wealth

Among the most prevalent sets of hypotheses put forth in the earlier writing by German students of the fertility decline was the so-called *Wohlstandstheorie*, which attributed the decline in German fertility to rising prosperity. Improvements in the standard of living were supposed to instill mobility aspirations as well as desires for even greater material wealth and the limitation of family size was seen as one way to realize these goals.[15] Attempts to substantiate the theory relied in part on statistical data suggesting richer sectors of the population had

[15] Among the proponents of *Wohlstandstheorie* were Mombert (1907), Brentano (1909), Wingen (1915), and May (1916).

fewer children and poorer sectors more. Since direct calculations of fertility differentials by wealth were rarely possible, comparisons were frequently based on fertility rates of the population living in richer and poorer sections of a city as determined by the average rent, average apartment size, proportion of families with servants. Fertility differentials with respect to wealth or standard of living are of course closely related to differentials associated with economic activities. Both wealth and occupation are in large part measures of social class and any associated fertility differences reflect broader class influences.

One of the very rare instances in which data on fertility and wealth could be directly related for individuals was provided by the 1905 family survey in the city of Breslau. The average number of children ever born per married couple was cross-tabulated by the amount of rent each couple paid. Houseowners were treated as a separate category. If we can assume that the rent level serves as an index of income or standard of living, the results provide us with a measure of fertility differentials by wealth. Table 3.14 presents the average family

TABLE 3.14

CHILDREN EVER BORN PER MARRIED COUPLE, BY LEVEL OF RENT AND DURATION
OF MARRIAGE, BRESLAU: 1905
(average number)

Duration of marriage (years)	Rent level (in marks)				House owners
	Under 250	251–500	501–750	Over 750	
Over 25	5.58	5.52	4.71	4.02	4.74
20–24	5.54	5.30	3.92	3.40	3.98
15–19	4.98	4.24	3.35	3.08	3.77
Decline	.60	1.28	1.36	.94	.97

SOURCE: Derived from Manschke, 1916, p. 1,878.

size by rent level and marriage duration. Only marriages of over fifteen years duration are included in order to eliminate marriages in which childbearing is not at least close to completion. Of course some couples continue having children after fifteen years but their further fertility is certainly minimal. For all those durations of marriage, there is a clear inverse relationship between the level of rent and family size. The difference between the number of children ever born to couples who were married longer than 25 years and couples married between 15 and 19 years indicates a more moderate decline among the most well-to-do categories (home owners and those with the highest monthly rental) than among those paying middle-level rents. However, the very existence of a decline in family size among couples in the poorest category is in doubt, since the small difference in children ever born may simply reflect the fact that the couples married only 15 to 19 years had not quite finished bearing children.

Most studies of differential fertility by wealth compared the fertility of wealthier or poorer districts of cities rather than directly comparing the fertility of richer and poorer individuals. The results of these studies uniformly found a rather sharp inverse relationship between fertility and the indices of wealth. Studies of seven German cities around 1900 presented by Mombert (1907, pp. 149–160) are summarized in Table 3.15. The correlations between the level of fer-

TABLE 3.15

FERTILITY IN DISTRICTS RANKED BY APARTMENT RENT OR SIZE, SELECTED CITIES: CIRCA 1900

		Level of fertility in			Correlation between apartment rent/size and fertility	
Measure	City and date	Highest ranked district	Median district	Lowest ranked district	r	N
General marital fertility rate	Berlin, 1901	147	198	243	-.85	18
	Hamburg, 1900-1901	136	209	285	-.74	22
	Dresden, 1895-1896	176	221	269	-.76	9
	Magdeburg, 1900-1901	199	186	266	-.84	6
General fertility rate	Leipzig, 1900-1901	51	164	236	-.90	26
	Munich, 1901	37	134	186	-.91	24
	Frankfurt/M., 1900-1901	28	128	189	-.91	17

SOURCE: Derived from Mombert, 1907, pp. 149-160.

NOTES: Districts are ranked by average rent, except in Magdeburg and Munich, where the percentage of rents above 300 marks was used, and Frankfurt/Main, where the percentage of apartments with over 3 rooms was used.
The general marital fertility rate is the number of legitimate births per 1,000 married women aged 15-44.
The general fertility rate is the number of births per 1,000 women aged 15-39 in Leipzig, aged 16-49 in Munich, and aged 18-44 in Frankfurt/Main.
Data for the median district, in cities with an even number of districts, are based upon the higher rent of the middle pair.
N = the number of districts in each city.

tility and the indices of wealth for wards within each of the cities are high. The fertility of the richest district in each case is well below the fertility of the poorest district, and only in Magdeburg, which was divided into only six districts, was the fertility of the middle district not intermediate.

Apparently substantial differences in the level of fertility according to wealth were present in Germany at the turn of the century, at least in the large cities. Proponents of *Wholstandstheorie* usually interpreted these findings as evidence that the fertility decline occurred earlier among the richer classes and later or not at all among the poor. Unfortunately they rarely presented time series of fertility by wealth so evidence of differentials in fertility decline are rarer. Data for two cities however do indicate that a convergence in the fertility level of richer and poorer districts occurred after 1900. Data presented by Bürgdorfer (1929, p. 88) for Bremen in 1901, 1910 and 1925 show little change in the crude birth rate of wealthy districts, large reductions in the working class districts, and intermediate declines in the middle income sections. This convergence was already apparent between 1901 and 1910 and continued after World War I so that by 1925 much smaller differences in the birth rate were apparent in these different sections of the city. A less striking convergence is evident from data presented by May (1916, pp. 1649–50) on fertility in Hamburg in 1894–1898 and 1911–1913. The fall in the crude birth rate that occurred between these two periods however was greater in the middle and low income wards than in the high income districts.

In sum, the evidence on fertility and wealth in Germany fits in well with the findings on occupational differentials. Clearly during much of the period in which the fertility transition took place, the fertility level of persons in the higher social classes was well below the fertility experienced by the lower classes whether measured by occupation or wealth. The evidence on differentials in the actual process of fertility decline is more scanty but does suggest a substantially earlier start in the higher classes followed by at least a partial convergence in levels as fertility reductions spread throughout the entire class structure.

Religious Affiliation

Another important variable in theoretical considerations and empirical studies of fertility behavior is religious affiliation. Religious groups often take positions either explicitly or implicitly concerning birth control and sexual behavior. The active opposition of the Catholic church to most methods of birth control is a well-known example.

Also important, however, is the influence a person's religious affiliation has on his social interactions. Certainly in Germany social contact was much more common among persons of the same religion than between persons whose religious affiliations were different. Indeed, in much of Germany there was little possibility of contact between persons of differing religions since many areas were populated either almost entirely by Protestants or entirely by Catholics. Jews lived mainly in the larger cities. But even when the population of an area was mixed, social contact between persons of different religions was limited. For example, separate school systems for Protestants and Catholics were generally the rule. Thus there is reason to expect that communication and diffusion of new ideas and norms in general, or concerning family size or birth control in particular, proceeded differentially within the Protestant, Catholic, or Jewish subpopulations in Germany. In addition, indirect factors which were important in effecting the fertility decline such as infant mortality, urbanization, and changes in the occupational structure may well have operated differently among persons of different religious affiliation.

It is useful at this point to distinguish between religious affiliation and religiosity. In the present study we deal only with the former although both are important variables to consider when studying the influence of religion on fertility. Religious affiliation is a classificatory variable used to delineate major subgroups in the population that may have differed in their fertility behavior. However, it is a dimension that remains basically static over time and hence can not be used to explain changing patterns of fertility. In contrast, religiosity, which refers to the degree of adherence to a religion both in practice and attitude, may well change over time.[16] The process of secularization thought to characterize modernization and often incorporated in explanations of the fertility decline refers in large part to a reduction in religiosity and proceeds more or less independently of changes in religious affiliation unless of course persons start to denounce any religious affiliation altogether. Although religiosity as a dynamic variable has the explanative potential that religious affiliation lacks, it is

[16]Religiosity is sometimes called religousness in the literature. See e.g. Westoff et al. (1961) p. 194.

also much more difficult to measure quantitatively. At best the concept can be only crudely operationalized. The division of the population by religious affiliation on the other hand is much easier and straightforward, at least in Germany.

The influence of religion was a topic of prime interest to many of the earlier writers concerned with the decline of German fertility. At least two monographs were devoted exclusively to the topic (Rost, 1913; Forberger, 1914), and many others included substantial sections considering religious differentials and their implications (e.g. Mombert, 1907; Hindelang, 1909; Muller, 1924). The polemical nature of these studies colored to some extent their interpretation of the meaning of the decline of fertility. Rost, a Catholic, was primarily interested in demonstrating that the Catholicism was a vigorous force, particularly in comparison to Protestantism, in combating what he judged as the undesirable trend towards lower fertility. Forberger, a Protestant clergyman, devoted his study to showing that there was not much contrast in the fertility decline of Protestants and Catholics and that the apparent difference could largely be explained away by factors extraneous to religion. Nevertheless the data these authors present can be useful in describing the differentials that existed. They relied on two basic approaches, which we will also adopt, in estimating the extent of religious differences in fertility decline.

The most direct approach consists of calculating separate fertility indices for each religious group within an area. Unfortunately, however, the national statistical bureau did not publish data for Germany on the number of births according to the parents' religious affiliation. Some state statistical bureaus, notably those of Prussia, Bavaria, and Hesse, did publish these data for births and other vital events but since census tabulations rarely included age or marital status distributions of the populations according to religious affiliation, in most cases it is possible to calculate only the crudest fertility measures in order to examine religious differentials. Data for Berlin and Munich permit the calculation of short series of the marital fertility index (I_g) by religion, but elsewhere we have to rely on crude birth rates and ratios of legitimate births to marriages as the only direct measures possible.

[132]

An indirect approach adopted by many of the earlier writers in order to estimate fertility differentials by religion in Germany was to compare more refined fertility measures of areas according to the proportion of the population that was Catholic (or Protestant). When consideration is limited to areas in which the population is either overwhelmingly Catholic or overwhelmingly Protestant, the risk of committing the "ecological fallacy" is minimized. However in making such comparisons it is necessary to control for regional influences on fertility which may operate independently of the religious composition of an area. For this purpose a comparison of direct measures of fertility for the different religious grouping within each area is desirable. However it is still of interest to examine the results yielded by this indirect approach.

Table 3.16 shows the average values of several measures of marital

TABLE 3.16

MARITAL FERTILITY (I_g), MAGNITUDE AND DATE OF DECLINE, BY PERCENTAGE CATHOLIC
(unweighted averages)

Percentage population Catholic in administrative area	Maximum I_g		I_g 1898-1902		I_g 1931-1935		Decline, maximum -1910			Date of 10% decline	
	Level	Number of areas	Level	Number of areas	Level	Number of areas	Absolute	Percent	Number of areas	Year	Number of areas
90 or more	.860	7	.814	6	.415	4	.181	21.3	7	1900	7
60-89	.841	12	.735	13	.355	11	.195	23.3	12	1897	12
40-59	.804	12	.734	12	.339	6	.179	22.3	12	1900	12
10-39	.754	13	.653	14	.296	19	.193	25.6	13	1895	13
9 or less	.696	27	.587	26	.244	25	.229	33.1	27	1894	27

NOTE: For maximum I_g, the decline to 1910, and the date of 10% decline, the percentage Catholic refers to 1880 data. For I_g 1898-1902, the religious distribution according to the 1900 census was used and for I_g 1931-1935, the categories refer to the percentage Catholic in 1933.

fertility for administrative areas grouped according to the percent of their population that was recorded as Roman Catholic in the censuses. It is quite apparent that areas which were almost entirely Catholic (more than 90 percent) experienced considerably higher marital fertility than areas which were almost entirely Protestant (i.e. with fewer than 10 percent Catholics). This relationship held both for predecline levels of fertility as indicated by the maximum I_g experienced in an administrative area, at the turn of the century, and at the conclusion of the fertility decline in the 1930s. In addition, areas with more mixed religious composition were characterized by intermediate levels of I_g. Mixed areas with Catholic majorities experienced higher intermediate levels than mixed areas where Catholics formed only a minority of the population. These findings, of course, do not mean that Catholics in mixed religious areas necessarily had higher marital fertility than Protestants in those same areas. This can only be demonstrated by a comparison of separate fertility measures for each subpopulation. The relationship between the religious composition and fertility, however, does not appear as strong as when we consider measures of the time and extent of fertility decline. The overwhelmingly Catholic areas showed signs of reduced fertility somewhat later than areas where Catholics were almost entirely absent, but between these two categories no regular progression is evident. Also if we examine the extent of decline between the maximum value experienced in an area and the level found in 1910 (1908–1912), the year marking the approximate mid-point in the national decline of I_g, a fairly sharp contrast is found between the purely Catholic and the purely Protestant areas with respect to the percentage decline in fertility but not with respect to the absolute amount of decline. Catholic areas began their fertility declines from higher levels than Protestant areas, and even though I_g was reduced by almost the same absolute amount by 1910 in both, Protestant areas scored larger relative declines. In areas with mixed religious composition there appears to be little relation between the extent of decline by 1910 and the proportion that was Catholic or Protestant.

Another way of expressing the relationship between the proportion Catholic and levels or decline of marital fertility is through correlations. Table 3.17 presents two sets of correlation coefficients relating the percent Catholic in an administrative area with the measures of the level and the decline of marital fertility discussed above. One set represents the relationship found between the absolute values of the particular pair of indices being related. However a second set of correlations is also presented in an attempt to see if the relationships hold independent of regional influences. The proportion of Catholics in an administrative area as well as the level or decline of fertility is strongly associated with the region in which the area is located.[17] In order to

[17]For a discussion of the regional association of the fertility indices and the method of evaluating it see Chapter 2. Employing the analysis of variance to measure the extent of

TABLE 3.17

MARITAL FERTILITY (I_g), CORRELATIONS BETWEEN MAGNITUDE AND DATE OF DECLINE, AND PERCENTAGE CATHOLIC

	Correlation coefficients	
Variables	Absolute values of indices	Deviations from regional means
Maximum I_g, percentage Catholic 1880	.74	.40
I_g 1898-1902, percentage Catholic 1900	.69	.44
I_g 1931-1935, percentage Catholic 1933	.64	.48
Absolute decline in I_g, (maximum-1910), percentage Catholic 1880	-.18	-.20
Percent decline in I_g, (maximum-1910), percentage Catholic 1880	-.37	-.26
Date of 10% decline, percentage Catholic 1880	.20	.28

NOTE: N = 71, except for 1930's data when N = 66.

eliminate the common influence of regional locations on the variables being correlated, we can take advantage of one form of the analyses of covariance (Hagood and Price, 1952, pp. 473–498). To do this we compute the deviation of each variable from its regional mean and then correlate these deviations with each other rather than simply correlate the absolute values of the variables. The result shows the level of association between variables once the effects of regional associations have been removed. The second set of correlations expresses the degree of association between the deviations from regional means for the pairs of variables being considered. The rather strong association between the level of marital fertility in an administrative

regional association with respect to the proportion Catholic in an administrative area, we obtain the following values of the F-ratio and ϵ:

	F-ratio	ϵ
Percent Catholic 1880	15.2	.74
Percent Catholic 1900	15.2	.74
Percent Catholic 1933	12.5	.72

area and the proportion of the population that was Catholic which was already evident in Table 3.16 is reflected in the moderately high correlation coefficients calculated between regionally unadjusted values of the indices. As the correlations between the deviations of I_g levels from their regional means and the deviations of the percent Catholic from their regional means show, the relationship is weaker but still persists when the effect of regional association is removed.

The weak associations between the religious composition of an area and the date or extent of decline in I_g which was also apparent from the results given in Table 3.16 are reflected in the weak negative correlations between the proportion Catholic in an area in 1880 on the one hand and the indices of the date of decline and extent of decline by 1910 on the other hand. These weak relationships are hardly changed when we remove the regional effects by correlating the deviations from regional means.

For the states that published data on births according to the parents' religion, it is possible to calculate directly separate fertility rates for each religious group. In general however it was not possible to calculate our index of marital fertility (I_g) since age, sex, and marital status distributions by religion were not published. Munich and Berlin are exceptions in this respect and hence separate marital fertility rates for Catholics, Protestants, and Jews could be calculated for limited periods. The results are shown in Table 3.18. Although the series are very incomplete they do suggest that considerable differences in the level of marital fertility existed for the three main religious

TABLE 3.18

MARITAL FERTILITY (I_g), BY FEMALE'S RELIGION, MUNICH AND BERLIN: 1875 TO 1902

City	Date	Catholic	Protestant	Jewish
Munich	1875	.660	.534	.522
	1878–1882	.607	.497	.414
	1883–1887	.564	.459	.335
	1888–1892	.532	.384	.299
Berlin	1893–1897	.499	.448	.367
	1898–1902	.446	.393	.337

groups during the last decades of the nineteenth century. In both cities Catholics experienced the highest and Jews the lowest marital fertility while Protestants were intermediate. However it is clear that I_g was declining in all three subpopulations. By the 1890s, marital fertility even for Catholics was far below the overall national average, and the marital fertility of the Jews in Munich was as low as the post-World War I national rates.

Less refined measures of fertility such as the crude birth rates by religion presented in Table 3.19 for Prussia and Table 3.20 for Bavaria

TABLE 3.19

CRUDE BIRTH RATE, BY FEMALE'S RELIGION, PRUSSIA: 1842 TO 1934

Date	Catholic	Protestant	Jewish
1842-1844	41.0	39.2	37.2
1845-1850	--	--	35.3
1851-1856	--	--	34.9
1857-1862	41.0	39.6	33.9
1863-1865	41.1	41.2	32.8
1875-1876	44.0	41.5	33.8
1880-1881	40.5	38.3	30.5
1885-1886	41.5	38.3	27.0
1890-1891	41.1	37.4	24.5
1895-1896	42.1	36.4	21.9
1900-1901	42.3	34.9	19.9
1905-1906	39.9	32.0	18.5
1910-1911	36.2	28.0	15.9
1924-1926	24.6	19.7	13.3
1932-1934	18.8	15.8	5.7

NOTE: 1875-1876 population data estimated by linear interpolation between census data for 1871 and 1880.

and Hesse suggest a pattern of differential fertility similar to that indicated by the Berlin and Munich data. All groups reduced their fertility substantially during the decades under discussion, but the Jews clearly seem to have led the rest of the population in achieving lower, modern levels of reproduction. The data for Prussia suggest that Jews

TABLE 3.20

CRUDE BIRTH RATE, BY FEMALE'S RELIGION, BAVARIA AND HESSE: 1866 TO 1925

Date	Bavaria			Hesse		
	Catholic	Protestant	Jewish	Catholic	Protestant	Jewish
1866-1870	--	--	--	--	--	34.8
1871-1875	--	--	--	41.6	37.7	32.7
1876-1880	43.3	39.3	32.7	40.7	36.1	31.7
1881-1885	40.1	36.0	28.4	36.2	32.4	26.8
1886-1890	38.4	34.3	23.9	35.2	31.3	24.1
1891-1895	38.8	34.2	21.1	36.3	32.0	22.7
1896-1900	39.2	34.6	18.8	37.6	32.7	19.9
1901-1905	38.9	33.4	17.7	36.8	32.2	18.6
1906-1910	36.0	30.1	16.3	32.8	28.8	18.8
1925	24.6	20.6	12.1	--	--	--

SOURCES: Bavarian births by religion for 1876-1910 were estimated from data given in Rost, 1913, p. 32 and Forberger, 1914, p. 58. Hessian births by religion were taken from Forberger, 1914, p. 62.

probably started to reduce their fertility at least several decades prior to German unification and well ahead of the rest of the German population. The data for Bavaria and Hesse are quite consistent with this finding. In the 1870s, the first decade for which we have information, the Jewish birth rate is well below the level for Catholics or Protestants and declines steadily from then on suggesting that Jews might well have begun reducing their fertility earlier. The striking contrast in fertility between Jews and the rest of the population may stem in part from the marked tendency of Jews to live in urban areas, particularly large cities.[18] But as the marital fertility rates for Berlin and Munich demonstrated, even within large cities Jews had substantially lower fertility.

Some differences in the levels and trend of Catholic and Protestant fertility are also evident. Almost without exception the Catholic birth rate was above the Protestants at any given time in Prussia, Bavaria, and Hesse. In addition, the Prussian data indicate an earlier tendency among Protestants to experience declining birth rates. If we ignore the

[18]For example, according to the Prussian census of 1900, 24 percent of Prussian Jews lived in Berlin and 64 percent in cities with populations over 20,000. The comparable figures for Protestants were 7 and 32 percent respectively and for Catholics only 2 and 26 percent respectively.

unusually high birth rates for 1875–1876 in Prussia, the Protestant birth rate reached a level 10 percent below its maximum shortly after 1890, whereas the Catholic rate was not reduced by an equivalent amount until almost 1910. Catholics also appear to lag a bit behind Protestants in Bavaria although the difference is less pronounced than in Prussia. In Hesse the birth rates of both religious groups follow rather parallel courses with little difference evident in the timing of decline.

Forberger (1914, pp. 33–39) compared the Catholic and Protestant birth rates for all of the separate *Regierungsbezirke* of Prussia in 1880, 1901, and 1911 and for the largest cities in 1901 and 1911. According to his data in 1880 the Protestant birth rate was lower than the Catholic rate in only half of the 36 areas. However, due to earlier and larger declines in birth rates among Protestants, by 1901 their birth rate was lower than the Catholic rate in all but six areas and by 1911 in all but two. Between 1880 and 1900 the birth rate declined among Protestants in all but six areas whereas it showed an increase in over half of the areas for Catholics. In only four areas was the decline in the Catholic birth rate larger than the decrease in the Protestant rate. However the greater Catholic resistance to moderating their reproductive behavior patterns was only a temporary one. Between 1901 and 1911 the Catholic and Protestant birth rate declined in every Prussian *Regierungsbezirk* and in 14 areas the magnitude of the decrease was actually greater for the Catholics.

A comparison of Catholic and Protestant birth rates in 1925 indicates that a substantial differential still existed in most Prussian areas. In all but two the Catholic rate still exceeded the birth rate for the Protestants. However a comparison with the 1911 rates given by Forberger makes it clear that fertility declined for both groups almost everywhere and often in similar amounts. The Protestant rate showed a decline in every area between 1911 and 1925, the Catholic rate in all but three.

The data Forberger presents for large cities indicate similar differences between Protestant and Catholic rates. For the 31 cities in Prussia with at least 100,000 population in 1900, the Catholic birth rate exceeded the Protestant in all but eight. By 1911 this was the case in all but two. The birth rate fell between these two dates in every one of these cities for Protestants and in all but two for Catholics.

Attempts were made by earlier writers to estimate religious differentials in marital fertility by calculating the ratio of legitimate births to the number of marriages according to the religion of the parents and the religion of the marriage partners (e.g. Broesike, 1904; von Fircks, 1879; Rost, 1913). This measure clearly has many weaknesses as an index of marital fertility, some of which were already discussed above in reference to studies of differential fertility by economic activity. In general the patterns of fertility differentials by religious affiliations revealed by this measure are quite similar to those indicated by crude birth rates.

In summary, several findings emerge with respect to religious differentials in Germany during the course of the fertility transition. Essentially at any time between unification and the 1930s differences in the level of fertility of the three major religious groups were evident wherever data were available. Jews had the lowest fertility, Catholics the highest, and the Protestants occupied an intermediate position. The early and rapid decline of Jewish fertility and the very low levels achieved even before the turn of the century were truly exceptional. Protestant and Catholic fertility experience also differed from each other although not to the extent that both differed from the Jewish experience. Generally the decline in Protestant birth rates preceded the decline in the Catholic rate and at any given time was lower. In the end, however, the fertility of all three religious groups declined to substantially lower levels.

Identification of religious differentials is a relatively simple task in comparison to explaining them. The distinctive behavior of the Jews should not only provide a clue in the search for an explanation of the fertility decline but also is one of the apects of the decline which needs to be accounted for in any complete explanation. Perhaps the most important distinctive features of the Jews were the close cultural and social ties between them which resulted in their being a more self-contained, closed cultural entity than Protestants or Catholics and provided a situation in which changing norms regarding family size and family limitation could spread rapidly and relatively independently of the rest of German society.

One crucial question is to what extent religious differentials are attributable to factors not directly derivative from religion but associated with religious groups for other reasons. A vigorous debate took place in the earlier literature about whether the higher fertility and later decline of the Catholics was due to the active opposition of the Catholic church to birth control, its requirements concerning confession, and its allegedly greater control over its members (e.g. Bornträger, 1913; Rost, 1913; Neuhaus, 1907) or due rather to the social and economic circumstances characteristic of Catholics (e.g. Muller, 1924; Forberger, 1914; Mombert, 1907). It is virtually impossible in the analysis of religious differentials to control directly for most other factors with the exception of rural-urban residence. Data on births and population by religion were simply not cross-classified with other variables. It is clear, however, that Jews in particular and Protestants to a much lesser extent were more urbanized than the German population as a whole. Even though the lower urban fertility levels and earlier urban declines may therefore account in part for the differences among religious groups, it is also clear from the data presented above, that within urban areas striking differences also existed. Other differences among the religious groups such as those regarding occupations, wealth and social backwardness which were mentioned by writers who ascribed the religious differentials to non-religious factors can not be controlled for directly.

Ethnic Affiliation

A substantial proportion of the population in the eastern administrative districts of Prussia consisted of persons belonging to non-Germanic ethnic groups, primarily of Polish origin. Most spoke Polish as their native language although in a few areas the Polish dialects Masurish and Kassubish were commonly spoken. The distribution of the population in 1900 according to their native language, shown in Table 3.21, serves as a measure of ethnic composition. In three of the six administrative areas comprising the eastern region (Posen, Bromberg, and Oppeln) Polish was the mother tongue of the

TABLE 3.21

DISTRIBUTION OF THE POPULATION BY NATIVE LANGUAGE, BY
ADMINISTRATIVE AREA, EASTERN REGION: 1900

| Area | Percentage of population whose native language was | | | | | |
	German	German and another lang.	Polish	Masurish	Kassubish	Other languages
01 Ostpreussen	78.7	1.7	7.8	6.6	--	5.2
02 Danzig	71.7	0.9	14.0	--	13.3	1.0
03 Marienwerder	59.0	1.3	38.4	--	1.2	--
09 Posen	32.2	0.5	67.3	--	--	0.1
10 Bromberg	48.3	0.7	50.9	--	--	--
13 Oppeln	36.6	3.8	56.1	--	--	3.4

NOTE: Due to rounding, data do not always add up to 100%.

majority of the population and of sizable minorities in the other three. Masurish was fairly common in Ostpreussen and Kassubish was the native tongue of one in eight in Danzig. To be sure, other non-Germanic ethnic groups also lived in the eastern region as well as in the rest of Germany. Most notable were the large numbers speaking Lithuanian in Ostpreussen, Czech or Moravian in Oppeln, Wendish in Liegnitz, Frankfurt/Oder, and the Kingdom of Saxony, Danish in Schleswig, and French in Alsace-Lorraine. However, none of these minorities approach in numbers the Poles in the eastern administrative areas.

It is not possible to calculate directly the fertility of any of the non-Germanic ethnic minorities living in Germany during most of the period of fertility decline. Information regarding the parents' mother tongue was noted on birth registration certificates only since 1922 and then only in Prussia. Hence cross-classification of births by ethnic affiliation of the parents is not available for earlier years. However, since in the eastern region some of the small administrative districts (*Kreise*) were populated almost entirely by Poles while in others the population was almost entirely ethnic German, it is possible to estimate differential fertility by comparing the fertility of districts according to the proportion of the population that was Polish (including Masurish and Kassubish) in origin. Broesike attempted to estimate the fertility of the Polish in 1900 in this manner (Broesike, 1904, part A, pp. 21–22; part B, pp. 157–160). In his analysis he considered districts in the administrative areas comprising the four easternmost provinces of Prussia. This covers what we labeled the eastern region (see Chapter 1) as well as the two additional administrative areas of Breslau and Liegnitz. He found much higher marital fertility in the districts with large Slavic majorities than in districts where the population was almost entirely composed of ethnic Germans. An even progression of fertility levels from high to low characterized the intermediate levels. These findings strongly suggest that there was a substantial differential in the fertility *level* in 1900 between the Polish and non-Polish (primarily ethnic German) population. Mombert (1907, pp. 224–228) in discussing these findings attributes the higher fertility of the Slavs to their impoverished condition. Citing evidence from Wegener (1902), he points out that the Poles were at a significantly lower economic level than the ethnic Germans in the same areas.

Broesike did not extend his analysis of district fertility by the proportion of Poles in the population to cover any years other than 1900. Von Fircks (1879, pp. 19–22) used a similar method to estimate the birth rates of ethnic groups in Prussia for the period 1862–1874. He also found substantially higher fertility for Slavs. Unfortunately it is difficult to compare von Fircks' results directly with those of Broesike for 1900 in order to determine if differentials in fertility changes were evident between Slavs and Germans, because the two studies did not use the same criteria for grouping together districts with similar ethnic composition. However, it is possible to calculate crude birth rates at different years for the individual districts comprizing the groups used by Broesike and compare the results to see if any clear differentials in either the timing or extent of fertility decline existed. Table 3.22 presents the average marital fertility in 1900 as well as the average crude birth rate in 1880–1881, 1894–1896 and 1909–1911 of groups of districts in the eastern region arranged according to the proportion of the population that was Polish (i.e. spoke Polish, Masurish, or Kassubish as their native language). The districts in each group are essentially the same as those in the Broesike study except that districts from the practically pure German administrative areas of Breslau and Liegnitz were excluded.

TABLE 3.22

GENERAL MARITAL FERTILITY RATE AND CRUDE BIRTH RATE, BY PERCENTAGE OF POLISH ORIGIN,
DISTRICTS (KREISE) OF EASTERN REGION: 1880 TO 1910
(unweighted averages)

Percentage Polish in Kreis (1900)	General marital fertility rate (1900)	Crude birth rate				
		Levels			Absolute change	
		1880	1895	1910	1880-1895	1895-1910
75 or more	342.3	43.19	46.17	39.89	+2.98	-6.28
55-74	332.5	44.63	46.85	39.96	+2.22	-6.89
45-54	322.0	44.11	43.61	36.31	-0.50	-7.30
25-44	300.1	41.95	42.30	35.29	+0.35	-7.01
5-24	280.9	41.74	40.21	34.35	-1.53	-5.86
4 or less	271.8	37.30	38.79	31.96	+0.49	-6.83

NOTES: Population of Polish origin is defined as those speaking Polish, Masurish,
or Kassubish as a native language.
The general marital fertility rate refers to the number of legitimate births
(including stillbirths) per 1,000 married women aged 15-49.

The differences in fertility levels are striking, particularly as measured by the legitimate fertility rate in 1900, but also as seen in the crude birth rates at each of the three periods of observation. The districts with Polish majorities clearly experienced higher fertility than those with German majorities. Differences with respect to the decline in the birth rate during the three decades following 1880, however, are much less striking. In part, changes in the proportions married probably obscure some differences in fertility changes. Ostpreussen and Danzig, the two administrative areas with the largest proportions of ethnic Germans in the eastern region experienced rising proportions married between 1880 and 1895 as indicated by I_m (see Appendix Table 2.1), and thus the slight rise in the crude birth rate over this period for districts with very small proportions of Poles may be obscuring constant or even declining marital fertility. Of the three administrative areas with a Polish majority, i.e. Posen, Bromberg, and Oppeln, the first two experienced declines in I_m thus compensating for what might have been an even greater increase in the birth rate in districts with Polish majorities. Between 1895 and 1910 all three of these administrative areas experienced slight declines in I_m, possibly accounting for part of the decline in the crude birth rate during this period. However, in Ostpreussen I_m also declined a small amount although in Danzig I_m increased. Even with the slight effect of changing proportions married taken into account, no clear differences in fertility decline are apparent. In general the crude birth rate showed little sign of decline between 1880 and 1895 in the districts of the eastern regions regardless of their ethnic composition. In the decade and a half after 1895 birth rates declined substantially and approximately equally in districts in each of the six categories of ethnic composition. Thus it is difficult to speak of differences with respect to the fertility decline between Poles and Germans, at least in eastern areas of Prussia, even though differences existed in their characteristic levels of fertility.

It is also difficult to determine the level of fertility of non-German ethnic groups other than the Poles because they are much smaller in number and rarely constituted the majority of a district's population. The three northernmost districts of Schleswig (Hadersleben, Apenrade, and Sonderburg), however, were predominantly Danish, with well over three-quarters of the population of each speaking Danish as their native language. In a fourth district, Tondern, about half spoke Danish. After World War I the Danish areas were ceded to Denmark, but between 1866 and 1920 they were part of Prussia. Some impression of the fertility of the Danish minority group can be derived from Table 3.23, which compares birth rates in the three predominantly

TABLE 3.23

CRUDE BIRTH RATE, BY PERCENTAGE OF DANISH ORIGIN, DISTRICTS IN SCHLESWIG: 1870 TO 1910

District or area	Percentage Danish in 1900	Levels				Absolute change		
		1870	1880	1895	1910	1870-1880	1880-1895	1895-1910
Hadersleben	82.9	31.2	30.8	28.5	30.4	-0.4	-2.3	+1.9
Apenrade	76.8	30.4	29.3	30.3	31.6	-1.1	+1.0	+1.3
Sonderburg	81.7	25.6	26.4	26.7	29.0	+0.8	+0.3	+2.3
Unweighted average	80.5	29.1	28.8	28.5	30.3	-0.3	-0.3	+1.8
Tondern	45.4	30.6	30.7	32.3	30.0	+0.1	+1.6	-2.3
Schleswig Total	9.5	33.3	33.7	34.5	28.4	+0.4	+0.8	-6.1

SOURCE: 1870 data from von Fircks, 1879, p. 22.

NOTES: Population of Danish origin is defined as those speaking Danish as a native language.
1870 data are averages of 1867-1874 period, 1880 data are averages of 1880-1881 period, 1895 data are averages of 1894-1896 period, and 1910 data are averages of 1909-1911 period.

Danish districts with the half-Danish district and with the entire administrative area of Schleswig, which contained a total of 23 districts in 1900. The largely Danish districts experienced consistently lower birth rates during the last third of the nineteenth century than the rest of Schleswig and generally the half-Danish district occupied an intermediate position. Curiously, however, birth rates in the three Danish districts show little tendency toward decline even by 1910, although the rest of Schleswig experienced a distinct decline between 1895 and 1910. Evidence from Danish statistics indicate that marital fertility in the rural areas of Denmark was very stable between 1840 and 1901 but declined substantially during the first decade of this century (van de Walle, 1969). Thus the Danes of Schleswig appear to have been slow to join in the fertility decline in comparison to both Germans and Danish nationals. On the other hand, the low birth rates which characterized the Danish districts during the entire period of observation raises the possibility that substantial portions of the population were already practicing fertility control. Indeed van de Walle (1969) finds some suggestion of deliberate family limitation evident in the age specific pattern of marital fertility which characterized rural populations in Denmark in the 1870s. Age specific data are not available for the predominantly Danish districts of Schleswig, although their overall level of fertility appears similar to that of Danish nationals.

Conclusion

Five socially defined dimensions (rural-urban residence, economic activity, wealth, religious affiliation, and ethnic affiliation) have been used to differentiate the German population into aggregates which might differ with respect to their fertility behavior. The choice of the particular dimensions was dictated in large part by the availability of data which permitted either the direct or indirect calculation of separate fertility indices. However on the basis of past empirical investigations as well as theoretical considerations there is sufficient reason to expect subpopulations defined by these dimensions to exhibit differences in their fertility behavior.

The examination of social differentials in the level of German fertility at the turn of the century, for example, yielded results at least superficially consistent with conventional expectations such as those incorporated into demographic transition theory: rural fertility was higher than urban; persons in higher social classes, whether measured by occupation or wealth, had lower fertility than those in classes below them; Catholic fertility was above Protestant fertility and Jews had lower fertility than both; the Polish minority had higher fertility and the Danish lower than the national level.

Data with respect to differentials in changes in fertility or the date of decline were scantier but also largely agreed with conventional expectations. Perhaps even more important than the differences that were revealed is the finding that in almost all the major social categories described in our examinations fertility began to decline within the span of a few decades and was substantially reduced virtually throughout German society by 1930. Only a few small societal segments (most notably the Jews and possibly the highly educated occupational classes) may have preceded the general population in fertility decline by a generation or more. The low level of fertility they were experiencing by the 1870s suggests that a substantial degree of fertility control may have been widespread within these limited circles before German unification and hence prior to the historical period analyzed here.

CHAPTER 4: Demographic Change and Fertility Decline: Infant Mortality

In Germany, perhaps the most frequently and intensely debated issue in the *Geburtenrückgang* literature during the early decades of this century was the relationship between declining infant mortality and declining fertility. E. Würzburger (1912, 1914), the most outspoken proponent of the importance of infant mortality, argued for many years that concern over declining fertility was unwarranted since the reduction in the birth rate was simply the result of a commensurate reduction in infant and child mortality. He stressed the importance of the number of children reaching maturity rather than the number of births in any consideration of declining fertility. Even as late as 1931, when the birth rate was close to reaching its historic peacetime low, he maintained that the decline could be explained by reduced infant mortality in combination with several demographic changes (age and frequency of marriage, age distribution shifts, and remarriage) resulting from the World War, and insisted it did not indicate a genuine decline in the number of children desired (Würzburger, 1931). While some German writers supported Würzburger's views at least in part, others took direct issue with it. Perhaps the most adamant opponent was Karl Oldenburg (1916) who held that the influence of mortality on the fertility decline was quite minimal in comparison with other causes.

The extensive controversy found in the German literature is indicative of the alternative hypotheses that can be postulated concerning the interaction between infant mortality and the fertility decline and the difficulty in unambiguously interpreting the statistical evidence. Unfortunately even recent discussions of the subject rarely attempt to specify in much detail the character of the relationship. In the following discussion, we will distinguish several ways in which fertility and infant mortality could be related. In addition we will comment on their implications for the fertility decline with respect to the magnitude of the relationship and the timing of the related changes in the two variables.

[148]

The most frequently suggested relationship is that infant mortality has a determining influence on fertility. The basic argument was stated in the German literature as early as 1861 by Wappäus: "First of all, a mother whose child was stillborn or died soon after birth will generally give birth sooner to another than a mother who nurses and rears her live born child. Second, as a rule it can be assumed that each parental couple wishes to raise a certain number of children and therefore when they already have this number of living children they no longer so actively want to enlarge the family as when the desired number has not been reached due to the loss of infants shortly after birth" (Wappäus, 1861, p. 322).

Wappäus's statement suggests two ways in which a reduction in infant mortality could have brought about a reduction in fertility. If it is true that parents neither purposively attempted to hasten the next conception after an infant died nor, alternatively, postponed it if the infant survived, then lower infant mortality would have meant generally longer birth intervals. It is possible that even in the absence of attempts to limit the ultimate family size, parents regulated the spacing of their children in response to the death or survival of each previous infant. A couple might lack the intention to restrict their final number of offsprings but still make some effort merely to delay births of any rank. Under such circumstances if a newborn infant survived, the parents might want to control their fertility for a short period in order to delay the next conception. If the infant died prematurely, fertility control would be abandoned. It is even possible to postulate a relationship between the length of the birth interval and infant mortality that results from fertility-limiting practices, but involve no intent either to control the ultimate family size, or to space subsequent births. For example when a newborn infant survives, the sexual behavior of the parents might be different in some unconscious way from what it is when the infant dies, so that a new pregnancy becomes less likely. The presence of an infant — or on the contrary his premature death — might affect reproductive behavior in several ways. For instance, his presence might reduce the frequency of intercourse. It may be that sleeping arrangements would be altered; mothers may sleep in another room close to the child, without the husband. Or they may be overburdened with work as a result of the new child, and their desire for intercourse may be reduced (Knodel and van de Walle, 1967, p. 132).

Another way in which a reduction in infant mortality would result in longer birth intervals is through the effect of lactation. There is considerable medical evidence that lactation inhibits conception through prolonging postpartum amenorrhea (Tietze, 1961; Slaber, Feinlieb, and MacMahon, 1965). Breastfeeding clearly affects the duration of temporary sterility in women immediately following confinement. The interruption of lactation on the other hand allows ovulation to be resumed sooner and, in the absence of contraception, causes an earlier pregnancy. An infant death that interrupts breast feeding could lead to a conception sooner than if the infant survived. An analysis of family histories in three Bavarian villages during a time when birth control apparently was not practiced revealed just such a mechanism. In two villages where breastfeeding was almost non-existent, birth intervals following infant deaths were almost as long as those following the birth of an infant that survived. In a village where prolonged breastfeeding was customary, birth intervals following infant deaths were considerably shorter than those coming after a surviving infant (Knodel, 1968). A number of other studies of pre-industrial populations (for which no direct information on breast feeding habits were available, however) also reveal shorter intervals following infant deaths (Knodel, 1968, pp. 316–318). Thus even where the practice of family limitation is not common, a reduction in infant mortality could plausibly lead to some reduction of fertility by lengthening the average birth interval. Very little time is required for this effect of changes in infant mortality to be translated into changes in fertility. A lag of a year or two at most seems likely. The actual magnitude of the effect would not be large however. Even a very substantial reduction in infant mortality would yield no more than a reduction in fertility by a few percent as a result of this mechanism.[1]

[1] The magnitude of this effect can be roughly estimated on the basis of studies of birth intervals and infant mortality in pre-industrial populations. Assume two cohorts of women marrying at the same age and ceasing to bear children at the same age. Suppose that for one cohort the probability of a child dying before reaching age one is approximately the same as in Germany just prior to the fertility decline (.250) and for the other

The most common hypothesis linking infant mortality and fertility is suggested in the second part of Wappäus's statement. It links infant mortality directly to family limitation, i.e. the use of birth control with the intent to restrict the ultimate number of surviving children. According to this argument, lower infant mortality creates pressure for fertility control because fewer births are needed to produce a given number of children surviving to any specified age or alternatively unrestricted fertility results in more surviving children than previously was the case. Implicit in this line of reasoning is the assumption that couples either have a fixed idea at marriage of the number of children they want or construct such a goal in the process of family building. When this number is attained, the couple limits its fertility through some form of deliberate birth control. The magnitude of the resultant fertility reduction should be greater than if infant mortality influences birth intervals only, but should still be no greater than would be needed to ensure constant average family size. In other

---

cohort the probability is that prevailing in Germany around 1935 (.080). Contraceptive practice is assumed the same for both cohorts. According to a survey of local historical population studies, the population of Mömmlingen, a village in Bavaria, showed the greatest difference between birth intervals following infant deaths and intervals following infant survival (Knodel, 1968, p. 317). If we assume that the interbirth intervals found in Mömmlingen (1.62 years following an infant death and 2.50 years following an infant survival) were characteristic of both cohorts, we can calculate what percent fewer second and higher order births the cohort experiencing lower infant mortality would have than the cohort experiencing higher infant mortality (the number of first order births would obviously be the same). The average interbirth interval for the high mortality cohort would be .25(1.62) + .75(2.50) or 2.28, and for the low mortality cohort .08(1.62) + .92(2.50 or 2.43. The relative difference in the number of second and higher order births occurring to the two cohorts is (average interval with low mortality/average interval with high mortality) minus one, or about six percent. The difference in the total number births would be less since each cohort has the same number of first births. The difference would be still smaller if we based the calculations on other populations where infant mortality had less effect on birth intervals. In Mömmlingen extended nursing was universal and thus the effect of an early infant death on the birth interval was maximized. The increasing use of contraception during the actual fertility decline would further reduce the effect of lactation. It is true of course that in some areas of Germany infant mortality prior to the decline was much greater than the national average, and in these areas the decline in infant mortality was correspondingly greater. However, high infant mortality during the last half of the nineteenth and early twentieth century was often associated with the lack of breast feeding or with breast feeding of short duration.

In such situations, the effect of a reduction in infant mortality would be much less than in an area like Mömmlingen where prolonged breast feeding was universal.

words, on this basis, we would expect the fertility decline to be more or less commensurate with the reduction in infant and child mortality, but not to exceed it. Thus in order to keep constant "effective" family size (i.e. the number of children surviving to maturity, which we will define as age 15) while the probability of dying between birth and age 15 decreases as it did in Germany from .376 in 1871–1880 to .107 in 1932–1934, on the average the number of births per family would have to decrease by about 30 percent.[2]

It is possible to argue that the effect of a reduction in infant and child mortality on fertility would be greater than the resulting increase in effective family size — the above calculation assumed that infant and child mortality exerted an influence on a couple's fertility only through their replacing children who actually die. If on the other hand couples have some idea of infant and child mortality risks based perhaps on their perception of the prior experience of their relatives, friends, and neighbors as well as the wisdom or lore passed on to them, they may adjust their fertility to anticipate possible deaths. Heer (1966) and Schultz (1971, p. 157) argue that in situations of high child mortality couples have additional births not only to make up for the expected number of deaths but also to compensate for the greater risks of exceeding the average number of deaths when mortality is high. They indicate that high mortality has a high variance and, therefore, high uncertainty) associated with it and as a consequence a larger allowance is needed in order to keep high the probability that any given couple will not fall short of a specified minimum. A reduction in mortality, provided it is more or less accurately perceived by the population, would result in a more than commensurate reduction in births because the necessity of a couple having additional children on hand as "insurance" against possible future child deaths would diminish.[3]

[2]The required proportionate reduction is equal to $1 - .624/.893$ or 30.1 percent. See discussion later in this chapter.

[3]The statistical point is correct that higher variance is associated with higher mortality and therefore more additional births are required to assure the same probability of achieving *at least* a given minimum effective family size than under circumstances of lower mortality. However the assumption this model carries with it that families somehow engage in such probabilistic calculus seems far-fetched. In general it seems implausible that the prevailing mortality probabilities influence a couple's fertility behavior. More likely it is the couple's actual experience with child deaths, perhaps altered a bit by the

Several possibilities exist with respect to the time lag that would elapse between the beginning of the mortality decline and the start of the fertility decline if the effect operates as stated in the second part of Wappäus's statement and expanded on above. If we postulate that adequate methods of fertility control were known and accepted at the time infant and child mortality declined, then the response in fertility behavior would simply be a natural accommodation to the new mortality conditions. A lag of only five or ten years would be expected, i.e. the time required for the parents affected by the lower mortality of their children to reach their desired family size. If, on the other hand, the increasing family size resulting from reduced mortality were the source of pressure leading to a newly created acceptance of methods of fertility control, the lag should be longer. We would expect that infant mortality would have to decline significantly before it could generate enough pressure to change basic attitudes and behavior. Transition theory postulates a considerable time lag between the mortality and fertility decline for more or less this reason and in this way treats mortality as a *cause* of the fertility decline.

The causal significance of reductions in infant mortality would not necessarily be contradicted by a finding that fertility declined much more than needed to compensate for the reduction of infant mortality. Infant mortality could be the initial cause leading to the acceptance of fertility control which would then set the stage for fertility to respond to the many other factors involved in modernization.

It is also possible to interpret the reduction of infant mortality not as the primary cause but as a secondary factor affecting the extent and pace of the fertility decline. Thus until knowledge and acceptance of fertility limitation practices spread throughout a population, let us say as a result of causes other than changes in infant mortality, fertility would respond to mortality changes at most because of the intervening effects on lactation. As increasing proportions of families controlled fertility, the number of children they desired would be responsive to prevailing norms and social-economic situations. Parents however would adjust their fertility performance to the level of infant mortality

experience and beliefs of their kin and neighbors, that exerts this influence. Thus it seems more credible that they would only replace children that actually die rather than to have replacements on hand in case any die in the future.

they experienced in order to achieve their desired family size. Using this interpretation, it is difficult to specify the direction and extent of the time lag between changes in mortality and fertility.

Up to now we have discussed the influence of mortality on fertility. The inverse relationship is also of interest, i.e. the influence fertility exerts on mortality. There are several reasons to expect a change from high to low fertility to reduce infant mortality, at least to some minor extent. A mother with fewer children should be able to devote more and better care to each. With less children in a family the probability of a child catching a disease from a sibling might be lower. In addition, a mother who bears children with longer intervals between each birth may be physiologically stronger and find it easier to cope with infant care. Several studies have demonstrated empirically that infants born after a relatively short interval experience higher mortality than those born after longer intervals (Woodbury, 1925, pp. 60–67; Gordon and Wyon, 1962, pp. 24–27; Knodel, 1968, pp. 315–316).

It is also possible that there was no direct effect of mortality on fertility during the demographic transition but that the decline in each was due to a set of common influences. It is not difficult to imagine that industrialization, changing standards of living, developing technology, or a host of other factors could have the effect of reducing both fertility and mortality. Under these circumstances it becomes difficult to predict how closely associated we would expect changes in fertility and mortality to be. If the pattern of changes in the relevant associated factors differed from area to area, the observed association between fertility and infant mortality would also differ.

The same social phenomena in different situations do not necessarily have the same causes. Thus with respect to the fertility decline, it may well be the case that in some contexts one of the above relationships with infant mortality holds while in other contexts a different relationship predominates (Müller, 1924, pp. 32–35). In the analysis of German data that follows, this possibility is explored.

In sum, there are a number of possible connections between infant mortality and fertility. They differ to some extent in their implications for the decline of fertility with respect to the magnitude of the effects and the timing of the related changes in both variables. Hence an investigation of the statistical evidence should enable us to eliminate at least a few of the possibilities. Unfortunately the available data are not sufficient to test most of the proposed connections. We hope at least to gain a general impression of the extent of the infant mortality decline and its potential impact on effective family size if not a detailed insight into the mechanisms that operated.

In the following analysis, we will rely almost exclusively on an index of infant mortality (i.e. mortality to infants under one year of age) rather than child mortality (i.e. mortality of children above one) as the measure we relate to fertility. Statistics on infant mortality are far more available than statistics on the mortality of older children. Only in rare instances are life tables giving the proportions surviving to age 5, 10, and 15 available for administrative areas. In contrast, abundant data exist on the number of deaths to infants under one year of age, and they can easily be related to the number of live births.

Our operational definition of infant mortality is the ratio of infant deaths in a given time period to live births in the same period (times 1,000). This measure is less than ideal because deaths of children under one in any calendar year do not occur only to infants born in that same year but also to infants born in the previous year. The inaccuracy introduced is generally very minor, particularly when the rates refer to periods of several years duration and is inconsequential for our study of long term trends.[4]

Trends in Infant Mortality

Uniform statistics on infant deaths for each state were not published by the National Statistical Bureau prior to 1901, and only from 1904 were these data given in enough detail to permit calculation of infant

---

[4]Infant deaths in a given year result not only from births in that year but from births in the preceding year. Likewise children born in a given year who die before reaching age one die not only in their birth year but also in the following year. This causes two related disturbing effects for our index. First, if the number of births fluctuates greatly from year to year, annual infant mortality rates calculated according to the above method would fluctuate as well (in an inverse manner), even though the actual risks of dying before age one might remain constant. Second, if the number of births is increasing from year to year the measure will slightly underestimate the probability of an infant dying. If the births are decreasing the reverse will hold. In most instances the rates used in the subsequent analysis are based on birth and death statistics covering periods of several years which minimizes both of these disturbing effects. In other instances annual rates which had already been computed were averaged over several years which minimizes at least the first effect.

mortality for each administrative area. However, individual state statistical bureaus frequently included some data on infant mortality in their own publications during the latter part of the nineteenth century. A number of states published infant mortality statistics for much of the first half of the century as well. Continuous data for the older Prussian provinces, for example, are available from 1816 to 1866. In addition several comprehensive articles on infant mortality provide useful data for periods prior to 1900 (Würzburg, 1887 and 1888; Prinzing, 1899 and 1900). From a combination of these sources it was possible to reconstruct a series of infant mortality rates for most administrative areas, usually covering five-year periods from the 1860s to the 1930s. The National Statistical Bureau reconstructed infant mortality rates back to 1872 on the national level. Table 4.1 presents the series for Germany and Table 4.2 shows the life table

TABLE 4.1

INFANT MORTALITY RATE: 1872 TO 1940

Date	Average rate	Date	Average rate
1872-1875	244	1906-1910	174
1876-1880	227	1911-1915	160
1881-1885	226	1916-1920	145
1886-1890	224	1921-1925	120
1891-1895	221	1926-1930	94
1896-1900	213	1931-1935	75
1901-1905	199	1936-1940	63

SOURCE: Based on rates reconstructed by the National Statistical Bureau, Germany.

NOTE: The infant mortality rate refers to the number of infant (under one year of age) deaths per 1,000 live births.

values indicating the probability of dying between exact ages 0 and 1 and exact ages 1 and 15. Only a very gradual decline in infant mortality is evident during most of the later decades of the nineteenth century. In sharp contrast, a steady sharp reduction proceeds after the turn of the century. A similar course is evident in the mortality at older childhood ages.

[156]

TABLE 4.2

PROBABILITIES OF DEATH IN INFANCY AND CHILDHOOD, BY SEX: 1871 TO 1934

| | Probability of death between specified ages | | | | | |
| | Male | | | Female | | |
Date	0-1	1-15	0-15	0-1	1-15	0-15
1871-1880	.253	.185	.391	.217	.184	.361
1881-1890	.242	.177	.376	.207	.178	.347
1891-1900	.234	.133	.335	.199	.132	.304
1901-1910	.202	.097	.280	.170	.097	.251
1910-1911	.181	.082	.248	.153	.080	.221
1924-1926	.115	.045	.155	.094	.041	.131
1932-1934	.085	.035	.118	.068	.031	.097

A table with the infant mortality rates for each of the administrative areas of Germany between the 1860s and the 1930s is presented in Appendix Table 4.1. The decline of infant mortality shows a monotonicity similar to that characteristic of the fertility decline. In almost every administrative area, once the rate of infant deaths declined by any moderate amount from its maximum, the decline (as portrayed by averages computed over several years) continued uninterrupted to the 1930s. In the few areas where this was not strictly the case, the interruption was always of minor proportions.

The pattern of the infant mortality decline experienced in an individual administrative area apparently depended on the level of infant mortality at the beginning of an observation period. Several examples of typical patterns are shown in Figure 4.1. In areas where infant mortality was particularly high during the 1860s and 1870s, a constant decline is apparent from the very first observations, and by the turn of the century infant mortality was typically 30–40 percent below its maximum. In contrast, areas that were experiencing exceptionally low infant mortality in the 1860s and 1870s show little tendency to decline until much later. Typically the rate of infant deaths would fluctuate within a narrow range until the first decade of this century and then join a general trend toward decline. Areas with intermediate levels of infant mortality during the initial period showed at most a moderate trend towards decline prior to 1900. In some cases a slight

[157]

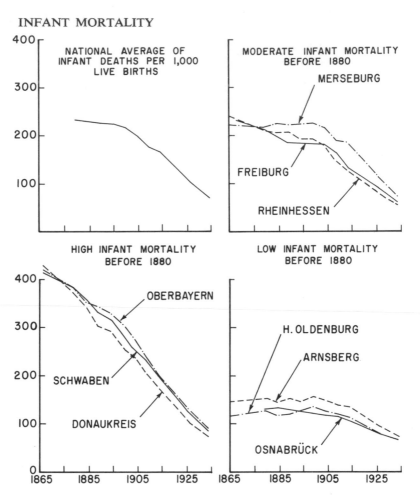

Figure 4.1. Infant Mortality Rate, Selected Administrative Areas and Germany: 1862 to 1934

tendency to rise is observed. But after 1900 a relatively precipitous decline occured for most areas in this category as well. The national trend of a slow decline prior to the turn of the century and a sharper decline thereafter results from the combination of these quite different patterns.

An examination of the relationship between the infant mortality and fertility decline must give particular attention to the timing of the declines, especially with respect to their onset. In order to date the beginning of the mortality decline we will use the data presented in the

Appendix Table 4.1. First, however, we must direct our attention to the possibility that the decline began prior to the 1860s, since our series begins only then. Areas where the observations in the Appendix show a continuous infant mortality decline from the 1860s or where the earliest observations indicate low although not declining levels of infant mortality merit particular attention. In the first case we may have caught infant mortality mid-course in its decline; in the second case a substantial decline may have taken place prior to 1860.

Data on infant mortality for Prussia is available from 1816. As Table 4.3 indicates, in Prussia as a whole the number of infant deaths

TABLE 4.3

INFANT MORTALITY RATE, PRUSSIA: 1816 TO 1885

Date	Average rate	Date	Average rate
1816-1820	168	1861-1865	208
1821-1830	174	1866-1870	214
1831-1840	183	1871-1875	224
1841-1850	185	1876-1880	205
1851-1860	197	1881-1885	207

per 1,000 live births actually shows a slow and rather steady increase lasting for more than half a century. Infant mortality in the individual provinces and administrative areas follows a similar pattern. Prinzing (1899, p. 587) compares rates averaged over fifteen-year periods between 1819 and 1863 with infant mortality during 1864–1870 in the individual Prussian provinces. In almost every province infant mortality rose steadily, and in no province was infant mortality higher in any prior period than it was during 1864–1870. This is true both for provinces with particularly low infant mortality in the 1860s and 1870s and those which showed a steady tendency to decline thereafter.

It is difficult to determine the extent to which the increases indicated in infant mortality are genuine. Von Fircks (1879, p. 87) assumed that the rates prior to 1866 were underestimated. He suspected that the church officials, who submitted the basic tabulations from the church registers, frequently classified only deaths of children who were born and died in the same calendar year as infant deaths rather than including all deaths to infants under one year of age. Prinzing (1899, pp. 585–587) argues that some omission may well have occurred prior to 1866 but doubts that it would have affected the trend. He points to the similar trends in infant mortality found in each of the separate provinces and argues that it is unlikely that the patterns of decreasing omissions would have coincided so closely. He attributes the increase prior to 1870 instead to the unfortunate situation of the working classes and indifference of the officials towards the situation. In contrast he cites public health measures in combination with an improved economic situation for workers and social legislation as the causes for the decline after 1875.

Without attempting to settle the question regarding the accuracy of the rates, it can at least be stated that the available evidence contains no indication that infant mortality declined during the half century prior to 1870 in Prussia. Inclusion of unadjusted infant mortality rates for years earlier than 1862–1866 would not affect calculations of the date at which the infant mortality decline began in the Prussian administrative areas.

In southern Germany, where infant mortality declined continuously from the 1860s, the evidence also indicates that a decline was not taking place during the preceding decades. Prinzing (1900, pp. 600–610) also reported on infant mortality in the South German states. In all eight Bavarian administrative areas, infant mortality was higher in 1862–1868 than in the previous decades, at least when compared to rates averaged over periods five or six years each from 1835 on. Of the four administrative areas in Württemberg between 1812 and 1868, only Donaukreis registered a slight decrease in the infant mortality rate prior to 1862–1868. In Baden, where the series extended back only to 1852, infant mortality showed an increase between 1852–1863 and 1864–1870.

In the remaining German states for which some data are available for the years prior to 1860, there is again no evidence of declining infant mortality to be found. In the administrative areas of Oldenburg and Birkenfeld where infant mortality was very low in the 1860s, it was just as low a decade earlier. No decline was evident in Bremen between 1826 and 1875, in Lübeck between 1846 and 1865, or Saxony between 1832 and 1875.

In sum, there is no evidence that infant mortality had been declining in Germany during the decades prior to the 1860s. Of course it is possible that infant mortality fluctuated within broad limits or declined from significantly higher levels during the seventeenth and eighteenth centuries or even during the first couple of decades in the nineteenth century. For example, Knapp (1874) found considerably higher infant mortality in the city of Leipzig between 1751 and 1820 than between 1821 and 1860. The important point for the study of the decline in fertility, however, is that the steady decline in infant mortality which resulted in the low levels that prevailed by the 1930s began in the 1860s or later from a plateau or a temporary maximum. It is true that infant mortality may have declined in the seventeenth and eighteenth centuries and may even have influenced fertility at that time; but it seems reasonable to assume that any decline so long in the past could not have been a dynamic factor in the modern fertility decline. None of the propositions we explored relating mortality and fertility posited a time lag between the decline in mortality and its effect on fertility to take as long as two or three generations.

Two methods were used to estimate the date at which infant mortality began to decline in each administrative area. Both utilize the series of rates in Appendix Table 4.1. The first method estimates the date of decline as the year in which infant mortality attained a sustained reduction of ten percent from its maximum value. The second dates the decline by determining the year in which a sustained decline of 50 points (i.e. by 50 infant deaths per 1,000 live births) from the maximum occurred. In both methods the dates were determined by linear interpolation between the mid years of the periods for which we have observations.[5]

[5] It should be noted that no infant mortality rates for the period 1867–1874 are included in the series of rates used for the dating of the infant mortality decline. Prussia did not publish data on the number of infant deaths for those years, so to increase comparability, infant mortality rates for 1867–1874 were excluded for all administrative areas. Estimates of infant mortality during 1871–1875 made by Prinzing (1899, p. 587) indicate that Prussian provinces experienced their maximum infant mortality during those years. Thus the

The date of a 10 percent reduction catches the very beginning of the decline. Fluctuations of somewhat less than 10 percent are common prior to any sustained fall. But once infant mortality is reduced to a level of 90 percent of its maximum value, the subsequent course is usually one of continuous decline to much lower levels. In the event infant mortality subsequently rose above the 90 percent benchmark the decline is dated according to the last time infant mortality fell below the 90 percent level. If the hypothesis is correct that a decline in infant mortality reduces fertility by reducing the number of births required to attain a given family size, we might expect that a 10 percent reduction in infant mortality, especially where infant mortality is characteristically low, would be so small that it is unlikely to have any observable effect on fertility. Therefore we also include in our analysis the second set of dates based on a reduction by an absolute amount of 50 points. Since in no administrative area was the maximum number of infant deaths per 1,000 births ever as high as 500 during the period under consideration, the date of a 50 point decline is always later than the date of a 10 percent decline.

Both types of dates for the decline in infant mortality should be considered only as rough indicators. Although they should not be interpreted literally, they do convey a general impression of when the shift to lower infant mortality levels took place and permit a crude comparison to be made among the administrative areas. For Germany as a whole, our calculations indicate that infant mortality did not decline by 10 percent until the turn of the century (1901) and was not reduced by 50 points until several years later (1907). However, as will be indicated in more detail in the following section, there was considerable variation in the timing of the infant mortality decline among the various administrative areas. Some experienced a 10 percent de-

---

dates of decline are somewhat distorted by this omission. In most cases the distortion appears to be insignificant. Another distrubing influence in the calculation of the date of decline results from the non-availability of data for several areas for some periods. For example, no infant mortality rates are available for 1862–1866 for most of the administrative areas acquired by Prussia in 1866. In several areas wide gaps exist in the series of rates between 1880 and 1900. Fortunately most areas with incomplete data showed relatively low infant mortality rates in 1875–1880 and do not appear to be the type which experienced a sharp decline in infant mortality during the end of the 19th century.

cline as early as the 1870s, whereas in others an equivalent reduction was not evident until after 1910.

Territorial and Regional Variation

Considerable territorial variability in infant mortality levels was present in Germany during the time of the fertility decline. Table 4.4,

TABLE 4.4

INFANT MORTALITY RATE, VARIABILITY
AMONG ADMINISTRATIVE AREAS: 1875 TO 1934

Measure	Date	Unweighted mean	Extreme values			Standard deviation	Coeff. of var.	N
			High	Low	Range			
Level of infant mortality	1875-1880	213.9	383	114	269	65.0	.303	71
	1901-1905	187.8	308	94	214	46.3	.246	71
	1911-1914	154.9	265	72	193	37.3	.240	71
	1924-1926	100.8	205	60	145	26.2	.259	66
	1932-1934	70.2	137	45	92	15.8	.225	66
Date of decline	By 10%	1895	1916	1872	44	13.2	--	71
	By 50 points	1907	1930	1876	54	14.5	--	71
Magnitude of decline	From maximum to 1932-1934							
	Absolute	72.7	357	60	297	160.5	--	64
	Percent	67.3	85	51	34	9.5	--	64

NOTE: Boundaries for data under magnitude of decline do not include areas lost after World War I.

which is based on the infant mortality rates for each administrative area (given in Appendix Table 4.1) and the date and magnitude of the decline derived from them, presents several measures of variability for selected infant mortality measures. Both the range and standard deviation of infant mortality levels decline substantially as the levels themselves fall. Even the coefficient of variability exhibits a declining trend as uniformly low levels of infant mortality spread throughout Germany. In fact, if we would include comparable statistics based on the infant mortality rates of the 39 administrative areas in West Germany for 1961, we would find that infant mortality was greatly reduced from the pre-war levels and that regional variation all but disappeared. The highest rate of infant mortality in 1961 was 42, which was below the lowest level in 1932. The range, standard deviation, and coefficient of variation were reduced to 18, 4.2, and .127 respectively.

Substantial variation is also evident in the two measures of the date of the decline in infant mortality and the magnitude of the decline (as measured by the absolute and percent changes in the rates between their maximum predecline values and the 1932–1934 level). Since the main usefulness of the coefficient of variation is to depict trends in the variation of the same index over time, it is not presented for the indices of the timing and magnitude of the infant mortality decline.

The territorial distribution of infant mortality in Germany during the later half of the 1870s is shown by Map 4.1. A diagonal drawn

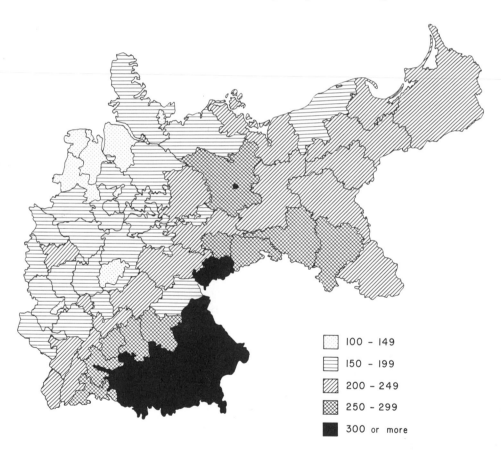

	100 - 149
	150 - 199
	200 - 249
	250 - 299
	300 or more

Map 4.1. Infant Mortality Rate, by Administrative Area: 1875–1880

from the southwest corner to the northeast corner rather effectively divides areas of low or moderate infant mortality from areas of higher levels. Areas falling along the diagonal occupy an intermediate position. Particularly striking are the high mortality rates experienced in Southern Germany. In part, the high rates of the South can be attributed to economic backwardness of the areas, but probably most important were the particular habits of child feeding prevalent in the region (Prinzing, 1899, pp. 597–599). The peculiar custom of early weaning or not breast feeding a child at all was widespread in Southern Germany as well as parts of Saxony, Bohemia, and neighboring areas of Austria (Knodel and van de Walle, 1967). There is abundant evidence connecting early weaning or the lack of breast feeding with high infant mortality during the latter part of the nineteenth century and the early twentieth century. For example, the proportion of mothers in 103 Bavarian districts who reported in a survey in 1904–1906 that they breast-fed their children is correlated −.81 with infant mortality for 1869–1878 in the districts (Knodel and van de Walle, 1967, p. 123). The particularly low infant mortality in the northwest is in sharp contrast to the southern areas.

Changes in the relative position with respect to infant mortality among the administrative areas in Germany occurred slowly. Thus the average correlation between infant mortality rates for any two successive five-year periods is in the order of .96 to .99. However, the greater the time separating two periods the greater the divergence in the relative order of infant mortality rates by administrative area. For example, the correlation between infant mortality in 1875–1880 and 1901–1906 is .80 but only .44 between 1875–1880 and 1932–1933.

The territorial pattern showing the year in which infant mortality fell ten percent below its maximum is presented in Map 4.2. The distribution on the map bears a resemblance to the distribution of infant mortality rates for 1875–1880 giving the general impression that areas with higher infant mortality began their descent to more modern lower levels sooner than areas where infant mortality was more moderate prior to the decline. The degree of association can be summarized by the correlation coefficient (−.51) that holds between the maximum predecline value of infant mortality in an area and the date of a ten

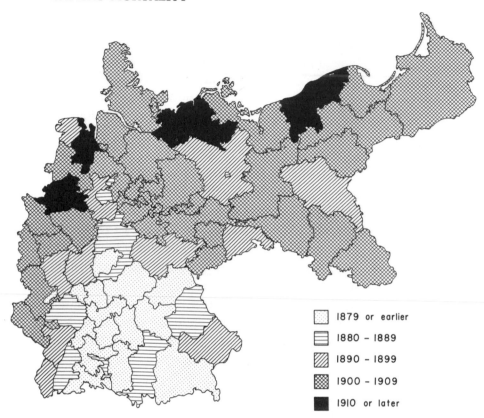

	1879 or earlier
	1880 – 1889
	1890 – 1899
	1900 – 1909
	1910 or later

Map 4.2. Infant Mortality Rate, Date of 10% Decline, by Administrative Area

percent decline. An even higher correlation ($-.83$) exists between the maximum predecline infant mortality and the year the infant mortality index sustained a decline of 50 points.

Clearly the level of infant mortality (at least in 1875–1880) and the date of its decline are not randomly distributed on the maps. The question arises as to what extent these variables exhibit an areal pattern which conforms to the regional classification set forth in Chapter 1. We will again utilize the analysis of variance to estimate the extent of regional association in infant mortality and its decline. The F-ratio compares the variation within each region at the administrative area level with the variation between regions. More exactly, the F-statistic represents the ratio of the mean square variance "within" each region with the mean square variance "between" regions. *F*-ratios substantially above one indicate a distinct regional association in the variable being tested. The strength of the association is indicated by the statistic ϵ. The results of the regional analysis of selected measures of infant mortality are summarized in Table 4.5. All the *F*-ratios indicate a

TABLE 4.5

INFANT MORTALITY RATE, ANALYSIS OF VARIANCE BETWEEN
ADMINISTRATIVE AREAS AND GEOGRAPHICAL REGIONS

Measure	Date	F ratio (df. = 6,64)	Unbiased correlation ratio (ϵ)
Level of infant mortality	1875-1880	13.6	.79
	1901-1905	12.9	.71
	1911-1914	11.4	.69
	1932-1934	4.6	.50
Date of decline	By 10%	15.4	.74
	By 50 points	15.1	.74

significance level of .001 or better. The degree of association between an administrative area's level of infant mortality and the region to which it belongs declined considerably after World War I, when infant mortality became uniformly lower throughout Germany. The date at which infant mortality declines shows strong regional association, whether measured in terms of a 10 percent reduction or a 50 point decline. Clearly these strong regional associations need to be considered in the analysis of the relationship between infant mortality and the fertility decline.

Infant Mortality Differentials

(a) *Legitimacy.* The mortality of infants born out of wedlock was higher than mortality of legitimate infants throughout Germany. In 1875–1880, the average illegitimate infant mortality was 62 percent higher than the legitimate rate among the 64 administrative areas for which rates by legitimacy were available. In 1906–1910, the comparable difference was 72 percent for the 58 areas with available data.

Thus the differences are substantial. Since we are concentrating in this study on the decline of *marital* fertility, it would seem preferable to employ rates of legitimate infant mortality in the anlaysis. However not all states cross-classified infant mortality by legitimacy, and thus the series of legitimate rates is less complete than those for total rates. In addition, there is an extremely high correlation between the levels of legitimate and total infant mortality in administrative areas. For example, total and legitimate infant mortality correlated .996 ($N = 64$) with each other in 1875–1880 and .995 ($N = 58$) in 1906–1910. Legitimate and illegitimate infant mortality also correlate with each other (.73 in 1875–1880 and .62 in 1906–1910) although the strength of the relationship is considerably weaker.

(b) *Rural-urban residence*. Distinct differences in the patterns of infant mortality levels and trends existed between rural and urban populations in Germany. Generally mortality risks for infants were higher in the cities than in the countryside prior to the secular decline in mortality. Decreases occurred sooner and initially at a faster pace in the cities, so that after several decades of decline the differentials reversed in many areas. In 1875–1877, for example, the rural population experienced higher infant mortality than the urban in only 8 (11 percent) of the 71 administrative areas or states for which Würzburg (1887 and 1888) presents relevant data. Rural-urban rates of infant mortality are not readily available for many states for later years although both Prussia and Bavaria provide rather complete records. In Prussia during 1875–1877 only one of 33 administrative areas experienced higher infant mortality in the rural than urban populations. By 1910 the number had risen to 16. Among the 8 administrative areas in Bavaria those with higher rural infant mortality increased from 3 during 1875–1877 to 6 in 1908–1912.

Rural and urban infant mortality rates for the Prussian and Bavarian administrative areas are presented in Appendix Tables 4.2 and 4.3. The rural and urban rates for both the Prussian and Bavarian states are summarized in Table 4.6, which also includes a calculation of the year in which infant mortality in each category achieved a 10 percent and a 50 point decline. In both states infant mortality was highest in the capital cities and lowest in the countryside at the beginning of the

TABLE 4.6

INFANT MORTALITY RATE, URBAN/RURAL,
PRUSSIA AND BAVARIA: 1862 TO 1937

| Measure | Date | Prussia | | | Bavaria | | |
		Berlin	All cities	Rural	Munich	All cities	Rural
Level of infant mortality	1862-1870	297	241	208	398	355	340
	1871-1875	--	--	--	404[a]	353	335
	1876-1877	308	233	193	--	328	317
	1878-1882	290	228	193	359	313	307
	1883-1887	276	232	198	331	300	304
	1888-1892	251	222	196	311	280	292
	1893-1897	229	214	195	290	253	264
	1898-1902	214	206	190	267	244	255
	1903-1907	194	191	184	219	222	240
	1908-1912	159	162	168	173	185	215
	1923-1927	90	101	107	111	112	148
	1928-1932	75	88	86	81	85	118
	1933-1937	--	--	--	71	69	91
Date of decline	By 10%	1885	1893	1902	1879	1878	1881
	By 50 points	1889	1905	1912	1881	1883	1890

NOTES: Prussian figures dated 1862-1870 are for years 1865-1866 and exclude
         provinces acquired in 1866-1867.
        Prussian figures dated 1876-1877 are for years 1875-1877; those dated
         1903-1907 are for years 1904-1906; and those dated 1923-1927 are for
         years 1924-1926.
        Bavarian data through 1892 do not include 37 Pfalz.

[a]1871-1874.

observation period. Earlier and steeper declines in the cities reversed
the differentials shortly after the turn of the century. The decline in
the rural rates proceeded swiftly during the next several decades. By
the 1930s both urban and rural rates were much lower and the differentials were no longer consistently in one direction.

The date of the onset of the infant mortality decline and the level
from which it started are presented for the rural and urban portions of
each administrative area in Prussia and Bavaria in Table 4.7. The
figures for the Prussian and Bavarian areas are not strictly comparable
since the series of rates on which the Prussian figures are based do not
extend back as far as the Bavarian series. In Prussia, the maximum
level of infant mortality experienced prior to its systematic decline was
higher in the urban than the rural portion of every administrative area

[169]

TABLE 4.7

INFANT MORTALITY RATE, MAXIMUM RECORDED AND DATE OF DECLINE,
URBAN/RURAL, BY ADMINISTRATIVE AREA, PRUSSIA AND BAVARIA

| | Maximum level | | Date of decline | | | |
| | | | By 10% | | By 50 points | |
Prussia	Urban	Rural	Urban	Rural	Urban	Rural
01 Ostpreussen	259	215	1897	1909	1903	1916
02 Danzig	281	236	1900	1909	1904	1915
03 Marienwerder	244	227	1906	1910	1911	1917
05 Potsdam	276	261	1897	1902	1904	1906
06 Frankfurt/O.	255	226	1903	1909	1908	1914
07 Stettin-Str.	276	235	1904	1910	1908	1915
08 Köslin	219	162	1906	1913	1913	1922
09 Posen	243	214	1899	1898	1907	1912
10 Bromberg	236	219	1908	1911	1913	1916
11 Breslau	305	278	1892	1908	1900	1911
12 Liegnitz	333	278	1889	1904	1893	1908
13 Oppeln	227	216	1898	1909	1911	1920
14 Magdeburg	247	220	1907	1908	1912	1914
15 Merseburg	226	221	1908	1908	1913	1914
16 Erfurt	195	185	1906	1906	1813	1914
17 Schleswig	193	144	1905	1911	1913	1921
18 Hannover	191	156	1905	1909	1909	1920
19 Hildesheim	175	160	1900	1905	1910	1916
20 Lüneburg	195	145	1904	1909	1911	1920
21 Stade	158	136	1908	1909	1919	1922
22 Osnabrück	157	125	1889	1906	1913	1925
23 Aurich	152	106	1890	1892	1912	1934[a]
24 Münster	187	163	1907	1910	1914	1919
25 Minden	171	152	1879	1891	1908	1916
26 Arnsberg	167	151	1907	1907	1919	1920
27 Kassel	177	167	1885	1884	1905	1902
28 Wiesbaden	174	163	1893	1880	1909	1906
29 Koblenz	197	177	1891	1893	1904	1908
30 Düsseldorf	178	173	1906	1908	1914	1916
31 Köln	242	205	1902	1906	1907	1912
32 Trier	170	157	1908	1909	1919	1925
33 Aachen	236	200	1900	1908	1907	1915
34 Sigmaringen	314	334	1880	1880	1881	1883
Bavaria						
35 Oberbayern	408	421	1878	1879	1881	1881
36 Niederbayern	390	360	1876	1895	1886	1904
37 Pfalz	201	171	--	--	--	--
38 Oberpfalz	357	353	1900	1891	1903	1895
39 Oberfranken	224	221	1880	1877	1902	1903
40 Mittelfranken	319	336	1875	1876	1886	1886
41 Unterfranken	259	251	1876	1875	1880	1879
42 Schwaben	449	408	1877	1881	1878	1883

SOURCE: Based on Appendix Tables 4.2 and 4.3.

[a]By extrapolation.

except one. In only three areas was the date of a 10 percent decline earlier in the rural than in the urban population. In just two areas did the rural portions exhibit a 50 point drop earlier than the urban section. To a lesser extent the same general pattern of higher urban predecline levels of infant mortality and earlier urban dates of decline is observed in Bavaria.

There is a strong association within Prussia both between rural and urban levels of infant mortality and between the dates at which rural and urban mortality declined. The correlation coefficients between the rural and urban level of infant mortality in 1875–1877, 1898–1902, and 1930–1932 in Prussia using each administrative area as a unit of observation are .92, .86, and .76 respectively. The correlations in Prussia between the rural and urban date of the infant mortality decline are .77 for the date of a 10 percent decline and .80 for the date of a 50 point decline. The association in Bavaria between rural and urban levels of infant mortality is also very strong although the association between the dates of decline is considerably weaker.

(c) *Religion, ethnic composition, and wealth.* In the previous chapter we examined social differentials in the level and decline of fertility according to several variables besides rural-urban residence. It will be interesting to see if there are similar differentials in infant mortality. Perhaps we can account for the fertility differentials in this way. Unfortunately, there is not a great deal of information readily available concerning social differentials (other than rural-urban residence) in infant mortality and we will have to rely on indirect estimates.

Direct data on infant death by the religious affiliation of the parents are rarely if ever available in the official statistical publications. Some idea of the difference between Catholic and Protestant infant mortality can be indirectly derived from a comparison of administrative areas that are almost entirely Catholic or almost completely Protestant. Table 4.8 presents the average infant mortality rates of groups of administrative areas categorized according to their religious composition. The almost purely Catholic areas were characterized by higher infant mortality than their Protestant counterparts both with respect to the maximum predecline level experienced and the level in 1906–1910. However the overall relationship between religious composition

[171]

TABLE 4.8

INFANT MORTALITY RATE, MAXIMUM RECORDED AND MAGNITUDE
OF DECLINE, BY PERCENTAGE CATHOLIC
(unweighted averages)

Percentage Catholic in administrative area (1880)	Level of infant mortality		Magnitude of decline		N
	Maximum	1906-1910	Absolute	Percent	
90 or more	312	210	102	33	7
60-89	247	170	77	31	12
40-59	223	173	50	22	12
10-39	219	149	70	32	13
9 or less	210	158	52	25	27

and infant mortality is not particularly strong as indicated by the correlation between percent Catholic in 1880 and maximum infant mortality ($r = .34$) or the infant mortality in 1906–1910 ($r = .32$). The larger decline in marital fertility before 1910 in the Protestant areas, which was indicated in the previous chapter (Table 3.16) is clearly not accounted for by religious differentials in the decline of infant mortality. The predominantly Protestant areas experienced less of a decline in infant mortality by 1906–1910 than did the largely Catholic areas, which is in the reverse direction from the one expected.

Ethnic differences in infant mortality can be indirectly estimated in the same way as ethnic fertility differentials were. Again we will focus our attention on the differences between the predominantly Polish and predominantly German districts (*Kreise*) in the six easternmost administrative areas of Prussia. Table 4.9 relates to the ethnic composition of the districts in the same manner as was done with fertility in Table 3.22. There is little difference in the infant mortality of the predominantly Polish districts in 1880–1881 and the purely Germanic districts. By 1910 infant mortality had fallen more in the Polish districts than in the Germanic ones and thus some difference in levels is apparent. If we compare the ethnic differences in fertility indicated in the previous chapter (Table 3.22) with the corresponding differences in infant mortality, it appears that infant mortality has no ability to

[172]

TABLE 4.9

INFANT MORTALITY RATE, BY PERCENTAGE OF POLISH ORIGIN,
DISTRICTS (KREISE) OF EASTERN REGION: 1880 TO 1911
(unweighted averages)

Percentage Polish in district (Kreis)	Level of infant mortality		Magnitude of decline	
	1880-1881	1909-1911	Absolute	Percent
75 or more	248	173	75	30
55-74	251	188	63	25
45-54	239	186	53	22
25-44	256	202	54	21
5-24	238	204	34	14
4 or less	246	202	44	18

NOTE: Population of Polish origin is defined as those speaking Polish, Masurish, or Kassubish as a native language.

account for ethnic fertility differentials, at least in the way in which they have been indirectly estimated in our analysis. Indeed if we limit ourselves to a comparison between districts with over 75 percent Polish and with under 5 percent Polish the difference in infant mortality is in the reverse direction as fertility in 1909–1911. With respect to the declines in both variables between 1880 and 1910, the predominantly Polish districts show a lesser decline in the crude birth rate but a greater decline in infant mortality.

Similarly, there is apparently no direct connection between infant mortality and the difference in the fertility behavior of the Danish districts of Schleswig in comparison to the remainder of the administrative area. Between 1875 and 1909–1911 the Danish districts experienced a greater decline in infant mortality even though the crude birth rate actually registered a rise. In the entire area of Schleswig, infant mortality declined less whereas the crude birth fell substantially (see Table 3.23 in the previous chapter).

The studies relating birth rates or other fertility measures in different sections of cities to the indices of wealth, such as average rent, rarely provided information on infant mortality. Hence it is difficult to describe differentials in infant mortality by wealth comparable to the differences described in fertility. An exception was the study done by

[173]

May (1916) on Hamburg. He found that both in the late 1890s and in 1911–1913 infant mortality was lowest in the affluent city districts, highest in the poorest districts, and intermediate in the middle-income districts, thus conforming to the fertility differentials he found. Between these two periods both the crude birth rate and infant mortality declined. However the decline in infant mortality was greatest in the poorest sections and least in the wealthiest sections whereas the decline of the birth rate was greatest in the middle income districts and least in the wealthiest. Thus there was not a perfect correspondence in the declines of both rates.

Infant Mortality and Fertility

(a) *Levels.* As an initial step in analyzing the relationship between infant mortality and fertility, the level of infant mortality was correlated with the level of the overall, marital, and illegitimate fertility (I_f, I_g, I_h) for different periods during the fertility decline. The results are offered in Table 4.10. For each set of correlations the infant mortality index refers to a period about two years prior to the period of

TABLE 4.10

INFANT MORTALITY RATE, CORRELATIONS WITH
FERTILITY INDICES: 1862 TO 1934

Registration period		Correlation coefficients between infant mortality rate and			
Infant mortality rate	Fertility indices	Overall fertility (I_f)	Marital fertility (I_g)	Illegitimate fertility (I_h)	N
1862–1866	1866–1868	.283	.405	.788	43
1862–1866	1869–1873	.425	.484	.715	54
1875–1880	1878–1882	.496	.406	.681	71
1881–1885	1883–1887	.376	.285	.716	63
1886–1890	1888–1892	.281	.234	.725	65
1896–1900	1898–1902	.257	.204	.727	65
1906–1910	1908–1912	.265	.264	.641	71
1924–1926	1923–1927	.453	.345	.655	66
1932–1934	1931–1935	.591	.474	.624	66

the fertility indices with which it is paired. Since the number of areas for which infant mortality data was available was not the same each year, the correlations for several periods are not based on the full complement of German administrative areas. If couples purposely adjusted their fertility to the level of infant mortality, we would expect that, as the fertility decline progressed and more couples were adopting practices of fertility control, the correlation between infant mortality and marital fertility would increase. As infant mortality reached low levels everywhere we might expect the correlation to disappear as small absolute differences in infant and child mortality would no longer create much difference between the number of births and the number of children who survived to maturity. Such results, however, are not evident. In fact the course of the correlation seems to follow the opposite path, becoming weaker during the initial stages of the fertility and mortality declines and becoming stronger as the declines reached their lowest levels. It is interesting that the strongest correlations are found between infant mortality and illegitimate fertility. It seems unlikely that these variables are directly connected; more probably, they are related to some other common factors. Perhaps the prevalence of illegitimacy and infant mortality reflect social disorganization, poverty, etc. In the absence of further analysis, however, we can only offer speculations.

It is logically preferable, of course, to correlate legitimate infant mortality with marital fertility and illegitimate infant mortality with illegitimate fertility. As explained earlier, statistical series of infant mortality by legitimacy are incomplete for many German administrative areas and thus in Table 4.10 overall infant mortality was related with the three measures of fertility. Nevertheless infant mortality indices by legitimacy were available for most administrative areas for 1875–1877 or 1875–1880. Table 4.11 presents the correlations between these indices and the fertility measures by legitimacy for 1878–1882. In addition, the comparable correlations for infant mortality 1906–1910 and fertility 1908–1912 are also given, although the data were available for fewer areas. The correlation coefficients between total infant mortality and the fertility indices do not agree exactly with those presented in the previous table since the several administra-

TABLE 4.11

INFANT MORTALITY RATES, LEGITIMATE AND ILLEGITIMATE, CORRELATIONS
WITH FERTILITY INDICES: 1875-1880 AND 1906-1910

	Registration period		Correlation coefficients between infant mortality rate and			
Measure	Infant mortality rate	Fertility indices	Overall fertility (I_f)	Marital fertility (I_g)	Illegitimate fertility (I_h)	N
Total infant mortality	1875-1880[a]	1878-1882	.50	.40	.70	64
Legitimate			.52	.44	.66	64
Illegitimate			.37	.34	.47	64
Total infant mortality	1906-1910	1908-1912	.23	.25	.65	58
Legitimate			.27	.30	.60	58
Illegitimate			.47	.40	.28	58

[a]In some cases 1875-1877 or 1876-1877.

tive areas that lacked infant mortality data by legitimacy are excluded in the present correlations. As expected, marital fertility is more closely associated with legitimate than total infant mortality. The difference in results is not great, however, and it appears that the inaccuracy introduced by using total infant mortality in our analysis of marital fertility is not serious. Also, illegitimate fertility during both periods is correlated more closely with legitimate infant mortality than is legitimate fertility. In addition, it is interesting to note that I_h no longer bears such a strong association to mortality when only illegitimate infant deaths are considered. This lends some support to the suggestion that illegitimacy and general infant mortality are not directly related but instead reflect common social and economic conditions.

We found previously that both infant mortality and fertility were subject to strong regional influences. The amount of variance for each variable within the seven regional groups of German administrative areas was small in comparison to the variance between these regions. This suggests that there might be a common regional influence exerted on both infant mortality and fertility that affects their relationship. An analysis of covariance permits us to see if there is a partial association between infant mortality and fertility when differences in the regional averages of the seven regions of Germany specified in Chapter 1 are taken into account. As in the analysis of covariance described in the previous chapter, we will correlate the deviations of variables from their regional means rather than the absolute values of the variables. The result is the average "within region" correlations. Actually the initially low correlations between the levels of infant mortality and marital fertility do not appear to be greatly affected by regional influences. For example, the "within region" correlation between infant mortality in 1875–1880 and I_g 1878–1882 is .42 versus the overall correlation .41; for infant mortality 1906–1910 and I_g 1908–1912 the "within region" correlation is .26 and thus identical with the correlation between the unadjusted values; and for infant mortality in 1932–1934 and I_g 1931–1935 the "within region" correlation was .42 versus .47 for the overall relationship.

We also observed in our survey of infant mortality trends and differentials that a distinct pattern of rural and urban differences existed. In order to test if differences in the relationship between levels of fertility and infant mortality existed between rural and urban populations, data from Prussia have been analyzed. Before we examine the results, it should be pointed out that among the 34 administrative areas of Prussia there was very little association between marital fertility and infant mortality when rural and urban populations were not considered separately. For example, the coefficient of correlation between infant mortality in 1875–1880 and I_g in 1878–1882 is −.04. The corresponding correlation between infant mortality in 1896–1900 and I_g 1898–1902 was zero. The correlations between infant mortality and I_g are given separately for the rural and the urban populations of Prussian administrative areas in Table 4.12. Considering the negligible overall correlation among the Prussian administrative areas, it is not surprising to find weak correlations between I_g and infant mortality in both the rural and the urban sectors. For most of the period under consideration there is a weak inverse association for the urban areas and a weak positive association for the rural areas.

Contrary to the hypothesis that high fertility is associated with high infant mortality, rural areas usually had lower infant mortality at the end of the nineteenth century but at the same time generally experienced higher marital fertility. Nevertheless it is still possible that rural-urban differentials in one of the variables influenced the differentials in

TABLE 4.12

INFANT MORTALITY RATE, CORRELATION WITH MARITAL
FERTILITY (I_g), URBAN/RURAL, PRUSSIA: 1875 TO 1912

Registration period		Correlation coefficients					
Infant mortality	Marital fertility (I_g)	Urban	N	Rural	N	Urban/Rural difference	N
1875-1877	1880-1881	-.221	31	.053	30	.159	30
1878-1882	1880-1881	-.199	31	.076	30	.142	30
1888-1892	1890-1891	-.070	34	.103	33	.376	33
1893-1897	1895-1896	-.069	34	.083	33	.471	33
1898-1902	1900-1901	-.064	34	.046	33	.417	33
1904-1906	1905-1906	-.075	34	.044	33	.306	33
1908-1912	1910-1911	.096	34	.177	33	.360	33

the other variable in a way that conforms to the hypotheses linking higher fertility with higher infant mortality. In other words, in areas where rural infant mortality was particularly lower than the urban level, the rural-urban differential in fertility might be diminished or even inverse. Conversely, in areas where rural infant mortality is higher than urban infant mortality the differences in rural-urban fertility might be accentuated. If this were the case, we would expect a positive correlation between rural-urban differences in infant mortality and fertility. Table 4.12 also reports the results of these correlations which are positive but not very strong.

(b) *Timing and change.* Although an analysis of the levels of infant mortality and fertility is interesting in itself, it is not appropriate for studying the connection between the mortality and fertility declines. To do this we must concentrate on analyzing the association between changes and the timing of such changes in both of the variables. If a reduction in infant mortality causes the onset of the fertility decline, we must demonstrate that infant mortality began to decline earlier. We have already calculated several dates signifying the onset of both the fertility and mortality decline. The question now arises as to which dates are appropriate for comparison. The most common hypothesis linking the fertility and mortality declines suggests that couples began to reduce their fertility in order to compensate for the increasing number of children which survive as a result of declining mortality. Perhaps the most theoretically satisfying comparison then would be to compare the dates by which infant mortality had declined by some given percentage or amount with the date fertility had declined by the amount needed to offset the increase in the children who would survive to maturity (or to some younger age since the impact of the mortality decline would be felt in the increasing number of children surviving to age 1, 5, 10, etc.). Actually a 10 percent reduction in infant mortality is offset by a considerably smaller decrease in fertility in most areas. The proportionate decrease in fertility required to offset a decline in mortality in order to insure that "effective" fertility (i.e. relating to children surviving to a given age) remain constant can be estimated without great difficulty. If the number of children surviving to some age a remains constant, it follows that $B \cdot l_a = B' l'_a$ where prior to the mortality change the initial number of births and the life table function indicating survivors to age a are represented by B and l_a respectively and the corresponding values after the mortality change are B' and l'_a. Consequently if mortality declines, reduced births as a proportion of initial births must be the reciprocal of the increased survival function to age a as a proportion of original survival function $B'/B = l_a/l'_a$. Thus, for example, if 25 percent more children survive to age a, the offsetting reduction in births would be 20 percent (since $.8 = 1/1.25$).

Using the above formula, we can estimate how large a decline in fertility in each of the 71 administrative areas is required to offset a 10 percent or a 50 point decline in infant mortality from the maximum level experienced so that "effective" fertility to age 1 and 15 remains unchanged. The maximum infant mortality rates can be translated directly into values of l_1. The values of l_{15} were estimated from the "East" model life tables published by the Office of Population Research, Princeton University (Coale and Demeny, 1966). The amount of fertility reduction required to offset a 10 percent reduction in infant mortality ranged from 1.2 percent to 7.0 percent to ensure that "effective" fertility to age 1 remained unchanged and from 2.1 percent to 10.8 percent to ensure that "effective" fertility to age 15 was constant. The exact amount depended on the level of the maximum infant mortality experienced in the administrative area. Alternatively a 50 point reduction in infant mortality from the maximum level would require

[179]

reductions in fertility ranging from 5.4 percent to 8.0 percent to ensure constant "effective" fertility to age 1 and 9.1 percent to 12.4 percent to age 15. Rather than recalculate a date of fertility decline corresponding to the exact level required to offset a 10 percent or 50 point reduction of infant mortality, we can simply compare the date of a 10 percent decline in I_g with the two dates of infant mortality decline and acknowledge the biases involved. Of the 71 administrative areas in Germany, a comparison of the dates of a 10 percent decline in both variables shows that infant mortality declined sooner in 36 areas, I_g declined sooner in 34, and in one area the years of the declines were equal. Among those areas where infant mortality declined earlier than I_g, the average lag was about 11 years. In the areas where the reverse was true the average lag was about 9 years. Since a 10 percent decline in infant mortality requires a smaller reduction in fertility to ensure constant "effective" fertility even to age 15, the date of mortality decline calculated on this basis yields particularly early figures for comparison with the dates of a 10 percent I_g decline. On the other hand, a 50 point reduction in infant mortality is approximately equivalent to a 10 percent reduction in the fertility needed to maintain "effective" fertility to age 15 and thus may be a more appropriate counterpart of the date of a 10 percent decline in I_g. Such a comparison yields quite different results. In only 15 of the 71 German administrative areas did infant mortality decline 50 points before I_g fell 10 percent. Among these 15 the average lag was about 9 years. In the other 56 areas I_g started to decline earlier by an average of 15 years.

In sum, the comparison of the dates of the onset of the fertility and mortality declines indicates that the decline in infant mortality could not have been an *initiating* cause of the fertility decline in most areas since the latter began before the former. This does not mean that infant mortality could not have assumed a causal role during the course of the fertility decline. However we can not determine this from our data. There does appear to be an association between the extent of decline in both variables. The more infant mortality declined in an area the greater was the decline in I_g. A correlation coefficient of .655 exists between the absolute decline in infant mortality from its maximum level to the 1932–1934 level and the absolute decline in I_g from its maximum value to the 1931–1935 level.

A comparison of the national trends in marital fertility and infant mortality reveals a striking parallel, especially when we compare index numbers. Figure 4.2 shows the course of the index values of I_g and

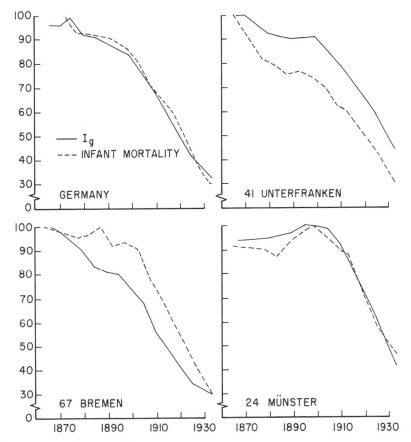

Figure 4.2. Infant Mortality Rate as Related to Marital Fertility (I_g), Index Values (Maximum = 100), Bremen, Münster, Unterfranken, and Germany: 1870 to 1930

infant mortality (maximum value of each series equal to 100) for the period between the 1860s and the 1930s for Germany and selected German administrative areas.[6] The curves on the national level are

[6]For the national figures, infant mortality during 1872–1876 was included as the first observation since estimates for earlier years are not available. Therefore I_g for 1873–1877 was included in the fertility series. In the curves for the administrative areas, I_g for 1873–1877 was not included since infant mortality for the early 1870s is excluded from the series we have presented in the appendix. Since the curves are based on different numbers of observations, caution should be exercised in their comparison.

practically identical. For contrast, the curves were plotted for three administrative areas: (1) Unterfranken, chosen because there was a particularly long lag between the onset of the infant mortality decline (as measured by both a 10 percent and a 50 point reduction) and the fertility decline (as measured by a 10 percent reduction in I_g); (2) Bremen, chosen because there was a particularly long lag in the opposite direction; and (3) Münster, because the difference in dates of fertility and mortality decline were close to the median differences for all administrative areas. The national average covers up the diversity found among the administrative areas. Nevertheless even in Unterfranken and Bremen, which represent extreme cases of divergence from the overall pattern, a considerable parallel between the courses of I_g and infant mortality is evident.

The coincidence between trends in infant mortality and fertility in German administrative areas is demonstrated by a number of correlations between the variables. We have already seen that the amounts of decline in both variables from their maximum level to their level in the 1930s were associated with each other. A positive correlation also exists between the changes that occurred during the initial phases of both declines. Among the 71 administrative areas in Germany, the absolute change in infant mortality between 1875–1880 to 1906–1910 is correlated .50 with changes in I_g between 1869–1873 and 1908–1912. Relative changes were correlated .45. In every case the change in I_g represented a decline and in most areas the change in infant mortality also represented a reduction between the two periods.

Even though a very mixed pattern emerged from our attempt to determine which of the two variables declined first, the dates of the onset of both declines are associated with each other. For the 71 administrative areas the date of a 10 percent decline in I_g is correlated .46 with the date of a 10 percent reduction in infant mortality and .55 with the date of a 50 point reduction.

At the beginning of the chapter we suggested that the relationship between infant mortality and fertility might not be the same in all contexts. For example, we might expect that in situations where infant mortality is particularly high fertility behavior would be more sensitive to a decline in infant mortality, since under such conditions mortality has a considerable impact on the number of children which reach maturity. Thus correlations between the dates of the fertility and mortality declines were calculated using only observations for the 35 areas whose maximum infant mortality exceeded the median computed from all administrative areas. The coefficients increased to .57 using the 10 percent criterion of decline for infant mortality and to .58 using the 50 point criterion. We might also expect that among areas where fertility is high, the beginning of an infant mortality decline would be more closely associated with a decline in fertility. In these areas, the particularly high fertility might be partially responsible for high infant mortality and thus a decline in fertility could bring about a reduction in mortality. Whether or not this is the correct reason, correlation coefficients between the date of a 10 percent decline in I_g and the dates of the infant mortality decline are even higher when we limit the cases to the 35 administrative areas where the maximum level of I_g exceeded the median value of the maximum I_g of all areas in Germany. The coefficients in this case increased to .69 and .71 respectively.

Both the date of the infant mortality decline and fertility decline showed strong patterns of regional association as revealed previously by analysis of variance. In order to see if a partial association between the variables persists when differences in regional averages are taken into account, an analysis of covariance was done. As before, the deviations of the variables from their regional means were correlated with each other. The "within region" correlation (.30) between the dates of a 10 percent decline in both infant mortality and I_g was considerably reduced from the overall correlation (.46). Using the date of a 50 point decline in infant mortality the "within region" correlation (.49) was only slightly lower than the correlation between the regionally unadjusted values (.55).

In order to see if the association between the timing of the fertility and infant mortality declines was different for rural and urban areas, the data for Prussia were analyzed. Separate correlations were calculated for rural and urban parts of each administrative area. The results are presented in Table 4.13. The association appears stronger in the urban areas, although the differences are not large. In most Prussian administrative areas the decline of both infant mortality and fertility

TABLE 4.13

INFANT MORTALITY RATE, DATE OF DECLINE, CORRELATION
WITH DATE OF 10% DECLINE IN MARITAL FERTILITY (I_g),
URBAN/RURAL, PRUSSIA

	Correlation between decline in I_g by 10% and decline in infant mortality		
	By 10%	By 50 points	N
Urban	.454	.630	31
Rural	.310	.517	30
Total	.379	.542	34

occurred earlier in the urban than in the rural populations. Perhaps the rural-urban differences in timing in both declines are associated with each other. In order to explore this possibility, the *differences* between the rural and urban dates of decline in I_g by 10 percent were correlated with *differences* in rural and urban dates of a 10 percent decline in infant mortality ($r = .27$) and the *differences* in the rural and urban dates of a 50 point decline in infant mortality ($r = .34$) among the 30 areas for which differences could be calculated. The results, although in the expected direction, are weak.

Even though the data we have examined so far have given little indication of a direct causal link between the declines in fertility and infant mortality experienced in Germany between unification and World War II, it still remains true that the mortality decline had a considerable impact on "effective" family size. There can be no question that the reduction in infant and childhood mortality tempered substantially the effect of the fertility decline on the number of living children per family. In order to estimate for each administrative area the amount of the fertility decline that was compensated for by the mortality reduction, we have used the following procedure. On the basis of the infant mortality rates for each area, the probability of a child surviving from birth to age 15 (l_{15}/l_0) was estimated using "East" model life tables (Coale and Demeny, 1966). The appropriate values were found which corresponded to the maximum level of infant mortality and the 1932–1934 level in each area. The amounts that fertility would have to decline in order to keep "effective" fertility to age 15 constant were calculated according to the formula discussed above. This result can then be compared to the actual amount of fertility decline in order to estimate the extent to which mortality changes compensate for fertility changes. The results are presented in Table 4.14. The implications of the mortality decline for "effective" fertility were substantial. For Germany over 40 percent of the fertility decline was offset by mortality reductions. In some areas well over two-thirds of the fertility decline was compensated for by the mortality decline and in only one area was this less than one-fifth.

Conclusion

It is apparent that the type of data surveyed in this chapter is not adequate to answer many of the questions raised in the introductory section concerning the nature of the relationship between fertility and infant mortality. However some implications can be drawn. It appears that the usual description of the demographic transition which postulates a prior decline in mortality (particularly infant and child mortality) as an initiating cause of the fertility decline does not fit the facts in Germany. Rather, they appear to decline more or less simultaneously. Indeed, not only the postulates incorporated in the transition model but any of the propositions discussed in the beginning of the chapter which posit a prior reduction in infant mortality with a perceptible lag in the timing of the fertility decline can not be accepted for the German experience without modification to account for the concurrence of these phenomena. Nevertheless associations between the amounts of change in each variable as well as in their timing suggest that the reduction of fertility and mortality in Germany may not have been independent phenomena. Whether or not a direct link in the variables existed or if they both occurred in response to a common set of changing conditions can not be readily determined. In addition, the striking parallelism between the decline in fertility and infant mortality remains to be explained. Both began at the same time and proceeded at the same pace, at least on a national scale. Can this be only coincidental?

Although the evidence examined in this chapter gives little support to hypotheses which causally relate the German fertility and mortality

INFANT MORTALITY

TABLE 4.14

FERTILITY DECLINE, ESTIMATED PERCENTAGE OFFSET BY INFANT
MORTALITY DECLINE, BY ADMINISTRATIVE AREA: MAXIMUM TO 1931-1935

Area	Probability of survival from birth to 15 years with infant mortality at a level of — Recorded maximum	1932-1934	Decrease in fertility by 1932-1934 required to keep family size constant despite decline in infant mortality (percent)	Decline in marital fertility (I_g), maximum to 1931-1935 (percent)	Amount of fertility decline compensated by infant mortality decline (percent)
01 Ostpreussen	665	881[a]	24.6	52.0	47.3
02 Danzig	626	881[a]	28.9	55.4	52.3
03 Marienwerder	652	881[a]	26.0	57.8	45.0
04 Berlin	551	914	39.7	76.5	51.9
05 Potsdam	600	900	33.3	66.9	50.0
06 Frankfurt/O.	643	892	27.9	66.5	42.0
07 Stettin-Str.	613	889	31.1	62.1	50.1
08 Köslin	733	892	17.9	56.4	31.7
09 Posen	659	884[b]	25.5	54.2	47.0
10 Bromberg	653	884[b]	26.2	55.3	47.4
11 Breslau	580	874	33.7	61.4	54.9
12 Liegnitz	571	883	35.4	61.5	57.6
13 Oppeln	661	844	21.7	49.2	44.1
14 Magdeburg	649	881	26.3	68.5	38.4
15 Merseburg	659	899	26.7	69.4	38.5
16 Erfurt	712	909	21.6	66.9	32.3
17 Schleswig	755	905	16.6	62.2	26.7
18 Hannover	742	925	19.7	69.1	28.5
19 Hildesheim	755	918	17.8	60.1	29.6
20 Lüneburg	763	920	17.1	54.8	31.2
21 Stade	793	917	13.5	59.3	22.8
22 Osnabrück	804	912	11.8	40.7	29.0
23 Aurich	833	926	10.1	46.3	21.8
24 Münster	749	892	16.1	58.9	27.3
25 Minden	774	920	15.9	58.6	27.1
26 Arnsberg	768	899	14.6	69.8	20.9
27 Kassel	754	933	19.2	61.1	31.4
28 Wiesbaden	758	937	19.2	68.9	27.9
29 Koblenz	730	915	20.3	56.8	35.7
30 Düsseldorf	735	905	18.9	72.1	26.2
31 Köln	668	914	26.9	71.9	37.4
32 Trier	765	896	14.6	47.6	30.7
33 Aachen	675	896	24.6	64.3	38.3
34 Sigmaringen	534	897	40.5	55.1	73.5
35 Oberbayern	411	871	52.9	67.3	78.6
36 Niederbayern	484	796	39.2	48.8	80.3
37 Pfalz	703	904	22.2	62.9	35.3
38 Oberpfalz	489	820	40.3	49.2	81.9
39 Oberfranken	662	892	25.8	57.5	44.9
40 Mittelfranken	511	897	43.0	67.6	63.6
41 Unterfranken	620	894	30.7	54.6	56.2
42 Schwaben	420	881	52.4	63.6	82.4
43 Dresden	600	922	34.9	71.4	48.9
44 Leipzig	610	907	32.8	75.5	43.4
45 Zwickau	526	925	43.1	77.0	56.0
46 Neckarkreis	519	936	44.6	68.9	64.7
47 Schwarzwaldkreis	504	910	44.6	60.2	74.1
48 Jagstkreis	499	917	45.6	54.7	83.4
49 Donaukreis	402	902	55.5	57.9	95.9
50 Konstanz	528	914	42.2	58.0	72.8
51 Freiburg	655	920	28.8	53.8	53.5
52 Karlsruhe	565	914	38.1	66.6	57.2
53 Mannheim	591	915	35.5	66.1	53.7
54 Starkenburg	662	932	29.0	68.8	42.2
55 Oberhessen	754	942	20.0	58.4	34.2
56 Rheinhessen	643	926	30.5	66.4	45.9
57 Mecklenburg	730	884	17.5	55.8	31.4
58 Thüringen	669	909	26.4	65.8	40.1
59 H. Oldenburg	803	912	12.0	48.3	24.8
60 F. Lübeck	712	894	20.3	58.0	35.0
61 Birkenfeld	807	926	12.8	58.9	21.7
62 Braunschweig	712	899	20.7	65.7	31.5
63 Anhalt	706	889	20.6	67.7	30.4
64 Schaumburg-Lippe	828	925	10.4	69.0	15.1
65 Lippe	758	933	18.8	60.2	31.2
66 Lübeck	705	905	22.3	69.1	32.3
67 Bremen	730	932	21.7	70.5	30.8
68 Hamburg	624	920	32.2	71.2	45.2
69 Unterelsass	649	--	--	--	--
70 Oberelsass	646	--	--	--	--
71 Lothringen	708	--	--	--	--
Germany	655	896	26.9	65.2	41.3

NOTE: Probability of survival estimated from East model life table (Coale and Demeny, 1966).

[a] 3A Westpreussen.

[b] 9A Gr. Posen-Westpreussen.

declines, it would be inappropriate to dismiss mortality from consideration in any description of Germany's fertility transition. Our knowledge would be most incomplete if we failed to realize that the impact the fertility decline had on the number of living children per family was substantially tempered by mortality reductions. It is therefore worth repeating that for the nation as a whole reduced infant and childhood mortality compensated for over forty percent of the fertility decline. This is indeed an impressive fact even if it is of a descriptive rather than an explanative nature.

CHAPTER 5: Demographic Change and Fertility Decline: Emigration, Migration, and Urbanization

Germany's decline in birth and death rates was accompanied by a radical redistribution of the population through migration. The implications of changes in residence involving long distance moves are of considerable consequence for both the individual and the society in which he lives. The rural to urban migration which involved the movement of millions of persons has been particularly significant. Not only did the population of existing cities swell but many formerly rural areas became urban or suburban in character. This phenomena was not unique to Germany, of course, but prevailed throughout most of Europe during the last century (Weber, 1899; Davis, 1955 and 1963). In addition, several waves of German emigration which carried large numbers to the New World as well as the long-distance internal flows, particularly the stream from agricultural eastern provinces to the rapidly industrializing western ones, were also of substantial importance.

Recently Davis (1963) and Friedlander (1969) have explored the theoretical and, to some extent, the empirical connection between the demographic transition in vital rates and both external and internal migration. Basically, what Davis labeled the theory of the "multiphasic demographic response" suggests that populations can ease the "strains" created by sustained natural increase in more ways than by simply adopting widespread contraception. One possible response is out-migration. Friedlander deplores the fact that most treatments of long term population changes have concentrated on the declines in fertility and mortality with little regard to the significant changes which occurred in population distributions and migration. He feels that population change needs to be studied in terms of all its demographic components, i.e. not just fertility and mortality but also internal and external migratory movements, since they are interrelated in important ways. Following Davis' theory of the "multi-phasic demographic response" he suggests that the timing and extent of the fertility transition in a community depended to a significant extent on the difficulty of out-migration and the ease with which those who left could make their livelihood elsewhere. In situations where rapid urban and industrial expansion was taking place, strains created in the rural and non-industrial areas by sustained natural increase could in part be alleviated through out-migration to the areas where employment opportunities resulting from this expansion were abundant. Thus the pressure to reduce fertility in the areas of exodus was at least temporarily relieved. We might expect similar effects to result if external migration, for example to the New World, was also relatively easy.

More conventional descriptions of the demographic transition include references to urbanization, although in a different context. Urbanization is usually regarded as one of the factors involved in the general process of modernization and industrialization that was responsible for the decline in fertility. In this setting urbanization is not treated as a process which relieves pressures in rural populations but rather as a force of social and demographic change and as such implies quite different consequences for fertility.

In this chapter we will explore the empirical relation between fertility and the various forms of migration recorded in German data. The first section focuses on emigration from Germany as well as internal migration across provincial or administrative area boundaries; the latter section concentrates on urbanization within administrative areas.

Emigration, Inter-Provincial Migration, and Migration between Administrative Areas

During the nineteenth century large numbers of Germans left their homeland to take up residence in the New World. The flow of emigrants was by no means constant. It fluctuated in response to a number of social, legal, and economic factors. Of course, not all the Germans that left their country remained expatriated. As in other European countries, a counterstream of returning Germans from the main countries of immigration was also present. Nevertheless the net result was a substantial loss of population through external migration.

There are two major sources of information on international migration for Germany: direct statistics collected at ports of departure on the numbers and nationality of overseas emigrants and indirect net migration estimates derived by comparison of intercensal population growth with the excess of births over deaths during the intercensal period.[1] A summary of the information from both sources is presented in Table 5.1. The overseas emigrants represent only a part of the total

TABLE 5.1

EMIGRATION AND INTERCENSAL NET MIGRATION: 1872 to 1933

| | Annual Average (000) | | Annual Rate | | | |
Date	Overseas emigrants	Net intercensal migrants	Emigra- tion	Net migration	Natural increase	Intercensal increase
1872-1875	78.9[a]	-79.9	1.9[a]	-1.9	11.9	10.0
1876-1880	46.2	-76.2	1.1	-1.7	13.1	11.4
1880-1885	171.5	-196.0	3.7	-4.3	11.3	7.0
1886-1890	97.0	-65.8	2.0	-1.4	12.1	10.7
1891-1895	80.5	-89.8	1.6	-1.8	13.0	11.2
1896-1900	25.5	+18.8	0.5	+0.4	14.7	15.1
1901-1905	29.3	+10.5	0.5	+0.2	14.4	14.6
1906-1910	26.6	-32.0	0.4	-0.5	14.2	13.6
1925-1933	41.1	-29.3	0.6	-0.4	4.9	4.5

NOTES: Emigrant data derived from number of persons leaving for overseas
countries as reported by German and some foreign ports of departure.
Net migrant data derived from difference between the increase in
population enumerated by the census and the excess of births over
deaths registered during the intercensal period.

[a]1871-1875.

persons migrating out of Germany during any period since some moved to other European countries. This probably accounts for the finding in Table 5.1 that the *net* loss of Germans between censuses sometimes exceeded the number of overseas emigrants during the

[1]This refers to estimates derived through the so-called balancing equation. If all statistics are correct then $P_2 = P_1 + B - D + I - E$ where P_2 refers to the population recorded at second census; P_1 refers to the population recorded at the first census; B and D refer respectively to the number of births and deaths which occurred within the country between the censuses; I and E refer respectively to the total number of immigrants and emigrants crossing the nation's boundaries. Thus net external migration $(I - E) = P_2 - P_1 - B + D$.

[190]

same period. Nevertheless for much of the period under consideration the overseas emigrants constituted the bulk of the external out-migration.

Both types of estimates are subject to error. Emigration statistics at ports of departure are notorious for their inaccuracy. In addition they were not available for all possible foreign ports of departure, although for much of the period of observation data was available for the most important ports. Estimates of net external migration based on the difference between census statistics and registered births and deaths are extremely sensitive to inaccuracies in either and thus also should be considered as only an approximate guide to the balance of loss and gain through international migration.

Between unification and the beginning of World War I the total number of registered German emigrants sailing for overseas ports exceeded two and a half million. The net loss through external migration in general during the same period was approximately the same. External migration, whether overseas or otherwise, was far from constant during this period. Overseas emigration was particularly heavy between 1880 and the early 1890s but tapered off considerably in the following decade and a half. Germany appears to have actually experienced a net gain in population between 1895 and 1905 through migration. In sum, on the national level emigration was most intense just prior to the decline in fertility and dropped off considerably once the decline was firmly on its way.

Prior to unification there were also periods of heavy emigration. According to immigration statistics from the United States alone, over two million German nationals entered between 1820 and 1870, the majority arriving in the two decades preceeding unification (Phillipovich, 1890). Estimates of total external migration indicate that Germany suffered a net loss of over two million between 1841 and 1871 (Hoffmann, 1965, pp. 172–173).

As extensive as external migration was, it retarded the growth of the German population only very moderately. A comparison of the rates of emigration, net migration, natural increase, and intercensal increase reveal that even during 1880–1885, the peak period of overseas emigration and net migratory loss, the rate of population growth was less than 40 percent smaller than the rate of natural increase. During the entire period between 1871 and 1910 external migration reduced the population growth that would have accrued from natural increase alone by only 10 percent.

Not all Germans who decided to leave the home province went overseas. Increasing internal mobility within Germany characterized the decades of rapid industrial expansion. Köllmann (1964, p. 102) has called internal migration "the greatest mass movement in German history." He divides internal migration into two phases during modern German history. Prior to the 1880s internal migration was dominated by short distance moves and an attraction to the nearby towns. Long distance internal moves were infrequent with the exception of those to Berlin. After 1890 moves involving considerable distances gained importance all over Germany and were particularly evident in the migration from the economically stagnant agricultural areas of the East to the rapidly expanding industrial areas of the West, especially the Ruhr area (Köllmann, 1964; cf. Köllmann, 1959).

There is abundant statistical evidence to document the extent of internal mobility for the German population. According to the 1871 census, 38 percent of the native-born population resided in a locality (*Ort* or *Gemeinde*) different from the one in which they were born. By 1907 almost half (48 percent) had moved from their place of birth.[2] Census statistics on the place of birth also give an impression of the rising trend in long distance internal movement. The proportion of the native-born population that lived in a state or Prussian province other than the one of birth as indicated by the censuses are as follows:[3]

> 1880: 7.9 percent
> 1890: 11.2 percent
> 1900: 13.7 percent
> 1907: 14.7 percent.

[2] The 1871 figure excludes troops stationed in France. The 1871 and 1907 figures are only roughly comparable since the number of localities were not identical due to boundary changes, divisions and consolidations in the interim.

[3] The 1907 figure is taken from the occupational census of that year and slightly underestimates the proportion of native born living outside their state or province of birth since for purposes of tabulation several smaller neighboring states and provinces were combined in the analyses and treated as if they were single states or provinces. Thus the

The proportion of long distance internal migrants measured in this manner almost doubled between 1880 and 1907. Köllmann (1964) suggests that there was an important connection between the decline in overseas emigration and the increase in long distance internal movement. He points to the fact that the eastern provinces of Prussia that contributed so heavily to inner German flows after 1890 had also contributed disproportionately to the overseas emigration prior to that time. He then argues that with the passing of the American frontier the excess agricultural population in Germany no longer had the opportunity to continue the rural way of life without capital in the United States. Given a choice between American or German industry, they opted more often to stay in their homeland. Hence the migratory currents which were going abroad before 1895 were diverted into the internal German migratory streams during the period of most rapid German industrial expansion.

The argument linking the passing of the American frontier with ebbing emigration from rural areas of northwest Europe is not new, but at least with reference to Germany it is probably incorrect. The great majority of German immigrants to the U.S. in the last half of the nineteenth century settled in American cities where they certainly did not continue their rural way of life. According to the 1900 U.S. census over 70 percent of the German-born population residing in either the states or American territories lived in cities with 25,000 or more inhabitants. German immigrants in America were far more urbanized than their relatives in Germany, where in 1900 less than 30 percent lived in cities with a population of 20,000 or more. Before 1895 German emigrants from agricultural areas were leaving their rural way of life behind to participate in American industrial and urban occupations. The rapid rise of German industry allowed them to move out of the agricultural sector and still remain in their native land. Thus while German industrialization probably was responsible for the decline in overseas emigration the passing of the American frontier was most likely of little consequence.

---

exchange of persons between the states (or provinces) within each particular combined area did not qualify as a long distance migrant as they had in the previous censuses.

There is sufficient evidence to suggest that German areas where emigration was most pronounced also lost considerable population through migratory exchanges within Germany.[4] For example, excluding Hamburg and Bremen, which were in peculiar positions since they were the major ports of departure, all but one of the nine states or provinces that experienced the highest overseas emigration rates (above 2.4 per 1,000 annually) during 1871–1895 had lost more persons through internal exchanges among German states than they had gained, as indicated by the 1900 census statistics on place of birth versus place of residence.[5] In contrast, among the nine states that experienced average emigration rates of under one per 1,000 annually between 1871 and 1895 only four showed a net loss with respect to population exchanges within Germany (see Table 5.2). Another way of looking at the relation between internal and external migration is to note that the median overseas emigration rate in 1885–1888 for the states or provinces that showed net losses through internal exchange in Germany according to the 1900 census was 2.11 per 1,000 population, practically twice as high as the median rate (1.07 per 1,000) of the states that gained through internal exchanges. These findings suggest that internal out-migration and overseas emigration were related phenomena probably arising from similar sets of pressures. They are treated together with respect to their effect on the fertility decline in most of our analysis. Before proceeding to a description of general migration rates, however, a few observations are in order concerning overseas emigration and fertility on the state and provincial level.

[4] A word of caution is appropriate when comparing registered overseas emigrations for states or provinces in Germany. Prior to 1899 and thus for the entire period during which we are comparing emigration rates, data on the state or province of origin was not reported for German nationals leaving from French or English ports. Also information from Dutch and Belgian ports was incomplete in this respect before 1887. Since emigrants from the areas in the south and west of Germany were more likely to leave from these ports than emigrants from other areas of Germany, their rates are somewhat depressed in comparison.

[5] The 1900 census results include cross-tabulations of the German population by state (or in the case of Prussia by province) of birth and by state (or province) of residence. Thus it is possible to compare the number born in a given state but residing outside it at the time of the census with the number born outside the state but residing inside. If the comparison is limited to native born Germans it is possible then to determine whether there was a net gain or loss through internal migration.

TABLE 5.2

EMIGRATION, INTERNAL MIGRATION, AND MARITAL FERTILITY (Ig),
BY SELECTED STATES AND PRUSSIAN PROVINCES: 1871 to 1900

Area	Overseas emigration rate (1871-1895)	Population change due to internal migration (1900)	Marital fertility (I_g) 1871	1900	Change (absolute)	Date of 10% decline
Highest emigration (1871-1895)						
West Prussia	6.81	loss	.826	.844	+.018	1911[a]
Pomerania	5.98	loss	.753	.679	-.074	1900
Posnania	5.24	loss	.799	.841	+.042	1913[a]
Schleswig	4.21	gain	.680	.595	-.085	1898
Mecklenburg	3.83	loss	.598	.518	-.080	1892
Hanover	3.16	loss	.668	.610	-.058	1901
Gd. Oldenburg	3.12	loss	.688	.684	-.004	1907
Württemberg	2.54	loss	.877	.732	-.145	1880
Pfalz	2.43	loss	.776	.690	-.086	1895
Lowest emigration (1871-1895)						
Alsace-Lorraine	0.37	gain	.765	.631	-.134	1887
Anhalt	0.56	gain	.672	.554	-.118	1892
Silesia	0.63	loss	.758	.735	-.023	1907
Ostpreussen	0.71	loss	.790	.781	-.009	1907
P. Saxony	0.71	loss	.711	.597	-.114	1894
Rhineland	0.82	gain	.863	.768	-.095	1898
Braunschweig	0.88	gain	.623	.547	-.076	1898
K. Saxony	0.98	gain	.722	.588	-.134	1893
Schaumburg-Lippe	0.99	loss	.717	.553	-.164	18?5

NOTES: Emigration rates (average number per 1,000 population) may be underestimated because overseas departures took place outside of Germany;
these were not uniformly reported by nationality.
Population change due to internal migration determined by a comparison
of the place of birth and the place of residence as given in the 1900
German census.
Hamburg and Bremen are not included in areas with highest emigration
because, as major ports of departure, their situation was peculiar.

[a]Determined by extrapolation of decline between 1905 and 1910.

Table 5.2 compares the states or provinces which registered the
highest and the lowest overseas emigrations during 1871–1895 with
respect to several measures of marital fertility. Again for the reason
noted above, Bremen and Hamburg are excluded. Neither the high
nor the low emigration states show a distinctive fertility level in 1871.
In both groups some are well above the national average and others

[195]

well below it. However in the high emigration states the decline in marital fertility seems to have been generally slower in getting underway as evident from both the change in I_g between 1871 and 1880 and the date of a sustained ten percent decline. Among this group only Mecklenburg and Württemberg experienced a ten percent decline prior to the national average, whereas among the nine low emigration states five started their declines earlier. Among the low emigration areas the two most marked exceptions with respect to having experienced little decline in I_g before 1900 and a rather late onset in fertility reduction are Ostpreussen and Silesia. It is interesting to note that although their rates of overseas emigration are quite low they both experienced population losses through internal German migration.

Overseas emigration rates and data on population exchanges through comparison of census results on the population by place of birth and place of residence are available only for states and Prussian provinces and not for administrative area units in general. In addition, it seems acceptable, if not preferable, to treat net effects of external and internal migratory movements simultaneously with respect to their repercussions on the fertility decline. From the perspective of the theory of the "multi-phasic demographic response" both emigration to another country and out-migration to a different province have the effect of relieving pressures associated with population growth. As a composite measure of migration we can calculate net migration estimates based on the "balancing equation," i.e. on the difference between natural increase and intercensal increase (or decrease) as indicated by successive population counts. The requisite data for determining net migration rate based on this method are available on the level of administrative areas from the census and vital statistics.[6]

Our primary concern is with the part played by migration in delaying the fertility decline, and since fertility began to fall substantially almost everywhere before World War I, we will limit our consideration to the period prior to 1910. Between unification and 1910 most administrative areas experienced negative net migration rates. Among

[6]Since the German census publications included net migration rates as well as the birth and death data used to compute them, direct reference need not be made to vital statistics publications.

[196]

the 71 areas, 55 apparently lost more population through migration than they gained. However, the rate of migration loss or gain varied substantially from area to area ranging from an average loss of over 12 per 1,000 in Marienwerder and Köslin to an average gain of over 15 per 1,000 in Potsdam and Hamburg during the period 1872–1910. The median position was held by Liegnitz with a net loss of 3.6 per 1,000.

Net migration rates exhibit only a weak regional association as indicated by an analysis of variance (for the average rate during 1872–1910 $F_{6,64} = 2.0$, $\epsilon = .28$), but as Map 5.1 indicates several distinct patterns existed. Most striking is the well documented exodus from

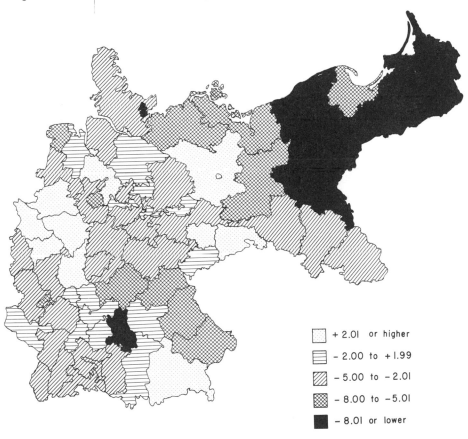

Map 5.1.   Net Migration Rate, by Administrative Area: 1872–1910

the eastern provinces of Prussia and the influx into the industrializing areas of the west and to some extent into the old industrial areas of the former Kingdom of Saxony. Berlin and the three city states of Hamburg, Bremen, and Lübeck all show migratory gains reflecting the more general process of urbanization that occurred during the four decades following unification. The areas of Southern Germany generally lost population. Areas containing large cities (i.e. Oberbayern with Munich, Schwaben with Augsburg, Mittelfranken with Nürenburg, and Neckerkreis with Stuttgart) were exceptions. They either gained population through migration or else held their own.

For a limited number of areas the migratory balance changed direction between 1871 and 1910 but generally areas either consistently lost or gained through the process. If we compare the period 1872–1890 with 1891–1910, we find that 47 areas experienced negative net migration rates in both periods, 15 experienced positive rates for both periods, and only 9 shifted from one category to the other. The correlation between migration rates during the two periods is .78; between 1872–1875 migration rates and rates in 1906–1910 a .61 correlation coefficient holds.

As a preliminary step in our investigation of the relationship between migration and fertility we can check if migration has had the effect of separating married couples and thereby depressing fertility through reducing the number of wives with husbands present. Under normal circumstances we would expect the number of married men to equal the number of married women in an area. If intense migration occurs and it involves married men who do not take their wives with them, a certain number of married women will remain in the area of origin who are not susceptible to the risk of conceiving a legitimate child until their husbands return. As a result, fertility as measured by most indices including I_g will be depressed. Livi Bacci (1965, pp. 15–21 and 1971, pp. 65–71) found this situation to exist in parts of Italy and Portugal and considered its effect severe enough to require adjusting his measures of marital fertility to allow for it.

One sign of an imbalance in the married population is a sex ratio (married women per 100 married men) which deviates very far from 100. In a sense this measure underestimates the phenomena since the absence of husbands through outmigration can be obscured by the presence of married male in-migrants who left their wives behind. Nationally the sex ratio of the married population was very close to 100. In 1880, for example, there were 100.45 married women per 100 married men indicating only a meager impact of emigration in this respect. In 1900 the sex ratio of 99.97 actually indicates a very slight excess of married men probably due to the presence of married male immigrants who left their wives behind. As indicated above, during the preceding five years Germany experienced a slight net gain through external migration. By 1910 the excess of married men is no longer evident and the sex ratio (100.12) is just slightly above unity.

Most administrative areas also indicated a very even balance between married men and women. According to the 1880, 1900, and 1910 censuses, the sex ratio of the married population exceeded 105 women per 100 men only in the following areas:

1880: Merseburg (105.3)

1900: Merseburg (105.8), Posen (106.3), Lippe (113.3)

1910: Posen (105.6), Lippe (112.5)

In addition, in each of the three years all but six areas indicated a sex ratio of under 102 married women per married men. Thus it is not likely that migration substantially affected marital fertility by separating married couples except in a very few administrative areas and hence no adjustments are made in the fertility indices. It is worth noting that in Lippe, where the situation appears most extreme, part of the decline in I_g between 1880 and 1900 probably is accounted for by the out-migration of married men without their spouses. Curiously, in Posen, where the number of "grass widows" also increased between 1880 and 1900, I_g rose as well. Deviations in the sex ratio of married persons in the opposite direction, which indicate an excess of married men in an area, are less extreme. They are also of less concern with respect to influencing measures of marital fertility such as I_g which relate legitimate births to married women. Married men present in an area without their wives contribute neither to numerator nor the denominator of such rates.

Oddly, the correlation between migration and the sex ratio of the married population is not as high as might be expected. The ratio of married women to married men in 1880 correlates −.33 with net migration rates during the previous five years. In 1900 and 1910 the equivalent correlations are −.47 and −.25 respectively. A closer examination of their covariation indicates that areas with a surplus of married women are usually areas of net out-migration. For example, all areas with sex ratios among the married population of 102 or more in any of the three censuses experienced negative net migration rates in the preceeding decade. However, areas with high migratory losses are not necessarily characterized by a large proportion of "grass widows." For example, Ostpreussen, Marienwerder, and Köslin all consistently experienced among the highest negative net migration rates in the four decades prior to 1910, and yet none was characterized by a ratio of 101 or more married women to married men. Apparently customs permitting men to migrate without their wives or conditions enabling wives to accompany their husbands in long distance moves varied from area to area. Thus the probability that a man would leave his wife behind might have depended on the distance of his move and the ease with which he could return home for temporary visits at least.

In order to examine the association between fertility and migration more generally we can relate through correlational analysis various measures of marital fertility and fertility decline with net migration rates. First we consider the association between the level of marital fertility and migration using the 71 administrative areas as units of observation. The relevant, zero order correlations are given in the first part of Table 5.3. Unfortunately we have no measure of migration for an earlier period than the 1870s. Thus to describe the empirical association between migration and fertility prior to the fertility decline, we must rely on migration rates for 1872–1880. The four largely urban administrative areas, Berlin and the three city states Lübeck, Bremen, and Hamburg, all experienced extremely high net in-migration for most of the period between unification and 1910 and therefore can exert a substantial influence on any correlations with net migrations. In order to see if the associations between fertility and migration are largely a result of these metropolitan centers rather than a more general phenomenon, a separate set of correlation coefficients is given based on all administrative areas except these four. The correlations

TABLE 5.3

NET MIGRATION RATE, CORRELATIONS WITH MARITAL FERTILITY (I_g): 1872 to 1910

Variables correlated		Correlation coefficients	
Net migration rate	Marital fertility (I_g)	All areas (N=71)	Excluding Berlin, Lübeck, Bremen, and Hamburg (N=67)
By time period	**By level**		
1872-1880	1880	-.28	-.08
1872-1880	Maximum	-.24	-.07
1872-1910	1910	-.56	-.45
1872-1890	Maximum	-.25	-.11
1891-1910	Maximum	-.18	-.10
1872-1910	Maximum	-.23	-.11
	By decline		
1872-1890	1871 to 1890	.37	.27
1891-1910	1890 to 1910	.52	.49
1872-1910	1871 to 1910	.57	.53
1872-1910	Maximum to 1910 (absolute)	.60	.55
1872-1910	Maximum to 1910 (percent)	.66	.57
	By date of decline		
1872-1890	By 10%	-.47	-.37
1872-1890	I_g = .600	-.47	-.30
1872-1890	I_g = .500	-.59	-.44
1872-1910	By 10%	-.47	-.37
1872-1910	I_g = .600	-.44	-.29
1872-1910	I_g = .500	-.56	-.42

between net migration in 1872–1880 and either I_g in 1880 or the maximum predecline I_g indicate that there was only a very weak association between the level of fertility and migration at the onset of the fertility decline when all administrative areas are considered. When the four metropolitan areas are excluded the association disappears almost entirely. However by 1910, which was the approximate chronological midpoint of the national fertility decline, some association between marital fertility and migration during the preceding decades became evident and was only partly due to the influence of the metropolitan areas. Apparently changes in marital fertility during the intervening period were related to migration rates.

Not only is it possible that out-migration may serve as a mechanism to relieve population strain and hence be an alternative to or a means of postponing fertility decline, but high fertility may lead to out-migration and low fertility may be conducive to in-migration. The last three pairs of correlations in the first part of Table 5.3 provide some information on this possibility. Apparently only a very weak association existed between the maximum levels of predecline marital fertility and migration during the subsequent decades and it is largely due to the influence of Berlin and the three city states.

To explore some of the implications of the theory of the "multiphasic demographic response," it is more interesting to examine the association between migration rates and changes in fertility or the timing of the fertility decline. Correlations between changes in I_g prior to 1910 and migration are presented in the second part of Table 5.3, and correlations between the date of decline and migration in the third part. The positive direction of the correlations between I_g changes and net migration rates indicate that net migratory gains are associated with larger declines in fertility and net migratory losses are associated with lesser declines or even with increases in I_g in the case of some areas prior to 1890. The strength of the relationship appears moderate and is reduced only slightly by the exclusion of the metropolitan administrative areas. The negative direction of the correlation between migration and the data of the fertility decline indicates that negative net migration was associated with later dates of decline and positive net migration with earlier dates of decline. Again the relationship is weakened but not eliminated by the exclusion of the metropolitan areas. In view of the positive correlation of migration with changes in I_g, the inverse association with the date of fertility decline is not unexpected.

Both sets of correlations are consistent with the proposition that out-migration can serve at least temporarily as an alternative to fertility reduction. Several other interpretations of the correlational results are also possible however. For example, the causation, if present, may run in the opposite direction. Areas which are slow to reduce fertility may be under greater pressure to relieve strains associated with population increase by maintaining a net loss in migration. The correlations *per se* can not indicate which interpretation, if any, is the correct one.

Another interpretation, with quite different implications concerning the link between migration and fertility also appears plausible. It may be that net out-migration occurs from areas that are economically and socially backward, e.g. largely agricultural with low incomes and little economic growth. It may be this backwardness that is responsible both for the net out-migration and for the slowness in fertility decline. It is difficult to find a suitable measure of socio-economic backwardness with which to test this interpretation. As very rough indicators we can use the proportion of the population in an administrative area that is dependent on agriculture for a livelihood and the porportion of recruits that were illiterate. Statistics on the proportion of the population dependent on the various branches of industry are readily available from the periodic occupational censuses (*Berufszählungen*) and will be discussed in more detail in the following chapter. Data on illiteracy among recruits will also be considered in Chapter 6. We introduce these indices here only in order to see if they might account for the association we have found between migration and fertility decline. Table 5.4 presents partial correlations between the net migration

TABLE 5.4

NET MIGRATION RATE, CORRELATIONS WITH MARITAL FERTILITY (I_g),
CONTROLLING FOR AGRICULTURE AND ILLITERACY: 1872 to 1910

Variable correlated with net migration rate 1872-1910	All areas (N=71)		Excluding Berlin, Lübeck, Bremen, and Hamburg (N=67)	
	Zero Order	Partial	Zero Order	Partial
Absolute decline in I_g 1871-1910	.57	.09	.53	.14
Absolute decline in I_g from maximum to 1910	.60	.14	.55	.18
Percentage decline in I_g from maximum to 1910	.66	.17	.57	.19
Date of 10% decline in I_g	-.47	-.10	-.37	-.08
Date I_g = .600	-.44	-.09	-.29	-.04
Date I_g = .500	-.56	-.09	-.42	-.06

NOTE: Control variables for agriculture and illiteracy are defined, respectively, as percentage dependent on agriculture in 1882 and percentage illiterate among recruits in 1875.

rate 1872–1910 and measures of extent and date of fertility decline with the proportion of the population dependent on agriculture in 1882 and the proportion illiterate among recruits in 1875 taken into account. In each case the partial association between migration and fertility becomes essentially negligible. The meaning of the zero order correlations between migration and fertility decline thus becomes ambiguous. The elimination of the association when we control for "backwardness" does not necessarily mean that out-migration is not an alternative to fertility decline. If there is a causal link between backwardness and net migration and between net migration and fertility decline then it makes little sense to control for "backwardness." If instead, "backwardness" is causally related both to net migration and fertility decline, the association between migration and fertility may be considered spurious. The partial correlations in Table 5.4 are consistent with both interpretations. Actually there are substantial intercorrelations among the three independent variables and removing the influence of any two through partial correlations reduces the correlation between the third and measures of fertility decline. However in the cases of proportion in agriculture and fertility or illiteracy and fertility the reduction is less than is the case with migration and fertility.

If out-migration occurs in response to rapid natural increase, we would expect to find an inverse association between rates of natural increase and rates of net migration. In other words, areas with relatively large net migratory losses should also have experienced high rates of natural increase and areas with a net inflow of migrants would be ones in which natural increase was more moderate. As the correlations presented in Table 5.5 indicate, such an association did not exist in Germany during the four decades following unification. When we consider all administrative areas, the correlation coefficients between rates of natural increase and rates of net migration are very close to zero. In addition, a comparison between the correlations during the first two and the last two decades indicates that the relationship did not emerge even after fertility began to fall in some areas. We might have expected the relationship to strengthen over time if out-migration was an alternative to fertility reduction in coping with the "strain" of high natural increase, since areas which responded by reducing fertility would also have directly reduced the rate of natural increase in the process. In contrast, the rates of natural increase would be only

TABLE 5.5

NET MIGRATION RATE, CORRELATION WITH
NATURAL INCREASE RATE: 1872 to 1910

Date	All areas		Areas with net out-migration		Areas with late fertility decline	
	r	N	r	N	r	N
1872-1890	-.09	71	-.32	54	-.30	34
1890-1910	-.05	71	-.30	49	.07	34
1872-1910	-.12	71	-.33	55	-.14	34

NOTE: Areas with late decline are those whose 10% decline in I_g occurred later than the median year (1896).

indirectly affected by migratory selections with respect to age, marital status, etc. in areas where out-migration was a substitute for fertility reduction.

Social and economic circumstances which were attractive enough to result in a net inflow of migrants such as occurred in some German administrative areas might also enable the area to absorb additions to the population through natural increase without creating any undue strains. Hence the relationship between migration and natural increase might differ in areas of net in-migration and areas of net out-migration in such a way that only in the latter areas is a "push" factor created by rapid natural increase. To check this possibility, a separate set of correlations based only on areas of net out-migration are presented. The association between migration and natural increase gains some strength under this condition but nevertheless is still relatively weak.

An argument can also be presented to support the hypothesis that the inverse reltationship between migration and natural increase is stronger in areas which were relatively late to reduce fertility in comparison to areas where fertility started to decline earlier. If some areas delayed the start of the fertility transition by responding to rapid natural increase through out-migration, it is among these areas that the strongest correlations would exist. The German data do not lend support to this hypothesis, at least when we limit consideration to areas which began their fertility decline later than the median year for all administrative areas.

In sum it appears that a simple relationship between natural increase and migration is not evident in Germany during the four decades between unification and 1910. Even when we limit consideration to selected areas in which we might expect stronger relationships to emerge on theoretical grounds, the associations remain rather weak.

Urbanization

The most important type of internal migration that has characteristically accompanied and indeed been part of the general process of modernization in the Western World has been the large scale movement of persons from rural to urban or suburban areas. In addition, many areas previously rural in character were transformed into essentially urban areas. Together these phenomena resulted in a "rural-urban transition" which had a profound impact on social and economic life. Indeed most descriptions of the demographic transition have included urbanization as one of the major factors in the process of modernization and held industrialization responsible for the decline in fertility. The meaning of urbanization has not always been clear in discussions relating it to fertility decline. Alternatively it has connoted implicitly if not explicitly an increasing proportion of the population living in cities, growth in the size of the urban population, and the development and diffusion of modern features of city life. Conventionally a strict definition of urbanization is limited to the first connotation and refers to a characteristic of an entire area including its rural parts. The second meaning is more properly labeled city growth and is a characteristic only of the urban areas themselves. The last meaning is better referred to as urbanism and refers more to a socio-cultural rather than a strictly demographic process. In testing empirically hypotheses concerning urbanization with respect to the German fertility decline we will be limited in large part to the first two meanings since they are more easily defined operationally with available demographic data.

Between the middle of the nineteenth century and the start of World War II, Germany was transformed from a predominately rural to a largely urban nation. Census data on the proportion of the population living in various sized municipalities (*Gemeinde*) document the

TABLE 5.6

POPULATION DISTRIBUTION, BY SIZE OF MUNICIPALITY: 1871 to 1933

Census year	Percentage in municipalities with populations of		
	Over 100,000	Over 20,000	Under 2,000
1871	4.8	12.5	63.9
1875	6.2	14.4	61.0
1880	7.2	16.1	58.6
1885	9.5	18.4	56.3
1890	11.4	20.7	53.0
1895	13.9	24.6	49.8
1900	16.2	28.8	45.7
1905	19.0	31.9	42.6
1910	21.3	34.7	40.0
1925	26.8	40.4	36.0
1933	30.4	43.3	33.2

change (Table 5.6). The transformation was rapid. The percent living in rural areas declined steadily and the proportions living in larger cities increased steadily. Part of the increase in the large cities and part of the decrease in the municipalities with less than 2,000 population is due to the shifting of some municipalities out of one category and into another. Since population was growing rapidly during most of the time span, the shift was usually in the direction of a more urban category. For example, between 1871 and 1910 the number of cities with 100,000 or more increased from 8 to 48. Nevertheless much of the increase in the percentage living in large cities reflects a genuinely faster growth in cities than rural areas due to heavy rural-urban migration. The three large cities, Berlin, Hamburg, and Munich serve as striking examples. Within the city boundaries of 1871, the populations of these three cities increased 143 percent, 207 percent, and 152 percent respectively between 1871 and 1910. The corresponding increase for the total population of Germany was only 57 percent (Zahn, 1918–19, p. 103).

The main impetus for urbanization apparently came from the growth of the industrial economy even where the cities were not primarily industrial in character as in the case of certain administrative centers or maritime cities (Köllman, 1964). Prior to the mid-nineteenth century when Germany was still largely a land of local industries producing for a local market, very little urbanization was apparent. The growth of cities coincided with the introduction and spread of factory industrialization (Weber, 1899, pp. 87–88). The proportion of the population living in the 25 largest cities (as of 1890) only rose from 4.7 percent in 1819 to 5.7 percent in 1852. By 1890

TABLE 5.7

POPULATION DISTRIBUTION, PERCENTAGE URBAN,
BY PROVINCE, PRUSSIA: 1819 to 1910

Province	1819	1831	1843	1855	1867	1880	1890	1900	1910
Ostpreussen	21.9	20.0	19.0	20.1	20.7	22.4	24.8	27.9	31.9
West Prussia	27.7	25.9	23.6	23.9	24.6	26.8	29.0	30.9	33.1
Brandenburg									
incl. Berlin	41.6	42.9	44.7	45.8	51.2	57.7	62.1	65.9	67.0
excl. Berlin	31.3	32.2	32.3	32.3	34.2	36.8	38.5	45.1	50.3
Pomerania	28.3	28.6	28.2	28.7	31.3	34.0	36.3	40.9	43.0
Posnania	28.1	27.5	26.7	26.8	27.1	28.0	28.9	32.6	34.4
Silesia	20.2	20.2	19.7	20.9	22.6	27.0	29.9	33.3	34.8
P. Saxony	35.2	36.3	35.9	36.5	38.5	41.3	44.5	47.2	49.2
Schleswig	--	--	--	--	29.9	35.0	39.3	43.3	48.0
Hanover	--	--	--	--	24.2	29.3	32.6	36.9	39.9
Westphalia	24.5	21.3	22.3	24.1	26.9	32.5	34.9	37.1	43.5
Hesse-Nassau	--	--	--	--	29.9	35.9	39.1	44.3	49.2
Rhineland	25.2	26.3	27.6	29.6	35.9	40.5	45.2	47.7	55.2
Sigmaringen	--	--	--	16.5	17.8	19.0	12.2[a]	12.8	14.9
Prussia	27.6	27.4	27.6	28.9	31.1	35.6	39.3	43.1	47.2

[a]Data on Sigmaringen affected by several municipalities losing their status as cities
between 1880 and 1890.

however it had risen to over 12 percent (Weber, 1899, p. 84). Data are also available for Prussian provinces from 1819 (Table 5.7). Since Prussia defined cities according to legal principles rather than by size, the Prussian data are not subject to the disturbing influence of municipalities shifting from one size category to another as is the case in Table 5.6. Although occasionally municipalities were redefined as urban or rural, this factor was insignificant in most cases. One conspicuous exception is the small province of Sigmaringen where the number of municipalities defined as cities was reduced from 7 to 2 between 1880 and 1890.

Judging from changes in the rural-urban distribution, in most provinces heavy migration from the rural areas is evidenced in Prussia only after 1867. Prior to this date the proportion living in cities was rather stable. Large scale movement to the city is evident only in the special case of Berlin where the population growth considerably outstripped the surrounding province of Brandenburg.

The trend in urban agglomeration in Germany during the latter part of the nineteenth century was a centralizing one resulting in a concentration in the largest cities (Weber, 1899, pp. 89–91). Metropolitan centers increased more rapidly than the population of all cities, and Berlin grew faster than either general category. The relationship between city size and growth rate is quite clear from a comparison of average annual growth rates between 1867 and 1885 of municipalities in different size categories. Irregularities caused by the passing of towns from one group to another between censuses are controlled by classifying all towns according to their size in the 1885 census. The municipalities with less than 2,000 population (i.e. officially rural) and villages with 2,000 to 5,000 inhabitants grew at only 0.2 percent and and 1.0 percent annually during this period. Towns with 5,000 to 20,000 and cities with 20,000 to 100,000 population grew at 1.8 percent and 2.4 percent respectively, while metropolitan areas with over 100,000 inhabitants grew at 2.7 percent annually (Weber, 1899, p. 91).

Several hypotheses can be advanced relating urbanization, city growth, and urbanism with the fertility decline. Most scholars concerned with the demographic transition would agree that the long run effect of these processes on reproductive behavior is to encourage the spread of family limitation and depress fertility. The exact mechanism through which this occurs is rarely made explicit in writings concerning the fertility transition.

Urbanization in the form of mere growth in the proportion urban without a transformation in the quality of city life might not be expected to have a substantial impact on fertility. Of course if prior to the start of significant urbanization fertility was much lower in the city than in the hinterland, an increase in the proportion urban would tend to reduce the overall fertility in an area simply by changing the weight of the urban population, provided the incoming migrants adopted city reproductive habits on their arrival. Some evidence accumulated from fertility surveys in the U.S., however, indicates that the urban population with a rural background has higher fertility (Goldberg, 1960). Even more to the point, the empirical evidence that differentials in rural-urban marital fertility were generally not very large in Germany prior to unification (see Chapter 3) renders it unlikely that urbanization would lead to the spread of family limitation or fertility decline if the character of urban life remained as it was in the cities of the preindustrial era. However it can still be argued that rapid urbanization itself or even simply rapid city growth act as catalysts for changes in the structure of urban life which are conducive to reduced fertility. For example, a rapid influx of migrants from the countryside into the city could create housing problems that might pressure a couple to limit their family size, or it may increase the amount of competition among those who wish to be socially mobile. If urbanization resulted in such pressures, then we would expect to find that changes in the pattern of urban growth preceded and accompanied declining fertility in the cities. Even if such a relationship between urbanization and urban fertility can be demonstrated, it helps little in the explanation of the decline in rural fertility.

Perhaps the most important interpretation of increases in the proportion urban in terms of the fertility decline is as an indicator of broad social changes connected with modernization in general. Even if the relative growth of the urban population may have no substantial independent effect on fertility, it may still signal the occurrence of associated socio-economic changes that do effect fertility, sooner or later. In this case we would expect urbanization to be correlated with the fertility decline of an entire area rather than merely the urban population, even though the direct linkage is vague.

The relationship between urbanization and rural fertility is also of considerable interest. Two opposing arguments can be made concerning the consequences of rapid urbanization on the fertility of the surrounding countryside. On the one hand arguments derived from the theory of the "multi-phasic demographic response" suggest rapid urbanization at least temporarily helps to keep rural fertility high and delay the onset of its decline. In referring to the European peasantry, Davis (1963) suggested, "If contraception was not at first adopted on a major scale in most agrarian sectors, it was because ready alternatives were available. One of these was migration. As the economic revolution advanced, the rural sections found in the rising cities an ever expanding outlet for their excess natural increase — an outlet that helped them capitalize on the opportunities offered by continued industrialization." Friedlander (1969) carried the argument further by suggesting that areas where large scale migration to the cities (and hence urbanization) was a feasible alternative for rural populations, their response to strains of high natural increase in terms of fertility reduction would be substantially delayed. In populations with no rapidly developing cities, the main response might be a sharp decline in rural fertility more or less coincidental with the urban fertility decline.

On the other hand arguments that cast the city in the role of a diffusion center for new ideas imply that rapid urbanization would hasten rather than retard the reduction of fertility in surrounding rural areas. Thus we can view the city both as the receiver of new ideas from urban centers in other areas and as the transmitter of these ideas to the surrounding countryside. In areas where rural to urban migration has been intense and hence rapid urbanization has occurred, a more extensive network of informal communication between the city and the rural hinterland seems likely. Among the urban norms and ideas that rural migrants transmit back to their friends and relations who remained behind would be values supporting low fertility and the use of birth control. It also seems likely that formal networks of communication whether through newspapers or business transactions are likely to be more highly developed between the urban center and the surrounding rural areas when the city is large rather than small. Hence an argument can be made that rapid urbanization and a high proportion urban in an area facilitate the spread of urbanism to the rural population and thereby act as a stimulus to a rural fertility decline.

The remainder of the chapter is devoted to examining the association of urbanization, proportion urban, and city growth with fertility

[211]

in Germany. The results should shed some light on the various hypotheses we have been discussing.

It is possible to calculate from census results the proportions of the population of administrative areas that live in rural or urban areas as defined by the size of municipality. Prior to 1885 the census tabulated the populations of each area into only two categories with respect to municipality size; municipalities with less than 2,000 inhabitants were considered rural and those with larger populations as urban. Starting with the 1885 census tabulations were given according to more categories and therefore it is possible to calculate not only the proportion of an administrative area's population that lives in communities with 2,000 or more inhabitants but also the proportion living in cities with at least 20,000 or 100,000·inhabitants for example. Actually there is a very high correlation between these indices at any given time as might be suspected. Also the ranking of administrative areas relative to each other with respect to proportions urban or proportions rural changed little between German unification and the 1930s. For example, the proportion of an area living in municipalities with under 2,000 population in 1871 correlates .89 with the 1900 values and .92 with the 1933 values.

Considerable differences exist between administrative areas with respect to the extent of urbanization. Even excluding Berlin and the three city states, the percent of the population living in rural municipalities (i.e. less than 2,000 inhabitants) in 1900 ranged from 87 percent in Sigmaringen to less than 9 percent in Düsseldorf. Six areas contained no cities with a population of 20,000 or more in 1900, whereas in Düsseldorf over half the population lived in cities of this size.

The absence of a clear geographical pattern in the extent administrative areas are urbanized is apparent from Map 5.2, which shows the percent of the population living in cities of 20,000 or more according to the 1900 census. The predominantly agrarian east is only minimally urbanized by 1900 but the rest of Germany shows a very mixed pattern. The lack of a distinct geographic pattern is reflected in the weak association between the regional classification described in Chapter 1 and the proportion living in cities of 20,000 or more in 1900 ($F_{6,64} = 1.19$, $\epsilon = .22$).

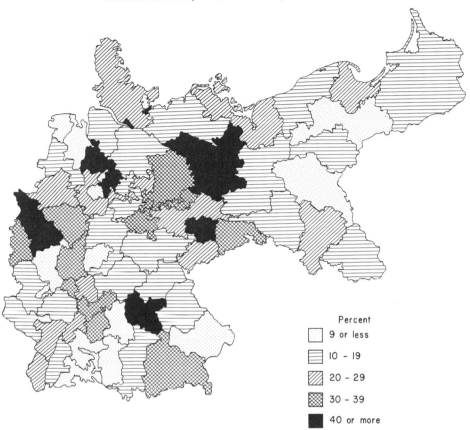

Map 5.2. Percentage of Population Living in Cities of 20,000 or More, by Administrative Area: 1895

The results of a correlational analysis between indices of urbanization and marital fertility are presented in Table 5.8. A separate set of correlation coefficients are given based on results which exclude the four metropolitan administrative areas in order to see if the observed associations for all areas are heavily influenced by them. The four metropolitan administrative areas occupy a special status with respect to urbanization and it could be misleading to include them in parts of the analysis, especially when considering changes in the proportion rural or proportion urban over time.

As is evident from the first part of Table 5.8, in general the more ru-

TABLE 5.8

URBANIZATION, CORRELATIONS WITH MARITAL FERTILITY (I_g): 1871 to 1933

Variables correlated		Correlation coefficients			
Urbanization	Marital fertility (I_g)	All areas		Excluding Berlin, Lübeck, Bremen, and Hamburg	
		r	N	r	N
By level	By level				
Percentage urban:					
1885	1885	-.37	71	-.10	67
1910	1910	-.50	71	-.40	67
1933	1933	-.53	66	-.47	62
Percentage rural:					
1871	1871	.24	71	-.10	67
1910	1910	.43	71	.35	67
1933	1933	.63	66	.57	62
By "pretransition" level	By decline				
Percentage rural:					
1871	Date by 10%	.44	71	.31	67
1871	1871 to 1910 (absolute)	-.57	71	-.55	67
1871	Maximum to 1933 (relative)	-.72	71	-.71	67
By urban growth	By decline				
Increase in percentage urban:					
1885-1910	1871 to 1910 (absolute)	.21	71	.22	67
1885-1933	Maximum to 1933 (relative)	.20	66	.25	62
Decline in percentage rural:					
1871-1890	Date by 10%	.15	71	-.21	67
1871-1910	1871 to 1910 (absolute)	-.07	71	.01	67
1871-1933	Maximum to 1933 (relative)	.05	66	.25	62

NOTES: Urban refers to the percentage in an administrative area living in cities with at least 20,000 residents; rural refers to the percentage living in municipalities with less than 2,000 residents.
Marital fertility in 1871 refers to 1869-1873, in 1885 to 1883-1887, in 1910 to 1908-1912, and in 1933 to 1931-1935.

ral the administrative area is, the higher is its marital fertility and conversely the greater the percent living in cities of 20,000 or more, the lower is its marital fertility. The degree of association in 1871 is very weak and when the four metropolitan administrative areas are excluded the correlation between I_g and percent rural takes an opposite sign. As the fertility decline progressed, urban-rural differentials with lower fertility in cities were created in areas where they did not exist before and were accentuated in areas where they were already evident (see Chapter 3). This development is probably responsible for the stronger correlations evident in 1910 and 1933. The negative correlation of fertility with percent in cities or the positive correlation with percent rural does not necessarily mean that *within* any areas the fertility in cities is lower than in the countryside. It simply means that areas with more of the population living in cities tend to have lower fertility than areas with less living in cities. Thus correlational analysis is no substitute for the actual calculation of separate rural and urban trends in fertility. The interpretation of the correlations becomes more meaningful in conjunction with data on the actual extent of rural-urban fertility differentials.

In order to examine the possibility that the fertility decline was conditioned by the extent to which an area was urbanized prior to the beginning of either the fertility transition or the rural-to-urban transition, we can examine correlations between the percent rural in 1871 and measures of fertility decline (Table 5.8, second part). The results indicate that an association did exist. The more rural an area was in 1871, the later its marital fertility declined ten percent from its pre-decline maximum. This finding is not surprising in light of the consistently earlier decline found in urban fertility in Chapter 3. Alternatively the less rural an area was in 1871 the greater was the magnitude of fertility decline it experienced whether measured by the absolute decline I_g between 1871 and 1910 or by the percentage decline between the maximum predecline value and the 1933 level. Exclusion of the four metropolitan areas has a noticeable effect only on the correlation with the date of decline which although reduced still persists in the same direction at a weaker level. The correlations with the extent of decline are barely affected.

So far we have only examined associations between the proportion urban (or rural) in an administrative area and fertility. If we are to test the hypothesis that the process of urbanization leads to the fertility decline, it is necessary to show that changes in the proportions urban (or rural) of cities are associated with declining fertility. In a very general sense we know from the evidence already presented that a period of rapid urbanization began prior to the fertility decline in much of Germany and continued to proceed along with it. In order to test this association more precisely, we can examine correlations between measures of the process of urbanization and fertility decline using administrative areas as units of observation. If urbanization fosters fertility decline, we would expect to find associations between the initial signs of urbanization and the date fertility started to descend as well as with changes over a longer run between the decline in fertility and changes in rural-urban composition.

With the exception of Berlin, which was already 100 percent urban by 1871, all administrative areas experienced a steady reduction in the proportion rural after 1871. In addition, the proportion of the population living in cities of 20,000 or more increased after 1885, the first census year for which such information is presented. Measurements of the change in percent living in either rural areas or cities are measurements of urbanization in its more narrowly defined sense. Nevertheless the correlations in the third part of Table 5.8 indicate that changes in the percent living in rural areas or cities appears to have exerted little influence over fertility whether or not the four metropolitan administrative areas are excluded. Thus there appears to be little association between the process of urbanization within an administrative area and the decline of fertility in the areas taken as a whole.

Many of the hypotheses suggested above deal specifically with the relationship between urbanization or city growth and either urban fertility or rural fertility considered separately. The series of rural and urban marital fertility indices for Prussian administrative areas permit us to test whether or not some of the suggested associations existed in the context of the German fertility decline.[7]

If urbanization creates pressures within the cities which result in the reduction of fertility, we would expect areas experiencing the fastest and earliest growth in the cities to show the earliest and largest declines in urban fertility. Three measures of urbanization and city growth are used in the analysis: (1) the year in which the size of the

[7]In the following analysis the *Regierungsbezirke* Stettin and Stralsund are treated as separate administrative areas. Correlations between indices which in whole or part are based on urban or rural I_g in 1880 excludes the administrative areas of Hannover and Aurich due to the unreliability of these measures (see Chapter 3). Also measures of urbanization or city growth which are based in whole or part on the size of the urban population after 1885 have not been calculated for Sigmaringen because of the sharp reduction in the number of municipalities officially considered urban after that date. Hence correlations incorporating these indices also exclude Sigmaringen.

urban population in each administrative area increased by 25 percent over the 1867 level (the year was obtained by interpolating between censuses); (2) the percentage increase in the urban population between 1867 and 1910; (3) the increase between 1867 and 1910 in the proportion of the total population that lived in urban municipalities. These measures are not perfect. They are sensitive to the changes in the number of municipalities which were legally defined as cities. With the exception of the administrative area Sigmaringen, which is excluded from the analysis when appropriate, the effect of these changes is not great. Table 5.9 presents the relevant correlations. Neither the date of

TABLE 5.9

URBAN GROWTH, CORRELATION WITH URBAN MARITAL FERTILITY (I_g),
PRUSSIA: 1867 to 1910

	Urban marital fertility (I_g)				Absolute decline, 1880 to 1910	
	Date of 10% decline				All cities	
	All cities		Cities over 20,000			
Measure of urban growth	r	N	r	N	r	N
Date of 25% increase in urban population over 1867 level	.19	32	.36	30	-.26	32
Increase in urban population , 1867-1910 (percent)	-.14	32	-.19	30	.31	32
Increase in proportion urban, 1867-1910 (absolute)	-.41	31	-.36	29	.47	31

NOTE: Berlin excluded from calculations on increase in proportion population urban.

the urban fertility decline nor the extent of decline in I_g between 1880 and 1910 are strongly related to the three indices of urbanization although the associations are in the expected direction. The increase in proportion urban (with the exclusion of Berlin since it was 100 percent urban in 1867) shows the strongest association. Perhaps more refined measures of both urbanization and fertility decline would yield different results. Until this can be shown, however, we must conclude that the evidence so far presented shows only weak support for a direct connection between urbanization and urban fertility decline.

Perhaps of even greater interest than the relationship between urbanization and urban fertility is its connection with rural fertility.

[217]

Correlational analysis has again been applied to the Prussian data to explore the possible associations which existed between measures of urbanization and measures of rural marital fertility during the decades prior to World War I. The results are reported in Table 5.10 and Table 5.11. In 1880, the first year for which we have reliable estimates of rural I_g in Prussia, there is no association between the proportion

TABLE 5.10

URBANIZATION, CORRELATION WITH RURAL MARITAL FERTILITY (I_g), PRUSSIA: 1880 to 1910

Variables correlated		Correlation coefficients	
Percentage urban	Rural marital fertility (I_g)	r	N
1880	1880	-.01	32
1910	1910	-.43	33
1880	Date of 10% decline	-.57	32
1880	Absolute decline, 1880-1910	-.36	32

NOTES: Rural I_g 1880 refers to 1880-1881, rural I_g 1910 refers to 1910-1911.

TABLE 5.11

URBAN GROWTH, CORRELATIONS WITH DECLINE IN RURAL MARITAL FERTILITY (I_g), PRUSSIA: 1867 to 1910

Measure of urban growth	Rural marital fertility (I_g)			
	Date of 10% decline		Absolute decline, 1880-1910	
	Zero order r	Partial r controlling for % urban 1867	Zero order r	Partial r controlling for % urban 1867
Date of 25% increase in urban population over 1867 level	.00	-.05	.05	.01
Increase in urban population, 1867-1910 (percent)	-.18	-.11	.30	.24
Increase in proportion urban, 1867-1910 (absolute)	-.37	-.45	.47	.65

N = 31.

urban in an administrative area and the level of rural marital fertility. However, the areas with higher proportions of the population living in cities experienced earlier declines in I_g, as indicated by the negative correlation between the date of I_g decline and the proportion urban in 1880. Also the more urban administrative areas experienced greater declines in I_g between 1880 and 1910 than the less urban areas. By 1910 the outcome was a negative association between proportion urban and rural I_g. These correlations then lend support to the suggestion that urban areas served as centers of diffusion for the spread of low fertility norms and family limitation into the surrounding countryside. It is also possible that more of the officially rural population in areas with high proportion urban are actually living in a suburban environment than in less urban administrative areas. If this were true the correlations between proportion urban and rural fertility decline might reflect the effect of the city on the suburbs rather than the true rural hinterland. Available data are insufficient to produce a measurement of this effect.

The date of the decline in rural I_g and the magnitude of its decline between 1880 and 1910 were correlated with the three measures of urbanization and city growth described in connection with the urban fertility decline. It seems plausible to assume that the size of the urban population relative to the rural population would influence the effect that urbanization or city growth had on rural fertility. For example, when the urban sector is small in comparison to the rural population, a rural to urban migratory stream of very modest proportions from the standpoint of the countryside could have a very large effect on changes in the city population. In order to allow for this effect, partial correlations were calculated between the fertility and urbanization measures controlling for the proportion urban 1867, the base date from which changes in the urban population were measured. Table 5.11 presents both the zero order and partial correlations.

Increases in the proportion urban between 1867 and 1910 exert the strongest influence on rural I_g. The greater the increase, the earlier the rural marital fertility declines and the greater the extent of its reduction between 1880 and 1910. The relationship is strengthened when we control for the initial proportion urban in 1867. One possible interpretation of this association is that the more rapid urbanization reflects greater rural to urban migration which helps' to establish informal communication networks between the cities and areas of origin of the rural migrants and thereby facilitates the spread of urbanism including low fertility norms and birth control. The results are contrary to the hypothesis that rural to urban migration retards fertility reduction. The interpretation of increases in the proportion urban in an administrative area as an indicator of rural-urban migration in the area even when we control for the initial proportion urban requires qualification. The rural migrants of any particular administrative area do not necessarily move to cities within the same area. Thus an area with slow urbanization is not necessarily characterized by a sedentary rural population. Also the rates of natural increase in both the rural and urban population influence the changes in the proportion living in cities even in the absence of migration. To complicate matters even further changes in rural fertility directly affect the rural rate of natural increase. Additional data are needed to determine the extent of these influences.

In order to further test the possibility that rapid urbanization retards the onset of the rural fertility decline, measures of urbanization and city growth are correlated with the differences between the years of ten percent decline in rural and urban I_g (Table 5.12). According to the theory of the "multi-phasic demographic response," greater and earlier increases in proportions urban and city growth should be associated with longer lags between urban and rural fertility decline. According to the diffusion hypothesis the opposite should hold. The results of the correlational analysis give little support to either position. Almost no association existed between the indices of urbanization or city growth and the lag in the dates of rural and urban fertility decline in Prussia. Controlling for the proportion urban in 1867 through partial correlation makes no difference. The lag between rural and urban decline was most strongly associated with the date of a 25 percent increase in the urban population. The negative correlation indicates that earlier increases in city size are associated with greater delays in rural fertility decline. Again the same reservations expressed above hold concerning the interpretation of city growth or

TABLE 5.12

URBAN GROWTH, CORRELATION WITH LAG BETWEEN URBAN AND
RURAL DECLINES IN MARITAL FERTILITY (I_g),
PRUSSIA: 1867 to 1910

| | Lag between urban and rural declines in marital fertility (I_g) | | | |
| | All cities (N = 31) | | Cities over 20,000 (N = 29) | |
Measure of urban growth	Zero order r	Partial r controlling for % urban 1867	Zero order r	Partial r controlling for % urban 1867
Date of 25% increase in urban population over 1867 level	-.20	-.20	-.38	-.38
Increase in urban population, 1867-1910 (percent)	-.10	-.10	.02	.03
Increase in proportion urban, 1867-1910 (absolute)	.15	.15	.10	.10

NOTE: Lag is defined as the difference between the dates of 10% decline in I_g for the urban and rural populations within each area.

increasing proportions urban as indications of the rural to urban migration in an administrative area.

Conclusion

In a very general way the period of fertility decline in Germany was also a time of substantial migratory movement. Long distance moves took Germans from agrarian administrative areas to industrializing ones or even further to the New World overseas. At the same time within each administrative area the population was shifting from the countryside to the urban centers. On the national level the broad social changes encompassed in modernization and the development of Germany into an industrial state were probably responsible for both the transformation of reproductive behavior and the intensified internal migrations.

A closer examination of the data on fertility decline and migration on the level of the administrative area suggests that the two demographic processes were also interrelated in a somewhat different manner. Areas of heavy out-migration were also areas where fertility declined later and more modestly, at least until 1910. Although this result is consistent with the hypothesis that net out-migration served as a temporary alternative to fertility decline, the association practically disappears when we control for the degree of social and economic backwardness through partial correlation. It seems equally plausible therefore that the conditions in "backward" areas, at least in terms of being highly agricultural and having higher proportions of illiterates, encouraged out-migration and impeded the spread of modern fertility levels.

The possible connections between urbanization and the fertility decline within the urban and rural sectors of an administrative area are complicated. Rapid and early urbanization and city growth appear to foster declines in urban fertility in Prussia but the association is weak. Very little evidence exists that migration from the countryside to the cities retarded the adoption of family limitation in the rural areas. Rather, fertility decline in the rural sectors was earlier and more intense in administrative areas in which the urban sector constituted a larger proportion of the population and was expanding most rapidly.

In conclusion, we might speculate that urbanization, rather than being a major cause of the fertility decline, was a response to the same general change in the social and economic structure that also resulted in changing attitudes towards family limitation. The cities, although not the cause, apparently served as the loci from which these new attitudes were diffused. The large number of newly arrived migrants from the countryside might have acted as effective communication links between the longer term urban dwellers and those who remained in the villages and on the farms.

CHAPTER 6: The Social Context of the German Fertility Decline

In the previous chapters we have dealt with the role of several social factors in connection with the decline of fertility in Germany. Urbanization and migration can be considered social processes as well as demographic ones, and the social differentials in fertility explored in Chapter 3 contribute to our understanding of the general social context in which the fertility transition in Germany took place. In this chapter we will examine the relationship of several additional social factors with marital fertility as well as reintroduce some of the variables we have previously considered.

The integral link between the demographic transition and modernization implies a host of relationships between the fertility decline and various aspects of the society in which it takes place (Notestein, 1945; Cowgill, 1963; Heer, 1966). Such relationships can be hypothesized both with respect to the societal norms and the socio-economic structure (Freedman, 1961–62). Many of the linkages which can be theoretically drawn, however, elude empirical exploration, particularly when we are dealing with the experience of countries over the last century. Very few of the many possible factors that might have influenced the basic changes occurring in reproductive behavior can be identified in the available statistics. Usually only rather crude indices can be constructed, yielding at best a very broad outline of socio-economic structure. Social historians who wish to detail the more intricate and complex facets of modernization need to resort to data outside the statistical realm. In particular, it is especially difficult to document changes in individually held norms and attitudes in a way that can be easily integrated into a statistical analysis of fertility. Almost no equivalent to the modern social survey existed at the time of the fertility decline in Europe, and hence investigators must infer attitudes and opinions from much less precise evidence.

The scope of the present chapter is limited to an investigation of a few selected social and demographic variables for which indices can be compiled on the administrative area level and thus be analyzed in relation to our measures of marital fertility with relative ease. No attempt will be made to provide a general social history of Germany. Indeed historical details are largely ignored.

The new variables to be introduced into our analysis include indices of the distribution of the population with respect to dependence on the major sectors of industry, an index of women's employment in non-agricultural labor, an index of the prevalence of savings accounts, and an index of illiteracy. In addition several social and demographic variables examined in previous chapters such as the proportion Catholic, infant mortality, and the index of proportion married will be reintroduced in order to produce a broader impression of the social context of the fertility decline in Germany. Nevertheless, it is clear that many other factors that may well have played an instrumental role in the German experience are not included. Julius Wolf (1912 and 1928), for example, has stressed the importance of changing sexual morality. Religiosity, higher education, inheritance patterns, and land tenure systems are other variables, to name but a few, which might be connected closely to major shifts in fertility behavior but either do not readily lend themselves to statistical measurement in general or else are not documented sufficiently to permit construction of indices on the administrative area level.

Before proceeding to the details about the data and their analysis, it seems appropriate to repeat a brief word of warning concerning the interpretation of the results. The main approach to be employed consists largely of attempts to associate levels of changes in independent variables with the onset or extent of fertility decline in the different administrative areas of Germany. Thus we are dealing with data for rather large aggregates; the unit of analysis is the population of an area rather than an individual or a family. Associations found between area characteristics and area fertility levels can not be automatically extended to the individual level although the temptation to do so is often great. It is all too easy to become entangled in the well known ecological fallacy.

Additional Social Variables

To evaluate the social context of the German fertility decline more fully, we introduce in this chapter several new social indices that should help us test some of the most commonly suggested associations between fertility decline and socio-economic structure. The first set of indices refers to the distribution of the population according to its dependence on the major sectors of the industry. On the basis of the occupational censuses (*Berufszählungen*) we have computed separately the percent of the population dependent on primary industry (largely agriculture but also forestry and fishing), secondary industry (manufacturing, mining, and construction), and tertiary industry (trade, transportation, and communications). We have chosen indices that refer to the dependence of the total population rather than a similar and perhaps more conventional set of measures indicating the distribution of the labor force (*Erwerbspersonen*) by economic sector. The reason for this decision was that the former indices avoid confusions in interpretations created by female employment in agriculture. Since wives more often assist their husbands in the primary sector than in other sectors and are often counted as part of the labor force, the percent of the labor force employed in primary industry is considerably larger than the percent of the population dependent on that sector and as an index is less sensitive to shifts in the socio-economic structure of the population.

The extent to which Germany was transformed from an agarian and newly industrializing nation at the time of Unification to a fully industrialized nation by the 1930s is reflected in the changing distribution of the population's dependence on the three main sectors of the economy (Table 6.1). The first occupational census was taken in 1882, more than a decade after unification and after the economic transformation of Germany had already gained a firm foothold. The 1871 census included some data on the occupation of respondents. The results, however, were conceded to be generally unsatisfactory by the national statistical bureau. Lack of specificity in the census questions and problems in coding rendered the results ambiguous. Although some of the data were published in the 1871 census volumes, they are accompanied by an explanation of the problems involved in their interpretation and a warning that comparisons of the results for the various German states would be misleading (*Statistik des Deutschen Reichs*, 1st Series, vol. 14, part IV, 189–196). The classification of respondents employed in or dependent on the secondary and tertiary

TABLE 6.1

SOCIO-ECONOMIC INDICES: 1871 TO 1939

Census year	Percentage population dependent on industrial sector			Nonagricultural female employment		Illiterate recruits (percent)
	Primary	Secondary	Tertiary	All women 14 or over (% employed)	Married women (% employed)	
1871	--	(32.8)[a]	(9.0)[a]	--	--	2.4[b]
1882	42.5	35.5	10.0	9.4	2.7	1.5
1895	35.8	39.1	11.5	11.7	4.3	0.2
1907	28.6	42.8	13.4	14.3	6.6	--
1925	23.0	42.0	16.7	18.0	9.1	--
1933	21.0	38.0	16.9	17.9	9.7	--
1939	18.2	--	--	19.4	--	--

NOTES: Definitions of industrial sectors are not consistent in all censuses.
Nonagricultural female employment refers to women employed in secondary and tertiary industries.
1933 data exclude the Saar.
1939 data exclude areas annexed after 1937.

[a] Figures of questionable reliability.
[b] 1875.

sectors was less affected than the other classifications, and therefore indices referring to these sectors were extended back to 1871 in Table 6.1 but bracketed to indicate the lack of strict comparability. In general, the results referring to occupation and economic activity in the 1871 population census and the 1882 occupational census are not comparable in either the national or the administrative area level (*Statistik des Deutschen Reichs*, new series, vol. 2, pp. 2*–3*). Our correlational analysis with fertility indices therefore does not utilize any of the data on economic activity from the 1871 census.

At any given time, administrative areas can be compared with respect to their population's dependence on each of three major industrial sectors in order to guage the agrarian or industrial character of the area. Of course for any year there are high inter-correlations among the three indices. For example in 1907 for the 71 administrative areas the percent dependent on primary industry was strongly correlated in a negative direction both with the percent dependent on secondary industry ($r = -.85$) and on tertiary industry ($r = -.70$).

Substantial differences existed within Germany. Some impression of the territorial differences in the extent to which an area was agrarian is given by Map 6.1, which depicts the percent dependent on primary

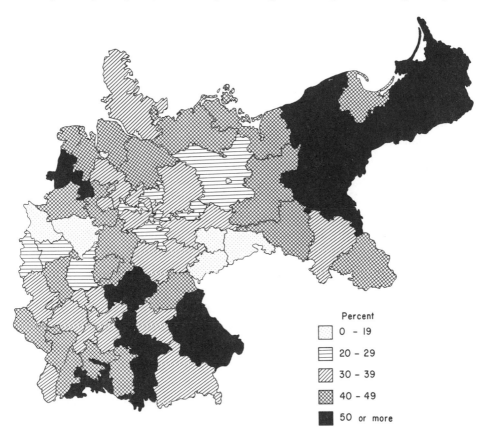

Percent

☐ 0 – 19

☰ 20 – 29

▨ 30 – 39

▩ 40 – 49

■ 50 or more

Map 6.1.   Dependence on Primary Industry, by Administrative Area: 1895

industry in 1895. Particularly striking is high dependence on agriculture in the eastern administrative areas of Prussia and much of Southern Germany. In contrast, agriculture was relatively unimportant not only in the four metropolitan administrative areas but in the largely industrial state of Saxony and the newly industrializing areas of Arnsberg and Düsseldorf. An analysis of variance ($F_{6,64} = 4.9$, $\epsilon = .50$) indicates a moderate association for 1895 between the percent dependent on primary industry and our regional classification.

A number of theoretical arguments can be made for expecting an association between fertility levels or fertility decline and the distribution of the population with respect to its dependence on the major branches of industry. In particular, high dependency in agriculture is thought to be associated with high fertility and late decline. Arguments reviewed in Chapter 3 in connection with differential fertility according to economic activity and rural residence come to mind. The economic utility of children in an agrarian context particularly when they can do a share of the labor is greater than in other situations and the cost of upbringing is less. Child labor in factories was not common in Germany during most of the 19th century. Substantial restrictions on the employment of minors in factories were legislated in 1839 and 1853 in Prussia, 1840 and 1854 in Bavaria, 1840 in Baden and 1861 in the kingdom of Saxony (Hamerow, 1969, pp. 76–77). In 1869 the Prussian laws were made applicable throughout the North German Confederation and after unification were adopted by many other states (von Landman, 1909). Such laws of course did not apply to the work of children under the direction of their father on the family farm. As industrialization proceeded and the labor force shifted out of the primary sector, the utility of child labor probably diminished thus removing one incentive for large families (Heer, 1968).

The immediate implications for fertility of increases in industrial employment however is not completely clear. In the long run changes brought about by industrialization surely act as a depressant on fertility at least in relation to pre-industrial levels. But the short range effect may be different. Wrigley (1961, p. 136) found that the coal mining and industrial districts of Rheinland and Westphalia had higher fertility than the adjacent rural areas during the period of rapid industrialization at the end of the nineteenth century. Heer (1966 and 1968) suggests that economic development in the narrow sense of rising real income per capita fosters fertility, but because it sets in motion other associated forces that act as fertility depressants it is frequently associated with fertility declines. Unfortunately we do not have data on average real income or average real wages for German administrative areas, although several detailed studies in the national level have been made (e.g. Bry, 1960; Desai, 1968). Thus we can not put this hypothesis directly to test for Germany.

Another process that accompanies modernization and has frequently been related to the decline of fertility, at least on a theoretical plane, has been the emancipation of women in an industrializing society. One index which should be sensitive to the changing status of women is their employement rate in non-agricultural occupations, especially in secondary and tertiary industry. Several indices of women's employment can be derived from data provided in the periodic occupational censuses in combination with information from the population censuses. Table 6.1 shows the national trend in two such indices. The first indicates the proportion of all women aged 14 and over employed in secondary and tertiary industry combined. The second index indicates the percent of married women holding jobs in these sectors. For both indices the number employed was taken from the occupational censuses and the number of women in the denominator was estimated from population census results by interpolation. Both measures show increases in women's employment that are larger than would be expected simply from the overall growth of the secondary and tertiary sectors. Employment of married women increased even faster than employment of women without regard to marital status.

There were considerable differences in female employment rates within Germany at any given time. In 1882 the percent of women 14 and over employed in secondary and tertiary industry ranged from 2.8 percent in the administrative area Marienwerder to 27.4 percent in Zwickau. Of course both at different times and in different places, the employment of women in Germany outside of agriculture depended not only on the status of women but also on the size of the secondary and tertiary sectors in general. Thus high correlations exist between our indices of women's employment and the indices of dependence on the various economic sectors. In 1882, for example, among the 71 administrative areas, the proportion of women 14 or over employed in secondary and tertiary industry was correlated negatively with the proportion of the population dependent on agriculture ($r = -.69$) and positively with proportion dependent on secondary ($r = .69$) or tertiary industry ($r = .41$).

Women's employment is just one facet of the changing status of women, but indices representing more subtle or varied aspects of the process are more difficult to extract from German statistics. Previous considerations of the impact of changes in the role of women in German society on fertility have centered not only on employment but on other aspects as well (e.g. Wolf, 1912 and 1928; Von Ungern-Sternberg, 1931, pp. 27–32 and 41–48). A monograph by Marie Bernays (1916) was devoted exclusively to exploring the connection between women's employment, particularly in factories, and fertility. The theoretical associations between women's employment and fertility is usually considered to be negative. High rates of employment outside of agriculture are thought to be a depressant on fertility. In addition, increases in women's employment were expected to foster the decline in fertility.

Another variable which could have been of considerable importance to the fertility is education. In order to investigate the influence of education we introduce into the analysis an index of illiteracy among recruits into the German forces. Unfortunately the German censuses never included questions on the number of years of schooling completed by the population. Since illiteracy was all but erased among adults by the 1870s in most German administrative areas, this index is a rather unsatisfactory measure of education in general. In 1875, the earliest year for which a national statistic exists, just 2.4 percent of the recruits could neither read nor write. Only among recruits from the eastern provinces of Westpreussen and Posnania was the percent illiterate in the vicinity of 10 percent or more. For most areas over 99 percent were classified as literates. By 1895 illiteracy was for all practical purposes nonexistent among recruits in all parts of Germany. Clearly the direct significance of illiteracy rates for fertility is minimal since such small numbers of uneducated could have only an insubstantial effect on the reproduction of the total population. However, to the extent that we can interpret illiteracy rates as indirect indicators of the educational status of the general population they can have some meaning for our analysis.

There is no doubt that substantial differences in the average level of education existed within Germany at the time of unification and that substantial changes in the educational level of the population were taking place throughout the nineteenth century and into the twentieth. According to the 1871 Prussian census, among the population over 10 who gave information on the topic, the number who could read and write was less than 60 percent in the administrative area of Bromberg and over 98 percent in Wiesbaden. The average for all of Prussia was 87.6 percent. Among recruits, however, the percent illiterate dropped from over 40 percent in 1837 in Posen and Bromberg to under 15 percent by unification, suggesting radical increases in the educational level even where illiteracy was the highest at the time of unification. Hamerow (1969, pp. 276–283), in reviewing the educational system in the German states during the two decades preceding unification, points out that classroom attendance and popular literacy were higher in the German Confederation than anywhere else in Europe. Education above the primary level, however, was designed largely to train a small elite who eventually filled positions in the bureaucracy, in skilled professions, and in important industrial and agricultural enterprises. For the lower classes only very elementary instruction was provided to help them practice their everyday occupations more effectively without arousing extravagant expectations. Thus although outright illiteracy was low, the average level of education was not high, at least in terms of modern standards. Hence following unification and during the period of the fertility decline there was substantial room for improvement in educational levels. Statistics on illiteracy unfortunately do not allow us to measure the progress made. Improvements in education above the most elementary levels may have had important implications for fertility but we are unable to incorporate an adequate measure of this into our analysis.[1] In general we would expect increases in education or literacy to have a depressing effect on fertility, at least during the initial phases of the fertility transition. Education should foster the flow of communications of all types and thus facilitate the

[1]Carl Schulze (1968, pp. 87–93) in a senior thesis for the Department of Sociology at Princeton University found a very strong association between cohort fertility in German states and provinces and the ratio of middle and high school students to elementary school students.

diffusion of new information and attitudes towards birth control and family size. Also increased education should contribute to the spread of rationality and secularism, which may be crucial to the acceptance of family limitation.

The last index we introduce in our analysis relates the number of bank accounts to the size of the population. Although the meaning of this measure may be subject to a variety of interpretations, it was used extensively by Mombert (1907, pp. 171–195) as a measure of prosperity. His purpose for introducing it was to show that a negative association existed between fertility levels and prosperity and a positive association between increases in prosperity and declines in fertility. We have taken the number of bank accounts per 100 population in 1900 largely from data provided by Mombert (1907, pp. 175–176).[2] Data were not readily available for a number of administrative areas for other years since the national statistical bureau published bank account statistics for states and provinces rather than for administrative areas. Mombert had supplemented this material through personal communications and thus could present a more detailed series. Even so his series lacks information for several areas.[3] Because the number of administrative areas which lacked the relevant data was much larger for other years, we utilize this index only for 1900.

Zero order correlations between the social indices described above and selected measures of marital fertility are presented in Tables 6.2 through 6.6. In Table 6.2 the level of fertility is correlated with the percent dependent on each of the three main sectors of industry. As expected, I_g is positively correlated with the percent dependent on primary industry and negatively with dependence on secondary or tertiary industry. However, the degree of association is rather weak

[2]A review of the published data for 1900 revealed that Mombert's figures for Lippe, Lothringen, and Berlin were incorrect. In our analysis we have substituted the correct figures for his incorrect ones. Thus for Lippe the number of bank accounts per 100 population was 53.8 not 30.3, for Lothringen 19.4 not 20.6, and for Berlin 37.4 not 37.3.

[3]Data is completely lacking for Braunschweig. Data were given only for the Grandduchy of Oldenburg and not separately for the three administrative areas. The figure for the Grandduchy was assigned to the administrative area of Oldenburg in our analysis and no values were assigned to F. Lübeck or Birkenfeld. Also data were given only for Württemberg and not for the four constituent administrative areas. However the overall figure for Württemberg was assigned to all four of the areas in our analysis.

TABLE 6.2

POPULATION DEPENDENT ON INDUSTRIAL SECTORS, CORRELATION WITH
MARITAL FERTILITY (I_g): 1882 TO 1933

Level of marital fertility (I_g)	Census year	Percentage population dependent on sector			$\underline{N}$
		Primary	Secondary	Tertiary	
Maximum	1882	.30	-.16	-.35	71
1880	1882	.33	-.17	-.37	71
1910	1907	.66	-.43	-.61	71
1933	1933	.77	--	--	66

TABLE 6.3

CHANGE IN POPULATION DEPENDENT ON INDUSTRIAL SECTORS, CORRELATION WITH DECLINE IN
MARITAL FERTILITY (I_g): 1882-1907

Decline in marital fertility (I_g)	Change in percentage population dependent on sector					
	All areas (N=71)			Excluding metro. areas (N=66)		
	Primary	Secondary	Tertiary	Primary	Secondary	Tertiary
Maximum to 1910 (absolute)	-.11	.19	-.38	.05	.06	-.41
Maximum to 1910 (percent)	-.11	.20	-.44	.10	.04	-.50
Date by 10%	.12	-.20	.36	-.05	-.07	.40
Date I_g = .500	.06	-.14	.43	-.19	-.03	.53

TABLE 6.4

NONAGRICULTURAL FEMALE EMPLOYMENT, CORRELATION WITH MARITAL
FERTILITY (I_g): 1882 TO 1907

Level of marital fertility (I_g)	Census year	Percentage of women employed, by sector		
		Secondary	Tertiary	Secondary and Tertiary
Maximum	1882	-.02	.03	-.01
1880	1882	-.05	-.03	-.05
1910	1907	-.38	-.37	-.43

N = 71

NOTE: Data on female employment exclude women under age 14.

TABLE 6.5

CHANGE IN NONAGRICULTURAL FEMALE EMPLOYMENT, CORRELATION WITH DECLINE IN MARITAL
FERTILITY (I_g): 1882-1907

	Change in percentage women employed, by sector					
	All areas (N=71)			Excluding metro. areas (N=66)		
Decline in marital fertility (I_g)	Secondary	Tertiary	Secondary and Tertiary	Secondary	Tertiary	Secondary and Tertiary
Maximum to 1910 (absolute)	.26	.44	.41	.36	.35	.43
Maximum to 1910 (percent)	.18	.43	.34	.31	.29	.37
Date by 10%	-.28	-.44	-.43	-.39	-.34	-.45
Date I_g = .500	.00	-.29	-.13	-.11	-.11	-.13

NOTE: Data on female employment exclude women under age 14.

TABLE 6.6

LEVEL OF ILLITERACY AND NUMBER OF BANK ACCOUNTS, CORRELATIONS WITH MARITAL FERTILITY (I_g)

Level of marital fertility (I_g)	Percentage illiterate among recruits in 1875 (N=71)	Bank accounts per 100 persons in 1900 (N=68)
Maximum	.30	-.51
1880	.32	-.52
1900	.48	-.62
1910	.54	-.63

prior to the turn of the century. When we examine the possibility that changes in economic activity are associated with fertility decline we find quite different results (Table 6.3). In all areas the percent dependent on primary industry decreased between 1882 and 1907, during the same period it increased in all areas for tertiary industry and in almost every area for secondary industry. If we consider all 71 administrative areas the magnitude of the decline in primary industry shows a very weak negative correlation with the magnitude of the decline in I_g prior to 1910 and a very weak positive correlation with the date of the fertility decline. Thus the correlations are in the opposite direction from that expected. The same is true for correlations between changes in dependence on secondary industry. Only changes in tertiary industry correlate in the expected direction with the date and magnitude of fertility decline. One reason for the unexpected direction of the correlations between decreases in primary industry results from the very low dependence on this sector in the four metropolitan administrative areas. Since very few persons earned their living in the primary sector in either Berlin or the three city states in 1882, there was almost no possibility for this index to decrease even though fertility could and did decrease substantially. When we eliminate these four areas from the correlations, the signs of the coefficients revert to the expected direction for dependence on primary industry but still are so low as to signify virtually no association.

The level of women's employment outside of agriculture shows almost no correlation with the level of I_g prior to the fertility decline (Table 6.4). By 1910 a weak negative correlation emerged indicating that higher levels of female employment are associated with lower levels of marital fertility as expected. Increases between 1882 and 1907 in the indices of female employment in secondary or tertiary industry are also weakly correlated in the expected direction with the magnitude and timing of the fertility decline (Table 6.5). These correlations are changed very little by the exclusion of the four metropolitan areas.

Correlations in the expected direction result when we relate the measure of illiteracy among recruits and the index of savings accounts to the level of I_g (Table 6.6). Correlations between changes in these indices and changes in fertility are not presented. Illiteracy rates were so low in most areas by 1875 that subsequent changes would be almost meaningless. Indeed the correlation between fertility levels and illiteracy among recruits in 1875 results largely from the fact that the few areas with exceptionally high illiteracy (i.e. the eastern Prussian administrative areas and to a lesser extent a few Bavarian areas) also had exceptionally high marital fertility. Among the remainder of the areas virtually no association existed. Statistics on savings accounts were not available for many administrative areas except in 1900 (from Mombert's study) and thus changes in this index could not be calculated. Mombert (1907, p. 194) presents data for 34 Prussian administrative areas on changes in marital fertility (as measured by legitimate births per 100 married women in the reproductive ages) and increases in the ratio of savings accounts to population between 1885 and 1900. The two measures show a substantial negative association ($r = -.63$)

indicating that the more the index of savings account increased the more marital fertility declined.

Zero order correlations were also calculated between the level of the socio-economic indices being discussed and the date marital fertility declined as well as the magnitude of its decline by 1910 (Table 6.7). The indices refer to the earliest year for which observations were

TABLE 6.7

SOCIO-ECONOMIC INDICES, CORRELATIONS WITH DECLINE IN MARITAL FERTILITY (I_g)

Decline in marital fertility (I_g)	Percentage population dependent on industrial sector, 1882			Nonagricultural female employment, 1882	Percentage illiterate among recruits, 1875	Bank accounts per 100 persons, 1900
	Primary	Secondary	Tertiary			
Maximum to 1910 (absolute)	-.66	.58	.46	.66	-.50	.43
Maximum to 1910 (percent)	-.73	.59	.56	.63	-.52	.55
Date by 10%	.51	-.39	-.41	-.50	.50	-.38
Date I_g = .500	.65	-.47	-.57	-.44	.38	-.61

NOTE: N=71 for all measurements except bank accounts, where N=68.
Nonagricultural female employment refers to the percentage of women aged 14 or over employed in secondary and tertiary industries.

available. Except for the savings account index which refers to 1900, the indices refer to years prior to or close to the onset of the fertility transition. These correlations enable us to examine possible associations between the socio-economic situation in German administrative areas just after unification and the subsequent decline in marital fertility. In general the degree of association found is moderately high and in each case in the expected direction. In sum, early and large reductions in marital fertility are associated with populations that prior to or at the onset of the decline were less dependent on primary industry and more dependent on secondary and tertiary industry, showed higher rates of female employment outside of agriculture, had very few illiterates among its recruits, and had a greater tendency to maintain savings accounts.

Multivariate Analyses of the Fertility Decline

In order to have a fuller picture of the social context of the German fertility decline, we want to know not only which simple associations

[236]

existed between socio-economic indices and fertility but also how each association is affected when the influences of the others are taken into account. We are also interested in the extent to which the variation in fertility can be statistically accounted for by all the other variables taken together. The method we have used for this purpose is partial and multiple correlation analysis. We will consider several of the indices introduced in the previous section as well as reintroduce several variables examined in previous chapters.

In the multiple and partial correlation analysis four measures of marital fertility serve as separate dependent variables: the maximum predecline level of I_g, the year I_g attained a sustained decline of 10 percent, and the absolute and relative decline in I_g between its maximum value and 1910. Four independent variables are related to each of the four fertility measures: the index of savings account for 1900, the percent dependent on primary industry in 1882, the index of illiteracy among recruits, and the proportion Catholic in 1880. In addition, a fifth independent variable referring to infant mortality is included in the analysis. However when we focus on the level of predecline marital fertility, the level of infant mortality in 1875–1880 is included, and when we focus on the date or magnitude of fertility decline, we substitute instead the estimated year that infant mortality declined by 50 points. Independent variables that were very highly correlated with each other and were conceptually very similar were not included in the analysis since it would make little sense to hold one constant while examining the association between the other and fertility. Therefore we did not include the percent rural, the percent dependent on secondary or primary industry, or the index of women's employment in non-agricultural occupations, since all are very closely related to the index of dependence on primary industry.

Table 6.8 presents the partial and multiple correlation coefficients between the selected independent variables and the four fertility measures. We have also reported the zero-order coefficients in the same table in order to facilitate the comparison. In all cases both the zero order and partial correlations are in the expected directions. However, the strength of the partial usually differs considerably from the simple correlations. Thus when the other variables are taken into account the

TABLE 6.8

SOCIO-ECONOMIC AND DEMOGRAPHIC INDICES, ZERO ORDER, PARTIAL, AND MULTIPLE CORRELATIONS WITH MARITAL FERTILITY (I_g)

			Decline in I_g					
Independent variables	Maximum I_g		Date by 10%		Maximum to 1910 (absolute)		Maximum to 1910 (percent)	
	Zero order r	Partial r	Zero order r	Partial r	Zero order r	Partial r	Zero order r	Partial r
Percentage dependent on primary industry 1882	.30	.05	.51	.40	-.66	-.61	-.73	-.65
Illiteracy 1875	.29	.08	.50	.25	-.50	-.23	-.52	-.21
Bank accounts 1900	-.51	-.10	-.38	-.06	.43	.05	.55	.06
Percentage Catholic 1880	.74	.56	.20	.19	-.18	-.08	-.36	-.31
Infant mortality rate:								
Level 1875-1880	.45	.34	--	--	--	--	--	--
At date of decline by 50	--	--	.55	.65	-.47	-.60	-.34	-.55
R^2	.60		.62		.68		.72	

NOTES: Illiteracy refers to the percentage of recruits illiterate.
Bank accounts refer to the number of bank accounts per 100 persons.

association between the maximum level of I_g and the indices of saving accounts, dependence on primary industry and illiteracy practically disappear. It appears that among the variables included religious composition and the level of infant mortality were the most important determinants of predecline fertility. The most notable feature of the partial correlations with the date and magnitude of fertility decline is the prominence of relationships with dependence on primary industry and the timing of the decline in infant mortality. The former is only slightly reduced when the other factors are taken into account while the latter is actually strengthened by this procedure. When all the independent variables are considered simultaneously, well over half of the variance in the fertility measures is statistically accounted for as indicated by the multiple correlations (R^2).

In Chapter 1 we introduced a classification scheme that grouped the 71 German administrative areas into seven broader regions. In subsequent chapters strong regional associations were found both for fertility and other variables. We have evaluated the strength of the regional influence through the analysis of variance and generally found that characteristics of administrative areas within the same region were much more similar than the average characteristics of the regions themselves. Although the statististical interpretation of these results is straightforward, the sociological meaning is less precise. It seems reasonable to assume however that areas within the same region are more likely to share a similar cultural heritage, history, or dialect as well as being alike with respect to their socio-economic structure than areas in different regions. Indeed, results of analysis of variance indicate some regional association for most of the socio-economic variables introduced into this study.

The question we now turn to is how the association between fertility and other variables is affected when we control for the influence of region. In order to remove the regional impact, we can compute for each administrative area the deviation of every variable from the mean value for the region in which it lies, and then using these regionally adjusted indices calculate the correlations between fertility and the independent variables. The results presented in Table 6.9 indicate

TABLE 6.9

SOCIO-ECONOMIC AND DEMOGRAPHIC INDICES REGIONALLY ADJUSTED, ZERO ORDER, PARTIAL, AND MULTIPLE CORRELATIONS WITH MARITAL FERTILITY (I_g) REGIONALLY ADJUSTED

| | Maximum I_g | | Date by 10% | | Decline in I_g | | | |
| | | | | | Maximum to 1910 (absolute) | | Maximum to 1910 (percent) | |
Independent variables	Zero order r	Partial r	Zero order r	Partial r	Zero order r	Partial r	Zero order r	Partial r
Percentage dependent on primary industry 1882	.08	.20	.62	.50	-.71	-.63	-.75	-.69
Illiteracy 1875	.02	-.06	.33	.13	-.23	-.03	-.21	.01
Bank accounts 1900	.00	.06	-.49	-.18	.44	.09	.44	.06
Percentage Catholic 1880	.39	.34	.28	.20	-.20	-.13	-.25	-.23
Infant mortality rate:								
Level 1875-1880	.43	.40	--	--	--	--	--	--
At date of decline by 50	--	--	.49	.30	-.45	-.28	-.42	-.25
R^2	.32		.54		.58		.63	

NOTES: Both independent and dependent variables are measured as deviations from regional means.
Illiteracy refers to the percentage of recruits illiterate.
Bank accounts refer to the number of bank accounts per 100 persons.

the level of association between variables once the effects of the region in which an administrative area is located have been removed. Both zero order and partial coefficients are indicated as well as the multiple correlations. In order to guage the effect of removing regional influence it is useful to compare Table 6.9 with Table 6.8 which presented the equivalent correlations for the regionally "unadjusted" values of the variables. The first point to note is the value of the multiple correlation (R^2) when all variables are in their original form and when all variables are measured in terms of deviations from the regional means. The amount of variance in the fertility variables "explained" by association with the independent variables listed in the stub of the table is sharply diminished in the first instance (the maximum value of I_g prior to decline) and much less substantially reduced when the independent variable is the date of decline in I_g or the amount of decline by 1910 in absolute percent terms.

The second point to note in Tables 6.8 and 6.9 is the change in the correlation coefficients (especially the partial correlation coefficients) that take place when the effect of "region" is removed by making measurements from regional means. Partial correlation coefficients with the proportion of the population dependent on primary industry are increased, and partial correlations between fertility variables and the date of infant mortality decline are greatly reduced. The partial correlation between percent Catholic and the level of I_g before decline is substantially diminished, but the partial relation to other fertility variables is hardly affected by holding region constant. The partial correlations in Table 6.9, where the influence of location by region has been minimized, can be briefly summarized as follows: with the influence of regional location controlled, the independent variables considered explain only a small fraction of the variance in marital fertility before the decline began; the most important operating variables are mortality and proportion Catholic. The variables most strongly associated with the decline in fertility — its date of inception and its extent by 1910 — are the proportion of the population dependent on primary industry and, at a distinctly lower level of correlation, the date of decline in infant mortality, and finally with still smaller coefficients of partial correlation, the percent Catholic. Note that the partial correlation between the proportion in primary industry and the fertility variables is either undiminished or actually increased when the variables are measured in terms of deviations from the regional averages.

It is quite possible that had we been able to introduce additional variables into our analysis a different or more complete picture would have resulted. The socio-economic indices we used were crude and perhaps covered up interesting results that would have emerged from more refined indices. The index of illiteracy seemed particularly tenuous as a measurement of education. The difficulties in constructing satisfactory indices which both maintain face validity and are available on a comparable basis for all administrative areas impose severe limits on the extent to which the analysis could be extended. Nevertheless, some aspects of the German fertility decline have been at least slightly clarified.

Conclusion

The theory of the demographic transition interprets the secular decline of fertility as a response to economic, demographic (largely with respect to mortality decline), and social changes when a society develops from a basically agrarian to a predominantly industrial sta te One implication is that a certain minimum level of socio-economic development is required before the processes that precipitate the fertility decline are set into motion. This "threshold" hypothesis has been stated recently by a U.N. report (United Nations, 1963, p. 143): "According to this (threshold) hypothesis, in a developing country where fertility is initially high, improving economic and social conditions are likely to have little if any effect on fertility until a certain economic and social level is reached; but once that level is achieved, fertility is likely to enter a decided decline and to continue downward until it is again stabilized on a much lower plane."

It seems a fitting conclusion to the study of the fertility decline in Germany to examine the experience of the different administrative areas in connection with the threshold hypothesis. It presents a last opportunity to bring together a number of the variables examined previously. As a first step, we will compare the diversity of areas with respect to selected socio-economic and demographic variables both at the time fertility began to decline in each and at some point prior to the general fertility transition.

If a clear threshold exists we would expect areas to be similar to each other with respect to socio-economic indices at the onset of the fertility decline, since it is at this time the crucial threshold level of socio-economic development is reached. Admittedly this is an overly simplistic interpretation of the threshold hypothesis. Any threshold would probably involve some complicated mix of social, economic, and demographic development, and thus there is no reason to assume that all areas would have identical values for each variable. Nevertheless, if the threshold hypothesis has much validity we would at least expect less dispersion in the socio-economic structure of areas at the onset of the fertility transition than at some given time prior to it.

The time of the onset of the fertility decline has been set for each area as the estimated year I_g sustained a 10 percent reduction from its maximum predecline level. The level of each socio-economic or demographic index at the onset of the fertility decline has been estimated for each administrative area by interpolation between years for which data are available. For example administrative area Oberbayern experienced a sustained decline of 10 percent in I_g by 1886. The percent dependent on primary industry for this year was then estimated by interpolating between the levels indicated in the 1882 and 1895 occupational censuses.[4] The distribution of each index among the 71 administrative areas can then be compared to the distribution of the index during the earliest year it is available for all areas. The results are presented in Table 6.10, which includes several measures of dispersion as well as an indication of the range of values for each index. Several points are worth noting. There is no striking contraction in the dispersion of social characteristics of the administrative areas between the years prior to the decline and the years of its onset. The interquartile range is larger as often as it is smaller for the eight variables considered. The standard deviations and coefficients of variation

[4]In cases where the data of fertility decline were estimated to be either earlier or later than any year for which we had data available, the value of the socio-economic index was estimated by forward or backward extrapolation. The years used as the basis for the interpolations or extrapolations were for each index as follows:

Percent dependent on primary industry: 1882, 1895, 1907, 1925
Percent dependent on secondary industry: 1882, 1907
Percent dependent on tertiary industry: 1882, 1907
Women's employment: 1882, 1907
Percent living in municipalities of under 2,000: 1871, 1880, 1885, 1890, 1900, 1910, 1925
Percent living in municipalities of over 20,000: 1885, 1890, 1900, 1910, 1925
Infant mortality: see Appendix Table 4.1
Index of proportion married (I_m): see Appendix Table 2.1.

TABLE 6.10

SOCIO-ECONOMIC AND DEMOGRAPHIC INDICES, VARIABILITY AMONG ADMINISTRATIVE AREAS: PRIOR TO DECLINE AND AT DATE OF 10% DECLINE IN MARITAL FERTILITY (I_g)

	Percentage population dependent on industrial sector						Nonagricultural female employment rate		Percentage living in municipalities of given population size				Infant mortality rate		Proportion married (I_m)	
	Primary		Secondary		Tertiary				under 2,000		20,000 or more					
	1882	10% decl. date	1882	10% decl. date	1882	10% decl. date	1882	10% decl. date	1871	10% decl. date	1885	10% decl. date	1875-1880	10% decl. date	1871	10% decl. date
Range of Values																
Lowest	0.8	0.8	16.2	19.7	5.5	6.0	2.8	5.0	0.0	0.0	0.0	0.0	114	94	.388	.420
1st quartile	37.3	30.5	26.1	30.7	7.5	9.1	5.7	8.4	57.6	43.4	5.4	12.4	162	161	.433	.470
Median	45.5	37.4	34.4	37.9	9.2	10.7	7.3	10.1	69.7	53.8	11.5	19.0	211	191	.466	.506
3rd quartile	53.2	47.4	41.0	45.0	11.0	13.2	10.6	12.7	78.3	66.6	20.9	28.3	254	241	.503	.536
Highest	66.7	63.2	67.7	68.1	34.2	34.6	27.4	29.7	89.7	87.2	100.0	100.0	383	349	.549	.598
Measure of Dispersion																
Interquartile range	15.9	16.9	14.9	14.3	3.5	4.1	4.9	4.3	20.7	23.2	15.5	15.9	92	80	.070	.066
Standard deviation	14.5	13.5	10.5	10.4	5.3	5.1	4.5	4.4	19.1	19.2	18.8	18.3	65.0	57.2	.040	.043
Coefficient of variation	.333	.364	.305	.274	.514	.433	.524	.397	.293	.370	1.135	.828	.304	.284	.088	.086

NOTES: Nonagricultural female employment rate refers to the percentage of women aged 14 or over employed in secondary and tertiary industries.
Infant mortality rate refers to the number of infant deaths per 1,000 live births.
First quartile refers to the 18th administrative area in rank; third quartile to the 54th in rank.

show little change. Perhaps the most striking feature of Table 6.10 is the wide diversity in the socio-economic structure indicated by the broad range of values each index shows at the time of the fertility decline. Areas that were still largely agrarian or had only a small minority of women employed outside of agriculture or had almost the entire population living in the countryside and villages entered the fertility transition along with areas showing much higher levels of urban-industrial development. Infant mortality and proportion married also varied widely among areas at the time of the fertility decline.

Perhaps other characteristics for which sufficient data were lacking would have indicated a greater homogeneity than the ones included in our analysis. Certainly illiteracy would have been one. In every German administrative area illiteracy was virtually eliminated, at least among adults in reproductive ages, by the time the fertility transition began. Whether similar homogeneity existed with respect to the educational levels in general however remains undetermined.

The data so far lend little support to the idea that any clearly identifiable threshold in socio-economic development was passed by areas in Germany prior to entering the fertility transition. The possibility exists however that there was a "moving threshold" that was easier to pass as the fertility decline spread from more modern or advanced areas to less developed ones. In order to examine this possibility we again look to the socio-economic and demographic indices explored above. However, we now classify administrative areas according to the date of the fertility decline in order to see if the characteristics of areas at the time fertility began to be reduced were different for late declines than for early declines. The results are included in Table 6.11.

Among the earliest declining areas were the four metropolitan administrative areas of Berlin, Bremen, Hamburg, and Lübeck. Although this is certainly of some significance in itself, it is also interesting to see, if we remove these areas from consideration, if the results of our comparison between early and late declining areas are very much affected. Therefore separate figures excluding these areas are given in parentheses when appropriate. In general, an even graduation from the early declining group of administrative areas to the late declining group is not evident. The earlier decliners included both highly agricultural and rural areas as well as industrial, commercial, and highly urbanized areas. The diversity in this group is decreased of course when we exclude Berlin and the city states. The 14 areas that started their fertility decline after 1905, however, appear in general to be slightly less "advanced" than were the other areas when they started on their fertility transition, thus lending a little support to "moving threshold" idea. On the other hand, these areas were more advanced in terms of infant mortality levels. Again the diversity among each group of areas is at least as impressive as their similarity.

In conclusion, it may be worthwhile to put the relationships exhibited in Tables 6.8 and 6.9 in perspective. These tables seem to indicate a moderately close association, at least, between socio-economic factors and the decline of fertility in the different areas of Germany. To be sure, to construct a close estimate for an area of the date of the initiation of fertility decline, or the extent of decline from the initial plateau until 1910, or some other parameter of its fertility experience from knowledge of socio-economic variables, it would be necessary to specify the region in which it lies as well as its social and economic characteristics. But perhaps the most remarkable aspect of the German fertility decline does not emerge from an examination of interrelationships of this sort; what we do not note in the examination of

TABLE 6.11

SOCIO-ECONOMIC AND DEMOGRAPHIC INDICES AT DATE OF 10% DECLINE IN MARITAL FERTILITY (I_g),
BY DATE OF DECLINE AMONG ADMINISTRATIVE AREAS

		Date I_g declined by 10%					
		1879-1885		1886-1895		1896-1905	1906 and later
Index	Value	All areas	Exc. Berlin, Bremen, & Hamburg	All areas	Exc. Lübeck	All areas	All areas
Percentage dependent on:							
Primary	Low	0.8	33.2	12.2	12.2	10.9	25.8
industry	High	55.1	55.1	53.7	53.7	63.2	58.1
	Mean	34.4	43.4	33.9	34.9	37.7	43.3
Secondary	Low	26.3	26.3	25.4	25.4	21.0	19.7
industry	High	47.7	43.8	68.1	68.1	66.2	53.7
	Mean	37.1	34.8	41.2	41.4	38.1	32.9
Tertiary	Low	6.8	6.8	6.0	6.0	6.2	7.7
industry	High	34.6	14.7	29.3	16.8	15.3	15.9
	Mean	14.4	9.9	12.1	11.2	10.9	10.1
Nonagricultur-	Low	5.1	5.1	5.0	5.0	5.2	5.2
al female em-	High	22.1	11.2	29.7	29.7	17.5	11.5
ployment rate	Mean	10.6	8.9	13.0	13.1	10.7	8.7
Percentage liv- ing in munici- palities with:							
Less than	Low	0.0	45.3	10.3	10.3	18.4	15.4
2,000	High	80.4	80.4	77.0	77.0	87.2	79.2
	Mean	47.9	60.7	47.6	49.1	56.6	55.0
More than	Low	0.0	0.0	0.0	0.0	0.0	0.0
20,000	High	100.0	30.1	82.9	45.9	36.0	41.1
	Mean	30.2	15.2	25.3	22.5	17.0	17.8
Infant mortal-	Low	114	114	136	136	126	94
ity rate	High	349	349	347	347	264	258
	Mean	216	211	227	229	186	170
Proportion	Low	.450	.450	.431	.431	.420	.424
married (I_m)	High	.537	.537	.585	.585	.598	.541
	Mean	.484	.487	.501	.501	.522	.501
N		13	10	22	21	22	14

NOTES: Nonagricultural female employment rate refers to the percentage of women, aged
14 or over, employed in secondary and tertiary industries.
Infant mortality rate refers to the number of infant deaths per 1,000 live births.
The mean refers to the unweighted mean of administrative areas in each category.

these relationships is the short span of time it took for the revolution in reproductive behavior to take hold everywhere in Germany. In many ways it is even more challenging to explain the similarity in the course of fertility among very diverse areas or groups than it is to attempt to account for differences in the timing of the decline within a period that from a historical perspective is short indeed.

[245]

Chapter 7: Summary of Findings

Between the mid-nineteenth century and the onset of World War II, German society experienced sweeping changes which together transformed Germany into a modern industrial state. This book focuses on one aspect of Germany's modernization — the transition in fertility from high, pre-modern levels to low, modern levels. It describes the fertility decline in detail and analyzes its components within the context of the social, economic, and demographic conditions that characterized Germany during this period.

Vital registration statistics and census reports published by the national and state statistical bureaus serve as the primary source of data for this study. In general these statistics are virtually complete and accurate, at least for the years since national political unification in 1871. The 71 administrative areas of Germany are the basic units of observation for much of the analysis. They are usually the smallest units for which detailed data are given in the official statistics. However, their use imposes limitations on the interpretation of results, since we cannot attribute to individuals the ralationships we find between the average characteristics of geographically defined population aggregates. Instead we must content ourselves with identifying the broad social and economic circumstances that made the different parts of Germany susceptible to the fertility decline.

A set of interrelated demographic indices, indirectly standardized for age, are employed in this study to describe trends in fertility and nuptiality. These indices include a measure of overall fertility (I_f), a measure of marital fertility (I_g), a measure of illegitimate fertility (I_h) and a measure of the proportion married (I_m). The main focus of the study, however, is on marital fertility and thus on I_g. Nevertheless, some attention is given to illegitimate fertility and to nuptiality and in particular to their in determining patterns of overall fertility.

Trends in Fertility and Nuptiality

On a national level, between unification in 1871 and the early 1930s, overall fertility declined by 60 percent, marital fertility by 65 percent,

[246]

and illegitimate fertility by 54 percent. Since the proportion of women in the fertile ages who were married actually increased and since illegitimate births never constituted much more than 10 percent of total births, it is clear that the decline in overall fertility was largely a result of reduced childbearing within marriage.

Prior to unification, uniform statistics on fertility and particularly marital fertility were not available for all administrative areas. The data which do exist, however, provide no evidence that fertility was declining prior to 1870. This is true whether we examine series of crude fertility measures calculated from official statistics between 1840 and 1870 or estimates of family size from local population studies based on parish records which cover a considerably longer period of time. It seems fair to conclude that the secular decline in German fertility which culminated in the low levels characteristic of modern times had its temporal origin in the decades immediately following German unification and not earlier. An image of relatively high and constant fertility seems appropriate for at least the century or so preceding 1870.

During the 1930s the fertility decline came to an end throughout Germany. Following the National Socialist takeover, fertility, whether measured by I_g or the crude birth rate, rose in every state and province. Following World War II, marital fertility can be calculated only for the administrative areas belonging to the Federal Republic (West Germany). A comparison between I_g in 1933–1935 and 1959–1963 in these areas reveals that in most cases marital fertility was either higher during the post-war years or only slightly lower, which suggests that we can treat the early 1930s as marking the end of Germany's fertility transition.

A close examination of the marital fertility series in each administrative area indicates that the fertility decline was a continuous process with a discrete beginning and a discrete end. Once fertility began to fall, the trend did not reverse until lower levels were reached. World War I caused only a temporary interruption of the process. Among the administrative areas, the decline in marital fertility ranged between 41 and 77 percent, with the vast majority experiencing declines of over 50 percent. Prior to and following the transition, fertility changes

[247]

appear to be merely fluctuations in comparison to the magnitude of the decline itself.

Administrative areas differed considerably in the level of marital fertility in the years before the start of the decline. The area with the lowest predecline marital fertility was characterized by a level only 60 percent as high as the area experiencing the highest level. It is difficult to determine if these substantial geographical differentials in predecline marital fertility reflected widespread use of deliberate family limitation in the areas with lower fertility. Even if this were the case, the modern fertility transition would still represent a distinct departure from past fertility trends if not a revolution in birth control practices.

If we measure the date of inception of the fertility decline by estimating the year by which I_g reached a level ten percent below its maximum predecline value, we find the earliest decline in an administrative area began in 1879 and the last decline began 35 years later in 1914. These dates are not intended to be taken as the literal years in which the decline began but rather as indices of the timing of the decline in each area.

The rate of fertility decline can be estimated from information on the date of its onset and its end in combination with the magnitude of decline. Correlations between the rate, date, magnitude, and level of predecline marital fertility yield some interesting results. There appears to be little association between the date of a sustained decline of ten percent in I_g and the level from which I_g declined. The maximum predecline level of marital fertility bears a positive relationship to the absolute magnitude of decline in I_g but only a very weak and negative association with the relative magnitude. The date of the onset of decline is related to both the rate and extent of decline. A later start in the transition is associated with a smaller fertility reduction but also with a faster pace of decline.

Illegitimate fertility in Germany has been high by European standards, averaging about ten percent of total births throughout most of the period between unification and World War II. Large regional differences, which persisted throughout the period, were not associated with either the level of marital fertility or the proportion married among females.

Subject to a secular trend very much like the long-term fall in marital fertility, illegitimate fertility in Germany underwent a substantial long-run decline during the seven decades preceding World War II. On a national level I_h, the index on non-marital fertility, fell by well over 50 percent, following a course remarkably parallel to that of marital fertility. However, among the individual administrative areas, the magnitude of the declines in I_h and I_g are only weakly correlated, and the timing of the onset of the declines are not associated at all.

In the absence of widespread acceptance of family limitation within marriage, the level of nuptiality is extremely important in determining a population's level of reproduction. In Germany prior to the fertility decline, as in most of Europe, the average age at first marriage was high (not far below 30 for men and over 25 for women), and around ten percent of the population was still single by the time they reached age fifty. Although there were substantial differences among the administrative areas, none was characterized by early marriage.

An examination of the trends in nuptiality during the period of the fertility decline makes it clear that changes in German marriage patterns could not have contributed to a decline in overall fertility. In fact there was a trend in most areas for the proportion married among women in the reproductive ages to increase slightly, working against the fertility decline. However, except for a short period just prior to and following unification when legal restrictions to marriage were eased in some areas, substantial changes in the direction of younger and more universal marriage took place only after the fertility decline had come to an end.

Correlational analysis lent no support to the suggestion that a larger proportion married prior to the fertility transition generated pressures for an earlier fertility decline. There also appeared to be very little relationship between changes in proportion married and changes in marital fertility, although at any given time the proportion of women married in the reproductive age was inversely related to the level of marital fertility.

Trends in overall fertility were very similar to trends in marital fertility. At any given period I_f and I_g are highly correlated among the administrative areas as are their dates of decline as well as the extent of decline.

SUMMARY

Within Germany substantial differences existed from area to area in almost every aspect of demographic behavior. An important question concerning this territorial variation is whether or not fertility or nuptiality was more uniform among administrative areas that are regionally associated than would be expected by chance. On the basis of a modified version of a regional classification used in the 1925 census, the 71 administrative areas of Germany can be divided into seven broader regions. Analysis of variance indicates that distinct regional clustering existed for virtually every measure of fertility and nuptiality employed in this study. Administrative areas within the same region were considerably more alike than were areas not in the same region. Regional location then, is an important factor to be considered when analyzing the German fertility decline. It probably reflects effects of regional cultural patterns that may be difficult or impossible to measure directly.

Social Differentials

Five socially defined dimensions have been used to differentiate the German population into aggregates which might differ in their fertility behavior: rural-urban residence, economic activity, wealth, religious affiliation, and ethnic affiliation. Although data availability was the main reason for their choice, past empirical investigations as well as theoretical considerations provide sufficient grounds to expect subpopulations defined by these dimensions to exhibit differentials with respect to the fertility decline.

A survey of rural-urban differentials in marital fertility and their part in the German fertility decline reveals several patterns:

(1) Just prior to the beginning of the fertility decline, marital fertility was generally higher in rural than urban areas. Within the urban category, fertility was usually lower in large cities than in smaller cities or towns. In only a few areas was urban I_g higher than rural and these cases can best be considered as exceptions. In general, the differences were not large in either direction. Whether or not the rural-urban predecline differences were the result of deliberate fertility control unfortunately cannot be determined from our data.

(2) The decline began first in urban populations but was followed

[250]

after a short time lag by a parallel decline in the rural population. In addition, fertility usually began to fall in large cities before it did in small cities and towns. Both with respect to the predecline level and the date of the decline, fertility of the rural population of an administrative area was closely associated with fertility of the urban population. Whatever the causes were that precipitated the fertility transition, they were apparently effective earlier in the cities than in the countryside. The short time lag between rural and urban fertility decline, however, indicates that these forces spread quickly from the urban setting into the hinterlands.

(3) Considerable differences existed among administrative areas within each rural-urban category both with respect to the level of marital fertility just prior to the decline and the date the decline began.

(4) Rural-urban differentials in the level of fertility persisted during the decline and because of the later date of decline in the rural populations, the differentials increased during the initial phases.

(5) By the time the decline had run its course in the early 1930s, rural-urban differentials still existed but on much lower levels of fertility. Both rural and urban populations experienced an increase in fertility between the beginning of the National Socialist period and World War II. The rise in marital fertility was somewhat less in rural populations. Nevertheless, in 1939 rural-urban differentials were still clearly evident.

Rural-urban indices of nuptiality and non-marital fertility provide some interesting information. An examination of rural-urban differences in the index of proportions married reveals a remarkably consistent pattern. Until the beginning of World War I, I_m was highest in rural populations and lowest in large cities. This appears to be true for almost every administrative area for which the relevant data were available. Only by the end of the fertility decline were rural-urban differences in marriage patterns no longer pronounced or distinctive.

Contrary to the conventional image of the city as the breeder of illegitimacy, the data for Germany indicate that where illegitimacy was high in the city, it was also high in the countryside. Where it was low in the countryside, it was also low in the city. As often as not when differences existed, the rural illegitimacy rate exceeded the urban one. The larger proportion of non-married women among women in the productive ages in the cities meant, however, that the ratio of illegitimate to total births was frequently higher for urban than for rural women, even though the same was not true for non-marital fertility rates. Lower I_m in the cities also meant that rural-urban differentials in overall fertility were often more pronounced than in marital fertility.

Prussian statistics permit the calculation of crude marital fertility rates classified by the industry in which the father worked, and by occupational position within each industry. In general the results conform to the differentials in fertility decline according to economic activity that have been described in most discussions of the demographic transition. Although it seems likely that some of the differentials in the level of fertility existed prior to the onset of the fertility decline, there can be no doubt that the leads and lags involved in the downward course of fertility created more pronounced differentials during the transition process. Civil servants, independent professionals, and persons engaged in trade and transportation, all predominantly urban economic activities, led the decline, whereas persons in agriculture and mining lagged behind. In all main branches of industry, workers apparently were slower to reduce fertility than persons in higher positions. All economic groups experienced substantial decline in marital fertility by the post-World War I period, although differences with respect to the level and extent of decline were still pronounced.

Additional evidence on fertility differentials by economic activity come from data on children ever born from the 1939 German census. These data indicate quite clearly that for couples married after the turn of the century, the average number of children born was declining for successive marriage cohorts for all economic segments. This finding remained unchanged when size of municipality was used as a central variable. For marriages of at least 20 years duration, workers experienced higher than average fertility, middle class white collar couples experienced lower than average fertility, and persons with independent positions were intermediate. This relationship held for both the agricultural and non-agricultural populations as well as rural and urban municipalities. Because the 1939 data did not refer to cohorts married far enough in the past, they did not permit the determination of differentials in the onset and pace of decline among economic groups.

The scattered evidence on fertility differentials by wealth in Germany during the period of the fertility decline fits in well with the findings on occupational differentials. Clearly during much of the period in which the fertility transition took place, the fertility level of persons in the higher social classes was well below the ferility experienced by the lower classes whether measured by occupation or wealth. The evidence on differentials in the actual process of fertility decline is more scanty but does suggest a substantially earlier start in the higher classes followed by at least a partial convergence in levels as fertility reductions spread throughout the entire class structure.

Several findings emerge with respect to religious differentials in Germany during the course of the fertility transition. Essentially at any time between unification and the 1930s differences in the level of fertility of the three major religious groups were evident wherever data were available. Jews had the lowest fertility, Catholics the highest, and the Protestants occupied an intermediate position. The early and rapid decline of Jewish fertility and the very low levels achieved even before the turn of the century were truly exceptional. Protestant and Catholic fertility experience also differed from each other although not to the extent that both differed from the Jewish experience. In most areas, fertility for Protestants began to decline earlier than for Catholics and at any given time was lower. Eventually, however, the fertility of all three religious groups declined substantially.

To some extent the distinctive fertility experience of the Jews may have reflected their greater social isolation from the rest of German society and their concentration in urban areas. Although less urbanized than Jews, Protestants were also more likely to live in cities than Catholics. By and large, however, the extent to which religious differentials could be attributed to non-religious factors is difficult to determine from available data.

Prior to the end of World War I, sizable Polish and Danish speaking minorities lived within the boundaries of Germany. By comparing the fertility of districts in which these groups formed the majority with neighboring districts where ethnic Germans predominated, some impression of differentials by ethnic affiliation could be gained. Predominately Polish districts in Eastern Germany generally experienced higher fertility than nearby districts with German majorities, at least during the three decades between 1880 and 1910. However, during the same period, the extent and timing of the fertility decline were roughly similar for Polish and German districts. In the administrative area of Schleswig, the districts with Danish-speaking majorities experienced consistently lower birth rates during the last third of the nineteenth century that the area's population as a whole. However, the Danish districts showed little tendency to decline even by 1910, although the rest of Schleswig experienced a distinct reduction between 1895 and 1910.

Social differentials found in the level of German fertility during the period of the fertility transition conform more or less to conventional expectations. Data with respect to differentials in changes in fertility or the date of decline were scantier but also largely agreed with expectations. Perhaps even more important than the differences that were revealed, however, is the finding that in almost all the major social categories described, fertility began to decline within the span of a few decades and was substantially reduced throughout German society by 1930. Only a few small segments (most notably the Jews and possibly the highly educated upper occupational classes) may have preceded the general population in fertility decline by a generation or more. The low level of fertility they were experiencing by the 1870's suggests that a substantial degree of fertility control may have been widespread within these limited circles before German Unification and hence prior to the historical period analyzed here.

Infant Mortality

During the same decades in which marital fertility fell by 65 percent in Germany, infant mortality declined by almost 70 percent. Just after political unification about one out of four children born alive died before reaching age one. By the 1930s only one out of fifteen did not survive.

There were substantial differences in infant mortality among the administrative areas in the earlier years. Territorial differences conformed to a considerable extent to the regional groupings of administrative areas used in this study; differences within each region tended to be small while differences between regions tended to be large.

The timing and extent of the infant mortality decline was dependent on the level of infant mortality at its inception. In areas where the rates were high in the 1860s or 1870s, an early and constant decline occurred. In contrast, areas that were experiencing initially low rates showed little tendency to decline until much later and then the reduction was of lesser proportions. The result was a constant reduction in the range of territorial differences within Germany. In more recent years, in fact, most of Germany was characterized by low, relatively uniform levels.

Substantial differentials in infant mortality existed according to legitimacy status. Children born out of wedlock were much more likely to die in infancy than those born to married couples. Distinct differentials also are found between rural and urban populations in Germany. Generally risks for infants were higher in the cities than in the countryside prior to the secular decline in mortality, which is opposite to the differences in fertility. Decreases occurred sooner and initially at a faster pace in the cities so that after several decades of decline the differentials reversed or disappeared in many areas. Thus rural-urban differences in the timing of the infant mortality and fertility decline coincided.

A comparison of the predominantly German districts in the eastern areas of Prussia reveals little difference in infant mortality in 1880. During the following three decades, however, the Polish areas experienced a somewhat larger decline so that by 1910 they were experiencing lower infant death rates than their German neighbors. Since at the same time the Polish areas were experiencing higher fertility, the fertility differentials are in the opposite direction.

There is no evidence that infant mortality had been declining in Germany during the decades prior to the 1860s. The modern decline in infant mortality appears to have its origin sometime after unification in virtually every area. On a national level, infant mortality and fertility began their descents practically simultaneously and followed remarkably parallel paths. In Germany, unlike the usual description incorporated in the demographic transition model, a decline in infant mortality did not precede the start of the fertility transition. It is thus difficult to argue that in Germany reduced infant mortality was an initiating cause of the fertility decline. If we compare the dates by which infant mortality and marital fertility underwent a sustained decline of ten percent, we find that in about half of the administrative areas infant mortality started to decline first and in the other half fertility began its descent earlier. In either case the average lag was only about a decade.

Correlational analysis of infant mortality and marital fertility of administrative areas yielded several findings:

(1) At any time just preceding or during the fertility decline, the greater the infant mortality in an area the greater the I_g. The degree of association, which is not strong at any time, is closer during the initial periods and final stages of the fertility transition and weakest during the middle.

(2) Infant mortality, as fertility, was subject to strong regional patterning. Nevertheless, controlling for the effect of regional location does not alter the association between the two variables. The average correlation within regions is practically identical to the correlation between regionally unadjusted values.

(3) For Prussian administrative areas it was possible to correlate fertility and infant mortality separately for the rural and urban sectors. The association was negligible in both divisions.

(4) The date of a ten percent decline in marital fertility is moderately correlated with both the date of a ten percent reduction in infant mortality and the date mortality risks declined by 50 infant deaths per 1,000 live births. Controlling for regional location reduces the degree of association somewhat. For Prussia, the dates of decline in infant mortality and I_g are moderately correlated both within the urban and the rural setting.

(5) The more infant mortality declined, the greater was the decline in I_g. This is true both for the total period of fertility decline as well as for the initial phases.

Associations between the amount of change in infant mortality and fertility as well as in their timing suggest that the reduction of fertility and mortality in Germany may not have been independent phenomena. However, it has not been possible to show with the available data that any direct causal link can be inferred. Nevertheless, from a different point of view, it is clear that the impact which the fertility had on the number of living children per family was substantially tempered by mortality reductions. Given the reduction in mortality to ages up to 15 which took place between unification and the 1930s, a 30 percent decline in the number of births per family would have left the number of children surviving to age 15 per family unchanged. This means that on a national level over 40 percent of the fertility decline was offset by mortality reductions. In some administrative areas well over two-thirds of the fertility decline was compensated for by the mortality decline and in only one area was this fraction less than one-fifth.

Emigration and Migration

Germany's decline in birth and death rates took place during a period of substantial migratory movement. Several waves of emigration carried large numbers to the New World. Long distance internal flows took Germans from agrarian areas to the newly industrializing ones. At the same time within each administrative area the population was shifting from the countryside to the urban centers.

Recently a number of theoretical connections between the demographic transition in vital rates and both external and internal migration have been suggested. One major theme of these suggestions is that out-migration can serve as an alternative to fertility reduction, as a response to rapid population growth and as a means of easing strains connected with it. The German data provide at least a partial test for this hypothesis.

In the three decades prior to unification, estimates indicate that Germany suffered a net loss of over two million through emigration. Even larger numbers left during the 1880s and early 1890s. As extensive as external migration was, it retarded national population growth only moderately. Even during the peak periods of exodus, emigration

[257]

was equal to less than half of the rate of national increase. During the entire period 1871 to 1910, external migration reduced the population growth that would have occurred from natural increase alone by only ten percent.

Some administrative areas were considerably more affected than others. In addition, areas where emigration was most pronounced also lost considerable population through migratory exchanges within Germany. Hence for some areas migration was a more important means of reducing population growth than for others.

In some European populations sex differentials in migration resulted in long periods of separation between husbands and wives and thereby depressed marital fertility. This does not appear to have happened in Germany, at least judging from the sex ratios of the married populations in the various administrative areas. In almost every area the number of married men is quite close to the number of married women.

A comparison of the data on fertility decline and migration on the level of the administrative area suggests that the two demographic processes might have been interrelated. Areas of heavy out-migration were also areas where fertility declined later and more modestly, at least until 1910. Although this result is consistent with the hypothesis that net out-migration served as a temporary alternative to fertility decline, the association practically disappears when we control for the degree of social and economic backwardness through partial correlation. It seems equally plausible therefore that the conditions in "backward" areas, at least in terms of being highly agricultural and having higher proportions of illiterates, encouraged out-migration *and* impeded the spread of modern fertility levels.

When we use correlational analysis to examine the relationship between natural increase and migration, almost no association between the two variables appears to exist. Even when we limit consideration to selected areas in which we would expect stronger relationships to emerge on theoretical grounds, the associations remain rather weak.

Between the middle of the nineteenth century and the start of World War II, Germany was transformed from a predominantly rural to a largely urban nation. This was a result both of large scale migration

[258]

from the rural areas to the cities as well as the transformation of areas previously rural in character into essentially urban areas. This process of urbanization is noticeable only after the mid-nineteenth century. The proportion of the population living in cities in the decades prior to this period remained rather stable.

The possible connections between urbanization and the fertility decline within the urban and rural sectors of an administrative area are complicated. Rapid and early urbanization and city growth appear to foster declines in urban fertility in Prussia but the association is weak. There is little indication that migration from the countryside to the cities retarded the adoption of family limitation in the rural areas. Rather, fertility decline in the rural sectors was earlier and more intense in administrative areas in which the urban sector constituted a larger proportion of the population and was expanding most rapidly.

Urbanization, rather than being a major cause of the fertility decline, may have been a response to the same general changes in the social and economic structure that also resulted in changing attitudes towards family limitation. The cities apparently served as the loci from which these new attitudes were diffused. The large number of newly arrived migrants from the countryside might have acted as effective communication links between the longer term urban dwellers and those who remained in the villages and on the farms.

The Social Context

The integral link between the demographic transition and modernization implies a host of relationships between the fertility decline and various aspects of the society in which it takes place. Many of the linkages which can be theoretically drawn, however, cannot be tested empirically when we deal with the experience of countries over the last century. Important social factors involved in the modern transformation of reproductive behavior often cannot be identified in the available statistics. At best, only very imperfect indices can be constructed to yield a rough outline of the socio-economic structure.

To help expand our exploration of the social context of the German fertility decline several additional variables can be introduced: indices of the distribution of the population with respect to dependence on the major sectors of industry, an index of women's employment in non-agricultural labor, an index of the prevalence of savings accounts, and an index of illiteracy. The decades of fertility decline where characterized by a rapid transformation in the distribution of the population's dependence on the three main sectors of the economy. Primary industry steadily declined in importance while the proportions who derived a living from manufacturing or service industries rose. At the same time the employment of women, both married and unmarried, outside of agriculture was rapidly increasing. Illiteracy, which was already uncommon by unification, virtually disappeared by the turn of the century. These changes of course represent only a small part of Germany's modernization.

Correlational analysis between these social indices and marital fertility yield several results:

(1) The level of marital fertility in an administrative area is positively associated with the percent dependent on primary industry and negatively associated with dependence on secondary or tertiary industry. The correlations strengthened as the fertility decline progressed. However, neither the date nor extent of fertility decline are associated with changes in the percent dependent on primary or secondary industry. Changes in dependence on tertiary industry does correlate moderately with both measures of fertility; the larger the increase in dependence on tertiary industry, the earlier and larger the fertility decline.

(2) The level of female employment outside of agriculture shows almost no correlation with the level of I_g prior to the onset of the fertility decline and only a weak negative relationship midway through. Early and large declines in marital fertility are weakly correlated with large increases in women's employment.

(3) The proportion of army recruits that could neither read nor write in 1875 is positively correlated with the level of marital fertility at least until 1910. This association results, however, mainly from the fact that the few areas with exceptionally high illiteracy also had exceptionally high fertility. Among the remaining areas no association existed.

(4) Areas with high ratios of savings accounts to population tended to have lower fertility. There is also evidence (based on Prussian ad-

ministrative areas) that the larger the increases in the savings account rate, the larger the decrease in marital fertility.

(5) Areas which experienced early and large reductions in marital fertility were likely to be characterized prior to the onset of the decline by low dependency on primary industry (and high dependency on secondary and tertiary industry), high female employment outside of agriculture, low illiteracy among recruits, and a high rate of savings accounts per capita.

In order to have a more complete understanding of the social context of the German fertility decline, it is important to know how each association between socio-economic indices and fertility is affected when the influences of the others are taken into account as well as to know the joint effect of all these variables on fertility. Partial and multiple correlation analysis provide a method for doing this. As independent social and demographic variables to be related to marital fertility, we selected indices of savings account prevalence, dependence on primary industry, illiteracy, percent Catholic, and infant mortality. It appears that among these variables, religious composition and the level of infant mortality were the most important determinants of predecline marital fertility. The closest partial associations with the date and magnitude of fertility decline are found with dependence on primary industry and the timing of the decline in infant mortality. When all factors are considered jointly they statistically account for well over half of the variance in the fertility measures.

When the influence of regional location is statistically controlled, the results of the multiple and partial correlation analysis change somewhat. The independent variables considered explain only a small fraction of the variance in the level of predecline marital fertility; the most important variables still appear to be infant mortality and the proportion Catholic, however. In contrast the date of inception and the extent of decline are still strongly associated with the joint effect of the independent variables; in particular, the proportion dependent on primary industry and at a distinctly lower level of correlation the date of decline in infant mortality are the two which appear to be most important.

The threshold hypothesis of the demographic transition postulates

[261]

that a population must reach a certain minimum level of socio-economic development before fertility will start to decline. If this hypothesis is valid, we would expect areas to be similar to each with respect to socio-economic indices at the onset of the fertility decline. Of course differences will exist as any threshold would probably involve some complicated mix of social, economic and demographic development. Nevertheless if the threshold hypothesis holds, there should be less dispersion in indices of socio-economic structure of areas at the onset of the fertility transition than at some given time prior to it. A comparison of the administrative areas in Germany lends no support to this hypothesis. A contraction in the dispersion of social characteristics of the areas between the years prior to the decline and the time of its onset is not evident. Indeed a comparison of areas at the time of their declines reveals a wide diversity in socio-economic structure. Areas that were predominantly agrarian, had only a small proportion of women working outside agriculture, or had high infant mortality entered the transition along with areas which could be considered much more modernized.

There is some indication that it was easier for an area (in terms of socio-economic development) to enter the fertility transition as the fertility decline spread from more modern and advanced areas to less developed ones. Areas which were late to decline appear to be slightly less advanced than areas which started on their fertility transition earlier. This suggests the possibility of a threshold which became progressively lower as the transition advanced. Again, however, the diversity among late or early declining areas is at least as impressive as the similarity.

Perhaps the most interesting aspect of the German fertility decline is obscured by attempts to account for differences between areas in their fertility trends or levels. By focusing on differences, it is easy to overlook the short span of time it took for the revolution in reproductive behavior to take hold everywhere in Germany. Finding an explanation for the similarity in the course of decline among diverse areas and social strata and the practical simultaneity of its occurrence is at least as challenging as trying to explain the differences.

Appendix 1A The Choice of a Regional Classification for Germany

As mentioned in Chapter 1, several possible regional classifications are available or could be constructed for use in the present study. Five variations were considered:

1. *Dialect regions excluding ambiguous administrative areas:* Administrative areas in which the population spoke the same or similar dialects were grouped together into regions. Administrative areas characterized by substantial portions of the population speaking different dialects were excluded altogether. This meant excluding eight administrative areas. On this basis seven dialect regions were formed.

2. *Dialect regions including ambiguous administrative areas:* Again, the linguistic map was used to form regions. However in this case the eight administrative areas in which substantial proportions of the population spoke different dialects were allocated to the seven dialect regions according to where the capital city was located on the linguistic map.

3. *The 1925 census regions as given:* The administrative areas were grouped into region according to the way the 1925 census group them in their presentation. This included six regions in total.

4. *A modified version of the regions given in the 1925 census:* The six easternmost administrative areas were grouped together into a region of their own. Otherwise the regions are the same as those given in the 1925 census. This meant there were a total of seven regions.

5. *A modified version of the regions given in the 1933 census:* Again, the six easternmost administrative areas were grouped together to form a region of their own. Otherwise the regions are the same as those given in the 1933 census.

In order to see if the regional classifications made any sense in terms of separating from each other areas which exhibited divergent demographic behavior, a crude test was used. All administrative areas which bordered on at least one other administrative area not in the same region were considered. Correlation coefficients were then calculated between the value of some selected demographic index (for example, marital fertility in 1869–1873) for each of these border areas and the average of the value of the same index for all contiguous administrative areas not in the same region. If, for example, an administrative area bordered on four other administrative areas which belonged to other regions, the index of the first mentioned area was paired with the average of the indices of the four contiguous areas outside its region. The resultant correlation coefficient was then compared to the correlation coefficient which resulted from an analogous pairing of index values of border administrative areas with the average value of the index found for contiguous areas *within* the same region. If region boundaries were discriminating with respect to demographic behavior, we would expect a low correlation between the indices of border areas and those of contiguous areas outside the border areas' region and a higher correlation with the indices of contiguous areas within the same region. Appendix Table 1.1 presents the results of

APPENDIX TABLE 1.1

REGIONALIZATION SCHEMES EXAMINED THROUGH SPATIAL PATTERNS OF MARITAL FERTILITY (I_g):
CORRELATIONS BETWEEN ADMINISTRATIVE AREAS ON REGIONAL BORDERS
AND CONTIGUOUS ADMINISTRATIVE AREAS

	Type of Regional Classification Used									
Measure of marital fertility (I_g)	Dialect region excluding ambiguous cases		Dialect regions including ambiguous cases		1925 census regions as given		Modified 1925 census regions		Modified 1933 census regions	
	Contiguous areas		Contiguous areas		Contiguous areas		Contiguous areas		Contiguous areas	
	outside region	inside region	outside region	inside region	outside region	inside region	outside region	inside region	outside region	inside region
Level 1869-1873	.48	.80	.55	.77	.20	.69	.20	.72	.56	.65
Level 1908-1912	.11	.75	.36	.74	.36	.73	.27	.87	.43	.86
Date of 10% decline[a]	.39	.66	.46	.70	.10	.63	.21	.78	.37	.78
Decline between maximum and 1910	.03	.62	.17	.62	.10	.50	.15	.73	.23	.66

[a]See Chapter 2 for an explanation of the variable.

such correlations using four different indices of demographic behavior for each of the five regional classifications.

On the basis of the crude test just described, it appears that the boundaries of the modified 1925 census region most consistently separate administrative areas with similar demographic behavior, at least with respect to the four indices examined, from areas of divergent demographic experience. For this reason the modified 1925 census regions were chosen as the regional classifications to be used in the present study.

APPENDIX 1B Comparison of the Demographic Indices with Conventional Measures Based on the German Experience 1800-1925

In order to evaluate the comparability of conventional and generally cruder measures of demographic behavior with the indices and in the present study, correlation coefficients have been calculated between them. The index of overall fertility (I_f) is compared with the general fertility rate, which is the ratio of total births to women aged 15–49 and the crude birth rate. The index of marital fertility (I_g) is compared with the general marital fertility rate, which is the ratio of legitimate births to married women 15–49, and the crude marital fertility rate, which is the ratio of legitimate births to all married women. The index of illegitimate fertility (I_h) is compared with the proportion of total births that is illegitimate and the general illegitimate fertility rate which is the ratio of illegitimate births to unmarried women 15–49. The index of proportion married (I_m) and its alternative index (I_{m*}) are both compared to the proportion of women 15–49 which is married (PM 15–49) and the proportion of the total population which is married (TPM). Comparisons are made for the periods 1800 (1878–1882) and 1925 (1923–1927) in Appendix Table 1.2. Correlations between changes in these rates (both absolute and relative) between 1880 and 1925 are also given. The basic units of observation are administrative areas.

The extremely high correlations between each of the basic fertility indices used in this study and the corresponding conventional rate which relates births of the appropriate legitimacy category to women 15–49 of the respective marital status indicate that the primary advantage of the basic rates in the German context is their intuitive interpretation (i.e. as a proportion of maximum natural fertility) rather than an increase in precision of measurement. Correlations between changes in these two groups of fertility measures are practically perfect in each case. Rarely, however, are data available for women by marital status for the total age group 15–49 when it is not also available by more detailed age categories. Thus the more pertinent question

APPENDIX TABLE 1.2

FERTILITY INDICES AND CONVENTIONAL DEMOGRAPHIC MEASURES,
INTERCORRELATIONS FOR LEVELS AND CHANGES: 1880 AND 1925

Measure	Levels		Change, 1880 to 1925	
	1880 (N=71)	1925 (N=66)	Absolute (N=64)	Relative (N=64)
Overall fertility				
I_f and general fertility rate	.988	.999	.992	.998
I_f and crude birth rate	.861	.982	.922	.982
General fertility rate and crude birth rate	.913	.985	.953	.986
Marital fertility				
I_g and general marital fertility rate	.967	.994	.983	.995
I_g and crude marital fertility rate	.815	.976	.915	.976
General marital fertility rate & crude marital fertility rate	.927	.990	.968	.989
Illegitimate fertility				
I_h and general illegitimate fertility rate	.999	.999	.998	.993
I_h and proportion illegitimate	.954	.874	.141	.646
Proportion illegitimate and general illegitimate fertility rate	.957	.852	.131	.643
Proportion married				
I_m and proportion married 15-49	.985	.992	.675	.975
I_m and total proportion married	.644	.808	.575	.605
Proportion married 15-49 and total proportion married	.709	.851	.702	.729
I_m^* and proportion married 15-49	.929	.930	.846	.857
I_m^* and total proportion married	.548	.637	.323	.381
I_m and I_m^*	.960	.958	.895	.905

concerns the use of cruder fertility measures as substitutes for the basic indices. Correlations between the I_f and crude birth rate and the I_g and the crude marital fertility rate are reasonably high, especially when relative changes are considered. In fact, even relative changes in I_g are correlated .92 with relative changes in the crude birth rate from 1880 to 1925. Of course, this correlation would have been reduced had the proportion married altered more drastically. The ratio of illegitimate births to total births is a poor measure of changes in the propensity of unmarried women to bear illegitimate children since it is influenced strongly by changes in marital fertility (Shorter, Knodel, and van de Walle, 1971, pp. 378–380). Thus correlations between changes in this ratio and I_h are not high.

The vulnerability of I_m to changes in age distribution is reflected in the higher correlations between the cruder indices of marriage and I_m than between the same indices and I_{m*}.

Since the primary focus of this study is in the decline in fertility and thus in changes in the variables over time, a comparison of the magnitude of *relative* changes in each of the basic indices with the relative changes in the substitute measures is of some interest. Appendix Table 1.3 indicates the changes that occurred in the national indices for Germany. In general, there is close agreement among the indices of either overall or marital fertility with respect to the extent that fertility decreased. Among the measures of illegitimacy the change in the proportion of births that are illegitimate is clearly out of line with the other two illegitimacy measures. This should not be surprising since the inadequacy of the former measure of illegitimacy is reasonably well known (Kumar, 1969). Among the measures of proportion married only the proportion of the total population that is married shows any substantial change between 1880 and 1925. The general agreement between the demographic measures employed in the present study and the more conventional and typically cruder measures does not insure that similar agreement would be found for different periods of Germany's demographic history. However it does suggest that we are not unduly disturbing the picture by use of the cruder measures for the decades prior to unification.

APPENDIX TABLE 1.3

FERTILITY INDICES AND CONVENTIONAL DEMOGRAPHIC MEASURES,
PERCENTAGE OF CHANGE: 1880 TO 1925

Measure	Change (percent)
Overall fertility	
I_f	-54.2
General fertility rate	-54.6
Crude birth rate	-47.4
Marital fertility	
I_g	-54.6
General marital fertility rate	-55.4
Crude marital fertility rate	-56.9
Illegitimate fertility	
I_h	-43.1
General illegitimate fertility rate	-42.9
Proportion illegitimate	+28.5
Proportion married	
I_m	- 2.2
I_m^*	- 3.3
Proportion married 15-49	- 0.8
Total proportion married	+19.4

APPENDIX 2A Democraphic Indices for Germany — I_f, I_g, I_h, I_m, and I_{m*} — for Each Administrative Area and for Each Province or State Consisting of More than One Administrative Area

The basic demographic indices were calculated whenever sufficient census and vital statistics were available. As is evident from Appendix Table 2.1 there is considerable variation among the areas with regard to the number of periods for which indices were calculated. This stems mainly from the independence possessed by the state statistical bureaus concerning collection and publication of vital statistics and census results. Differences in data availability from state to state is especially great prior to unification in 1871. Although it was possible to calculate the indices for most areas on the basis of the 1867 census, only a limited number of states published census data tabulated in sufficient detail to permit the calculation of indices for earlier periods. Even after the unification of Germany, the state statistical bureaus maintained considerable autonomy. The national statistical bureau (*Statistisches Reichsamt*) published annual birth statistics providing a uniform series after 1871 and the results of each census from 1871 and after. However the results for the 1875, 1895, and 1905 censuses did not include the necessary crosstabulations of age, sex, and marital status. The indices based on these censuses were calculated only for the states which independently published the required data. Also indices are not given after World War I for administrative areas lost by Germany.

All fertility indices based on censuses between 1880 and 1933 refer to the average annual births during five-year periods centered on the census year. The 1871 indices are likewise based on a five-year span surrounding the census year. Indices based on the 1875 census, however, utilize births for the four-year period 1874–1877. Since prior to 1871 censuses were usually taken at three-year intervals, the average annual births used in the calculation of the fertility indices in most cases refer to three-year periods centered on the census.

APPENDIX TABLE 2.1
DEMOGRAPHIC INDICES FOR GERMANY: INDEX OF OVERALL FERTILITY (I_f)

ADMINISTRATIVE AREA	1866-68	1869-73	1874-77	1878-82	1883-87	1888-92	1893-97	1898-02	1903-07	1908-12	1923-27	1931-35	1938-39
01 OSTPREUSSEN	.403	.403		.410	.420	.431	.432	.423	.391	.364	.251	.226	.253
02 DANZIG	.438	.420		.434	.436	.438	.446	.452	.431	.402			
03 MARIENWERDER	.470	.467		.474	.482	.479	.485	.491	.468	.438	.237	.222	
04 BERLIN	.328	.314	.355	.320	.283	.258	.238	.217	.204	.183	.085	.090	.145
05 POTSDAM	.380	.379		.400	.390	.380	.350	.302	.257	.209	.163	.156	
06 FRANKFURT/O.	.383	.390		.398	.394	.391	.374	.358	.327	.292	.188	.163	
07 STETTIN-STR.	.392	.393		.402	.401	.397	.392	.384	.346	.308	.206	.185	
08 KOESLIN	.410	.415		.422	.425	.421	.419	.421	.395	.366	.236	.210	
09 POSEN	.430	.443		.446	.439	.436	.442	.454	.445	.409	.237	.221	
10 BROMBERG	.466	.466		.471	.477	.471	.479	.483	.465	.428			
11 BRESLAU	.388	.398		.391	.384	.382	.382	.379	.352	.321	.206	.178	
12 LIEGNITZ	.351	.358		.373	.372	.371	.363	.360	.334	.312	.206	.173	
13 OPPELN	.447	.457		.426	.437	.452	.481	.491	.472	.441	.271	.244	
14 MAGDEBURG	.384	.383		.400	.404	.390	.375	.351	.310	.283	.176	.151	
15 MERSEBURG	.417	.421		.449	.456	.448	.426	.410	.371	.335	.212	.168	
16 ERFURT	.396	.410		.410	.402	.387	.369	.356	.332	.298	.187	.155	
17 SCHLESWIG	.354	.348		.374	.372	.372	.373	.356	.336	.305	.174	.165	.238
18 HANNOVER	.359	.356		.360	.352	.342	.341	.327	.288	.248	.143	.129	
19 HILDESHEIM	.362	.364		.374	.367	.366	.361	.351	.322	.292	.190	.163	
20 LUENEBURG	.319	.319		.329	.332	.330	.339	.334	.316	.297	.185	.167	
21 STADE	.373	.379		.392	.396	.390	.394	.389	.379	.348	.203	.177	
22 OSNABRUECK	.344	.358		.369	.372	.362	.367	.370	.366	.354	.245	.209	
23 AURICH	.328	.337		.364	.373	.379	.379	.371	.363	.350	.246	.196	
24 MUENSTER	.320	.329		.371	.384	.395	.414	.442	.459	.447	.268	.196	
25 MINDEN	.384	.386		.401	.397	.389	.386	.379	.356	.319	.198	.161	
26 ARNSBERG	.445	.471		.487	.482	.477	.474	.477	.461	.404	.205	.150	
27 KASSEL	.363	.374		.381	.361	.356	.344	.339	.326	.294	.197	.164	
28 WIESBADEN	.340	.343		.329	.307	.292	.290	.289	.274	.237	.149	.123	
29 KOBLENZ	.361	.372		.387	.372	.366	.363	.360	.345	.314	.213	.173	
30 DUESSELDORF	.406	.420		.430	.420	.407	.399	.400	.381	.325	.170	.140	
31 KOELN	.368	.380		.401	.390	.390	.375	.374	.350	.298	.173	.135	
32 TRIER	.401	.404		.423	.412	.414	.423	.433	.423	.386	.262	.197	
33 AACHEN	.373	.386		.395	.388	.389	.385	.381	.362	.331	.215	.172	
34 SIGMARINGEN	.386	.411		.422	.380	.352	.347	.360	.355	.334	.202	.177	.228
35 OBERBAYERN	.406	.418	.461	.434	.409	.388		.368		.292	.170	.144	
36 NIEDERBAYERN	.415	.439	.479	.477	.468	.453		.455		.425	.283	.240	
37 PFALZ	.374	.409	.454	.424	.406	.388		.395		.345	.210	.171	.195
38 OBERPFALZ	.414	.439	.484	.472	.464	.444		.449		.414	.281	.234	
39 OBERFRANKEN	.365	.379	.412	.384	.374	.357		.363		.325	.214	.178	
40 MITTELFRANKEN	.385	.401	.437	.408	.390	.371		.362		.292	.167	.144	
41 UNTERFRANKEN	.367	.377	.411	.376	.352	.339		.349		.327	.229	.189	
42 SCHWABEN	.399	.424	.469	.454	.428	.402		.382		.339	.200	.165	
43 DRESDEN	.362	.369		.385	.377	.366		.349		.247	.145	.119	
44 LEIPZIG	.394	.403		.423	.419	.406		.353		.256	.144	.119	
45 ZWICKAU	.475	.482		.485	.486	.467		.415		.296	.158	.119	
46 NECKARKREIS		.420	.467	.425	.384	.355		.340		.285	.156	.138	
47 SCHWARZWALD.		.454	.483	.448	.415	.394		.391		.350	.193	.167	
48 JAGSTKREIS		.452	.486	.454	.424	.394		.373		.345	.217	.185	
49 DONAUKREIS		.441	.480	.455	.422	.387		.381		.342	.200	.169	
50 KONSTANZ		.397		.395	.362	.343		.339		.310	.208	.177	
51 FREIBURG		.351		.348	.328	.315		.318		.286	.199	.174	
52 KARLSRUHE		.422		.405	.377	.356		.361		.308	.191	.154	
53 MANNHEIM		.413		.414	.396	.385		.388		.330	.196	.153	
54 STARKENBURG		.408		.392	.365	.353	.354	.365	.351	.306	.181	.148	
55 OBERHESSEN		.356		.346	.326	.310	.310	.307	.297	.275	.197	.162	
56 RHEINHESSEN		.367		.366	.345	.329	.315	.320	.302	.264	.175	.146	
57 MECKLENBURG	.307	.325	.349	.337	.338	.339		.326		.287	.212	.187	.247
58 THUERINGEN		.380	.412	.390	.392	.384		.374		.307	.193	.151	.200
59 H.OLDENBURG	.332	.329	.362	.353	.350	.355	.372	.381	.373	.349	.234	.206	
60 F.LUEBECK	.367	.365	.390	.385	.404	.395	.390	.385	.375	.350	.198	.171	
61 BIRKENFELD	.365	.376	.404	.389	.386	.383	.375	.385	.377	.352	.231	.173	
62 BRAUNSCHWEIG		.360	.395	.372	.369	.366	.356	.340	.301	.263	.169	.142	.188
63 ANHALT	.388	.383	.415	.402	.405	.398		.359		.275	.192	.161	.219
64 SCHAUMBURG-L.		.361		.357	.354	.328		.321		.270	.161	.139	.203
65 LIPPE		.380		.397	.393	.393		.374		.329	.198	.161	.203
66 LUEBECK	.307	.315	.345	.340	.332	.324		.309	.293	.252	.154	.131	
67 BREMEN	.319	.334	.366	.334	.305	.290	.297	.283	.279	.241	.144	.129	.193
68 HAMBURG	.292	.315	.349	.340	.322	.321	.294	.270	.238	.210	.118	.114	.168
69 UNTERELSASS		.378		.379	.366	.344		.330		.275			
70 OBERELSASS		.364		.359	.348	.337		.326		.249			
71 LOTHRINGEN		.326		.337	.329	.321		.344		.328			
GERMANY	.389	.396	.428	.404	.395	.389		.373		.312	.185	.157	.202

PROVINCE OR STATE WITH MORE THAN ONE ADM. AREA

	1866-68	1869-73	1874-77	1878-82	1883-87	1888-92	1893-97	1898-02	1903-07	1908-12	1923-27	1931-35	1938-39
P.WESTPREUSSEN	.457	.448		.457	.463	.462	.469	.474	.451	.422			
BRANDENBURG	.381	.385		.399	.392	.385	.360	.322	.279	.230	.175	.159	.206
POMERANIA	.399	.401		.410	.410	.405	.401	.397	.363	.328	.217	.194	.250
POSNANIA	.443	.451		.455	.452	.448	.455	.465	.452	.416			
SILESIA	.398	.408		.399	.400	.406	.415	.418	.395	.368	.226	.197	.241
P.SAXONY	.400	.403		.421	.425	.413	.395	.376	.339	.307	.193	.159	.206
P.HANOVER	.348	.352		.363	.362	.357	.359	.351	.328	.301	.190	.167	.220
WESTPHALIA	.395	.412		.438	.439	.438	.441	.449	.440	.398	.220	.166	.207
HESSE-NASSAU	.353	.360		.357	.335	.323	.315	.312	.297	.262	.170	.140	.187
RHINELAND	.386	.398		.413	.403	.397	.392	.393	.375	.327	.185	.149	.185
PRUSSIA	.391	.395	.427	.403	.398	.392	.388	.380	.357	.321	.186	.159	.205
BAVARIA	.391	.411	.451	.428	.410	.391		.386		.334	.208	.174	.216
K.SAXONY	.411	.419	.457	.431	.427	.413	.394	.373	.319	.267	.149	.119	.159
WUERTTENBURG	.415	.440	.478	.443	.408	.379	.369	.367	.321	.322	.183	.158	.209
BADEN	.373	.394	.422	.389	.366	.351	.347	.354	.343	.309	.197	.162	.202
HESSE	.359	.381	.410	.371	.348	.334	.330	.336	.322	.286	.183	.151	.186
GD.OLDENBURG	.339	.338	.370	.360	.359	.362	.374	.382	.374	.350	.230	.200	.269
ALSACE LORRAINE		.358	.387	.360	.349	.335		.333		.285			

APPENDIX TABLE 2.1
DEMOGRAPHIC INDICES FOR GERMANY: INDEX OF MARITAL FERTILITY (I_g)

ADMINISTRATIVE AREA	1866-68	1869-73	1874-77	1878-82	1883-87	1888-92	1893-97	1898-02	1903-07	1908-12	1923-27	1931-35	1938-39
01 OSTPREUSSEN	.744	.790		.794	.800	.794	.800	.781	.739	.692	.476	.384	.401
02 DANZIG	.815	.806		.806	.821	.807	.820	.812	.775	.730			
03 MARIENWERDER	.820	.838		.833	.861	.844	.861	.868	.841	.802	.433	.366	
04 BERLIN	.648	.636	.662	.594	.535	.494	.448	.394	.356	.303	.147	.152	.224
05 POTSDAM	.674	.680		.669	.652	.623	.573	.498	.430	.347	.263	.225	
06 FRANKFURT/O.	.693	.704		.685	.675	.666	.640	.595	.536	.472	.306	.236	
07 STETTIN-STR.	.713	.733		.709	.706	.690	.674	.638	.572	.501	.336	.278	
08 KOESLIN	.762	.786		.783	.801	.782	.785	.763	.723	.670	.446	.349	
09 POSEN	.787	.789		.792	.803	.797	.823	.834	.814	.778	.458	.382	
10 BROMBERG	.806	.817		.821	.852	.833	.855	.853	.832	.790			
11 BRESLAU	.740	.749		.724	.720	.715	.704	.680	.625	.569	.371	.289	
12 LIEGNITZ	.660	.671		.662	.654	.641	.623	.597	.552	.512	.342	.258	
13 OPPELN	.920	.827		.806	.836	.842	.870	.866	.846	.816	.568	.442	
14 MAGDEBURG	.669	.673		.649	.646	.622	.590	.544	.488	.427	.269	.212	
15 MERSEBURG	.731	.736		.734	.733	.711	.678	.644	.580	.506	.316	.225	
16 ERFURT	.732	.741		.704	.700	.669	.651	.617	.574	.508	.323	.245	
17 SCHLESWIG	.686	.680		.673	.664	.651	.640	.595	.546	.487	.297	.259	
18 HANNOVER	.679	.677		.651	.643	.616	.608	.562	.491	.420	.255	.210	.353
19 HILDESHEIM	.650	.661		.651	.645	.635	.628	.598	.546	.492	.335	.264	
20 LUENEBURG	.567	.573		.554	.562	.552	.557	.537	.503	.465	.313	.259	
21 STADE	.681	.688		.678	.676	.660	.667	.643	.611	.548	.348	.280	
22 OSNABRUECK	.744	.746		.737	.742	.730	.749	.737	.719	.686	.529	.444	
23 AURICH	.719	.743		.743	.760	.752	.765	.747	.726	.680	.499	.411	
24 MUENSTER	.827	.829		.835	.862	.858	.886	.868	.870	.811	.527	.364	
25 MINDEN	.796	.798		.783	.787	.768	.772	.739	.683	.619	.442	.330	
26 ARNSBERG	.818	.839		.815	.817	.811	.810	.781	.741	.644	.364	.253	
27 KASSEL	.724	.731		.702	.675	.673	.660	.634	.591	.530	.366	.284	
28 WIESBADEN	.700	.688		.642	.627	.599	.592	.566	.513	.435	.285	.218	
29 KOBLENZ	.769	.799		.783	.761	.750	.755	.739	.691	.626	.439	.345	
30 DUESSELDORF	.853	.872		.841	.835	.802	.784	.743	.677	.569	.314	.243	
31 KOELN	.846	.872		.850	.823	.803	.774	.734	.665	.554	.328	.245	
32 TRIER	.826	.844		.835	.832	.828	.844	.841	.793	.713	.599	.442	
33 AACHEN	.903	.931		.915	.917	.918	.913	.891	.827	.737	.456	.332	
34 SIGMARINGEN	.868	.888		.814	.764	.748	.776	.801	.764	.689	.474	.399	.503
35 OBERBAYERN	.842	.839	.838	.786	.762	.732		.680		.534	.323	.275	
36 NIEDERBAYERN	.923	.921	.931	.913	.916	.906		.912		.835	.574	.473	
37 PFALZ	.735	.776	.789	.736	.720	.707		.690		.568	.373	.288	.304
38 OBERPFALZ	.888	.889	.907	.880	.886	.876		.896		.803	.572	.455	
39 OBERFRANKEN	.717	.714	.732	.688	.679	.666		.664		.565	.397	.305	
40 MITTELFRANKEN	.759	.762	.765	.717	.694	.663		.624		.483	.297	.247	
41 UNTERFRANKEN	.782	.781	.789	.726	.711	.704		.711		.617	.459	.355	
42 SCHWABEN	.948	.942	.934	.860	.845	.814		.782		.669	.418	.345	
43 DRESDEN	.640	.651		.639	.625	.604		.552		.394	.237	.186	
44 LEIPZIG	.717	.730		.715	.698	.665		.564		.403	.230	.179	
45 ZWICKAU	.778	.786		.761	.760	.728		.640		.463	.256	.181	
46 NECKARKREIS			.845	.849	.781	.744	.710	.660		.505	.302	.263	
47 SCHWARZWALD.			.892	.893	.836	.814	.799	.780		.642	.417	.355	
48 JAGSTKREIS			.859	.876	.826	.801	.774	.746		.651	.459	.389	
49 DONAUKREIS			.921	.922	.868	.834	.793	.791		.678	.453	.388	
50 KONSTANZ				.848	.774	.720	.695	.694		.599	.437	.356	
51 FREIBURG				.742	.700	.677	.657	.650		.549	.412	.343	
52 KARLSRUHE				.851	.770	.746	.722	.689		.545	.365	.284	
53 MANNHEIM				.787	.750	.731	.719	.686		.556	.357	.267	
54 STARKENBURG			.763	.695	.679	.666	.667	.641	.583	.498	.320	.238	
55 OBERHESSEN			.614	.578	.562	.539	.542	.526	.489	.443	.346	.261	
56 RHEINHESSEN			.759	.705	.683	.663	.634	.609	.551	.471	.331	.255	
57 MECKLENBURG	.616	.598	.612	.579	.574	.566		.518		.440	.323	.272	.346
58 THUERINGEN		.644	.679	.634	.635	.621		.586		.477	.309	.220	.281
59 H.OLDENBURG	.695	.691	.731	.689	.694	.693	.710	.689	.649	.603	.437	.367	
60 F.LUEBECK	.644	.648	.678	.651	.672	.655	.646	.618	.595	.545	.352	.282	
61 BIRKENFELD	.652	.704	.729	.708	.694	.691	.700	.700	.673	.618	.434	.291	
62 BRAUNSCHWEIG		.623	.676	.608	.602	.595	.580	.547	.486	.420	.277	.214	.291
63 ANHALT	.661	.672	.682	.646	.639	.621		.554		.416	.287	.217	.290
64 SCHAUMBURG-L.			.717	.641	.648	.589		.553		.467	.291	.222	.299
65 LIPPE			.767	.732	.726	.726		.685		.595	.415	.305	.335
66 LUEBECK	.651	.643	.669	.635	.605	.582		.534	.488	.417	.254	.201	
67 BREMEN	.746	.728	.769	.668	.619	.603	.592	.550	.504	.417	.252	.220	.295
68 HAMBURG	.666	.662	.672	.630	.594	.582	.561	.474	.406	.346	.205	.192	.254
69 UNTERELSASS			.793	.729	.704	.666		.619		.484			
70 OBERELSASS			.802	.762	.740	.710		.638		.462			
71 LOTHRINGEN			.695	.670	.656	.637		.639		.557			
GERMANY	.761	.760	.791	.735	.726	.706		.664		.542	.334	.264	.316

PROVINCE OR STATE WITH MORE THAN ONE ADM. AREA

	1866-68	1869-73	1874-77	1878-82	1883-87	1888-92	1893-97	1898-02	1903-07	1908-12	1923-27	1931-35	1938-39
P.WESTPREUSSEN	.818	.826		.823	.845	.829	.844	.844	.812	.770			
BRANDENBURG	.683	.692		.677	.663	.641	.599	.532	.463	.380	.284	.231	.287
POMERANIA	.731	.753		.736	.741	.722	.711	.679	.621	.556	.373	.302	.368
POSNANIA	.794	.799		.802	.821	.810	.834	.841	.821	.782			
SILESIA	.749	.758		.738	.747	.745	.751	.735	.697	.656	.419	.326	.375
P.SAXONY	.705	.711		.693	.691	.666	.635	.597	.540	.474	.299	.224	.283
P.HANOVER	.661	.668		.655	.655	.639	.640	.610	.566	.512	.346	.282	.343
WESTPHALIA	.814	.826		.811	.819	.811	.817	.793	.758	.677	.415	.297	.343
HESSE-NASSAU	.713	.712		.674	.652	.636	.624	.598	.548	.478	.322	.247	.299
RHINELAND	.840	.863		.841	.831	.811	.800	.768	.705	.604	.357	.271	.307
PRUSSIA	.747	.759	.781	.741	.737	.719	.710	.679	.630	.561	.338	.267	.319
BAVARIA	.818	.824	.832	.786	.771	.750		.725		.605	.399	.322	.359
K.SAXONY	.710	.722	.748	.703	.694	.667	.640	.588	.507	.422	.242	.182	.232
WUERTTEMBURG	.981	.877	.883	.823	.792	.762	.769	.732	.674	.597	.382	.325	.367
BADEN	.802	.802	.831	.746	.718	.700	.697	.633		.557	.383	.302	.367
HESSE	.701	.716	.726	.663	.646	.629	.623	.602	.550	.477	.329	.248	.280
GD.OLDENBURG	.684	.688	.725	.688	.692	.689	.703	.684	.647	.600	.430	.351	.426
ALSACE LORRAINE			.765	.761	.720	.700	.670	.631		.504			

APPENDIX TABLE 2.1
DEMOGRAPHIC INDICES FOR GERMANY: INDEX OF ILLEGITIMATE FERTILITY (I_h)

ADMINISTRATIVE AREA	1866 -68	1869 -73	1874 -77	1878 -82	1883 -87	1888 -92	1893 -97	1898 -02	1903 -07	1908 -12	1923 -27	1931 -35	1938 -39
01 OSTPREUSSEN	.071	.069		.077	.085	.085	.084	.078	.069	.068	.055	.050	.051
02 DANZIG	.086	.076		.082	.084	.079	.076	.072	.066	.065			
03 MARIENWERDER	.064	.060		.068	.075	.072	.067	.060	.054	.052	.057	.053	
04 BERLIN	.082	.074	.087	.080	.069	.060	.062	.061	.065	.073	.028	.024	.037
05 POTSDAM	.075	.073		.083	.085	.081	.076	.064	.054	.048	.049	.045	
06 FRANKFURT/O.	.084	.084		.089	.092	.088	.086	.082	.074	.073	.049	.045	
07 STETTIN-STR.	.085	.083		.090	.093	.089	.092	.091	.081	.080	.073	.058	
08 KOESLIN	.073	.073		.078	.081	.078	.077	.073	.065	.062	.050	.048	
09 POSEN	.058	.059		.060	.062	.058	.053	.051	.046	.042	.043	.040	
10 BROMBERG	.064	.059		.065	.069	.066	.064	.058	.050	.046			
11 BRESLAU	.095	.092		.093	.096	.094	.098	.094	.087	.087	.065	.053	
12 LIEGNITZ	.087	.086		.094	.098	.096	.093	.091	.083	.081	.064	.058	
13 OPPELN	.061	.055		.053	.057	.057	.057	.054	.048	.049	.042	.035	
14 MAGDEBURG	.075	.071		.085	.091	.087	.092	.091	.082	.088	.065	.055	
15 MERSEBURG	.089	.089		.101	.106	.103	.103	.102	.093	.097	.075	.063	
16 ERFURT	.062	.058		.062	.063	.059	.057	.058	.054	.053	.039	.034	
17 SCHLESWIG	.066	.059		.069	.071	.070	.072	.068	.067	.068	.039	.035	.045
18 HANNOVER	.071	.062		.063	.064	.064	.068	.067	.058	.054	.031	.026	
19 HILDESHEIM	.085	.065		.061	.060	.056	.055	.056	.051	.051	.042	.032	
20 LUENEBURG	.063	.050		.051	.055	.055	.061	.058	.056	.057	.039	.033	
21 STADE	.053	.046		.047	.052	.049	.049	.048	.048	.051	.032	.027	
22 OSNABRUECK	.027	.021		.025	.028	.028	.028	.027	.025	.024	.017	.012	
23 AURICH	.034	.027		.026	.029	.026	.027	.024	.024	.025	.023	.019	
24 MUENSTER	.014	.012		.016	.016	.014	.016	.017	.018	.021	.021	.013	
25 MINDEN	.035	.028		.030	.030	.028	.028	.030	.029	.024	.016	.011	
26 ARNSBERG	.026	.023		.029	.028	.026	.027	.029	.030	.034	.022	.013	
27 KASSEL	.069	.054		.048	.046	.045	.043	.042	.038	.036	.028	.021	
28 WIESBADEN	.049	.038		.033	.031	.032	.033	.035	.037	.035	.021	.016	
29 KOBLENZ	.021	.019		.021	.022	.020	.020	.019	.017	.016	.014	.011	
30 DUESSELDORF	.023	.022		.025	.026	.025	.026	.028	.029	.029	.020	.013	
31 KOELN	.035	.035		.042	.045	.048	.050	.053	.050	.048	.029	.017	
32 TRIER	.024	.021		.023	.024	.024	.025	.025	.023	.023	.013	.010	
33 AACHEN	.015	.014		.016	.016	.017	.016	.015	.014	.014	.014	.010	
34 SIGMARINGEN	.091	.080		.064	.056	.051	.044	.041	.032	.026	.021	.023	.021
35 OBERBAYERN	.158	.140	.147	.144	.139	.136		.126		.100	.061	.049	
36 NIEDERBAYERN	.161	.134	.135	.135	.134	.128		.125		.112	.089	.080	
37 PFALZ	.072	.062	.053	.050	.048	.049		.053		.050	.035	.026	.027
38 OBERPFALZ	.152	.117	.107	.103	.101	.095		.086		.070	.059	.051	
39 OBERFRANKEN	.144	.116	.113	.107	.102	.092		.077		.066	.046	.037	
40 MITTELFRANKEN	.147	.130	.134	.130	.127	.121		.116		.094	.052	.044	
41 UNTERFRANKEN	.090	.073	.066	.062	.058	.053		.047		.039	.031	.025	
42 SCHWABEN	.100	.091	.094	.092	.088	.083		.078		.065	.047	.040	
43 DRESDEN	.107	.105		.110	.110	.102		.100		.080	.054	.046	
44 LIEPZIG	.110	.104		.107	.111	.110		.107		.090	.057	.048	
45 ZWICKAU	.138	.131		.133	.135	.124		.112		.091	.056	.045	
46 NECKARKREIS		.075	.069	.065	.064	.062		.062		.056	.030	.023	
47 SCHWARZWALD.		.083	.068	.068	.071	.067		.064		.054	.034	.027	
48 JAGSTKREIS		.112	.097	.089	.086	.082		.074		.057	.035	.031	
49 DONAUKREIS		.096	.090	.084	.080	.073		.065		.050	.033	.027	
50 KONSTANZ		.094		.071	.066	.059		.046		.034	.029	.027	
51 FREIBURG		.073		.053	.055	.049		.044		.039	.033	.029	
52 KARLSRUHE		.062		.050	.051	.049		.052		.051	.037	.029	
53 MANNHEIM		.073		.056	.057	.060		.065		.068	.045	.032	
54 STARKENBURG		.066		.057	.056	.054	.053	.054	.052	.053	.035	.025	
55 OBERHESSEN		.071		.061	.058	.055	.058	.058	.054	.050	.034	.023	
56 RHEINHESSEN		.061		.047	.046	.041	.043	.048	.044	.043	.032	.023	
57 MECKLENBURG	.073	.086	.092	.092	.093	.091		.087		.091	.090	.067	.072
58 THUERINGEN		.088	.091	.090	.095	.092		.091		.082	.057	.048	.051
59 H.OLDENBURG	.026	.022	.025	.028	.029	.030	.034	.035	.039	.040	.031	.023	
60 F.LUEBECK	.108	.099	.102	.100	.109	.103	.105	.105	.097	.099	.051	.041	
61 BIRKENFELD	.038	.035	.035	.037	.048	.046	.041	.038	.036	.035	.020	.015	
62 BRAUNSCHWEIG		.088	.082	.084	.087	.085	.084	.079	.071	.069	.050	.041	.040
63 ANHALT	.092	.072	.086	.085	.088	.084		.082		.080	.071	.057	.064
64 SCHAUMBURG-L.		.030		.030	.023	.017		.029		.023	.012	.011	.022
65 LIPPE		.040		.043	.049	.044		.039		.031	.020	.013	.020
66 LUEBECK	.052	.044	.053	.053	.055	.056		.059	.058	.058	.045	.034	
67 BREMEN	.035	.034	.035	.037	.034	.033	.013	.039	.043	.047	.031	.022	.032
68 HAMBURG	.054	.053	.061	.061	.065	.069	.072	.065	.062	.060	.028	.024	.037
69 UNTERELSASS		.064		.063	.067	.064		.059		.052			
70 OBERELSASS		.051		.047	.049	.048		.048		.036			
71 LOTHRINGEN		.035		.034	.034	.034		.038		.037			
GERMANY	.079	.071	.073	.072	.073	.070		.066		.059	.041	.033	.038

PROVINCE OR STATE WITH MORE THAN ONE ADM.AREA

	1866 -68	1869 -73	1874 -77	1878 -82	1883 -87	1888 -92	1893 -97	1898 -02	1903 -07	1908 -12	1923 -27	1931 -35	1938 -39
P.WESTPREUSSEN	.074	.067		.074	.079	.075	.071	.065	.059	.058			
BRANDENBURG	.080	.079		.086	.089	.084	.080	.070	.060	.054	.049	.045	.052
POMERANIA	.080	.079		.085	.089	.085	.086	.084	.075	.074	.065	.055	.059
POSNANIA	.060	.059		.062	.064	.060	.057	.053	.047	.043			
SILESIA	.082	.078		.079	.082	.081	.082	.079	.071	.070	.057	.048	.046
P.SAXONY	.078	.076		.087	.092	.089	.090	.089	.081	.085	.064	.054	.059
P.HANOVER	.059	.049		.049	.051	.050	.052	.051	.048	.047	.032	.025	.032
WESTPHALIA	.025	.021		.025	.025	.024	.024	.026	.027	.029	.021	.013	.018
HESSE-NASSAU	.060	.047		.041	.039	.038	.038	.038	.037	.035	.024	.018	.024
RHINELAND	.024	.023		.026	.027	.028	.028	.030	.029	.029	.020	.013	.019
PRUSSIA	.062	.059	.063	.062	.064	.061	.060	.058	.054	.053	.037	.029	.035
BAVARIA	.123	.110	.110	.107	.104	.100		.094		.079	.054	.045	.049
K.SAXONY	.119	.113	.123	.117	.119	.112	.108	.106	.093	.086	.056	.046	.045
WUERTTEMBURG	.101	.090	.079	.075	.074	.069	.068	.065	.048	.054	.032	.026	.031
BADEN	.087	.074	.061	.056	.056	.054	.053	.053	.050	.050	.037	.029	.029
HESSE	.092	.066	.060	.055	.053	.050	.051	.053	.050	.049	.034	.024	.026
GD.OLDENBURG	.036	.031	.034	.036	.038	.038	.041	.041	.043	.044	.032	.023	.027
ALSACE LORRAINE		.052	.050	.049	.052	.050		.049		.043			

APPENDIX TABLE 2.1
DEMOGRAPHIC INDICES FOR GERMANY: INDEX OF PROPORTION MARRIED (I_m)

ADMINISTRATIVE AREA	1867	1871	1875	1880	1885	1890	1895	1900	1905	1910	1925	1933	1939
01 OSTPREUSSEN	.494	.464		.464	.469	.488	.486	.491	.481	.475	.465	.527	.578
02 DANZIG	.483	.471		.486	.478	.493	.497	.514	.515	.506			
03 MARIENWERDER	.537	.523		.531	.518	.528	.527	.533	.526	.515	.480	.538	
04 BERLIN	.434	.427	.467	.467	.459	.456	.455	.467	.477	.479	.477	.512	.578
05 POTSDAM	.508	.504		.541	.538	.552	.551	.548	.540	.537	.532	.613	
06 FRANKFURT/O.	.491	.493		.518	.518	.524	.521	.538	.548	.549	.539	.616	
07 STETTIN-STR.	.489	.478		.505	.501	.511	.515	.537	.539	.542	.506	.579	
08 KOESLIN	.489	.479		.488	.478	.487	.484	.504	.502	.501	.468	.537	
09 POSEN	.510	.526		.527	.508	.512	.506	.515	.519	.498	.467	.527	
10 BROMBERG	.542	.537		.536	.521	.528	.525	.535	.531	.514			
11 BRESLAU	.453	.466		.472	.461	.464	.468	.486	.492	.487	.461	.530	
12 LIEGNITZ	.460	.466		.491	.492	.505	.510	.531	.536	.536	.512	.574	
13 OPPELN	.509	.521		.495	.488	.503	.521	.538	.532	.511	.436	.512	
14 MAGDEBURG	.520	.518		.557	.564	.567	.569	.573	.563	.577	.544	.614	
15 MERSEBURG	.511	.514		.550	.559	.568	.562	.568	.570	.581	.566	.648	
16 ERFURT	.499	.515		.542	.532	.538	.525	.533	.534	.538	.519	.575	
17 SCHLESWIG	.464	.465		.505	.508	.521	.530	.547	.561	.565	.524	.580	.626
18 HANNOVER	.473	.478		.505	.497	.503	.506	.524	.530	.531	.497	.560	
19 HILDESHEIM	.490	.503		.530	.526	.536	.534	.545	.546	.545	.506	.565	
20 LUENEBURG	.508	.514		.553	.546	.552	.561	.577	.581	.588	.532	.591	
21 STADE	.509	.519		.546	.552	.557	.559	.573	.587	.598	.541	.593	
22 OSNABRUECK	.442	.464		.484	.481	.475	.469	.483	.491	.498	.444	.457	
23 AURICH	.429	.433		.471	.470	.486	.478	.479	.483	.496	.469	.510	
24 MUENSTER	.377	.388		.434	.435	.451	.458	.490	.517	.539	.489	.520	
25 MINDEN	.459	.465		.493	.485	.487	.482	.492	.499	.496	.427	.470	
26 ARNSBERG	.529	.549		.583	.575	.575	.571	.595	.607	.606	.536	.571	
27 KASSEL	.449	.473		.510	.501	.496	.489	.502	.522	.523	.500	.545	
28 WIESBADEN	.447	.469		.486	.464	.460	.459	.477	.499	.506	.483	.526	
29 KOBLENZ	.454	.453		.481	.474	.474	.467	.474	.487	.488	.469	.486	
30 DUESSELDORF	.461	.469		.496	.487	.491	.492	.521	.543	.549	.510	.552	
31 KOELN	.410	.412		.445	.443	.452	.449	.471	.488	.493	.483	.517	
32 TRIER	.470	.465		.492	.480	.484	.486	.501	.520	.526	.425	.433	
33 AACHEN	.403	.405		.422	.413	.412	.411	.418	.429	.439	.455	.504	
34 SIGMARINGEN	.379	.409		.478	.458	.432	.414	.420	.442	.465	.400	.409	.429
35 OBERBAYERN	.363	.398	.454	.452	.433	.423		.437		.442	.416	.419	
36 NIEDERBAYERN	.334	.388	.431	.440	.427	.417		.419		.433	.401	.409	
37 PFALZ	.455	.487	.545	.545	.533	.516		.538		.569	.517	.553	.607
38 OBERPFALZ	.357	.417	.471	.475	.462	.447		.449		.469	.433	.453	
39 OBERFRANKEN	.386	.439	.483	.477	.471	.462		.487		.519	.479	.526	
40 MITTELFRANKEN	.388	.428	.480	.474	.464	.460		.484		.509	.471	.494	
41 UNTERFRANKEN	.400	.430	.477	.473	.450	.439		.455		.497	.463	.498	
42 SCHWABEN	.353	.391	.447	.460	.449	.436		.432		.453	.413	.407	
43 DRESDEN	.478	.484		.520	.519	.526		.549		.531	.496	.524	
44 LIEPZIG	.468	.478		.519	.524	.533		.537		.532	.501	.540	
45 ZWICKAU	.527	.537		.562	.562	.567		.575		.553	.509	.547	
46 NECKARKREIS		.448	.511	.503	.471	.452		.466		.510	.463	.475	
47 SCHWARZWALD.		.458	.504	.495	.464	.446		.458		.503	.416	.427	
48 JAGSTKREIS		.454	.499	.495	.473	.451		.446		.484	.430	.431	
49 DONAUKREIS		.418	.470	.474	.453	.437		.434		.466	.399	.392	
50 KONSTANZ		.402		.461	.453	.447		.452		.489	.440	.456	
51 FREIBURG		.415		.456	.440	.437		.452		.485	.440	.462	
52 KARLSRUHE		.456		.493	.469	.456		.485		.519	.468	.491	
53 MANNHEIM		.476		.516	.503	.493		.520		.537	.484	.515	
54 STARKENBURG		.492		.525	.496	.488	.490	.529	.561	.569	.514	.580	
55 OBERHESSEN		.525		.551	.533	.527	.521	.533	.562	.574	.522	.584	
56 RHEINHESSEN		.438		.485	.470	.462	.460	.485	.508	.515	.479	.532	
57 MECKLENBURG	.431	.467	.496	.503	.508	.522		.554		.561	.524	.583	.638
58 THUERINGEN		.526	.546	.553	.549	.552		.572		.570	.538	.602	.647
59 H.OLDENBURG	.457	.459	.478	.491	.483	.491	.499	.530	.547	.549	.499	.534	
60 F.LUEBECK	.483	.484	.501	.517	.523	.529	.527	.546	.558	.564	.487	.540	
61 BIRKENFELD	.532	.510	.532	.525	.523	.522	.506	.525	.535	.544	.511	.571	
62 BRAUNSCHWEIG		.509	.527	.550	.547	.550	.548	.558	.555	.553	.521	.587	.590
63 ANHALT	.520	.518	.553	.565	.575	.584		.587		.578	.561	.647	.685
64 SCHAUMBURG-L.		.481		.535	.530	.544		.558		.557	.533	.607	.656
65 LIPPE		.467		.514	.507	.512		.519		.529	.451	.509	.581
66 LUEBECK	.425	.453	.473	.493	.503	.509		.526	.546	.541	.523	.576	
67 BREMEN	.400	.433	.452	.481	.463	.450	.470	.477	.512	.525	.510	.542	.612
68 HAMBURG	.389	.430	.471	.491	.485	.491	.493	.501	.513	.526	.511	.536	.604
69 UNTERELSASS		.430		.475	.469	.465		.484		.516			
70 OBERELSASS		.417		.437	.432	.436		.471		.498			
71 LOTHRINGEN		.441		.476	.475	.476		.509		.558			
GERMANY	.454	.472	.495	.501	.494	.497		.513		.524	.490	.534	.590

PROVINCE OR STATE
WITH MORE THAN
ONE ADM. AREA

	1867	1871	1875	1880	1885	1890	1895	1900	1905	1910	1925	1933	1939
P.WESTPREUSSEN	.515	.502		.512	.501	.513	.514	.525	.521	.511			
BRANDENBURG	.500	.498		.530	.529	.540	.539	.545	.542	.540	.536	.614	.654
POMERANIA	.489	.478		.498	.493	.502	.504	.526	.527	.528	.492	.564	.618
POSNANIA	.521	.530		.531	.513	.518	.513	.522	.524	.504			
SILESIA	.474	.485		.485	.479	.489	.498	.517	.518	.508	.467	.536	.591
P.SAXONY	.513	.516		.552	.556	.562	.559	.566	.561	.572	.549	.621	.659
P.HANOVER	.480	.490		.519	.515	.522	.522	.535	.542	.546	.502	.552	.604
WESTPHALIA	.470	.486		.525	.521	.527	.526	.551	.565	.570	.505	.538	.582
HESSE-NASSAU	.448	.471		.499	.483	.477	.473	.488	.509	.513	.491	.534	.592
RHINELAND	.444	.447		.474	.467	.472	.471	.493	.513	.519	.489	.526	.576
PRUSSIA	.480	.481	.506	.502	.497	.503	.504	.519	.526	.527	.496	.547	.598
BAVARIA	.380	.421	.473	.473	.459	.449		.462		.484	.447	.466	.539
K.SAXONY	.494	.502	.533	.535	.536	.543	.538	.555	.547	.539	.502	.537	.606
WUERTTENBURG	.403	.445	.496	.492	.466	.447	.432	.453	.436	.494	.433	.440	.532
BADEN	.400	.439	.468	.483	.467	.460	.457	.482	.503	.512	.462	.486	.546
HESSE	.439	.485	.526	.520	.498	.490	.488	.516	.545	.553	.506	.567	.628
GD.OLDENBURG	.468	.467	.486	.497	.491	.498	.502	.531	.547	.550	.499	.538	.605
ALSACE LORRAINE		.429	.474	.464	.459	.460		.488		.525			

APPENDIX TABLE 2.1
DEMOGRAPHIC INDICES FOR GERMANY: ADJUSTED INDEX OF PROPORTION MARRIED (I_{m^*})

ADMINISTRATIVE AREA	1867	1871	1875	1880	1885	1890	1895	1900	1905	1910	1925	1933	1939
01 OSTPREUSSEN	.537	.508		.525	.519	.524	.524	.530	.532	.538	.513	.536	.584
02 DANZIG	.530	.518		.541	.530	.539	.544	.559	.562	.559			
03 MARIENWERDER	.604	.588		.602	.588	.592	.590	.590	.589	.589	.527	.552	
04 BERLIN	.469	.462	.503	.491	.481	.483	.480	.494	.501	.500	.472	.477	.525
05 POTSDAM	.559	.549		.583	.575	.585	.582	.577	.570	.564	.562	.594	
06 FRANKFURT/O.	.541	.541		.564	.561	.567	.568	.579	.586	.592	.570	.599	
07 STETTIN-STR.	.539	.525		.554	.548	.558	.562	.577	.579	.584	.542	.571	
08 KOESLIN	.547	.534		.549	.536	.540	.541	.553	.554	.562	.519	.543	
09 POSEN	.563	.569		.582	.569	.573	.568	.568	.569	.560	.514	.533	
10 BROMBERG	.606	.597		.603	.586	.592	.592	.591	.589	.584			
11 BRESLAU	.492	.495		.510	.502	.506	.509	.519	.522	.522	.494	.521	
12 LIEGNITZ	.493	.495		.526	.529	.541	.548	.564	.567	.573	.543	.563	
13 OPPELN	.553	.557		.556	.547	.554	.563	.572	.571	.566	.485	.507	
14 MAGDEBURG	.566	.563		.602	.604	.609	.611	.617	.613	.620	.576	.600	
15 MERSEBURG	.559	.563		.597	.604	.611	.608	.614	.618	.625	.599	.631	
16 ERFURT	.534	.545		.582	.575	.586	.577	.583	.585	.590	.555	.567	
17 SCHLESWIG	.504	.506		.551	.553	.567	.578	.592	.599	.606	.557	.571	.615
18 HANNOVER	.516	.523		.554	.543	.551	.555	.568	.567	.572	.527	.543	
19 HILDESHEIM	.522	.536		.575	.572	.579	.578	.587	.587	.589	.547	.559	
20 LUENEBURG	.547	.551		.591	.586	.593	.602	.614	.617	.628	.573	.590	
21 STADE	.552	.556		.591	.589	.599	.605	.617	.626	.636	.583	.595	
22 OSNABRUECK	.495	.510		.536	.533	.533	.530	.538	.540	.547	.501	.478	
23 AURICH	.479	.478		.518	.518	.531	.532	.536	.538	.552	.519	.524	
24 MUENSTER	.426	.432		.485	.487	.506	.520	.546	.565	.584	.550	.537	
25 MINDEN	.523	.520		.553	.546	.550	.550	.558	.561	.557	.486	.481	
26 ARNSBERG	.575	.584		.623	.618	.623	.625	.641	.643	.643	.584	.567	
27 KASSEL	.493	.506		.547	.543	.547	.546	.550	.561	.564	.542	.542	
28 WIESBADEN	.488	.499		.527	.510	.511	.512	.522	.529	.534	.514	.510	
29 KOBLENZ	.500	.491		.526	.521	.521	.515	.522	.530	.531	.515	.490	
30 DUESSELDORF	.512	.514		.542	.536	.546	.546	.551	.573	.586	.589	.552	.544
31 KOELN	.462	.460		.491	.487	.499	.500	.518	.526	.530	.519	.508	
32 TRIER	.518	.508		.544	.534	.535	.541	.554	.567	.573	.480	.447	
33 AACHEN	.448	.445		.462	.454	.454	.457	.467	.474	.483	.499	.506	
34 SIGMARINGEN	.423	.440		.496	.482	.473	.466	.465	.469	.486	.444	.415	.419
35 OBERBAYERN	.382	.420	.475	.475	.461	.462		.477		.467	.447	.414	
36 NIEDERBAYERN	.354	.413	.458	.472	.469	.468		.467		.475	.451	.424	
37 PFALZ	.519	.532	.580	.586	.582	.578		.594		.603	.569	.553	.589
38 OBERPFALZ	.385	.446	.498	.505	.501	.501		.500		.509	.484	.464	
39 OBERFRANKEN	.416	.464	.508	.510	.513	.515		.534		.555	.526	.523	
40 MITTELFRANKEN	.422	.460	.506	.506	.505	.512		.533		.539	.506	.487	
41 UNTERFRANKEN	.431	.458	.504	.508	.492	.487		.503		.525	.511	.501	
42 SCHWABEN	.381	.418	.469	.484	.481	.481		.483		.489	.453	.414	
43 DRESDEN	.518	.524		.559	.557	.565		.588		.568	.521	.499	
44 LEIPZIG	.520	.531		.567	.569	.579		.586		.576	.525	.520	
45 ZWICKAU	.580	.589		.616	.619	.626		.627		.609	.543	.530	
46 NECKARKREIS		.478	.533	.530	.513	.512		.521		.535	.501	.478	
47 SCHWARZWALD.		.475	.514	.515	.505	.502		.504		.526	.466	.436	
48 JAGSTKREIS		.479	.515	.520	.512	.502		.495		.513	.474	.444	
49 DONAUKREIS		.449	.487	.492	.485	.485		.485		.497	.443	.407	
50 KONSTANZ		.425		.483	.481	.486		.495		.514	.483	.455	
51 FREIBURG		.437		.488	.481	.485		.495		.512	.482	.461	
52 KARLSRUHE		.490		.530	.519	.521		.540		.550	.514	.488	
53 MANNHEIM		.510		.553	.551	.552		.571		.566	.528	.513	
54 STARKENBURG		.524		.559	.547	.552	.556	.575	.589	.597	.565	.570	
55 OBERHESSEN		.553		.585	.576	.576	.576	.579	.595	.607	.565	.581	
56 RHEINHESSEN		.482		.523	.519	.522	.522	.533	.543	.546	.519	.521	
57 MECKLENBURG	.478	.515	.536	.540	.545	.565		.593		.602	.556	.579	.634
58 THUERINGEN		.560	.575	.591	.593	.598		.613		.614	.575	.587	.629
59 H.OLDENBURG	.501	.499	.519	.538	.530	.540	.553	.578	.595	.597	.547	.546	
60 F.LUEBECK	.522	.525	.542	.564	.568	.577	.574	.591	.604	.611	.542	.560	
61 BIRKENFELD	.582	.565	.588	.588	.583	.578	.565	.590	.598	.602	.570	.580	
62 BRAUNSCHWEIG		.556	.574	.592	.589	.593		.598		.597	.552	.569	.549
63 ANHALT	.566	.571	.598	.608	.616	.624		.631		.619	.592	.629	.670
64 SCHAUMBURG-L.		.538		.586	.580	.591		.613		.612	.572	.599	.637
65 LIPPE		.509		.564	.555	.565		.570		.575	.501	.511	.566
66 LUEBECK	.463	.487	.513	.532	.542	.554		.568		.576	.544	.554	
67 BREMEN	.457	.490	.506	.519	.504	.505		.533		.558	.531	.528	.580
68 HAMBURG	.435	.468	.504	.513	.509	.524		.532		.554	.513	.504	.558
69 UNTERELSASS		.461		.509	.504	.506		.525		.537			
70 OBERELSASS		.443		.480	.480	.483		.508		.522			
71 LOTHRINGEN		.469		.510	.507	.512		.543		.582			
GERMANY	.501	.511	.535	.543	.538	.544		.557		.564	.525	.526	.568

PROVINCE OR STATE
WITH MORE THAN
ONE ADM.AREA

	1867	1871	1875	1880	1885	1890	1895	1900	1905	1910	1925	1933	1939
P.WESTPREUSSEN	.574	.559		.576	.563	.570	.570	.577	.577	.575			
BRANDENBURG	.550	.545		.574	.569	.577	.576	.578	.574	.571	.566	.596	.632
POMERANIA	.542	.528		.552	.544	.552	.555	.569	.570	.576	.534	.561	.611
POSNANIA	.578	.579		.590	.575	.579	.577	.577	.576	.569			
SILESIA	.514	.517		.531	.526	.533	.539	.550	.552	.551	.505	.528	.575
P.SAXONY	.557	.560		.596	.599	.606	.604	.610	.610	.617	.582	.608	.643
P.HANOVER	.522	.530		.565	.560	.567	.570	.580	.582	.589	.543	.551	.591
WESTPHALIA	.522	.529		.573	.571	.580	.585	.604	.610	.613	.559	.543	.566
HESSE-NASSAU	.491	.503		.537	.527	.528	.527	.535	.543	.547	.526	.524	.568
RHINELAND	.493	.491		.521	.514	.522	.525	.544	.555	.560	.532	.521	.554
PRUSSIA	.526	.523	.537	.549	.543	.549	.551	.562	.566	.569	.531	.538	.577
BAVARIA	.410	.450	.499	.508	.498	.498		.510		.516	.489	.467	.525
K.SAXONY	.542	.549	.580	.582	.582	.591	.588	.601	.592	.585	.530	.516	.573
WUERTTENBURG	.446	.470	.513	.515	.504	.501	.490	.505	.518	.521	.476	.449	.513
BADEN	.450	.468	.490	.516	.511	.514	.516	.531	.537	.540	.506	.485	.527
HESSE	.488	.520	.553	.555	.546	.549	.550	.563	.576	.583	.551	.558	.604
GD.OLDENBURG	.512	.509	.530	.546	.540	.548	.556	.581	.596	.599	.549	.551	.599
ALSACE LORRAINE		.458	.502	.500	.498	.501		.525		.540			

APPENDIX 2B Notes on Data Adjustments Involved in
the Computation of the Basic Demographic Indices in
Appendix Table 2.1

The computation of the basic demographic indices (I_f, I_g, I_h, I_m, and I_{m*}) presented in Appendix Table 2.1 requires data on the annual number of live births classified by legitimacy and the number of married or unmarried (single, widowed, and divorced) women in five-year age categories from age 15 through 49 and the number of total women in each age category. Most of the indices in Appendix Table 2.1 are based on such data taken directly from either the national or state statistical publications. Occasionally, however, the published data were presented in a slightly different format than the required one and adjustments had to be made. From 1871 on, the national statistical bureau published the annual number of live births in each administrative area by legitimacy until 1938, and hence no adjustments of the birth data during this time were necessary. Prior to this date, several states published the total number of live births without specifying legitimacy, or they published the number of births by legitimacy without differentiating live from still births. Live births by legitimacy were estimated by using the ratios of live to still births in each legitimacy category during the several years after 1871 when such information was first available. Separate birth data were not available for the four administrative areas in Baden and the three administrative areas of Alsace-Lorraine before 1872. The births for 1869–1871 for each of these administrative areas was estimated by assuming the proportions of the births in the entire state (i.e. in either Baden or Alsace-Lorraine) which occurred in each of the constituent administrative areas were the same as the corresponding proportions were in 1872–1874. For 1939, apparently due to difficulties arising from World War II, the scheduled volume of vital statistics was not published. Live births by area were available, however, without specification of legitimacy status. By assuming the ratio of illegitimate live births to total live births to be the same in 1939 as it was in 1937 and

1938, the number of illegitimate and legitimate live births in 1939 could be estimated.

Age distributions for some states for the 1871 census and earlier censuses were frequently tabulated by ten-year age intervals over age 20 rather than by five-year age intervals. In such situations, the ten-year age intervals were divided into five-year age intervals according to the ratio of the corresponding five-year age group to the corresponding ten-year age group in the first census which tabulated five-year age groups. Thus, for example, the 1867 Prussian census was tabulated by ten-year age groups over age 20. The 1871 Prussian census tabulated five-year intervals until age 40 after which ten-year intervals were given. Five-year intervals were given for all ages in the 1880 census. Accordingly, the age group 40–49 in the 1871 census was divided into two five-year groups (both for total women and married women) in the same proportion as the five-year age groups 40–44 and 45–49 were of the ten-year age group 40–49 in the 1880 census. The ten-year age groups 20–29 and 30–39 in the 1867 census were divided into five-year age groups in the same proportion as the corresponding five-year age groups were of the corresponding ten-year age group in the 1871 census. The ten-year age group 40–49 in 1867 was divided in the same proportion as the 1880 census.

The 1933 census presented a different problem. Age distributions by administrative areas were available in the national statistical publications only for total women and single women. For some states, the number of widowed and divorced women was available from state statistical publications. For the majority of areas, however, the number of widowed and divorced women had to be estimated. The number of widowed and divorced women by age was available for Germany as a whole. The national ratios of widowed and divorced women to single women by age group served as correction factors for administrative areas for which more detailed data on marital status were not available. It is unlikely that this procedure introduced much error into the calculations since the proportions of widowed and divorced women is not high at any age under 50. The range of error could be estimated from the examples of Berlin and Baden, for which exact data on marital status were available for 1933. In Berlin the ratios of widowed and divorced women to single women are higher for all age categories than are the corresponding ratios for Germany. In Baden, the same ratios are lower than for Germany. Thus use of the national ratios to estimate widowed and divorced women in Berlin would lead to an underestimate of marital fertility and an overestimate of illegitimate fertility and proportions married. The reverse is true for Baden. Overall fertility, of course, is not affected by this procedure. The amount of error introduced, however, is small as seen in the results presented in Appendix Table 2.2 which compares the true indices

APPENDIX TABLE 2.2

DEMOGRAPHIC INDICES, ACTUAL VS. ESTIMATED, BERLIN AND BADEN: 1933

Demographic index	Berlin		Baden	
	Actual	Estimated	Actual	Estimated
I_f	.090	.090	.162	.162
I_g	.152	.147	.302	.306
I_h	.024	.025	.029	.029
I_m	.512	.528	.486	.479
I_{m*}	.477	.492	.485	.476

NOTE: Estimations made by author.

calculated on the basis of complete marital status data and the indices which result from using the procedure described above to estimate the number of widowed and divorced women (indices refer to live births 1931–1935).

APPENDIX 3 Rural-Urban Marital Fertility for Selected German States and Administrative Areas

General Notes to the Tables

The indices for the total state or administrative area do not always correspond exactly with those presented in Appendix 2. In some cases, the number of births used for the computation of the indices were based on a lesser number of years. This was necessary because of the problems involved in matching the rural-urban classification in the census with the same classification in the vital statistics. In other cases, the census distribution for the rural-urban categories were divided into broader age groups than by five-year divisions. The value of the index for the state was then calculated on the same basis to aid comparability.

In Appendix Table 3.1 separate figures are given for *Regierungsbezirke* Königsberg, Gumbinnen, and Allenstein which together form the administrative area Ostpreussen and for *Regierungsbezirke* Stettin and Stralsund which together form the administrative area Stettin-Stralsund. In addition, Kassel excludes Waldeck. See footnote 3 to Chapter 1 and footnote 4 to Chapter 3.

APPENDIX 3

APPENDIX TABLE 3.1
MARITAL FERTILITY (I_g), URBAN/RURAL, BY ADMINISTRATIVE AREA, PRUSSIA: 1880 to 1911

	1880 -81	1885 -86	1890 -91	1895 -96	1900 -01	1905 -06	1910 -11
1K KOENIGSBERG	.778	.802	.799	.805	.763	.693	.649
1K TOTAL RURAL	.807		.845	.861	.828	.777	.742
1K TOTAL URBAN	.702		.690	.679	.638	.585	.539
1K CITIES 20000+	.660	.647	.632	.606	.574	.557	
1K OTHER URBAN	.735		.739	.742	.701	.632	
1G GUMBINNEN	.773	.806	.812	.812	.781	.726	.678
1G TOTAL RURAL	.783		.829	.837	.812	.762	.714
1G TOTAL URBAN	.698		.705	.670	.635	.578	.534
1G CITIES 20000+	.729	.713	.730	.637	.646	.584	
1G OTHER URBAN	.691		.699	.679	.632	.575	
1A ALLENSTEIN						.804	.783
1A TOTAL RURAL						.848	.837
1A TOTAL URBAN						.654	.630
01 OSTPREUSSEN	.776	.804	.804	.808	.770	.732	.691
01 TOTAL RURAL	.796		.838	.850	.821	.792	.759
01 TOTAL URBAN	.701		.693	.676	.638	.597	.556
01 CITIES 20000+	.668	.649	.644	.610	.585	.561	
01 OTHER URBAN	.722		.726	.721	.678	.627	
02 DANZIG	.792	.829	.820	.833	.818	.779	.724
02 TOTAL RURAL	.823		.876	.910	.901	.884	.857
02 TOTAL URBAN	.724		.716	.695	.681	.638	.557
02 CITIES 20000+	.710	.712	.706	.671	.663	.609	
02 OTHER URBAN	.770		.750	.773	.743	.724	
03 MARIENWERDER	.820	.872	.854	.873	.869	.839	.799
03 TOTAL RURAL	.836		.887	.910	.912	.891	.865
03 TOTAL URBAN	.758		.737	.747	.736	.693	.644
03 CITIES 20000+	.673	.677	.672	.649	.624	.579	
03 OTHER URBAN	.767		.746	.760	.751	.708	
04 BERLIN	.590	.536	.504	.439	.399	.361	.292
05 POTSDAM	.662	.653	.637	.579	.500	.439	.345
05 TOTAL RURAL	.659		.649	.592	.531	.469	.381
05 TOTAL URBAN	.666		.617	.558	.468	.408	.315
05 CITIES 20000+	.652	.609	.600	.529	.427	.367	
05 OTHER URBAN	.673		.629	.585	.493	.430	
06 FRANKFURT/O	.678	.679	.668	.642	.589	.529	.466
06 TOTAL RURAL	.683		.686	.675	.631	.581	.524
06 TOTAL URBAN	.668		.640	.593	.532	.463	.392
06 CITIES 20000+	.652	.638	.628	.574	.499	.428	
06 OTHER URBAN	.677		.646	.604	.550	.483	
7A STETTIN	.725	.728	.706	.684	.644	.567	.481
7A TOTAL RURAL	.761		.745	.727	.696	.620	.556
7A TOTAL URBAN	.669		.653	.630	.595	.519	.414
7A CITIES 20000+	.622	.627	.622	.587	.581	.487	
7A OTHER URBAN	.701		.681	.675	.619	.572	
7B STRALSUND	.645	.662	.649	.654	.618	.565	.513
7B TOTAL RURAL	.675		.674	.676	.653	.596	.555
7B TOTAL URBAN	.603		.614	.624	.574	.525	.459
7B CITIES 20000+	.575	.559	.579	.630	.548	.464	
7B OTHER URBAN	.616		.630	.635	.586	.553	
07 STETTIN-STRAL.	.707	.714	.694	.677	.639	.566	.487
07 TOTAL RURAL	.743		.730	.718	.687	.614	.556
07 TOTAL URBAN	.654		.645	.628	.591	.520	.422
07 CITIES 20000+	.613	.615	.616	.589	.577	.485	
07 OTHER URBAN	.680		.667	.662	.610	.567	
08 KOESLIN	.772	.804	.788	.795	.758	.726	.662
08 TOTAL RURAL	.785		.814	.825	.789	.768	.718
08 TOTAL URBAN	.731		.719	.719	.690	.639	.559
08 CITIES 20000+	.698	.696	.678	.694	.664	.659	
08 OTHER URBAN	.737		.727	.723	.696	.635	

APPENDIX TABLE 3.1 (cont).

09 POSEN	.767	.810	.803	.837	.833	.805	.779
09 TOTAL RURAL	.782		.830	.874	.884	.859	.859
09 TOTAL URBAN	.723		.726	.732	.720	.699	.634
09 CITIES 20000+	.677	.664	.660	.657	.702	.694	
09 OTHER URBAN	.735		.743	.749	.728	.702	
10 BROMBERG	.803	.865	.842	.870	.856	.831	.789
10 TOTAL RURAL	.828		.882	.916	.910	.891	.862
10 TOTAL URBAN	.733		.743	.766	.748	.712	.653
10 CITIES 20000+	.633	.670	.646	.650	.605	.548	
10 OTHER URBAN	.756		.768	.796	.787	.755	
11 BRESSLAU	.710	.727	.718	.708	.676	.623	.560
11 TOTAL RURAL	.740		.767	.774	.748	.699	.654
11 TOTAL URBAN	.653		.640	.610	.580	.527	.453
11 CITIES 20000+	.626	.618	.617	.583	.555	.504	
11 OTHER URBAN	.695		.677	.660	.627	.573	
12 LIEGNITZ	.652	.660	.642	.622	.597	.547	.505
12 TOTAL RURAL	.661		.669	.660	.642	.591	.557
12 TOTAL URBAN	.631		.584	.549	.517	.468	.416
12 CITIES 20000+	.623	.586	.550	.524	.501	.429	
12 OTHER URBAN	.635		.602	.563	.526	.491	
13 OPPELN	.787	.853	.851	.881	.870	.843	.818
13 TOTAL RURAL	.800		.877	.910	.907	.889	.874
13 TOTAL URBAN	.729		.751	.770	.757	.707	.657
13 CITIES 20000+	.739	.799	.788	.827	.823	.755	
13 OTHER URBAN	.726		.736	.745	.727	.685	
14 MAGDEBURG	.645	.655	.626	.587	.542	.483	.418
14 TOTAL RURAL	.642		.622	.596	.560	.511	.460
14 TOTAL URBAN	.648		.631	.577	.525	.455	.385
14 CITIES 20000+	.623	.650	.608	.545	.473	.404	
14 OTHER URBAN	.664		.652	.607	.572	.502	
15 MERSEBURG	.735	.743	.712	.677	.648	.577	.500
15 TOTAL RURAL	.750		.733	.712	.690	.622	.552
15 TOTAL URBAN	.710		.683	.630	.596	.521	.437
15 CITIES 20000+	.646	.643	.638	.570	.552	.472	
15 OTHER URBAN	.726		.697	.650	.616	.543	
16 ERFURT	.698	.704	.678	.648	.624	.575	.496
16 TOTAL RURAL	.718		.713	.692	.684	.645	.568
16 TOTAL URBAN	.671		.638	.598	.562	.505	.426
16 CITIES 20000+	.647	.640	.617	.576	.539	.480	
16 OTHER URBAN	.712		.678	.643	.608	.559	
17 SCHLESWIG	.664	.665	.658	.648	.597	.545	.483
17 TOTAL RURAL	.674		.676	.602	.641	.598	.559
17 TOTAL URBAN	.645		.634	.603	.544	.487	.409
17 CITIES 20000+	.642	.616	.626	.572	.506	.457	
17 OTHER URBAN	.647		.644	.644	.592	.530	
18 HANNOVER	.642	.645	.621	.615	.562	.486	.412
18 TOTAL RURAL	(.703)*		.650	.653	.617	.575	.524
18 TOTAL URBAN	(.570)*		.591	.585	.523	.419	.348
18 CITIES 20000+	.608	.588	.577	.575	.508	.397	
18 OTHER URBAN	(.458)*		.638	.627	.588	.516	
19 HILDESHEIM	.646	.662	.638	.627	.598	.545	.478
19 TOTAL RURAL	.654		.651	.645	.621	.572	.508
19 TOTAL URBAN	.629		.615	.596	.561	.503	.434
19 CITIES 20000+	.635	.656	.631	.598	.548	.471	
19 OTHER URBAN	.627		.612	.596	.565	.511	
20 LUNEBURG	.548	.560	.557	.557	.540	.504	.462
20 TOTAL RURAL	.539		.542	.545	.533	.510	.474
20 TOTAL URBAN	.583		.602	.590	.554	.493	.436
21 STADE	.668	.678	.668	.670	.645	.613	.541
21 TOTAL RURAL	.668		.678	.682	.663	.635	.578
21 TOTAL URBAN	.667		.634	.627	.593	.555	.446
22 OSNABRUCK	.724	.744	.730	.752	.745	.719	.689
22 TOTAL RURAL	.735		.749	.776	.774	.762	.745
22 TOTAL URBAN	.693		.684	.692	.679	.629	.578
22 CITIES 20000+	.673	.690	.657	.648	.638	.579	
22 OTHER URBAN	.714		.714	.742	.731	.702	
23 AURICH	.732	.761	.761	.764	.748	.727	.681
23 TOTAL RURAL	(.776)*		.782	.799	.796	.784	.761
23 TOTAL URBAN	(.604)*		.704	.671	.632	.595	.506

APPENDIX TABLE 3.1 (cont.)

24 MUENSTER	.835	.870	.866	.901	.913	.883	.813
24 TOTAL RURAL	.847		.883	.924	.940	.922	.852
24 TOTAL URBAN	.804		.829	.852	.858	.803	.725
24 CITIES 20000+	.770	.782	.774	.747	.720	.683	
24 OTHER URBAN	.818		.850	.892	.903	.846	
25 MINDEN	.784	.794	.769	.775	.745	.682	.613
25 TOTAL RURAL	.791		.792	.814	.792	.740	.681
25 TOTAL URBAN	.763		.717	.692	.654	.575	.500
25 CITIES 20000+	.745	.731	.687	.627	.593	.465	
25 OTHER URBAN	.770		.728	.721	.688	.638	
26 ARNSBERG	.810	.830	.823	.819	.808	.744	.627
26 TOTAL RURAL	.826		.848	.851	.845	.777	.672
26 TOTAL URBAN	.795		.786	.769	.755	.712	.587
26 CITIES 20000+	.786	.790	.769	.753	.738	.681	
26 OTHER URBAN	.802		.798	.781	.768	.736	
27 KASSEL	.692	.668	.675	.658	.639	.595	.517
27 TOTAL RURAL	.712		.703	.688	.673	.629	.561
27 TOTAL URBAN	.644		.611	.594	.573	.532	.449
27 CITIES 20000+	.560	.545	.543	.550	.532	.480	
27 OTHER URBAN	.686		.655	.625	.608	.578	
28 WIESBADEN	.638	.629	.608	.595	.580	.517	.423
28 TOTAL RURAL	.671		.656	.650	.649	.586	.515
28 TOTAL URBAN	.591		.552	.534	.519	.463	.361
28 CITIES 20000+	.546	.504	.508	.497	.480	.432	
28 OTHER URBAN	.672		.628	.621	.620	.546	
29 KOBLENZ	.778	.761	.757	.752	.743	.691	.613
29 TOTAL RURAL	.787		.773	.772	.774	.734	.665
29 TOTAL URBAN	.743		.699	.685	.647	.587	.490
29 CITIES 20000+	.666	.642	.636	.647	.617	.543	
29 OTHER URBAN	.764		.716	.698	.658	.603	
30 DUESSELDORF	.843	.839	.815	.790	.766	.685	.557
30 TOTAL RURAL	.894		.904	.904	.888	.819	.718
30 TOTAL URBAN	.813		.768	.733	.695	.623	.503
30 CITIES 20000+	.801	.786	.755	.712	.670	.607	
30 OTHER URBAN	.836		.793	.774	.741	.661	
31 KOELN	.847	.831	.817	.777	.749	.669	.538
31 TOTAL RURAL	.886		.908	.904	.883	.815	.704
31 TOTAL URBAN	.792		.748	.687	.660	.588	.453
31 CITIES 20000+	.749	.709	.733	.672	.649	.578	
31 OTHER URBAN	.895		.827	.766	.724	.643	
32 TRIER	.832	.838	.841	.848	.854	.798	.706
32 TOTAL RURAL	.842		.857	.870	.884	.837	.752
32 TOTAL URBAN	.771		.758	.738	.732	.650	.550
32 CITIES 20000+	.732	.754	.764	.741	.708	.664	
32 OTHER URBAN	.781		.756	.736	.738	.647	
33 AACHEN	.913	.926	.926	.915	.904	.830	.725
33 TOTAL RURAL	.934		.974	.987	.995	.934	.861
33 TOTAL URBAN	.880		.855	.816	.785	.688	.554
33 CITIES 20000+	.860	.830	.833	.788	.747	.648	
33 OTHER URBAN	.900		.877	.845	.836	.743	
34 SIGMARINGEN	.803	.760	.739	.796	.806	.776	.662
34 TOTAL RURAL	.821		.762	.831	.836	.805	.696
34 TOTAL URBAN	.729		.561	.534	.597	.597	.473
PRUSSIA	.733	.743	.727	.715	.685	.631	.554
TOTAL RURAL	.758		.774	.779	.764	.716	.659
TOTAL URBAN	.689		.656	.625	.589	.536	.449
CITIES 20000+	.660	.637	.619	.576	.541	.491	
OTHER URBAN	.719		.702	.686	.651	.596	

* OF QUESTIONABLE RELIABILITY; SEE TEXT

APPENDIX TABLE 3.2

DEMOGRAPHIC INDICES, URBAN/RURAL, BAVARIA: 1867 TO 1939

Census year	Birth registration period	Overall fertility (I_f)				Marital fertility (I_g)			
		Munich	Other cities	Rural	State	Munich	Other cities	Rural	State
1867	1866-1868	.352	.329	.405	.391	.658	.693	.862	.820
1871	1869-1872[a]	.341	.344	.433	.418	.650	.704	.874	.838
1875	1873-1877	.361	.363	.467	.447	.627	.678	.860	.823
1880	1878-1882	.338	.342	.451	.428	.589	.647	.823	.786
1885	1883-1887	.301	--	--	.410	.540	--	--	.771
1890	1888-1892	.290	.318	.421	.391	.506	.614	.806	.750
1895	1893-1897	.294	--	--	--	.513	--	--	--
1900	1898-1902	.285	--	--	.386	.488	--	--	.725
1910	1908-1912	.199	.262	.387	.334	.326	.447	.713	.602
1925	1924-1926	.115	.165	.245	.210	.188	.284	.491	.401
1933	1931-1935	.108	--	--	.174	.190	--	--	.321
1939	1938-1939	.134	--	--	.205	.227	--	--	.359

Census year	Birth registration period	Illegitimate fertility (I_h)				Proportion married (I_m)			
		Munich	Other cities	Rural	State	Munich	Other cities	Rural	State
1867	1866-1868	.207	.139	.128	.129	.321	.344	.375	.380
1871	1869-1872[a]	.165	.117	.115	.112	.362	.388	.419	.421
1875	1873-1877	.160	.113	.115	.110	.430	.443	.468	.473
1880	1878-1882	.160	.098	.103	.106	.415	.445	.483	.473
1885	1883-1887	.147	--	--	.104	.390	--	--	.459
1890	1888-1892	.148	.089	.097	.100	.395	.436	.458	.449
1895	1893-1897	.144	--	--	--	.406	--	--	--
1900	1898-1902	.131	--	--	.094	.432	--	--	.462
1910	1908-1912	.104	.080	.075	.080	.429	.496	.489	.487
1925	1924-1926	.061	.055	.053	.055	.429	.480	.436	.447
1933	1931-1935	.048	--	--	.045	.421	--	--	.466
1939	1938-1939	.049	--	--	.049	.475	--	--	.539

NOTE: Under Other cities and Rural, data for 1867, 1871, and 1875 excludes Pfalz.

[a]Excluding 1871

APPENDIX TABLE 3.3

MARITAL FERTILITY (I_g), URBAN/RURAL, BY ADMINISTRATIVE AREA, BAVARIA: 1867 TO 1925

Census	Birth registration period	35 Oberbayern				36 Niederbayern			37 Pfalz			38 Oberpfalz		
		Munich	Other urban	Rural	Total	Urban	Rural	Total	Urban	Rural	Total	Urban	Rural	Total
1867	1866-1868	.658	.831	.899	.848	.735	.935	.924	--	--	.737	.742	.898	.886
1871	1869-1872ᵃ	.650	.819	.907	.847	.756	.943	.932	--	--	.803	.769	.918	.906
1875	1873-1877	.627	.803	.903	.828	.713	.938	.924	--	--	.779	.729	.913	.897
1880	1878-1882	.589	.713	.870	.786	.687	.932	.912	.714	.742	.736	.682	.899	.880
1885	1883-1887	.540	--	--	.762	--	--	.917	--	--	.720	--	--	.886
1890	1888-1892	.506	.673	.874	.733	.665	.928	.906	.676	.718	.707	.676	.900	.876
1900	1898-1902	.488	--	--	.680	--	--	.912	--	--	.690	--	--	.896
1910	1908-1912	.326	--	--	.534	--	--	.835	--	--	.568	--	--	.803
1925	1924-1926	.188	.302	.454	.325	.337	.612	.578	.312	.408	.374	.345	.651	.572

Census	Birth registration period	39 Oberfranken			40 Mittelfranken			41 Unterfranken			42 Schwaben		
		Urban	Rural	Total	Urban	Rural	Total	Urban	Rural	Total	Urban	Rural	Total
1867	1866-1868	.683	.717	.714	.660	.806	.764	.634	.796	.782	.748	.991	.951
1871	1869-1872ᵃ	.670	.726	.720	.667	.816	.771	.662	.817	.801	.749	1.001	.953
1875	1873-1877	.671	.732	.725	.653	.805	.757	.693	.800	.781	.703	.983	.926
1880	1878-1882	.613	.699	.688	.605	.768	.716	.576	.747	.725	.651	.939	.878
1885	1883-1887	--	--	.679	--	--	.694	--	--	.710	--	--	.845
1890	1888-1892	.599	.681	.666	.571	.722	.663	.564	.729	.704	.589	.885	.814
1900	1898-1902	--	--	.664	--	--	.624	--	--	.711	--	--	.782
1910	1908-1912	--	--	.565	--	--	.483	--	--	.617	--	--	.669
1925	1924-1926	.319	.434	.401	.223	.423	.297	.340	.506	.464	.275	.509	.419

ᵃExcluding 1871.

APPENDIX TABLE 3.4

MARITAL FERTILITY (I_g), URBAN/RURAL, KINGDOM OF SAXONY: 1864 TO 1895

Census year	Birth registration period	Large cities	Other cities	All cities	Rural	State
1864	1863-1865	.644	.745	.714	.714	.714
1867	1866-1868	.630	.736	.703	.715	.710
1871	1869-1870	--	--	.684	.715	.703
1875	1873-1877	--	--	--	--	.736
1880	1878-1882	.577	.713	.662	.733	.703
1885	1883-1887	--	--	--	--	.694
1890	1888-1892	--	--	--	--	.667
1895	1893-1897	--	--	.584	.692	.640

NOTE: Dresden, Leipzig, and Chemnitz are classified as Large cities.

APPENDIX TABLE 3.5

MARITAL FERTILITY (I_g), URBAN/RURAL, BRAUNSCHWEIG: 1871 TO 1910

Census year	Birth registration period	City of Braunschweig	Other cities	Rural	State
1871	1869-1873	.658	.646	.610	.623
1875	1874-1877	--	--	--	.676
1880	1878-1882	.603	.630	.604	.608
1890	1886-1895	.563	.617	.606	.596
1900	1896-1905	.478	.549	.568	.539
1905	1905	.397	.510	.519	.482
1910	1906-1915	.326	--	--	.406

APPENDIX TABLE 3.6

MARITAL FERTILITY (I_g), URBAN/RURAL, LÜBECK: 1862 TO 1905

Census year	Birth registration period	City proper	Rural surrounding	State
1862	1860-1865	.624	.575	.610
1867	1866-1869	.673	.603	.657
1871	1869-1873	.654	.612	.643
1875	1874-1877	.680	.632	.669
1880	1878-1882	--	--	.635
1900	1898-1902	--	--	.534
1905	1903-1907	.476	.596	.488

APPENDIX 3

APPENDIX TABLE 3.7

MARITAL FERTILITY (I_g), URBAN/RURAL, BREMEN: 1861 TO 1925

Census year	Birth registration period	City proper	Rural surrounding	State
1861	1860–1862	.705	.746	.719
1864	1863–1865	.724	.731	.726
1867	1866–1868	.748	.719	.738
1871	1869–1873	.738	.741	.739
1880	1878–1882	.659	.709	.673
1885	1883–1887	--	--	.619
1890	1889–1891	.584	.669	.611
1895	1893–1897	--	--	.592
1900	1899–1901	.532	.605	.553
1905	1903–1907	.502	.528	.506
1910	1908–1912	.416	.444	.421
1925	1924–1926	.247	.272	.250

APPENDIX TABLE 3.8

MARITAL FERTILITY (I_g), URBAN/RURAL, HAMBURG: 1867 TO 1933

Census year	Birth registration period	City and suburbs	Rural surrounding	State
1867	1866–1868	--	--	.666
1871	1869–1873	.662	.641	.656
1875	1874–1877	--	--	.672
1880	1878–1882	.627	.659	.630
1885	1883–1887	.592	.614	.594
1890	1888–1892	.578	.633	.582
1895	1894–1896	.555	.624	.560
1900	1898–1902	.469	.536	.474
1905	1903–1907	--	--	.406
1910	1908–1912	.340	.424	.346
1925	1923–1927	.201	.262	.205
1933	1931–1935	.196	.197	.196

APPENDIX TABLE 3.9

MARITAL FERTILITY (I_g), URBAN/RURAL, NECKARKREIS: 1871 TO 1925

Census year	Birth registration period	Stuttgart	Remaining area	Total Neckarkreis
1871	1871-1873	.726	.897	.868
1875	1874-1877	--	--	.849
1880	1878-1882	--	--	.781
1885	1883-1887	--	--	.744
1890	1888-1892	.544	.756	.709
1895	1893-1897	.544	--	--
1900	1898-1902	.520	.706	.660
1905	1903-1907	.449	--	--
1910	1908-1912	--	--	.505
1925	1923-1927	.273	.319	.302

APPENDIX 4 (Tables 4.1, 4.2, & 4.3)

APPENDIX TABLE 4.1

INFANT MORTALITY RATE, BY ADMINISTRATIVE AREA: 1862 TO 1934

Area	1862-1866	1875-1880	1881-1885	1886-1890	1891-1895	1896-1900	1901-1905	1906-1910	1911-1914	1924-1926	1932-1934
01 Ostpreussen	209	218	220	221	221	221	209	187	195	120	084
02 Danzig	245	235	230	243	239	248	231	207	206	132[a]	084[a]
03 Marienwerder	226	226	230	227	222	229	217	202	200	132[a]	084[a]
04 Berlin	279	304	278	263	242	218	202	165	152	090	064
05 Potsdam	211	254	256	267	267	245	226	180	172	118	072
06 Frankfurt/O.	195	220	227	236	236	233	223	195	189	117	077
07 Stettin-Str.	192	215	222	230	246	258	243	213	201	127	079
08 Köslin	164	166	165	165	167	177	173	166	165	106	077
09 Posen	213	216	225	214	204	203	192	174	170	124[b]	082[b]
10 Bromberg	224	215	228	225	217	229	215	203	197	124[b]	082[b]
11 Breslau	275	274	282	281	279	268	262	231	212	138	089
12 Liegnitz	278	289	289	289	282	265	250	215	198	125	083
13 Oppeln	224	212	223	213	216	206	198	193	189	147	108
14 Magdeburg	204	219	226	220	232	230	221	196	193	123	084
15 Merseburg	219	214	221	220	223	225	214	189	184	112	073
16 Erfurt	190	186	190	185	176	174	173	151	146	096	067
17 Schleswig	148[c]	150	146	159	163	161	158	142	137	092	069
18 Hannover	--	165	161	171	170	169	160	139	127	081	057
19 Hidlesheim	--	161	159	163	160	158	146	129	122	080	061
20 Lüneburg	--	150	144	153	158	156	152	136	130	081	060
21 Stade	--	137	136	136	139	138	134	123	122	080	062
22 Osnabrück	--	129	132	129	123	120	116	113	105	078	065
23 Aurich	--	114	109	106	103	101	100	098	094	072	056
24 Münster	153	150	144	155	161	167	161	152	147	097	077
25 Minden	151	151	145	146	137	133	128	119	113	079	060
26 Arnsberg	144	151	144	151	146	155	148	137	134	094	073
27 Kassel	--	164	157	149	140	130	124	102	099	073	051
28 Wiesbaden	--	162	154	151	143	141	137	113	100	072	048
29 Koblenz	173	179	175	170	164	157	149	123	118	083	063
30 Düsseldorf	146	166	169	175	172	176	165	144	139	092	069
31 Köln	172	202	211	225	219	217	201	174	162	094	064
32 Trier	154	157	152	156	157	156	149	139	138	106	075
33 Aachen	189	193	196	211	214	207	194	174	167	098	075
34 Sigmaringen	317	317	282	261	242	224	225	190	166	107	074
35 Oberbayern	420[d]	383	353	343	329	306	272	236	202	132	091
36 Niederbayern	361[d]	348	342	333	336	317	308	290	265	205	137
37 Pfalz	196[d]	179	176	177	176	171	166	153	144	093	070
38 Oberpfalz	356[d]	327	330	323	313	303	293	270	246	191	122
39 Oberfranken	223[d]	192	189	190	175	174	169	163	153	119	077
40 Mittelfranken	335[d]	286	281	278	267	259	245	211	179	109	074
41 Unterfranken	253[d]	207	199	190	193	188	179	161	151	111	076
42 Schwaben	412[d]	383	354	329	314	282	258	230	199	124	084
43 Dresden	250	267[e]	259	256	243	227	205	168	153	088	059
44 Leipzig	256	266[e]	260	259	261	249	237	185	182	099	068
45 Zwickau	279	303[e]	314	316	323	309	267	226	197	087	057
46 Neckarkreis	329[f]	278	251	239	237	223	207	171	177	071	049

[a]Rates are for 3A Westpreussen.
[b]Rates are for 9A Grenzmark Posen-Westpreussen.
[c]1864-1870.
[d]1862-1869.
[e]1875-1877.
[f]1862-1868.
[g]1876-1880.
[h]1863-1865.
[i]1863-1870.
[j]1867-1870.

[k]For Mecklenburg-Schwerin only.
[l]1868-1877.
[m]1876-1877.
[n]1904-1905.
[o]For Stadt Lübeck only.
[p]1867.
[q]1888-1892.
[r]1893-1897.
[s]1911-1913.

APPENDIX TABLE 4.1 (cont.)

47 Schwarzwaldkreis	342^f	290	269	248	251	230	221	183	152	091	066
48 Jagstkreis	347^f	289	265	241	240	220	202	175	150	093	062
49 Donaukreis	428^f	376	339	302	291	260	237	201	171	105	071
50 Konstanz	322^c	266^g	238	211	199	188	165	145	121	089	064
51 Freiburg	228^c	211^g	197	184	183	182	179	163	129	090	060
52 Karlsruhe	293^c	245^g	239	229	229	233	218	193	166	101	064
53 Mannheim	274^c	240^g	237	237	237	227	216	184	155	096	063
54 Starkenburg	223^h	198^g	195	194	187	177	163	142	116	074	052
55 Oberhessen	164^i	140^g	131	125	115	107	106	080	072	060	045
56 Rheinhessen	236^h	212^g	203	206_k	190_k	191_k	175	142	120	081	056
57 Mecklenburg	154^j	$158^{g,k}$	156	162^k	166^k	163^k	177	170	179	102	082
58 Thüringen	--	218^l	--	--	--	--	194	164	157	137	067
59 H. Oldenburg	115	126	115	119	126	133	124	119	112	078	065
60 F. Lübeck	165	135^m	--	--	--	--	190^n	170	182	107	076
61 Birkenfeld	130	109^m	--	--	--	--	094^n	094	090	071	056
62 Braunschweig	--	190^e	--	190	187	186	176	156	155	095	073
63 Anhalt	--	187^e	--	--	--	--	194	163	173	115	079
64 Schaumburg-Lippe	--	117^e	--	--	--	--	107	105	094	081	057
65 Lippe	--	162^e	--	--	--	--	120	109	107	068	051
66 Lübeck	195	178^e	--	183°	165°	171°	165	156	143	097	069
67 Bremen	179	171	172	178	164	166	161	139	123	079	052
68 Hamburg	162^p	219	229	250	220	182	171	148	130	081	060
69 Unterelsass	--	232	227	219	216^q	200^r	192^n	162	146^s	--	--
70 Oberelsass	--	226	234	226	222^q	214^r	193^n	162	147^s	--	--
71 Lothringen	--	182	177	182	184^q	178^r	193^n	167	169^s	--	--
Germany		228	226	224	221	213	199	174	164	102	075

APPENDIX 4

INFANT MORTALITY RATE, URBAN/RURAL,
BY ADMINISTRATIVE AREA, PRUSSIA: 1875 TO 1932

Area	1875-1877	1878-1882	1888-1892	1893-1897	1898-1902	1904-1906	1908-1912	1924-1926	1930-1932
				URBAN					
01 Ostpreussen	252	259	246	249	222	202	172	110	91
02 Danzig	263	281	268	273	254	227	197	121	99
03 Marienwerder	244	237	237	238	236	222	201	121	99
04 Berlin	308	290	251	229	214	194	159	90	70
05 Potsdam	276	270	273	262	231	224	171	114	89
06 Frankfurt/O.	255	242	255	247	239	221	191	111	88
07 Stettin-Str.	255	253	267	276	275	244	211	118	90
08 Köslin	212	213	206	217	219	203	181	114	94
09 Posen	235	243	231	230	217	205	176	124	95
10 Bromberg	236	234	236	234	236	223	203	124	95
11 Breslau	296	305	281	267	254	239	196	122	95
12 Liegnitz	333	321	296	277	254	244	203	113	88
13 Oppeln	224	227	225	212	200	203	181	132	118
14 Magdeburg	247	238	241	245	242	233	207	122	94
15 Merseburg	224	225	225	225	226	219	190	114	86
16 Erfurt	195	189	189	181	177	178	158	93	76
17 Schleswig	192	186	193	181	181	174	152	102	88
18 Hannover	182	179	191	189	185	171	135	83	69
19 Hildesheim	175	166	164	159	158	140	125	79	73
20 Lüneburg	187	176	192	195	183	173	148	83	65
21 Stade	155	158	158	149	158	152	137	90	78
22 Osnabrück	150	157	140	135	133	136	113	86	69
23 Aurich	152	143	137	123	126	120	105	86	66
24 Münster	185	185	186	187	187	177	151	103	91
25 Minden	171	151	149	143	140	134	114	81	66
26 Arnsberg	165	163	160	157	167	157	141	101	92
27 Kassel	177	169	150	142	138	128	105	75	59
28 Wiesbaden	169	174	165	153	153	147	116	76	54
29 Koblenz	197	194	181	164	160	144	130	81	75
30 Düsseldorf	175	173	178	174	175	163	139	94	80
31 Köln	220	217	242	226	227	208	173	97	80
32 Trier	162	156	167	159	170	164	148	101	70
33 Aachen	219	219	233	236	213	197	169	94	84
34 Sigmaringen	314	280	165	167	134	179	136	87	52
				RURAL					
01 Ostpreussen	202	211	213	215	213	197	192	123	97
02 Danzig	212	224	220	236	233	224	211	143	91
03 Marienwerder	227	219	217	224	224	208	202	143	91
04 Berlin	--	--	--	--	--	--	--	--	--
05 Potsdam	246	237	261	253	241	222	182	120	80
06 Frankfurt/O.	211	201	220	226	223	198	198	120	83
07 Stettin-Str.	197	192	212	232	235	231	212	134	90
08 Köslin	153	148	146	156	157	162	157	102	84
09 Posen	208	214	199	202	188	178	169	123	90
10 Bromberg	207	211	209	218	219	207	202	123	90
11 Breslau	253	269	276	278	272	268	235	149	108
12 Liegnitz	270	278	277	273	263	245	213	130	90
13 Oppeln	208	214	216	210	198	202	192	152	125
14 Magdeburg	203	198	205	212	220	214	188	123	96
15 Merseburg	211	207	213	217	221	214	192	111	78
16 Erfurt	185	179	175	164	168	169	146	99	79
17 Schleswig	126	127	138	144	146	142	134	83	70
18 Hannover	156	145	147	142	150	147	130	79	58
19 Hildesheim	158	152	160	154	152	144	128	80	61
20 Lüneburg	145	133	137	139	145	140	128	80	64
21 Stade	136	129	135	130	128	126	120	77	65
22 Osnabrück	125	119	121	115	106	114	107	74	68
23 Aurich	106	106	99	91	93	93	95	68	60
24 Munster	137	130	144	149	150	163	148	90	79
25 Minden	152	139	139	130	128	124	117	78	66
26 Arnsberg	144	134	139	138	151	140	128	86	65
27 Kassel	167	155	143	131	122	111	98	72	52
28 Wiesbaden	163	146	113	129	127	116	97	68	50
29 Koblenz	177	172	167	155	153	135	120	84	65
30 Düsseldorf	151	155	164	162	173	172	146	88	68
31 Köln	189	193	205	197	203	187	168	89	67
32 Trier	157	151	156	150	152	151	139	107	80
33 Aachen	179	173	193	193	200	188	176	101	81
34 Sigmaringen	334	296	259	243	219	227	185	110	87

NOTES: 02 Danzig/03 Marienwerder data under 1924-1932 are for 3A Westpreussen.
        09 Posen/10 Bromberg data under 1924-1932 are for 9A Gr. Posen-Westpreussen.

APPENDIX TABLE 4.3

INFANT MORTALITY RATE, URBAN/RURAL,
BY ADMINISTRATIVE AREA, BAVARIA: 1862 TO 1935

Area	1862-1870	1871-1875	1876-1877	1878-1882	1883-1887	1888-1892	1893-1897	1898-1902	1903-1907	1908-1912	1913-1915	1924-1926	1931-1935
35 Oberbayern													
Urban	407	408	372	362	336	317	295	271	228	183	156	106	74
Rural	421	415	387	373	361	344	327	311	282	242	224	143	105
36 Niederbayern													
Urban	390	372	349	348	348	310	301	298	286	256	254	163	110
Rural	354	260	343	347	339	337	324	320	306	277	275	205	143
37 Pfalz													
Urban	--	--	--	--	--	201[a]	188	192	189	171	149	91	78
Rural	--	--	--	--	--	171[a]	165	161	153	139	137	93	67
38 Oberpfalz													
Urban	357	343	337	313	324	312	309	322	300	259	215	180	113
Rural	353	342	338	325	329	320	302	294	290	264	250	191	129
39 Oberfranken													
Urban	224	219	213	200	199	181	172	181	161	147	127	094	063
Rural	221	202	204	182	190	184	170	173	169	162	165	125	084
40 Mittelfranken													
Urban	319	300	272	269	274	257	248	250	240	186	159	091	065
Rural	336	326	297	286	290	274	267	257	242	211	188	122	082
41 Unterfranken													
Urban	259	257	228	209	206	192	188	186	180	148	135	093	068
Rural	251	238	216	196	198	193	185	183	178	160	157	115	080
42 Schwaben													
Urban	426	449	413	369	340	314	290	264	241	215	197	104	072
Rural	408	406	381	372	351	3?1	298	276	252	219	196	126	090

[a]1890-1892.

Official Statistical Sources

(Note: The bulk of data which served as the basis for the computation of indices used in the present study were taken directly from the official national and state statistical publications. Because the number of specific volumes used was extremely large, only the title of each series is listed below.)

A. National Statistical Publications

Statistisches Reichsamt, *Erste Reihe der Statistik des Deutschen Reichs*
———, *Neue Folge der Statistik des Deutschen Reichs*
———, *Statistik des Deutschen Reiches*
———, *Statistisches Jahrbuch für das Deutsche Reich*
———, *Wirtschaft und Statistik*
———, *Monatshefte*
———, *Vierteljahrshefte zur Statistik des Deutschen Reichs*
Statistisches Bundesamt, *Statistik der Bundesrepublik Deutschlands, Bevölkerungsstand und Bevölkerungsentwicklung*
———, *Statistik der Bundesrepublik Deutschlands, Natürlche Bevölkerungsbewegung*

B. State Statistical Publications

Prussia, Statistical Bureau, *Preussische Statistik*
———, *Zeitschrift des Preussischen Statischen Landesamts*
———, *Jahrbuch für die amtliche Statistik des Preussischen Staates*
———, *Statistisches Jahrbuch für den Preussischen Staat*
Saarland, Statistical Bureau, *Statistik des Saarlands*
Bavaria, Statistical Bureau, *Beiträge zur Statistik Bayerns*
———, *Statistisches Jahrbuch für Bayern*
———, *Zeitschrift des Bayerischen Statistischen Landesamts*
———, *Bericht über das Bayerische Gesundheitswesen*
Saxony, Statistical Bureau, *Zeitschrift des Sächsischen Statistischen Landesamtes*

————, *Statistisches Jahrbuch Sachsen*

Württemberg, Statistical Bureau, *Württembergisches Jahrbücher für Statistik und Landeskunde*

Baden, Statistical Bureau, *Beiträge zur Statistik Badens*

————, *Statistisches Jahrbuch Baden*

Hesse, Statistical Bureau, *Beiträge zur Statistik Hessens*

————, *Statistisches Handbuch für das Grossherzogstum Hessen*

————, *Mitteilungen der Hessischen Centralstelle*

Mecklenburg Schwerin, Statistical Bureau, *Statistisches Handbuch für das Land Mecklenburg-Schwerin*

————, *Beiträge zur Statistik Mecklenburg-Schwerins*

Oldenburg, Statistical Bureau, *Statistisches Nachrichten über das Grossherzogtums Oldenburg*

Braunschweig, Statistical Bureau, *Beiträge zur Statistik Braunschweigs*

Lübeck, Statistical Bureau, *Statistik des Lübeckischen Staats*

Bremen, Statistical Bureau, *Statistik des Bremischen Staates*

————, *Jahrbuch für Bremische Statistik*

————, *Bremische Statistik*

————, *Statistisches Jahrbuch der freien Hansestadt Bremen*

Hamburg, Statistical Bureau, *Statistik des Hamburgischen Staats*

Other References

Agarwala, S. N., (1962). *Age at marriage in India.* Allahabad, Kitab Mehal.

Banks, J. A., (1954). *Prosperity and parenthood.* London.

Berger, L., (1912). "Untersuchungen über den Zusammenhang zwischen Beruf und Fruchtbarkeit unter besonderer Berücksichtigung des Königreichs Preussen." *Zeitschrift des Preussischen Statistischen Büreaus* 52, 225–250.

Bernays, Marie, (1916). *Untersuchung über den Zusammenhang von Frauenfabrikarbeit und Geburtenhäufigkeit in Deutschland.* Berlin.

Beshers, J. M., (1967). *Population processes in social systems.* New York.

Blalock, Hubert, (1960). *Social statistics.* New York.

Bornträger, Johannes, (1913). *Der Geburtenruckgang in Deutschland.* Würzburg.

Brentano, Lujo, (1909). "Die Maltussche Lehre und die Bevölkerungsbewegung der letzten Dezennien." *Abhandlungen der Historische Klasse der Kgl. Bayerische Akademie der Wissenschaften* 24, part 3. Munich.

Broesike, Max, (1904). "Rückblick auf die Entwicklung der preussische Bevölkerung von 1875 bis 1900." *Preussische Statistik* 188.

Bry, Gerhard, (1960). *Wages in Germany.* Princeton.

Buissink, John, (1971). "Regional differences in marital fertility in the Netherlands in the second half of the nineteenth century." *Population Studies* 25, 353–374.

Burgdörfer, Friederich, (1929). *Der Geburtenrückgang und seine Bekämpfung.* Berlin.

Carlsson, Gösta, (1967). "The decline of fertility: Innovation or adjustment process," *Population Studies* 20, 149–174.

Carlsson, Gösta, (1970). "Nineteenth century fertility oscillations." *Population Studies* 24, 413–422.

Coale, Ansley J., (1967). "Factors associated with the development of low fertility: an historic summary." United Nations, *World Population Conference, 1965* 2, 205–209. New York.

———— (1969). "The decline of fertility in Europe from the French Revolution to World War II." In *Fertility and family planning*, ed. S. J. Behrman, Leslie Corsa, Jr., and Ronald Freedman, pp. 3–24. Ann Arbor.

———— and Paul Demeny (1966). *Regional model life tables and stable populations*. Princeton.

Cowgill, Donald, (1963). "Transition theory as general population theory." *Social Forces* 41, 270–74.

Cutright, Phillips, (1971). "Illegitimacy: myths, causes and cures." *Family Planning Perspectives* 3, 25–48.

Davis, Kingsley, (1955). "The origin and growth of urbanization in the world." *American Journal of Sociology* 60, 429–437.

———— (1963). "The theory of change and response in modern demographic history." *Population Index* 29, 345–366.

———— (1965). "The urbanization of the human population." *Scientific American* 213, 40–53.

Desai, Ashok V., (1968). *Real wages in Germany 1871–1913*. Oxford.

Forberger, Johannes, (1914). *Geburtenrückgang und Konfession*. Berlin.

Freedman, Ronald, (1961–62). "The sociology of human fertility: a trend report and bibliography." *Current Sociology* 11, no. 2.

Friedlander, Dov, (1969). "Demographic responses and population change." *Demography* 6, 359–381.

Glass, D. V., (1940). *Population policies and movements in Europe*. Oxford.

Goldberg, David, (1960). "Another look at the Indianapolis fertility data." *Milbank Memorial Fund Quarterly* 38, 23–36.

Grassl, Josef, (1904). "Die Gebärfähigkeit der Bayerischen Frauen." *Allgemeines Statistisches Archiv* 6 (2nd Halbband), 282–293.

Hagood, Margaret and Daniel Price (1952). *Statistics for sociologists*. Rev. ed. New York.

Hajnal, John, (1953a). "Age at marriage and proportions marrying." *Population Studies* 7, 111–132.

———— (1953b), "The marriage boom." *Population Index* 19, 80–101.

Hamerow, Theodore S., (1969). *The social foundations of German unification 1858–1871*. Princeton.

OTHER REFERENCES

Hawthorn, Geoffrey, (1970). *The sociology of fertility*. London.

Heckh, G., (1939). "Bevölkerungsgeschichte und Bevölkerungsbewegung des Kirchspiels Böhringen auf der Uracher Alb vom 16. Jahrhundert bis zur Gegenwart," *Archiv für Rassen und Gesellschafts biologie* 33, 126–169.

Heer, David, (1966). "Economic development and fertility." *Demography* 3, 423–444.

—————— (1968). "Economic development and the fertility transition." *Daedalus* 97, 447–462.

Henry, Louis, (1961). "Some data on natural fertility." *Eugenics Quarterly* 8, 81–91.

Hindelang, Hans, (1909). "Die eheliche und uneheliche Fruchtbarkeit mit besonderer Berücksichtigung Bayerns." *Beiträge zur Statistik des Königreichs Bayern*, 71.

Houdaille, J., (1970a). "Quelques resultats sur la démographie de trois villages d'Allemagne de 1750 à 1879." *Population* 25, 649–654.

—————— (1970b). "La population de Remmesweiler en Sarre aux XVIIIe et XIXe siècle." *Population* 25, 1181–1191.

Kirk, Dudley, (1942). "The relations of employment levels to births in Germany." *Milbank Memorial Fund Quarterly* 20, 126–138.

Kirk, Dudley, (1971). "A new demographic transition?" In National Acadamy of Sciences, *Rapid population growth*, vol. II, Baltimore.

Klenck, W., (1959). *Das Dorfbuch von Mulsum*. Frankfurt a. M.

Knapp, G. F., (1874). "Die Kindersterblichkeit in Leipzig 1751–1870." *Mitteilungen des Leipzigen Statistischen Büreaus*, no. 8.

Knodel, John, (1967). "Law, marriage and illegitimacy in nineteenth century Germany." *Population Studies* 20, 279–294.

—————— (1968). "Infant mortality and fertility in three Bavarian villages: an analysis of family histories from the 19th century." *Population Studies* 22, 297–318.

—————— (1970). "Two and a half centuries of demographic history in a Bavarian village." *Population Studies* 24, 353–376.

—————— (1972). "Historische Demographie und Genealogie." *Genealogie*, 20.

—————— and T. Espenshade (1972). "Genealogical studies as demographic data." In *Population Analysis and Studies*, ed. I. Husain. Bombay and New Delhi.

———— and E. van de Walle (1967). "Breast feeding, fertility, and infant mortality: an analysis of some early German data." *Population Studies* 21, 109–131.

Köllmann, Wolfgang, (1959). "Industrialisierung, Binnenwanderung und 'Sociale Frage': Zur Entstehungsgeschichte der deutschen Industriegrossstadt in 19. Jahrhundert." *Vierteljahrschrift für Sozial- und Wirtschaftgeschichte* 46, 45–70.

———— (1964). "The population of Germany in the age of industrialism." *Population movements in modern European history*, ed. Herbert Moller. New York.

Kosic, Mirko, (1917). "Die soziologischen Grundlagen der Geburtenbeschränkung." *Allgemeines Statistisches Archiv* 10, 427–483.

Kumar, Joginder, (1969). "Demographic analysis of data on illegitimate births." *Social Biology* 16, 92–103.

Leasure, William, (1963). "Factors involved in the decline of fertility in Spain 1900–1950." *Population Studies* 17, 271–285.

Livi Bacci, Massimo, (1965). "Il declino della fecondità della popolazione italiana nell'ultimo secolo." *Statistica*, 25.

———— (1971). *A century of Portugese fertility*. Princeton.

Manschke, R., (1916). "Beruf und Kinderzahl." *Schmollers Jahrbuch* 40, 1867–1937.

May, R. E., (1916). "Zur Frage des Geburtenrückganges." *Schmollers Jahrbuch* 40, 1645–1684.

Mombert, Paul, (1907). *Studien zur Bevölkerungsbewegung in Deutschland*. Karlsruhe.

Müller, Johannes, (1922). "Der Strcit um die Ursache des Geburtenrückganges." *Jahrbücher für Nationalökonomie und Statistik* 119, 396–424.

———— (1924). *Der Geburtenrückgang*. Jena.

Müller, Ilse, (1939). Bevölkerungsgeschichtliche Untersuchungen in drei Gemeiden des Würztembergischen Schwarzwaldes." *Bevölkerungswissenschaft und Bevölkerungspolitik* 9, 185–206, 247–264.

Neuhaus, George, (1907). "Konfession und natürliche Bevölkerungsbewegung." *Hochland* 4.

Notestein, Frank, (1945). "Population — the long view." In *Food for the world*, ed. T. W. Schultz. Chicago.

Oldenburg, Karl, (1911). "Über den Rückgang der Geburten und

Sterbeziffer." *Archiv für Sozialwissenchaft und Sozialpolitik* 32, 319–377.

———— (1916). "Geburtenrückgang und Aufwuchsziffer." *Schmollers Jahrbuch* 40, 241–311.

Philippovich, E., (1890). "Die Auswanderung aus einzelnen europäischen Staaten." In *Handwörterbuch der Staatswissenschaften*, ed. J. Conrad et al., 1, 1018–1041. Jena

Prinzing, Friederich, (1899). "Die Entwicklung der Kindersterblichkeit in den europäischen Staatan." *Jahrbücher für Nationalökonomie und Statistik* 72, 577–635.

———— (1900). "Die Kindersterblichkeit in Stadt und Land." *Jahrbücher für Nationalökonomie und Statistik* 75, 593–644.

———— (1902). "Die uneheliche Fruchtbarkeit in Deutschland." *Zeitschrift für Sozialwissenschaft* 5, 37–46.

———— (1911). "Uneheliche Geburten," in *Handwörterbuch der Staatswissenschaften*, ed. J. Conrad et al. 3rd edition. Jena.

Rost, Hans, (1913). *Geburtenrückgang und Konfession, eine Untersuchung*. Cologne.

Salber, E., M. Feinlieb, and B. MacMahon (1965). "The duration of postpartum amenorrhea." *American Journal of Epidemiology* 82, 347–358.

Scheidt, W., (1928). "Erbbiologische und bevölkerungsbiologische Aufgaben der Familiengeschichtesforschung." *Archiv für Sippenforschung und alle verwandten Gebieten* 5, 289–315.

Schultz, T. Paul, (1971). "An economic perspective on population growth." In National Academy of Sciences, *Rapid population growth*, vol. II, Baltimore.

Schulze, Carl, (1968). *Analysis of completed cohort fertility in Germany*. Senior Thesis, Department of Sociology, Princeton University (unpublished).

Shorter, E., J. Knodel, E. van de Walle. "The decline of non-marital fertility in Europe, 1880–1940," *Population Studies* 25, 375–393.

Simonis, Aloys, (1939). "Sippen- und bevölkerungskundliche Untersuchung eines Eifeldorfes." *Archiv für Bevölkerungswissenschaft und Bevölkerungspolitik* 6, 36–46.

Stys, W., (1957). "The influence of economic conditions of the fertility of peasant women." *Population Studies* 11, 136–148.

Tietze, Christopher, (1916). "The effect of breastfeeding on the rate of conception." *International Population Conference*, New York, II, 129–136.

Trubenbach, A., (1962). *Ortssippenbuch Tottleben.* Frankfurt a. M.

United Nations, (1963). *Population Bulletin* 7, New York.

van de Walle, Etienne, (1968). "Marriage and marital fertility." *Daedalus* 97, 486–499.

——— (1969). "Problèmes de l'étude du décline de la fécondité européene." *Recherches économiques de Louvain* 4, 271–287.

——— and J. Knodel (1967). "Demographic transition and fertility decline: the European case." International Union for the Scientific Study of Population, *Contributed Papers*, Sydney Conference, pp. 47–55.

von Fircks, A. (1879). "Rückblick auf die Bewegung der Bevölkerung in Preussische Staats." *Preussische Statistik* 48A.

——— (1889). "Die Berufs- und Erwerbsthätigkeit der eheschliessenden Personen in ihrem Einflüsse auf deren Verheirathbarkeit, die Wahl des Gatten bezs. der Gattin, das durchschnittliche Heirathsalter, die eheliche und unehelich Fruchtbarkeit sowie das Geschlecht und die Lebensfähigkeit der Kinder." *Zeitschrift des Preussischen Statistischen Büreaus* 29, 165–203.

von Landman, Dr., (1909). "Die Arbeiterschutzgesetzgebung in den einzelnen Staaten." In *Handwörterbuch der Staatswissenschaft*, ed. J. Conrad et al. 3rd edition. Jena.

von Ungern-Sternberg, Roderich, (1931). *Causes of the decline in birth rate within the European sphere of civilization.* Cold Spring Harbor.

Wappäus, J. E., (1861). *Allgemeine Bevölkerungsstatistik*, vol. II. Leipzig.

Weber, Adna F., (1899). *Growth of cities in the 19th century.* Columbia University Studies in History, Economics and Public Law, no. 11. New York.

Wegener, (1902). *Der Wirtschaftliche Kampf der Deutschen mit den Polen um die Provinz Posen.* Posen.

Westoff, C. F., R. G. Potter, P. Sagi, and E. Mishler (1961). *Family growth in metropolitan America.* Princeton.

Wingen, Oscar, (1915). "Die Bevölkerungstheorien der letzten Jahre." *Münchener Volkswirtschaftliche Studien* 136. Stuttgart and Berlin.

OTHER REFERENCES

Wolf, Julius, (1912). *Der Geburtenrückgang: die Rationalisierung des Sexualslebens unserer Zeit.* Jena.

Wolf, Julius, (1928). *Die neue Sexualmoral und das Geburtenproblem unser Tage.* Jena.

Woodbury, R. M., (1925). *Causal factors in infant mortality.* Washington.

Wrigley, E. A., (1961). *Industrial growth and population change.* Cambridge.

——— (1966). "Family limitation in pre-industrial England." *Economic History Review* 19, 82–109.

Wülker, Heinz, (1940). *Bevölkerungsbiologie niedersächsischer Dörfer.* Leipzig.

Würzburg, Arthur, (1887, 1888). "Die Säuglingssterblichkeit im Deutschen Reich während der Jahre 1875 bis 1877. *"Arbeiten aus dem Kaiserlichen Gesundheitsamte,* vols. 2 and 4.

Würsburger, Eugen, (1912). "Ist die Besorgnis über den Geburtenrückgang begründet?" *Zeitschrift des Sächsischen Statistischen Büreaus* 1912, 112–114.

——— (1914). "Der Geburtenrückgang und seine Statistik." *Schmollers Jahrbuch* 38, 1259ff.

——— (1931). "Die Ursachen des neueren Geburtenrückganges." *Schmollers Jahrbuch* 55, 109–117.

Wyon, J. B. and J. E. Gordon, (1962). "A long-term prospective-type field study of population dynamics in the Punjab, India." In *Research in Family Planning,* ed. C. Kiser. Princeton.

Zahn, Friederich, (1918–19). "Die deutsche Bevölkerung vor dem Kreig." *Allegemeines Statistisches Archiv* 11, 79–144.

Index

INDEX

economic activity, *see* occupation
education, 224. *See also* illiteracy
"effective" fertility, *see* infant mortality
emigration, *see* migration
employment, *see* occupation
ethnic affiliation: fertility differentials, 141–146, 253–254; infant mortality differentials, 172–173
expectation of life, 4

family size: relation with child labor, 228; estimates from parish records, 46–49, 247; relation with infant mortality, 149–154; Jewish population, 140–141; by occupation, 120–127, 252–253; by rent in Breslau, 128–129, urban-rural trends, 107, 109, 122, 123, 125, 127
female employment, 224, 236, 237, 243, 261; growth outside of agriculture, 3–4, 229–230; correlations with marital fertility (I_g), 235, 260
fertility decline: date began, 55–59, 64, 87, 248; date ended, 50–52, 87, 247; determinants, 240, 261; hypothesis on relation with infant mortality decline, 149–154, 178–179, 185–187; similarities in course of, 245, 262; timing compared with rest of Europe, 64–65
fertility measures, *see* birth rate, family size, fertility decline, illegitimate fertility (I_h), marital fertility (I_g), marital fertility rates, natural increase rate, net reproduction rate, overall fertility (I_f), predecline fertility
F. Lübeck, 14n, 232n
Freiburg, 11n

Gd. Oldenburg, 10, 14n, 232n
Gumbinnen, 10n, 95n

Hadersleben, 145
Hambühren, 48
Hamburg, 21n, 90, 130, 244; infant mortality, 174; migration, 194, 195, 197, 198, 200–202 *passim*; urbanization, 207, 212; urban-rural trends in marital fertility (I_g), 101–103
Hannover (area), 14n, 95, 216n
Hanover (province), 14n
Heidelberg, 11n

Hesse, 10, 14n, 21n, 103, 132; birth rate by religion, 137–139
Hesse-Nassau, 14n, 21n
Hohenzollern, *see* Sigmaringen
H. Oldenburg, 14n, 160, 232n

illegitimate fertility, 68; infant mortality, 167–168. *See also* illegitimate fertility index (I_h)
illegitimate fertility index (I_h): compared with rest of Europe, 75, 78–79, 248; defined, 34; correlation with infant mortality, 174–176; magnitude of decline, 78, 247, 249; relation with marital fertility (I_g), 77–80, 248; contribution to overall fertility (I_f), 76, 247; relation with proportion married (I_m), 77–248; regional patterns, 76–77, 82–83, 248; urban-rural trends, 110–111, 251–252. *See also* illegitimate fertility
illiteracy, 224, 236, 243, 261; correlations with marital fertility (I_g), 235, 237–238, 260; and migration, relation with fertility, 203–204, 222; as a variable to measure fertility, 230–232
immigration, *see* migration
industrialization, *see* modernization
infant mortality, 224; administrative area trends, 157–158, 255; relation with breastfeeding, 60; date of decline, 158–163, 169–171, 255–256; decline compared with marital fertility (I_g) decline, 157, 179–185, 256; defined, 155; relation with "effective" fertility, 151–152, 178–180, 184–185, 187, 257; ethnic affiliation, 172–173, 255; relation with fertility decline, 244, 261; hypotheses on relation with fertility decline, 149–154, 178–179; correlation with illegitimate fertility (I_h), 174–176; levels by legitimacy, 167–168, 255; magnitude of decline, 4, 254; correlations with marital fertility (I_g), 174–176, 237–238, 240, 256; national trend, 156, 158, 254; correlations with overall fertility (I_f), 174–176; predecline fertility, 61, 261; regional patterns, 163–167, 176–177, 243, 255–256; religious affiliations, 171–172;